FROM *Hester Street*
TO
HOLLYWOOD

JEWISH LITERATURE AND CULTURE
Series Editor, Alvin Rosenfeld

FROM *Hester Street*
TO
HOLLYWOOD

The Jewish-American Stage and Screen

EDITED BY

Sarah Blacher Cohen

INDIANA UNIVERSITY PRESS
BLOOMINGTON

Manufactured in the United States of America

*Library of Congress Cataloging in Publication Data
Main entry under title:*

From Hester Street to Hollywood.

   *1. Jewish theater—United States—Addresses, essays,
lectures. 2. American drama—Jewish authors—History
and criticism—Addresses, essays, lectures. 3. Jews
in motion pictures—Addresses, essays, lectures.
4. Jews in literature—Addresses, essays, lectures.
I. Cohen, Sarah Blacher. II. Title: Jewish-American
stage and screen.*
PN3035.F76   1983   791.4'089924   82-47924
  2 3 4 5 87 86 85 84 83

ISBN 0-253-32500-5

ONCE MORE FOR GARY

Contents

FROM *Hester Street*
TO
HOLLYWOOD

Yiddish Origins and Jewish-American Transformations

Sarah Blacher Cohen

JEWISH-AMERICAN DRAMA IS NOT AN ORPHANED ART FORM OF UNKNOWN OR uncertain parentage. Unlike Jewish-American poetry, it does not lack a readily discernible tradition. Nor has Jewish-American drama suffered the fate of modern Hebrew drama, whose independence has been curtailed and its vitality diminished by the intrusive presence of powerful relatives: the majestic but intimidating drama of Hebrew scriptures. The immediate ancestor of Jewish-American drama is the vibrant but not awesome Yiddish theater, whose valuable legacy has not overwhelmed its heirs but enabled them to use only what they most cherished and could comfortably assimilate.

Among its treasures the Yiddish theater generously made available its serious literature: its weighty dramas of filial disobedience and parental anguish, of loyalties divided between Old World and New, of Jew-Gentile confrontations, of personal versus communal betterment. It also provided intentional and unintentional humorous fare: its saccharine melodramas, eclectic musicals, and macaronic comedies. By both stressing and diminishing the importance of being earnest, the Yiddish theater created its own brand of parables and parodies, a rich source of didacticism and levity for Jewish-American drama. But the most influential gift the Yiddish theater bequeathed to its American offspring was the emotional impact it had on its immigrant audience, the majority of the 1,300,000 Yiddish-speaking Jews who between 1882 and 1903 left Eastern Europe for a better life in America. By recreating *shtetl* life and types, the Yiddish theater preserved the familiar within the unknown and made the new aliens less homesick. It was the common meeting place, the common topic of conversation, the common dispeller of estrangement. Its heartrending plots permitted the immigrants to give full vent to their feelings, "to bathe in this homey theatrical bathhouse."[1] Its makeshift spectacles and grandiloquent acting provided a glamorous respite from their grim Hester Street lives. Its self-ordained playwright-preachers—the Gordons, the Pinskis, the Aschs—became their New World rabbis whose moralizations replaced Old World Torah instruction and spiritual counsel. The Yiddish theater generated such a consuming passion for works of the imagination that it became their secular temple where they regularly worshipped the aesthetic. Or if the mode of dramatic expression was not to their liking and they opposed the values depicted, the Yiddish theater became an arena for cultural debate, a place to exercise their newly gained freedom of expression. As journalist Lincoln Steffens observed: "A remarkable phenomenon it was, a community of thousands of people fighting over an art question as

1

savagely as other people fought over political or religious questions, dividing families, setting brother against brother, breaking up business firms and finally actually forcing the organization of a rival theater with a company pledged to realism against the old theater which would play any good piece."[2]

Despite such differences of artistic opinion, the establishment by 1918 of some twenty Yiddish theaters in New York City alone suggested that these enterprises were catalysts for social cohesion rather than sources of communal disruption. The Jewish immigrants may have had heated arguments over the aesthetic merits of a given play, but the Yiddish theater was still their own theater. It offered them, as Nahma Sandrow points out, the "intimate atmosphere of an 'insider's event' for people who were still outsiders in America. The play was for them and, often about them, and in their own language."

Most of the music in the Yiddish theater was their own as well, since it was based on cantorial compositions and *klezmer* music, the *shtetl* folk songs and instrumental accompaniment of Jewish wandering minstrels. Directors and playwrights used this liturgical and *klezmer* music in its unaltered state or, in the case of Abraham Goldfaden and Joseph Lateiner, theatricalized it to make it more conspicuous. More accomplished composers like Joseph Rumshinsky did not depend solely on Yiddish folk music but, according to Mark Slobin, constantly struggled "to create an international style within ethnic boundaries," a practice the reverse of George Gershwin's, for within the American mainstream Gershwin attempted to "suggest the world of tradition through minor keys and turns of phrase." But whatever kind of music it was, a superabundance of it was used in the Yiddish theater so that it often upstaged other elements of the play. So popular were the musical interludes heightening sentiment and enlivening action that audiences demanded entire evenings of them. They, in turn, were presented with earthy Yiddish musicals based for the most part on their own lives in contrast to the Broadway musicals, which were "mostly hothouse flowers, operettas imported from Europe, or homegrown imitations . . . [with] romantic swains, lavish costumes, and outlandish plots set in exotic lands."[3] These Yiddish musicals, with their excess of frivolity, broad comedy, and sentimentality, so appealed to the uneducated masses that the Yiddish idiom for their success was that "they wallowed in a *schmaltzgrub*," a tub of chicken fat.

The more serious Yiddish patrons, however, were not pleased with this "greasy" fare. The religious ones hoped the theater would depict a more pious way of life to revitalize their faith and convert their disaffected American-born children. The Yiddishists wanted the theater to be a much cherished museum preserving precious samples of Yiddish language and literature. The cultural elitists, infected by the " 'Russian Flu,' that yearning for high artistic and moral ideals,"[4] insisted that the Yiddish theater be elevating in form and content. The ideologues demanded that it be an instrument of social and political reform. But the majority of the uncommitted audience, the industrious immigrants eager for social and professional advancement, regarded the Yiddish theater as a Dale Carnegie course that would teach them how to succeed in America and hasten their transformation from *Yidn* to Yankees. Fortunately for them and unfortunately for the Yiddish theater, they quickly learned their lessons. Though the Yiddish theater flourished during the twenties and early thirties, the immigrant audience rapidly became more Americanized, more affluent. Changing their names, language, and occupations, they moved from the Lower East Side to settle in better parts of the city and suburbs. They left the clannish "theatrical bathhouse" to jump into the nonsectarian melting pot to wash away their greenhorn identity. The more talented actors and actresses—Paul Muni, Stella Adler, Molly Picon—also abandoned the sinking Yiddish theater for smoother sailing on Yankee showboats. The few fans who remained loyal to the Yiddish theater could no longer see a variety of engaging plays by gifted playwrights, for once an impoverished company had a success, they performed it for an entire season. And the hit, more often than not, was a form of *Shund* [trash], the low-brow fare which in the earlier Yiddish theater was a mishmash of "classical Yiddish songs, topical jokes, pilfered dialogue, irrelevant new show tunes," all expressed in a "diluted, crippled, macaronic, or eviscerated Yiddish."[5] The distinguishing feature of this newer brand of *Shund* was that it was performed in "'potato Yiddish'—a corrupt version diluted with English words and Americanisms."[6] The appeal of this new Yiddish theater, itself a prime casualty of the acculturation it had instigated, was the bastardization of the language it so lovingly nurtured. Promoted as bilingual hilarity, its fractured Yiddish and English, its crude puns and malapropisms, its obscene jests struck audiences as terribly funny. Yiddish in this context was so held up to ridicule that even the sound appeared comical, especially to the young who did not speak or understand the language.[7]

The juxtaposition of Yiddish with English for humorous purposes may have been a sign of the ebbing vitality of the Yiddish theater, but it added new comic gusto to the emerging vaudeville routines of American Jewish entertainers and Borscht Belt comedians who themselves were the irreverent descendants of the *shtetl badkhn*, the facile-tongued wedding jester and itinerant funnyman. While Weber and Fields performed a variation of Yiddish dialect humor in America as early as the 1870s and "Hebe comedians" devised trite Yiddish parodies at the turn of the century, not until the next decade did the street-trained Eddie Cantor, Georgie Jessel, Sophie Tucker, Al Jolson, and Fanny Brice begin infusing new life into ethnic song and jest. In crowded vaudeville and burlesque halls, primarily owned and operated by Jews, they catered to former Yiddish theater fans who now wanted entertainment that was more American than Yiddish but still had a Jewish flavor. Mingling breezy Americanisms with racy Yiddishisms, these performers became comic universe-changers, importing into one sphere an entire "universe of discourse with all sorts of associations from an entirely different sphere."[8] Eddie Cantor, singing "Cohen Owes Me Ninety-Seven Dollars" and "Yiddle on Your Fiddle, Play Some Ragtime"; Fanny Brice as Rosie Rosenstein performing "I'm an Indian" in a Jewish accent; Al Jolson, the cantor's son in blackface, belting out "Mammy"; and Sophie Tucker with her Yiddish and English tear-jerker, "My Yiddish Mamme," capitalized on the rich humor of their hyphenated origins. Unashamed of being Jewish, they seasoned their acts with spicy Yiddish to amuse, not malign, their people. Fanny Brice's justification for her Jewish routines expressed their general attitude: "In anything Jewish I ever did, I wasn't standing apart, making fun of the race, and what happened to me on the stage is what could happen to them. They identified with me, and then it was all right to get a laugh, because they were laughing at me as well as at themselves."[9] Many of these entertainers used Yiddish to establish an immediate intimacy with their Jewish audiences, to evoke the bittersweet experiences of a shared immigrant background. The language's earthy expressions also brought the luminaries down to earth and briefly transformed them into commoners once again. As Irving Howe perceptively states, for "a Jolson or a Cantor, Yiddish had served as a kind of secret sign, a gleeful or desperate wave to the folks back home by a performer who liked it to be known that he was still a Jewish boy faithful to the old plebeian ways and the bracing street vulgarisms."[10]

The female performers' use of Yiddish had a somewhat different effect, however. Fanny Brice's Yiddish accent in Irving Berlin's "Sadie Salome Go Home," the song of a clumsy Jewish girl eager to become a shimmy dancer, both differentiates her from more agile Gentile girls and underscores her ineptitude. Her enactment of Jewish ladies in distress, whose English is faulty as well, makes her doubly vulnerable. She is still the oppressed greenhorn girl beneath her glamorous Ziegfeld Follies exterior. Sophie Tucker, on the other hand, used Yiddish, especially its four-letter vocabulary, to establish her sexual equality with men. In her off-color numbers she candidly expressed her sexual needs and destroyed the stereotype of the frigid Jewish woman. By being lascivious, she also violated the code of gentility observed by respectable Jewish women. But she did not alienate her audience with her breaches of decency. Her Yiddish equivalents of foul language made her act more comic than shocking. It also enabled her to more effectively mask her hostility so she could mock men with impunity.

Fanny Brice and Sophie Tucker were not Molly Picons. The use of Yiddish phrases, intonations, and character types was not a principal feature of their routines. According to June Sochen, "both Brice and Tucker ultimately used their femaleness rather than their Jewishness to make their enduring point, but their Jewish heritage surely added a deep and subtle layer to the meaning of vulnerability and the need to be assertive." This was also true of the Jewish male comedians of the same period. Their Jewishness was not the predominant trait of their theatrical personas, nor in their acts did they examine their Jewishness in any great depth. In blackface they facilely combined Negro spontaneity and Jewish sentimentality. As paleface vaudevillians, they rattled off innocuous Jewish jokes, related clever but uncomplicated dialect stories, improvised benignly comic skits of ethnic misunderstanding. Their chief distinction was the invention of themselves as stars, fired by the need to rise above their immigrant depths and sustained in the heights by their Jewish energy and talent. But theirs were not parochial Stars of David shining on one segment of the people, but the more worldly, show-biz variety illuminating the entire tribe. Only later in the century did the Jewish comic appear undisguisedly as a Jew. True of both a smiling Milton Berle and a seething Lenny Bruce, this later comic's "Jewishness," Anthony Lewis claims, "may embarrass, motivate or anger him, but the connection between performance and cultural background is clear to him, and, he assumes, the audience as well." Instead of hiding or subordinating his Jewish identity, he virtually advertised the fact.

Such an uninhibited presentation of the Jew had been possible in the intimate quarters of a nightclub stage. But such an uncamouflaged portrait of the Jew could not be the focal point in the beginnings of Jewish-American drama, in, for example, the 1920s melting-pot plays of Elmer Rice. Just as the more established German-Jewish community tried to suppress the early Yiddish theater for making "spectacles of themselves before all of New York,"[11] so the newly assimilated Eastern European Jews of the 1920s did not want Jewish-American dramatists to depict them as significantly different from their fellow Americans. Reinforcing their desire for a low dramatic profile were the passage in the same decade of the National Origins Act restricting immigration and an upsurge of anti-Semitism fomented by the Ku Klux Klan. Moreover, Broadway producers, knowing that drama evoking prejudice or battling it would be bad for business, backed only those plays that would not offend any sizable group. Thus, the most popular play of the times, the one that best kept the peace and the profits, was Gentile playwright Ann Nichol's *Abie's Irish Rose* (1922), the amiable comedy of Jewish and Irish star-crossed lovers and their feuding fathers. The Old World prejudices and exaggerated dialects of the stereotypical immigrant parents, Solomon Levy and Patrick Murphy, provide the engaging humor of the piece; the New World triumph of romantic love and brotherhood over religious clannishness—the blissful union of Abie and his Irish Rose—contributes an even more winning sentimentality. To dispel any reservations about the appropriateness of intermarriage, Ann Nichols has two liberal clergymen, Father Whalen and Rabbi Jacob Samuels, give their respective blessings to the happy couple and try to gain their parents' approval. Assuming that all faiths and creeds are essentially the same, both clergymen express pleasure at the merging of customs and ceremonies in the young couple's home: "a Christmas tree in the parlor, kosher food in the cabinets, and a ham in the oven."[12] But most important, the inflexibilities of Jewish tradition and Irish Catholicism have been eliminated and the goal of total assimilation achieved.

Had Elmer Rice, born Elmer Leopold Reizenstein, written plays about Jews significantly more subtle than the more obvious acculturation plays of an Ann Nichols, he would have been deemed illegitimate on the legitimate stage. Jules Chametzky tells us that Rice, rather than openly dramatizing the complexities of the Leo Frank case, the 1913 lynching in Atlanta of a northern Jew, treated the subject ten years afterwards "in the more oblique and stylized expressionistic manner of *The Adding Machine* (1923)," depicting "the potential for mindless violence in the average man frustrated by forces beyond his comprehension." Even in Rice's less oblique Pulitzer Prize play, the 1929 *Street Scene*, Jews appear as one of many minorities in a crowded urban tenement, a miniature

United Nations of warring factions. Here the Kaplan family and their ethnic neighbors are powerless to prevent the domestic tragedy enacted before them— the murder of the oppressed Mrs. Maurrant and her milkman lover by her authoritarian, drunken husband. Unlike the indifferent Irish, Italian, German and Scandanavian witnesses of the event's prelude and aftermath, the Kaplans are the more sympathetic choric figures, the more articulate armchair critics of American slum conditions that brutalize the individual. Yet despite their heart-felt condolences and perceptive social criticism, these Jews are not fully de-lineated. They are eclipsed by the street they inhabit—the kaleidoscopic setting for the sensational dramas of city life. Thus Rice's remark about his Jewish background, "I have never paraded my origin, but I have never tried to deny it,"[13] applies to the Jewish characters of *Street Scene* and his later plays *Coun-sellor-at-Law* (1931) and *Flight to the West* (1940). His protagonists are liberal intellectuals who accept the external world's designation of them as Jews, but do not act the part with any distinctiveness.

Such ethnic blandness is certainly not the case in Clifford Odets's *Awake and Sing!* (1935), his most celebrated play of the 1930s and certainly America's best dramatic treatment of the Depression. Though Baird Shuman believes that "Odets will be remembered historically more as a proletarian playwright than as a Jewish playwright, nevertheless," he acknowledges that [Odets's] "back-ground and upbringing imposed a Jewishness upon his work, a Hébrewtude," reflected in his use of theme, character, and language. Unlike other leftist dramatists, Odets did not write about the generalized proletariat but about the social class and institution he knew best: the Jewish bourgeois family. In one respect, he agrees with Jacob Berger, the Marxist grandfather in *Awake and Sing!* who wants to "abolish such families," since they breed selfishness and hypocrisy, stifle personal growth, destroy spiritual values. Yet Odets also ad-mires the personal sacrifice the Jewish mother, Bessie Berger, makes for the economic survival of her family and the revolutionary zeal Jacob imparts to his grandson, inspiring him to improve the family of humankind.

Such a desire to better society at large is clearly Marx-inspired, but it can also be traced to the universalist concerns of Judaism, for the title Odets chose to replace the original one of *I Got the Blues* is taken from Isaiah 26:19, which prophesies the resurrection of all peoples: "Awake and sing, ye that dwell in dust: for the dew is as the dew of herbs, and the earth shall cast out the dead." Thus the Jewish prophetic tradition as well as Marxism were responsible for Odets's commitment to social reform in the thirties.

Such lofty Biblical allusions lent depth to *Awake and Sing*'s thematic con-cerns, but the more earthy Yiddishized English gave the play its great vitality. Of its street-tough dialogue, Alfred Kazin appreciatively remarked: "In Odets' play there was a lyric uplifting of blunt Jewish speech, boiling over and explo-sive, that did more to arouse the audience than the political catchwords that brought the curtain down."[14] Odets's inimitable use of the ironic echoes of Old World Yiddish mingled with the sassy banter of New World colloquialism produced an original idiom for the theater. Unconcerned with correctness or the niceties of expression, brimming with raciness and impudence, this idiom enabled Odets to fashion a new Jewish literary style that subsequently induced Jewish-American fiction writers to take similar liberties with language.

However, the other two leading social dramatists who were Jewish, Lillian Hellman and Arthur Miller, did not in the majority of their plays cultivate Odets's brand of Yinglish, nor did they intentionally create recognizably Jewish characters. The de-Semitization of their drama in the late thirties and most of the forties was in keeping with the general trend of the times: the eviction of the Jew as a figure in popular culture due in large measure to the emergence of Hitler whose presence Henry Popkin believes had the following effect: "When Hitler forced Americans to take anti-Semitism seriously . . . the most eloquent reply that could be made was dead silence: the American answer to the banishment of Jews in public life in Germany was the banishment of Jewish figures from the popular arts in the United States."[15] Even in Lillian Hellman's two World War Two plays, *Watch on the Rhine* (1941) and *The Searching Wind* (1944), there were no Jewish characters nor any direct reference to the persecution of the Jews. Her primary concern was to alert Americans to the encroaching evils of Fascism, to rally impotent liberals to combat the powerful enemy in their midst.

Undoubtedly, Lillian Hellman's a-Semitic dramas were a response to the period's unwritten censorship of things Jewish in the arts. But they also seem to reflect her own anti-Jewish feelings. Her memoirs reveal that she wanted to banish objectionable Jews and Jewish traits from her life, and she apparently wanted to banish them from her plays as well. The notable exception to this is her adaptation, *My Mother, My Father and Me* (1963), where she focuses on the Jewish middle class but then with caustic humor indicts them for their hypocrisy and philistinism. In her original dramas, what she values most is the physical and emotional bravery of Gentiles, a kind of Hemingwayesque "grace under pressure," in contrast to the Jews in her life, whom she sees as unduly fearful and self-seeking. Thus Bonnie Lyons concludes that Hellman's "negative image of the Jew coupled with her Hemingwayesque world view suggests a flight from her own Jewishness."

Arthur Miller's attitude toward his Jewish heritage in his plays is more complex than Hellman's and more subject to change through the years. His earliest works of the 1930s, *Honors at Dawn* and *No Villain*, plays of social protest that he wrote as a student at the University of Michigan, are about a middle-class Jewish family in the Depression, torn between principle and the need for profit. Miller, however, did not continue in this vein, for in his 1940s bid for Broadway, he, like Elmer Rice in the 1920s, sensed that the climate was unfavorable for homegrown ethnic drama. Moreover, he himself did not want to be known as a producer of parochial stock, but aspired to be a great public playwright able to capture the essence of the generic American, the universal tragedy of the common man. The result, of course, was the rough-hewn *All My Sons* (1947) and the superbly crafted *Death of a Salesman* (1949) in which errant fathers struggling with self-righteous sons try to make "of the outside world a home."[16] True to Miller's new ecumenicalism, the homes of Joe Keller and Willy Loman are purposely not identified as Jewish, nor do the family members reveal any specific religious or ethnic affiliation. For these omissions Miller was chastened not by a Jewish critic but by the Irish-Catholic Mary McCarthy: "A disturbing aspect of *Death of a Salesman* was that Willy Loman seemed to be Jewish, to judge by his speech-cadences, but there was no mention of this on stage. He could not be Jewish because he had to be 'America,' which is not so much a setting as a big, amorphous idea; the puzzle for the audience . . . is to guess where these living-rooms, roughly, are and who is living in them, which might make it possible to measure the plausibility of the action."[17] Miller's reply to such a charge was that the themes of these particular plays did not require their characters to be Jewish. Who they were was not determined by their cultural or religious background. He does concede, however, that two of his later plays, *Incident at Vichy* (1964), depicting the plight of Jews in Nazi-occupied France, and *The Price* (1968), with its comically sage Jewish appraiser of furniture and life, and, I would add, his 1980 television drama, *Playing for Time*, based on Fania Fénelon's Auschwitz memoirs, and his semi-autobiographical Depression play, *The American Clock* (1980), have Jewish characters in them because historical verisimilitude demands they be there. Moreover, the Jewish values they embody advance the complexities of meaning Miller intended for these works. Why he chose to write about these subjects at the particular time he did suggests another shift in his reaction to his own and the public's Jewish concerns. During the philo-Semitic 1960s, the period Leslie Fiedler insightfully describes as the "Judaization of American culture" when "Zion" became Main Street,"[18] Miller, now the successful playwright, could afford in *The Price* to create a Gregory Solomon, the Jew as resilient survivor, and allow him to be the play's resident oracle. And America's belated confrontation with the Holocaust gave Miller permission to tough-mindedly confront the subject in *Incident at Vichy* and later in *Playing for Time* where he intricately reveals the ambiguities of individual and collective guilt for the destruction of the Jews. But in all of these plays "ethics not ethnicity," the Old Testament prophetic virtues of social responsibility and righteous conduct toward Jew and Gentile alike, are Miller's primary concern, for, according to Enoch Brater, Miller finds in "traditions more Judaic than Jewish the real conflicts he might still portray on stage."

The reverse is true of Paddy Chayefsky's Jewish-flavored dramas of the early sixties, *The Tenth Man* (1960) and *Gideon* (1962), where popularized ethnicity rather than probing ethics is the chief appeal for audiences yearning to recapture their vibrant immigrant pasts. In the fifties such Broadway favorites as *The Fifth Season* (1953), *A Hole in the Head* (1955) and *A Majority of One* (1959), had accustomed theatergoers to folksy comedies with sentimentalized stock characters, risibly mistaken uses of the English language, and implausibly optimistic endings. It, therefore, did not matter to audiences that *The Tenth Man*'s underlying theme was a rather hackneyed one—the healing powers of human love—as long as the play retained its amusing mixture of exotic Jewish mysticism, blatant satire of attenuated American Judaism, and the greenhorn vaudeville routines of the synagogue's elders. Similarly, theatergoers were not bothered that the thematic concerns of *Gideon*, Chayefsky's Biblical drama, were more temporal than celestial. They were delighted that he transformed a lofty debate between man and God into a domestic quarrel between ethnically Jewish family members employing comic anachronism and ironic hindsight to win their arguments. However, the playful but facile reduction of profound theological issues in *Gideon* and the whimsical but simple formula for the renewal of religious faith and love in *The Tenth Man* moved Robert Brustein to dub Chayefsky "the Mahomet of Middle Seriousness."[19] Yet he is a Mahomet with a large Jewish following, for Leslie Field maintains that Chayefsky "has produced Jewish drama as forthright, perceptive, and enjoyable as any written today in America."

Neil Simon has an even larger following, perhaps because he rarely tries to inject Jewish "middle seriousness" in his plays. He is, for the most part, a nondenominational Pied Piper, who, with his fast-paced urban comedies, rescues people from their tedium-infested lives. When he does deal with recognizably Jewish types and topics, he unwittingly follows the same ingratiating practices which Gertrude Berg claimed made the Molly Goldberg radio and television show so successful for twenty-five years:

"You see, darling, I don't bring up anything that will bother people. . . . Unions, politics, fund-raising, Zionism, socialism, intergroup relations, I don't stress them. And, after all, aren't all such things secondary to daily family living? The Goldbergs are not defensive about their Jewishness, or especially aware of it. . . . I keep things average. I don't want to lose friends."[20]

Neil Simon doesn't "lose friends" with such Jewish-style comedies as *Come Blow Your Horn* (1961), *The Odd Couple* (1965), *The Sunshine Boys* (1973), *God's Favorite* (1974), and his most recent *Fools* (1981). In then. Judaism takes the form of amusing eccentricities of character, language, and gastronomical preference. Be it in Manhattan, Long Island, or Chelm, ethnically exaggerated modes of behavior are highlighted for humorous response, but there is no attempt to grapple with any Jewish issue that does not provide immediate comic relief. Moreover, Simon's Jewish-seasoned comedies are often indistinguishable from his secular urban comedies where conditions of residence take precedence over religious affiliation. Yet Daniel Walden argues that though Simon is not a practicing Jew, certain of his plays are more than nominally Jewish, since his earliest, most formative "points of reference are to an upwardly-mobile Jewish lower and middle-class culture, politically and socially liberal." Or, as Lenny Bruce expressed it, "if you live in New York or any other big city, you are Jewish. It doesn't matter even if you're Catholic, if you live New York, you're Jewish."[21]

If we accept Bruce's equation of urban and religious origins, then the cabaret revues and full-length satires of lifelong New Yorker Jules Feiffer are Jewish, though they lack explicitly Jewish themes and other visible Semitic earmarks and forelocks. With their neurotic dread and defensive wit, their intellectual pretensions and schoolboy irreverence, their quick tempos and tempers, they are not much different from Neil Simon's brand of predictable urban comedies. Both are producers of what some see in the sixties and seventies as the waning of minority culture and the waxing of an American mass culture absorbing all of its distinctiveness. Yet others claim that the highly ethnic metropolitan context in which these plays are written rather than their specific content is what makes them Jewish, if only through association. In Jules Feiffer's cartoons and in their stage metamorphosis in such works as *Crawling Arnold* (1961), *Little Murders* (1967), *Grownups* (1974) and *Knock Knock* (1976), there is an unmistakably Jewish ambiance derived in part from the larger world of the popular arts, many of whose creators are Jewish. Though Feiffer has not demonstrably pledged allegiance to Judaism in his life or works, Stephen Whitfield finds that his "satiric animus, his leftist perspective, his urban irony and his psychoanalytic spirit help give his work a Jewish component in the sense that a Jew is most likely to have created it."

The Last Analysis (1965) the only full-length play by Nobel Laureate Saul Bellow is also endowed with "urban irony" and the "psychoanalytic spirit," but there is no doubt a Jew created it. While his play does not possess his novels' subtle interplay of Jewish and American values or their rich humor of verbal retrieval,[22] it does present a convincing depiction of another of his "suffering joker" heroes: Philip Bummidge, ex-television comedian. Like Tommy Wilhelm and Moses Herzog, he makes a career of his problems and is compulsively funny as a way of enduring his wretched circumstances, but as he ruefully acknowledges: "When the laughter stops, there's still a big surplus of pain."[23] A clown driven to being a theoretician, Bummidge is another of Bellow's visionary creatures who, disappointed with his fallibility, strives to become a *mensch*, a person of substance. But his Jewish family stands in the way of his self-improvement. In this respect the generational conflicts of *The Last Analysis* resemble those of *Awake and Sing!*, since Bummidge, like Jacob Berger, struggles to become "drenched with new meaning" despite his money-hungry family's clamoring that he be content with the old meaning. Though Berger's god is Marx and Bummidge's is Freud, they each adopt one exclusive metaphor for salvation and the interpretation of experience which ultimately isolates them from society. Jacob Berger commits suicide and Bummidge retreats from the predatory world to his platonic academy. The fact that Bummidge severs ties with his associates and "ends up alone, like the American cowboy with a sidekick or two," makes Keith Opdahl initially think that *The Last Analysis* is a "notably non-Jewish play." But, on second thought, he considers that Bummidge's case of "humanitis", his inability to tolerate other people, may be the "personal or emotional equivalent to the very real Jewish ambivalence about assimilation," for to affiliate with a larger group is to risk forfeiting one's identity. Therefore, Bummidge in his hermetic Institute of Nonsense may be alienated from the Jewish community, but he is all-consumed with his psychoanalysis, that Jewish talking science wherein the most profound conversations are with oneself. Unfortunately, the critics did not regard these conversations as terribly profound. *The Last Analysis* closed after twenty-eight performances on Broadway.

The inability of one Nobel Laureate to adroitly shift gears from the fictional to the theatrical and have a long-running production did not prevent another American Nobel Laureate, the Yiddish writer Isaac Bashevis Singer, from creating, at age 68, his own vehicles for the stage. Foreign in appearance and antiquated in design, Singer's plays were not manufactured from their own raw materials, but were, with the help of collaborators, adaptations of his short stories and children's tales. Singer, however, was not the first to provide English adaptations of Yiddish literature for the American theater. In the fifties and sixties Jewish-American dramatists, mourning the irrevocable loss of Yiddish-speaking Jews and their *shtetl* folkways, felt compelled to recapture their unique qualities and give them theatrical permanence. Since Sholom Aleichem was considered the most endearing chronicler of this quaint past, his stories became the primary source of Arnold Perl's *The World of Sholom Aleichem* (1953)[24] and *Tevya and His Daughters* (1957) as well as the enormously successful musical version of the Tevya stories, Joseph Stein's *Fiddler on the Roof* (1964). These works ostensibly offered an intimate view of familiar Jews within their confining but accustomed quarters who, despite poverty and persecution, had a durable sense of humor and an abiding faith in God. But a close reading of Sholom Aleichem's original stories and historical accounts of the *shtetl* reveals that these Broadway versions greatly sentimentalized Jewish life in pre-holocaust Eastern Europe and provided what audiences wanted: heartwarming stories about close-knit, tradition-bound families who triumph over adversity.

The *shtetl* of Isaac Bashevis Singer's dramas, by contrast, is not idealized. Though his fictional treatment of it departs from strict realism, his is an authentic depiction of its more sordid and anguished side. And since he is the principal adapter of his stories for the theater, his plays derived from his firsthand knowledge of the *shtetl* are certainly more authentic than those by American-born adapters produced almost a century later. Particularly in Singer's stage version of *Yentl* (1974), he accurately reveals the unalterable religious context of nineteenth-century Polish Jewry and captures the inner torment of a young woman forced to choose between the illicit study of sacred texts and the lawful performance of wifely duties. To lend ready-made depth to commonplace scenes, Singer also incorporates eloquent orthodox rituals, yet shocks us by employing them to commemorate unorthodox events, such as the marriage ceremony uniting two women. In Hollywood's projected musical version of *Yentl*, it seems highly unlikely they will retain Singer's rare combination of the authentic and his imaginative profanation of it, since they have not asked him to write the screenplay and have given artistic control to Barbra Streisand, who will direct the movie and portray the eighteen-year-old Yentl. What Singer has said about his participation in the theater, therefore, applies even more strongly to the cinema's appropriation of his art: "I like art to be pure. A book is written by one man. In the theater you have too many partners—the director, the producer, the actors, the writers. In a way it is already a collective."[25]

Even though the cinema's "collective" is sure to have its Jewish members, there is no guarantee the Jewish quality of Singer's work will retain its full strength. Indeed in the 1930s at the height of Jewish control of the movie industry—the period of uncontested rule by such moguls as Adolph Zukor, Jesse Lasky and B. P. Schulberg at Paramount; William Fox at Twentieth Century; Louis Mayer and Samuel Goldwyn at MGM; Carl Laemmle and Harry Cohn at Columbia and the Warner brothers at their own studio—there was a concerted effort to ban most Jewish subject matter from Hollywood films. To escape from their Jewish immigrant backgrounds, the moguls eliminated all traces of it on the screen. To confirm their new-found identities as devoted United States citizens, their pictures reflected the America of their heart's desire—a place where people have the same non-distinctive names, speak the same unaccented language, and share the same undivided national loyalties. Eager to win the favor of that vast unseen audience somewhere in the center of the country, the studio heads had Jewish actors and actresses change their names to less Semitic ones. Scripts depicted tepid mixed marriages as the happy resolutions for too heated religious conflicts. They substituted WASP identities for minority ones in screen adaptations of ethnically particularized Broadway plays. Even the anti-Nazi films they produced in the forties were intriguing tales of adventure and romance that ignored the grim realities of Jewish persecution. If they included a Jewish character, it was usually as a token minority soldier in melting-pot battle scenes against the Axis. The notable exception to Hollywood's Semitic invisibility was Charlie Chaplin's *The Great Dictator* (1940), which comically yet seriously addressed the plight of the Jews. However, the fact that Chaplin hilariously played a crazed Hitler and the innocent Jewish barber mistaken for him caused the isolationist Senators Wheeler and Nye to cite the film as one of those designed to "drug the reason of the American people into an unreasoning hatred and fear" of Hitler. They attributed such "pro-war, pro-interventionist propaganda in Hollywood movies" to Jewish studio heads who they claimed were committed to "foreign causes."[26] This charge was especially grievous to those movie-makers who had cultivated their Americanism at the expense of their Judaism. Yet they dared not express their anger at these unjust government accusers, but lashed out at the Jews for their present difficulties. " 'Relief Fund for the Jews!'" Harry Cohn yelled at Ben Hecht. " 'Somebody should start a fund for relief *from* the Jews. All the trouble in the world has been caused by Jews. . . .' "[27]

Similarly in the 1950s Hollywood was more responsive to the witch-hunting of the House Un-American Activities Committee than to the demands for truthful depiction of religious and political minorities. Since a number of Jewish artists supposedly had Communist affiliations in the thirties, Hollywood conducted its own inquisition and carried out its own character assassinations. Fired from the studios, Jews and their concerns were once again barred from the films. Moreover, since Germany was now America's ally in the Cold War against Russia, Hollywood created films showing the Germans of World War Two in a more positive light, devoid of Nazis and certainly of Communist-tainted Jews.

By the end of the 1950s, however, the witch-hunters had retreated to the political hinterlands and Hollywood, no longer under the control of universalist moguls, permitted itself to catch the fever of ethnicity infecting the country. Pride in the emergence of Israel caused second- and third-generation Jewish producers and screenwriters, more artistically sure of themselves than their predecessors had been, to create extravagant film epics championing the exploits of ancient and modern Israel and cinematographically transforming frail Jews into formidable giants. Since recent history enabled them to celebrate Jews as victors, it obligated them to show Jews as victims as well. Unlike the ultra-cautious moguls, the younger, more secure film-makers, such as Sidney Lumet, the superb adapter of Jewish-American fiction, were not afraid of showing kinship with oppressed European Jewry or making too great a claim for their special suffering. Even if it meant accusations of dual allegiance, they were committed to producing films that honestly revealed the fate of the Jews in the Holocaust. Yet despite their good intentions and those of the Broadway playwrights whose works they adapted for the screen, many of them failed to capture the horrors of the nightmare experience. Relying on moral simplicities, outmoded notions of heroism, and facile plot resolutions, their Holocaust dramas tried to avoid the depths of hopelessness. In both the stage and movie versions of *The Diary of Anne Frank* and *The Wall*, for example, Lawrence Langer states that "the American vision of the Holocaust" . . . continued to insist that millions have not died in vain, "trying to parlay hope, sacrifice, justice, and the future into a victory that will mitigate despair." Like Anne Frank, they led audiences to believe that "people are really good at heart," yet her ultimate destruction belies such affirmation. In the course of the play, however, they deleted the somber knowledge that an innocent young girl and countless like her were killed simply because they were Jewish. Such a dark truth Broadway and Hollywood were unwilling to convey.

But in the sixties and seventies there were many lighter truths Hollywood told about Jews who were neither victors nor victims, but unpretentious members of ordinary reality whose urban agonies, ecstasies, and follies captivated the pluralistic movie public. Since there were more young film-makers, the Jewish characters they depicted were invariably sons and daughters whose destinies were shaped by their place in the family structure, not by their position in the social and political context. They were more consumed with personal rights than with religious rites. Yet they felt no need to conceal their Jewish identity. On the contrary, the Jewish stars who portrayed them left behind the ethnic striptease of former years to prominently display their minority profiles and in so doing became majority cult figures. Barbra Streisand, obeying the commandment of not changing your noses or your Moses, became a funny girl whom everyone thought beautiful. Woody Allen, assuming the persona of the Jewish schlemiel as sexual loser, was a huge box-office winner and set the standard for a more realistic kind of American masculinity. His Jewish imagination of disaster legitimized the suppressed fears of most city-dwellers and made it respectable to be a neurotic. His Jewish humor of self-irony and veiled contempt for the overly intellectual joined forces with his American humor's disdain of the highbrow to produce what Mark Shechner describes as "the comedy of cultural revenge" whereby "inferiority is brandished as a point of pride." Yet Allen's cultivated pose of inferiority is such a crowd-pleaser that it leads to a superiority he must mock in, for example, *Manhattan* and *Stardust Memories*, if he is to retain his reputation as a successful Jewish failure.

Mel Brooks's reputation, on the other hand, does not rest on the popularity ratings of a single, thinly disguised autobiographical figure. Though he often appears in his movies as the "short Hebrew man" he is in real life, he does not focus on only one person's misadventures. Reflecting what Sanford Pinsker terms "the deeply divided impulses in American Jewish life," Brooks wants to consume all of popular culture, "to assimilate everything," yet at the same time, his Jewish marginality and cynicism distance him from it and cause him to mock its values in film parodies which encompass his ambivalence. *Blazing Saddles*, for example, may mark his love affair with the American Western, yet he bastardizes it by having Yiddish-speaking Indians incongruously shout, "*Shvartzers?*"to express their dismay at the presence of Blacks in their territory. Unlike the early screen moguls who wanted to de-Semiticize American movies, Brooks tries to over-Semiticize them. Indeed, at the end of his *History of the World, Part One*, he has bearded Jewish astronauts in Flying Stars of David gleefully destroying Gentile space ships to the strains of lively Jewish music.

Of course, such Jewish assaults upon the major bastions of Gentile dominance are but playful fantasy. However, what is not fantasy is that the recent film image of the Jew, inextricably linked with the antic and the anguished in contemporary urban life, has become a highly saleable product readily purchased by both Gentile and Jewish consumers of mass entertainment. Yet beneath this product's appealing Semitic surface, it lacks cultural and religious density. Jews may be ubiquitous in these new films, but they make no profound, lasting impression as Jews. The fact that some film-makers have allowed amorphous or caricatured ethnicity to substitute for "ancestral and familiar uniqueness" causes Alan Spiegel to ask such disturbing questions as: "Aren't we witnessing to some extent the process whereby a Jewish style unmoors itself from a Jewish content and both vanish into the anonymous social sea? And how legitimate is it when Jewish identity becomes just another all-purpose insignia of urban contemporaneity? We have seen how marketable a commodity Judaism can be, but does marketable also mean exportable?"

Unfortunately, commercial Hollywood and Broadway are thriving exporters of nominally Jewish, quickly forgotten goods. Yet the seventies and now eighties have seen the emergence of a small but growing number of knowledgeable importers of authentic Jewish content. For the Jewish Opera Series at New York's 92nd Street Y, David Schiff combined the motives of Torah cantillation with the idioms of Yiddish folk and contemporary music for his opera, *Gimpel the Fool*, which used Isaac Bashevis Singer's original Yiddish for its libretto. Lazar Weiner, the recently deceased octogenarian composer of Yiddish art songs and synagogue liturgy, drew upon the Jewish mysticism of his Eastern

European past for his opera, *The Golem;* and Ezra Laderman and Joe Darion looked to the Bible for the source of their opera, *And David Wept*. Two highly professional off-Broadway companies have dedicated themselves to presenting plays with memorable Jewish themes and characters—Stanley Brechner's American Jewish Theater at the Y and Ran Avni's Jewish Repertory Theatre. Just as the Group Theatre of the thirties motivated dramatists to write plays of social protest, so these companies encourage neophyte and veteran dramatists to write plays "about Jewishness, about roots, their values, the loss of them, the search for them, the distaste for them, the joy of them."[28] The results have been works covering a wide range of Jewish experience by playwrights of diverse national origins. The Jewish Repertory Theatre, for example, presented the American premieres of two dramas by Israeli writers: A. B. Yehoshua's *A Night in May*, an account of an Israeli family in the besieged Jerusalem of 1967, and Leah Goldberg's *Lady of the Castle*, an exploration of what Israel offered the Holocaust survivor whose identity was tied to pre-war Europe. It also featured such new American plays as Edward M. Cohen's *Cakes with the Wine*, a domestic drama about a New York lower-class Jewish family in the 1950s and Isaac Metzger's semi-documentary, *East Side Justice*, written especially for the company. Similarly, the American Jewish Theatre at the Y presented such new works as *Capella* by Israel Horovitz and David Boorstin, a painfully funny treatment of the relationship between an elderly Jewish refugee and a young American, as well as a revival of the original dramatic version of Herman Wouk's *The Caine Mutiny Court Martial*, a study of anti-Semitism and its effect upon the Navy's Jewish prosecuting attorney.

Sensitive new films have also been produced which capture the subtleties of Jewish life in both the Old and the New Worlds. One of the best is Joan Micklin Silver's low-budget but high-quality *Hester Street*. Based on Abraham Cahan's *Yekl*, it unsparingly reveals the Lower East Side's high cost of living for the turn-of-the-century immigrant who divorces his orthodox Yiddish-speaking wife to marry a crass, assimilated dance-hall teacher. Another exceptional Jewish-American film is Josh Waletzky's NEH-funded documentary, *Image Before My Eyes*, which fondly and meticulously recreates the felt and unfelt realities of Polish Jewry between the two World Wars. Through the use of home movies of the period, rare historical footage, thirty explanatory interviews, authentic music, and the most evocative of 15,000,000 photos from the YIVO Institute for Yiddish Research, Waletzky hopes that audiences seeing *Image Before My Eyes* will no longer "retain the idea that all the Jews in Eastern Europe were like characters in *Fiddler on the Roof*."[29]

Out of the remnants of Hester Street and the ashes of the Holocaust the Joan Micklin Silvers and the Josh Waletzkys have caused the phoenix of Jewish creativity to rise again. At the present time, however, it would be unrealistic to expect the mainstream Jewish-American stage and screen to hatch very many of these genuine Jewbirds which were so plentiful in the parent nest, the Yiddish theater. Indeed, its more emancipated, less informed heirs are more comfortable with nondescript starlings and loud-mouthed parrots who imitate accents but utter nonsense. Yet when these Jewbirds make their rare appearance, their ethnic exactitude, their original markings transport us to a vibrant past and cause our imaginations to soar with them. Then the Jewish-American stage and screen have the same lifting power as the Yiddish theater.

NOTES

1. Nahma Sandrow, *Vagabond Stars* (New York: Harper & Row, 1977), p. 210.

2. Quoted in Ronald Sanders, *The Downtown Jews* (New York: New American Library, 1969), p. 296.

3. Jack Gottlieb, "From *Shtetl* to Stage Door: The Jewish Influence on Musical Broadway," *Reform Judaism* 1 (November 1972):1.

4. Irving Howe, *World of Our Fathers* (New York: Harcourt Brace Jovanovich, 1976), p. 474.

5. Sandrow, p. 111.

6. Ibid., p. 294.

7. Such a response confirms Uriel Weinreich's observation in *Languages in Contact* that when a language becomes obsolescent for certain immigrant communities in America, the automatic reaction to it is laughter.

8. D. H. Monro, *Argument of Laughter* (South Bend, Indiana: University of Notre Dame Press, 1963), pp. 45-46.

9. Quoted in Norman Katkov, *The Fabulous Fanny: The Story of Fanny Brice* (New York: Knopf, 1953), p. 205.

10. Howe, p. 569.

11. Sandrow, p. 74.

12. Rhoda Silver Kachuck, "The Portrayal of the Jew in American Drama Since 1920" (Ph.D. diss., University of Southern California, 1971), p. 20.

13. Elmer Rice, *Minority Report: An Autobiography* (New York: Simon & Schuster, 1963), p. 164.

14. Alfred Kazin, *Starting Out in the Thirties* (Boston: Atlantic, Little, Brown, 1965), p. 81.

15. Henry Popkin, "The Vanishing Jew of Our Popular Culture," *Commentary* 13 (July 1952): 46.

16. Arthur Miller, "The Family in Modern Drama," *Atlantic Monthly* 197 (April 1956): 36.

17. Mary McCarthy, *Sights and Spectacles* (London: William Heinemann, 1959), p. xxiii.

18. Leslie Fiedler, *Waiting for the End* (New York: Dell Publishing Co., 1964), p. 67.

19. Robert Brustein, "All Hail, Mahomet of Middle Seriousness," *The New Republic*, 27 November 1961, p. 21.

20. Morris Freedman, "The Real Molly Goldberg," *Commentary*, 21 (April, 1956): 360.

21. Lenny Bruce, *How to Talk Dirty and Influence People* (Chicago: Playboy Press, 1965), p. 5.

22. For a fuller discussion of the humor in Bellow's novels, see my book, *Saul Bellow's Enigmatic Laughter* (Urbana: University of Illinois Press, 1974).

23. Saul Bellow, *The Last Analysis* (New York: Viking Press, 1966), p. 78.

24. Besides dramatizations of Sholom Aleichem's folktale *"The Melamed, His Wife, The Rabbi and the Goat of Chelm"* and his story "The High School," Arnold Perl's *The World of Sholom Aleichem* also contains an adaptation of I. L. Peretz's *"Bontsche Schweig."*

25. Quoted in Paul Kresh, *Isaac Bashevis Singer: The Magician of West 86th Street* (New York: The Dial Press, 1979), p. 308.

26. Quoted in Barry Gross, "Behaving Like a Jew": The Jewish Presence in American Films," an unpublished essay, p. 13.

27. Quoted in Gross, p. 14.

28. Edward M. Cohen, "The Jewish Repertory Theatre: A Subjective Account," an unpublished essay, p. 5.

29. Quoted in Annette Insdorf, "Rediscovering Polish Jewry," *New York Times*, 15 March 1981, p. 15.

Yiddish Theater and American Theater

Nahma Sandrow

YIDDISH THEATER IN AMERICA WAS INFLUENCED BY, AND IN TURN INFLU-
enced, the American (i.e., English-speaking) theater. Like most cross-cultural
interactions, these influences are hard to quantify. Although Yiddish theater's
development took place within the Yiddish-speaking cultural community,
neither the theater nor the community was ever totally isolated from the rest of
America. Just as American life and American theater influenced Yiddish theater, Yiddish theater, along with the cultural community that created it, nourished American theater. Since each theater so enriched the other, they share
many distinctive treasures.

Yiddish theater, is, obviously, theater in the Yiddish language. In the late
Middle Ages when the Rhineland was a major center of Jewish population, the
Yiddish language developed there out of old High German plus a great deal of
Hebrew, Romance, and other linguistic elements. As the Jewish population
emigrated eastward in the next few centuries, Slavic elements entered the
language. Yiddish, then, is the language of the Ashkenazic Jews of Central and
Eastern Europe and of their twentieth-century descendants, wherever in the
world they ended up—Western Europe, South Africa, Australia, South and
North America. Yiddish and English have many cognates, by the way, because
they both developed largely from German sources. Like English, Yiddish developed into a distinct language with its own syntax, flavor, and literature—
including drama.

By the seventeenth century, Jewish merrymakers in Poland were performing
ritual folk plays in Yiddish; by the mid-nineteenth century, Russian Jewish
intellectuals were writing satirical dramas for reading aloud in Yiddish; and in
1876 in a Rumanian cafe, a poet named Avrom Goldfadn joined a cabaret
entertainer to put on the first professional secular Yiddish theater production.
Six years later, in 1882, when a new wave of czarist oppression sent hundreds of
thousands of Jews emigrating westward, few of them had yet had a chance to see
Yiddish theater. But that same year brought the debut of professional Yiddish
theater on the Bowery of New York City. For the next several decades, although
Yiddish theater continued to develop in Europe, it was in the New World,
especially on New York's Lower East Side, that Yiddish theater first flourished.
It was in many ways a typical turn-of-the-century American theater.

Yiddish theater soon became in its own small way a get-up-and-go American
business. Like the American theater uptown on Broadway, it offered a full range
of types of shows. You could buy a ticket for a good laugh or a good cry. You
could enjoy operettas or musical comedies or musical revues. You could attend
a melodrama or domestic drama. You could revel in the classics: Shakespeare's

Othello, Schiller's *Maria Stuart*, Molière's *The Miser*—all in Yiddish translation. You could see the current avant-garde: naturalism, expressionism, sym-
bolism. You could even attend the current Broadway hits—*Dr. Jekyll and Mr.
Hyde*, *Uncle Tom's Cabin*, *Cyrano de Bergerac*, *Johnny Belinda*, *It Can't Happen Here*, and *Detective Story* all played the American Yiddish stage. Besides
such direct translations of Broadway successes, French or German plays sometimes ran simultaneously in Yiddish downtown and in English uptown.

By the First World War, there were some twenty Yiddish theaters in the New
York area alone, as well as music halls, vaudeville houses (which alternated
live acts with Yiddish or English films), cabarets, and roof garden cafés. Detroit, Chicago, Baltimore, Pittsburgh, Montreal, and other North American
cities had year-round Yiddish theater companies—sometimes two or three companies simultaneously. And Yiddish actors toured, particularly in summertime,
to smaller Jewish communities, such as Syracuse, New York, and Youngstown,
Ohio. (They also toured South America and Europe.) Companies from different
cities sometimes switched places for the summer season. Posters and handbills
papered the streets in Jewish neighborhoods. After the show, people gathered in
cafés to discuss it over a glass of tea and sometimes to ogle the actors at the next
table. So vital was the Yiddish theater in America that when Avrom Goldfadn
died in 1909, thirty thousand mourners followed his funeral procession on foot
over the Manhattan Bridge to his grave in Brooklyn.

Yiddish theater companies were organized in a variety of ways. There were
repertory groups formed for a season in one place or for a tour. There were
others playing a single hit. Companies were sometimes managed by a businessman, sometimes by a star, sometimes by a partnership, sometimes around a
core family group. Or when a star went on the road, he/she might follow the
nineteenth-century American tradition of taking nothing but some scenery,
costumes, and scripts; the supporting cast was picked up afresh in each new
town. In every case, the theater party benefit, organized to raise funds for a
charitable or fraternal association, was an important source of revenue. The
Hebrew Actors Union was organized in 1887, making it the second professional
union (as opposed to brotherhood) founded in the United States.

Almost every Yiddish-speaking Jew, except for the most religiously orthodox,
was touched in some way by Yiddish theater. If he did not go to shows himself,
at least he certainly knew people who went. He recognized show tunes and
heard the catch phrases of current hits. The same was true of his children, who
even if they did not speak Yiddish fluently, probably understood it.

Like the splendidly gaslit nineteenth-century American theater, the American Yiddish theater was an actor's theater, dominated by great and flamboyant
stars. Among the most famous were Jacob P. Adler and David Kessler, dramatic
heroes; Boris Tomashevsky, romantic lead; Sigmund Mogulesko, clown; and the
female stars, Bertha Kalich, Keni Liptsin, Sophie Karp, Sara Adler, and Bessie
Tomashevsky. The next generation, which played into the 1970s, included
Maurice Schwartz, Jacob Ben-Ami, Ludwig Satz, Aaron Lebedev, Samuel
Goldenburg, Menashe Skulnick, Celia Adler, Jennie Goldstein, and Mollie

Picon. Yiddish actors have always had a reputation for temperament and energy, for "truth" broadly and passionately portrayed. Brooks Atkinson's description of Maurice Schwartz is typical:

> He is not afraid of the theater. . . . The acting on Second Avenue has animation and latitude, with wide gestures and excitement; and you always know that you are not in a library.[1]

Fans [in Yiddish: *patriótn*] of these stars were tremendously loyal; fan clubs and claques lavished wild applause on their favorites and, for their benefits, flowers and gifts. For their stars' rivals there were hisses, heckling, or even occasional showers of cold water. Competing *patriótn* quarreled over their heroes' merits and occasionally even battled in the streets outside the theater, though none of their brawls ever went so far as the American theater's Astor Place riot of 1849, in which twenty-two died.[2]

In keeping with the nineteenth-century American star tradition, the mass audience tended to be more interested in the actors than in their material. Yet a number of professional Yiddish playwrights of stature lived in America. Avrom Goldfadn himself came first, and in the 1890s he was joined by Jacob Gordin, who aimed to reform Yiddish theater according to the principles of modern art theaters. The following decade brought the works of a number of distinguished dramatists. Sholom Aleichem not only dramatized some of his own stories and novels, most notably, *Tevye the Dairyman;* he also wrote original plays such as the comedies, *The Big Win* (also known as *The Two Hundred Thousand*) and *Hard to Be a Jew* and the one-acters, *People, The Divorce,* and *Mazel Tov.* David Pinsky, H. Leivick, Sholom Asch, Peretz Hirschbein, and others experimented with a variety of styles and settings (historical, Old World, and modern American). Many, though not all, of their more serious plays had some distinct message. Often they concerned themselves with the Jewish experience, with questions of religion, history, identity. Many of the plays addressed the political situation, often from a left-wing perspective, or depicted a universal ethical theme such as the role of the artist vis-à-vis his society.

In addition to these serious writers, every season brought work from the journeymen who turned out popular comedies or costume operettas about, say, a girl who gets her boy in the end though her parents intended her for someone else or a prince who discovers that the girl next door is the one he really loves. They turned out melodramas about families parted, to be reunited at the final curtain; they wrote most often about sacrifices for love. There was always at least one subplot involving a comic couple and their slapstick romance, along with interludes of singing and dancing. Other theater professionals dreamed up vaudeville sketches and gags. In addition, many actors wrote their own material or were at least able to dramatize and adapt for their own needs. There were professional lyricists. Finally, there were a number of fine composers—stars in their own right—such as Secunda, Olshanetsky, and Elstein.

Associated with theater were other allied industries. People liked to play on their victrolas recordings of Yiddish show music as well as of monologues, both comic and melodramatic. If a song made a hit, it was promptly published as sheet music, often decorated with the face of the actor who first sang it or of the theater building where it was first introduced. Publishers printed play texts in book or pamphlet form. For several decades Yiddish movies were produced, both short films and features.

The prominence of the theater in the American Yiddish press is an indication of the theater's vitality. Gossip columns provided the latest truths and untruths about the stars' careers and private lives. Daily papers printed critical reviews. Literary monthlies included reflective essays. In the twenties the *Jewish Daily Forward* sponsored a feature allowing readers to contribute letters to the editor on the subject of Yiddish theater. There were even whole magazines about theater in general and the theater scene in particular.

Nonprofessionals, too, took Yiddish theater seriously. Parallel with the American Little Theatre Movement, amateur Yiddish theaters formed across the country were so active that in 1916 and 1919 there were national conventions in Cleveland and Detroit at which groups presented plays for each other's pleasure and encouragement. *The Folksbiene*, the oldest continuously performing Yiddish theater in the world, began in New York as an amateur company in 1915, and even then it was a coalition of amateur groups which already existed. Aside from the interest of amateur performers, various intellectual and fraternal organizations, most notably the Workmen's Circle, have given support to theater endeavors. Intellectuals and community leaders considered it part of their responsibility to try to elevate Yiddish theater aesthetically and to use it as a didactic instrument.

Beginning in the nineteenth century, America appeared in many Yiddish plays as physical setting and as atmosphere. There might be the deck of an immigrant ship or Ellis Island. The most popular backdrop was obviously the tenement, its parlor and its kitchen. The other most common interior was the sweatshop, with its sewing machines and tables piled with piecework. Outside settings included the roof, the stoop, and the street. Other American scenes were evoked: Chinatown and other ethnic communities novel to Eastern Europeans; reform school and settlement house; union hall and dance hall. Sometimes real places and events such as the Johnstown Flood provided the play's very situation. Vaudeville and musical comedy drew on the more spectacular and exotic aspects of the New Land, such as Mexico or the wild West, which were American but still very far away. Such newly familiar character types as the landlady and her boarder, the sweatshop boss, the Yankee social worker and the Irish policeman quickly appeared on the Yiddish-American stage.

In many Yiddish plays America figures not only as a setting but also as an idea. In dramas of romance and suspense set in the old country, America signified freedom, the paradise to which the hero would eventually escape for his happy ending. In dramas set in the tenements of the Lower East Side, America was the evil power of materialism that caused the breakup of traditional ways and traditional relationships; it destroyed families' happiness, encouraged disrespect, and eradicated religious piety faster than any cruel czar ever could. In some serious plays, as well as in turn-of-the-century Yiddish-American lyric poetry, endless labor in the sweatshop crushed body and soul. In other plays, the corrupt protagonists who made fortunes as bosses at the expense of old political and religious ideals represented the dark side of American opportunities—of the streets paved with gold.

Even the American language—English—figures in Yiddish-American plays. Although literary playwrights struggled to maintain linguistic purity, English infiltrated the dialogue of popular Yiddish plays. As early as the 1880s, printed editions of Yiddish plays sometimes included glossaries in the back, explaining for European readers the Yiddish meanings of English words. Comic characters "broke their teeth" trying to master English; their malapropisms and inadvertent puns were a standard source of fun. Characters incorporated varying amounts of English into their dialogue as an indication of their type, social status, and degree of Americanization. Occasionally a character was supposed to be so affected, or so assimilated, that he spoke only English. By 1928, when Leon Kobrin wrote *Riverside Drive*, a drama about family alienation, he incorporated language into the action of the play by having the old characters speak and understand only Yiddish while their grandchildren speak and understand only English.

As in other American immigrant theaters, homesickness was a recurrent theme. Old country settings featured peasant girls in embroidered blouses and balalaika choruses. Songs like "Rumania, Rumania," "My Little Hometown Belz," and "I'm Homesick" profoundly moved the audience. Scenes of traditional ritual, such as lighting Sabbath candles, and reenactments of events out of Jewish history served to preserve and reinforce communal identity in the face of isolation and assimilation.

Scenes set in the new land, on the other hand, helped audiences to work through the painful problems of adjustment. For example, Gordin's play, *Homeless*, depicts an immigrant family in which the mother fails to adjust to American big city life, loses touch with her rapidly Americanized husband and children, and finally goes mad. The protagonist of Leivick's *Rags* is an old man who refuses to join his fellow rag sorters in a strike because, he explains bitterly, a dollar more a week cannot restore the dignity of their lives as respected scholars in the Old Country. Even the jokes about greenhorn blunders gave the audiences new courage. While they laughed at newcomers lost among big buildings and confused by new customs, such scenes reminded them that they had passed through their own early ordeals of initiation and were Americans now.

For many in the audience who were fresh from peasant villages, there was yet another way in which theater helped to educate them to become Americans. Yiddish dramatists sometimes used the classics of world literature *(Hamlet, Faust)* as a source of plots, and faraway times and places (fifteenth-century Spain, nineteenth-century France) as settings. Gordin, in particular, deliberately incorporated into his dialogue literary allusions together with explanations. All this brought Western culture to those in the audience who lacked it. Later, when Eastern Europe had come to seem a world as distant as Shakespeare's England, plays set in the old country taught an already alienated younger generation about their roots.

The theater event itself provided enrichment and support for the immigrant community. Its warmth was the intimate atmosphere of an "insiders" event for people who were still outsiders in America. The play was for them and, often, about them, and in their own language. They could relax in the theater among their own kind. In the lobby they ran into old friends or made new ones. Benefits to raise funds for a fraternal or charitable organization ensured that the evening would be practically a reunion. In other words, theatergoing took over some of the functions of the traditional community institutions back home. It even helped maintain a calendar separate from that of the rest of the world, by presenting a play in biblical setting in the appropriate holiday season, for example, or a play by Sholom Aleichem on the anniversary of his death. Most important of all, perhaps, the theater helped to maintain the Yiddish language and literature.

Since ancient times rabbinical opinion has been sternly against theater. The Talmudic commentators considered theater pagan, frivolous, and vulgar. In fact, the reference in the first psalm to the "seat of scoffers" has been traditionally interpreted as theater. All the same, in the phrase of one elderly man recalling a half century of attending Yiddish theater, audiences "ate theater for bread." Informants of his generation recall spending their last dime on a theater ticket instead of carfare or dinner. The show, they say, helped them forget hunger, cold, and homesickness. Indeed, memoirs of actors, newspaper accounts of "patriot" ovations, published critiques, letters to the editor, theatrical manifestos and semi-fictional vignettes testify to the strength of this feeling for theater—a feeling so unaccountably strong and widespread that it seems to be a basic element of modern Yiddish culture.

Yiddish theater, both professional and amateur, continues to be performed and in some seasons even to flourish. However, most American Jews with strong feelings for theater attend not only Yiddish but also American theater. For the majority, English theater has supplanted the Yiddish entirely. One result of this shift is that Ashkenazic Jews have had an impact on American theater vastly disproportionate to their numbers in the population as a whole.

In his book, *The Season (A Candid Look at Broadway)*, the playwright and novelist William Goldman estimated that in 1968 "a conservative guess would be that Jews account for 50% of the attendance on Broadway."[3] Inevitably the tastes and expectations of so many ticket buyers affected what was produced and what was successful. The institution of theater parties reinforces this influence. The large-scale theater party benefit seems to have developed from the Yiddish theater's practice of selling blocks of seats—sometimes entire houses—as a fund-raising activity for charity or fraternal organizations. Very many Jewish organizations still maintain the practice regularly. Furthermore,

Goldman estimates that a very large proportion of the professional theater party organizers are Jewish themselves.

Ashkenazic Jews make up a sizable proportion of the professionals of American theater (and film, and television). Among the actors, some actually began their careers in Yiddish theater; Molly Picon, Stella Adler, Paul Muni, Herschel Bernardi are among the best known examples. About half the American plays that opened in New York in the 1967–68 season (again according to Goldman) were written by Jews. And many of the producers, theatrical lawyers, agents, and public relations people were Ashkenazic Jews. When Actors Equity was organizing, the Hebrew Actors Union brought hot coffee and doughnuts to the picket lines; now the Hebrew Actors Union is affiliated with Equity.

Occasionally a play has come directly from the Yiddish stage to the American. Hirschbein's *The Idle Inn* and Pinsky's *The Treasure* are two examples. The best known example is Ansky's *The Dybbuk*, which in 1977 played at the Public Theater translated by Mira Rafelowicz. Paddy Chayevsky's *The Tenth Man*, produced on Broadway twenty years earlier, was based on *The Dybbuk*— not a translation, this time, but an adaptation of a Yiddish play. *Fiddler on the Roof* comes more obliquely from Yiddish theater, since it is taken not from the dramatization of Sholom Aleichem's stories that was popular on the Yiddish stage but directly from the stories themselves. There have been several plays about Yiddish theater, such as *Café Crown* and *The Prince of Grand Street*. Then there are other plays that have nothing to do with Yiddish theater at all but are about Jews (like *Milk and Honey*), or are played by actors with Yiddish mannerisms (Joseph Buloff in *The Price*), or seem congenial to the style or themes of Yiddish theater *(Majority of One, Square in the Eye, Family Business.)*

Granted, these connections do not seem firmly established. Yet it is undeniable that there are plays people describe as Jewish, just as people describe Barbra Streisand's style as Jewish, an impression that has nothing to do with her religious practices or her knowledge of Yiddish. (Even Fanny Brice, to whom Ms. Streisand is often compared, didn't really know Yiddish; she learned her Yiddish words and accent just to use them on stage.)

Ashkenazic Jews have been especially productive in the genre of musical comedy. In Eastern Europe, long before professional Yiddish theater existed, there were many groups of Jewish musicians specializing in weddings of Jews and non-Jews, too. It became a commonplace of Yiddish theater that every show had to have music. The popular plays inserted songs and dances lavishly into the action; more intellectual plays included fewer songs and tried harder to integrate them subtly into the plot. George Gershwin attended Yiddish musical theater and went backstage to compliment Tomashevsky in his dressing room. Obviously there is no reason to think that most Jewish musical comedy writers knew much about Yiddish theater. But what is not debatable is that since King David Jews have been drawn to the field of music, and it is striking how many famous American Jewish musical comedy writers there have been. William

Goldman lists twenty-two of them, including Rodgers, Hart, Lerner, Lowe, Kern, Romberg, Styne, and Sondheim. He concludes:

> In the last half century, the only major gentile composer to come along was Cole Porter. Without Jews, there simply would have been no musical comedy to speak of in America.[4]

Another genre which seems to have roots in Yiddish theater is stand-up comedy. The Jewish stand-up comic's ancestor is the *badkhon*, the wedding jester or wedding bard who to this day performs at Hasidic weddings. The *badkhon*'s monologue is in rhyme, much of it spontaneous or at least with the air of spontaneity. Each *badkhon* has his own style: benevolent, dignified, merry or slashing. His subjects are the members of the wedding party and their guests; marriage, birth, and death; religion, morals, and politics. His address is witty but also serious; traditionally a moment comes when the bride and guests weep at his sad reflections on life. The styles of Lenny Bruce, Shelly Berman, Mort Sahl, Woody Allen, Sam Levenson and many others retain the intimate quality of the *badkhon*. It is a personal style, as if addressing wedding guests rather than an anonymous audience; in some cases it is even aggressively personal, insistently naked, and this is part of what people mean when they refer to a "show biz" manner. Such comedians also retain the *badkhon*'s assumption that the universe is their material and that they should make their audiences not only laugh but think about their human condition.

Besides European sources—the *badkhon* and other varieties of Yiddish ritual jesters and folk preachers—American Jewish comedians have an authentically American Jewish source: the Catskills. Many American Jewish comedians actually began their careers entertaining in the "borscht belt" circuit (hotels in the Catskill mountains catering to a primarily Jewish clientele), and the intimacy and vulgarity of the borscht belt is often part of the stand-up comic routine. Comic patter sprinkled with Yiddish words and inflections, with allusions to *bar mitzvahs*, Jewish neighborhoods, and Jewish insecurities, is also an inheritance from the Catskills. To these sources Irving Howe adds the nervousness and aggressiveness of the immigrant, out on the street hustling for his life. When comedians performing in nightclubs or sitting on the guests' sofa on television talk shows have these characteristics, they seem to be part of the essence of show biz and of New York, both qualities which tend to blur in the popular mind with Yiddishness.

As for more serious dramatic genres, American Yiddish theater, like American German theater, served as a conduit for new currents that were stirring in the European theater from before the turn of the century. Stark Young, Brooks Atkinson, and other critics spread the word that the avant-garde could be found on the Lower East Side—sometimes sooner than uptown.

For example, Tolstoy's *The Power of Darkness* played on the Lower East Side in Yiddish translation beginning in 1905. Intellectually adventurous New Yorkers went downtown to taste its grim Russian naturalism, for no English production reached uptown New York till 1920. Similarly, Tolstoy's *Redemption* (also known as *The Living Corpse*) played downtown in Yiddish in 1911 and uptown in English in 1918; and Andreyev's *Anathema* downtown in 1910 and uptown in 1923. Gorky's *The Lower Depths*, which opened in both languages in 1919, remained in the Yiddish repertory for decades. Furthermore, besides these and other Russian originals, the Yiddish playwrights of the same period, many of whom were actually born or even educated in Russia, found them congenial models and developed works in the same mode. Such dramatists as Jacob Gordin *(God, Man, and Devil)* and Leon Kobrin *(Yankl Boyle)* made the naturalistic world view and its dark grotesque atmosphere accessible to American theatergoers.

In the 1920s, when expressionism became known as a mode for the avant-garde, it was almost a commonplace on the Yiddish stage for more ambitious efforts. Expressionism was especially useful for evoking the depths of religious experience and for presenting political abstractions, both of which were important subjects in Yiddish theater. Moreover, it was associated with central and Eastern Europe, "home" for most American Jews—or for their grandparents. *Bloody Laughter*, by the important German expressionist Ernst Toller, had its first New York production in Yiddish translation.

Indeed, Chekhov's *Uncle Vanya*, Strindberg's *The Father*, Romain Rolland's *Wolves*, Schnitzler's *Professor Bernardi*—all were performed in America in Yiddish translation before they were performed in English. Ibsen's *A Doll's House* and *An Enemy of the People* were staples in the serious Yiddish repertories, and Gordin and others consciously took the fusion of symbol and structure in Ibsen's problem plays as their inspiration.

In acting style, too, the Yiddish theater became both museum and laboratory for the uptown theater. The Yiddish popular theater preserved the mystique of the star, by then relatively outmoded on the American stage, as well as the nineteenth century's broad acting style. Diametrically opposite were the Jewish Art Theater, Irving Place Theater, and other Yiddish intellectual theaters, where the philosophy was Stanislavskian truthfulness and the style was modern ensemble work. (The Stanislavskian "method" was championed in America by the Group Theater whose leaders included Harold Clurman, familiar with Yiddish theater, and Stella Adler, an actress in it.) The leftist theater group Artef was a showcase for experimental expressionism, with its elaborately nonrealistic movement and speech.

Artef's impact on audiences was meant to be ideological as much as aesthetic. People who didn't even speak Yiddish came to Artef's performances of the *Yiddish Recruits*, Hallie Flanagan's *Drought* in Yiddish translation, and other leftist plays and stayed for political discussions with the cast. Other professional and amateur Yiddish theaters, too, presented plays with clear political messages. Artef was not the only American theater, nor even the only American foreign-language theater, to use the stage as a forum for reform, especially political reform. But it was the best known and perhaps the most influential. Furthermore, it is worth noting that the Workers Laboratory Theatre and other English-language groups included Yiddish-speaking Jews among their original organizers.

Increasingly over the last few years, young American Jews—most of whom speak no Yiddish—have tried consciously to use Jewish culture as a basis for theatrical experimentation. The American Jewish Theatre has produced Yiddish plays in English translation. More common are scripts created directly in English, either from existing Yiddish material (such as *Not Afraid of Failing*, adapted from a Peretz story by Avram Patt with the Barking Rooster Theatre) or from specifically American Jewish history (such as *A Jew in Kansas* written by Norman Fedder for the Jewish Heritage Theatre). In 1979 the Jewish Theatre Association emerged as a "service organization" intending to "articulate and promote . . . theatre relating to the Jewish experience"; its founding members included fifteen theater companies and thirty independent directors, producers and playwrights. The association's manifesto states that its first objective is "to serve as an advocate of theatre relating to the Jewish experience" and to "broaden its audiences within both the Jewish and general communities." A further, unstated objective seems to be to use theater as a personal link with Jewishness for both audiences and artists. This venture is an indication of the continued organized connection between the impulse to Jewishness and the impulse to theater.

The fans of popular Yiddish theater had an intense attachment to the theatergoing experience. More intellectual theatergoers associated theater and ideals, both aesthetic ideals and political. They attached to their theater a great range of hopes: that it would represent to Gentile Americans Yiddish culture at its highest; that it would teach morals, making the members of the audience more understanding people; that it would enlighten them politically; that it would make them more thoughtful and refined; that it would make them truly American, by portraying American life, or make them cosmopolitan by alluding to the history and literature of western civilization; that it would preserve and even elevate Yiddish literature and language; and furthermore that by portraying traditional Jewish life, it would make better Jews of the American-born generations who could see this tradition only on the stage. It is, therefore, not surprising that many of the passionate reformers of the twentieth-century American theater, so many critics, so many sponsors and patrons, so many experimenters, came out of Yiddish culture.

A feeling for theater seems to be an element in Ashkenazic Jewish culture. Ashkenazic Jews in America created a lively theater of their own in Yiddish and helped create the larger American theater as well. Why theater should be such a catalyst for their particular energies is, like all such cultural predilections, a mystery. Whatever the dynamics behind it, however, it has enriched American theater and American culture.

NOTES

1. Brooks Atkinson in a 1947 assessment of the Yiddish Art Theatre which appeared in the Sunday theater section of *The New York Times,* quoted in Nahma Sandrow, *Vagabond Stars: A World History of Yiddish Theater* (New York: Harper & Row, 1977), pp. 270–71.

2. The personal rivalry between the American tragedian Edwin Forrest and the English actor William Charles Macready, together with the American mob's anti-British feeling, led to mass rioting outside the Astor Place Opera House where Macready was to play Macbeth. An infantry regiment called out to quell the riot fired into the crowd, killing twenty-two.

3. William Goldman, *The Season* (New York: Harcourt, Brace & World, 1968), p. 149.

4. Ibid., p. 148.

Some Intersections of Jews, Music, and Theater

Mark Slobin

IN 1916 JOSEPH RUMSHINSKY WAS WRITING THE SCORE FOR THE OPERETTA
Broken Violin (Tsebrokhene Fidele), which was to help win him the title of "The
Jewish Victor Herbert." Eager to maintain complete secrecy, he presented the
score privately to Boris Thomashefsky, superstar of Yiddish theater, at the
latter's country estate. A teen-ager sneaked in to listen—his name was George
Gershwin.

This piquant moment can stand for an intersection of two overlapping worlds
which encompass the relationship of Jewish-American artists to musical theater. The world of a Rumshinsky is group-specific: songs are in a European
language, sensibilities have been trained in Old World contexts, but the composer constantly struggles to create an international style within ethnic boundaries. The world of Gershwin and his Jewish colleagues lies within the
American mainstream, but occasionally suggests the world of tradition through
minor keys and turns of phrase. At the point of contact of these two musical
spheres we find many intersections: countless mutual borrowings found on 78
rpm records like "The Yiddish Yackadula Hickadula," an imitation of the
Hawaiian sound, and the Original Dixieland Jazz Band's "Palesteena Fox Trot";
or messages from one world to another, such as Irving Berlin and Al Jolson
saluting the creation of the State of Israel with new songs.

In a brief essay there is no easy way to consider the many issues, personalities, and styles that arise from the evolution and collision of Jewish-
American musical worlds, even when we restrict the survey to theatrical
material. All we can do is focus on a few key intersections of Jews, music, and
theater in America; the first is in the 1890s, the last in the 1960s. Several cases
involve theatrical material that not only *is* entertainment but is about entertainment, more specifically about performers. The entertainer, the actual transmit-
ter of the musical style that characterizes the group or him/herself reflects the
concerns that make the entertainment important to its audience. This puts a
great burden on performers, who must simultaneously succeed professionally
while they serve as showcase representatives of the group's strivings for recognition. This responsibility was not borne lightly by immigrant entertainers, but
neither did it affect them adversely. At any rate, none of them crumbled under
the pressure of reflecting their generation the way rock stars like Janis Joplin or
Jimi Hendrix did. Instead, the energies of entertainers fueled the growth of their
individual careers and set off reactions throughout the culture, both within the
group and without. As Alfred Kazin has noted for American literature,

> The positive, creative role of the Jews as modern American, and above all as a
> modern American writer, was in the first years of this century being prepared

not in the universities, not even in journalism, but in the vaudeville theaters, music halls, and burlesque houses where the pent-up eagerness of penniless immigrant youngsters met the raw urban scene on its own terms.[1]

We begin, appropriately, with a theatrical moment hard to date precisely, since it stems from the immigrant era: *Shloyme Gorgel*, a play by the indefatigable Joseph Lateiner, author of some two hundred potboilers. Lateiner was a master theatrical "baker," to use the Yiddish term. Coming to America in the first massive wave of immigration (1882), he set up shop near his arch-rival from Rumania, "Professor" Hurwitz, and the two writers turned out at least one play a week during the brief season. Lateiner's works were enormously popular throughout the 1880s and 1890s, and were rapidly exported to Europe, where they played for decades. In America, Lateiner was able to make a comeback as late as the early 'teens. Scripts of his plays usually circulated in manuscript form; copies in the archives of YIVO (Jewish Research Institute, New York) come from locations as far as Capetown and as near as Cleveland. There are printed editions of a few of his plays—all are in Polish (pirated) versions and were printed long after the New York premiere.

Shloyme Gorgel, published in Warsaw in 1907, probably dates back to the 1890s, if not earlier. The play was typical of the musical melodramas held in contempt by writers and critics of Yiddish belles-lettres. This is evidenced by Sholom Aleichem's scornful mention of the piece in his novel *Blondzhende Shteren* ("Wandering Stars"), where the sleazy Lemberg impresario Getzel ben Getzel says: "The masses are asses," to which the author adds:

> Such modern dramas as "The Golden Land: A Bloody Tragedy" . . . were too heavy for Getzel's taste. Recently he had introduced a lighter repertory in a literary vein: "Hinke Pinke," "Shloima Gorgel," "Jump into Bed," and "Velvel Eats Compote."

Yet as Sholom Aleichem acknowledges about Getzel's audience, "Whatever he chose to give them, they would lick their fingers and come back for more."[2]

Lateiner's scissors-and-paste method, as described by the theater historian B. Gorin, was to take a non-Jewish (German, Rumanian, or whatever) play, insert songs, dances, and comedy, change the names of the characters to make them sound Jewish, and tack on a lively title. That music was an integral part of this theater is of particular interest to our concerns, though Gorin dismisses the interpolated songs as mere nonsense, designed to give the audience a theatrical smorgasbord. An analysis of how songs function in a typical Lateiner work like *Shloyme Gorgel*, however, shows that they carry much of the implied message of the melodrama and even develop characters.

The plot of *Shloyme Gorgel* is labyrinthine. The title character is a gifted cantor who has fallen on hard times, living as a perennially drunken street singer. Thus, we are dealing with a play that comments on the musician's lot. His fall was precipitated by his daughter Hadassah's arrest and seventeen-year imprisonment for murdering her infant. However, Hadassah was falsely charged: a wealthy baker whose son, Mesholem, had secretly married and impregnated Hadassah, had the marriage annulled and the baby stolen, substituting a dead child to implicate Hadassah. The baker died, leaving Mesholem and the baker's wife, Gitele, ignorant of the plot. Shifra, the erstwhile infant, now seventeen, is meant to be Mesholem's wife, though she loves a baker's apprentice, Solomon. By play's end, Solomon gets his Shifra, Hadassah is vindicated and reunited with Mesholem, and a double wedding is planned. Much of the happy ending is due to a missing right ear-lobe of Shifra's, which identifies her as Hadassah's child. This device, as well as the general style of plot and construction, indicates Lateiner's affinity with—and probably direct borrowing from—mainstream Euro-American melodrama.

Unlike Lateiner's more successful dramas (e.g. *David's Violin, The Jewish Heart*), *Shloyme Gorgel* had none of its songs published in sheet music form. However, songs are clearly labeled and are given with full texts in the script. There are eleven musical numbers, or about half the total for the more ambitious musical dramas of Abraham Goldfadn, founder of the Yiddish theater. Where music is not the main focus of attention, but shares the limelight with comedy and melodrama, Lateiner places his songs within the play strategically.

The first song appears as a climax to the play's opening scene in court, where Shloyme Gorgel sings a bit of cantorial music for his daughter Hadassah, who has been so traumatized by seventeen years of imprisonment that she no longer recognizes her father. The relief provided by the music after the tense melodrama of the courtroom scene is very useful. The introduction of cantorial music has a threefold dramatic relevance: 1) the Jewishness of the characters, in the strained setting of a Polish courtroom, is vividly stated through music; 2) the better nature of Shloyme Gorgel, depicted heretofore as a rambling drunkard, is suggested; 3) the sentimental scene of the father-daughter reunion is expressively marked—no doubt tears flowed at this point in the old days.

In the second song, Mesholem, seemingly digressing from the action, asks: "When will truth come to light? How long can falsehood reign?" Unrelated as it may be to the moment at hand (as Gorin and other drama critics would charge), the song nicely sets up the suspense that marks any melodrama based on a series of delayed recognitions and vindication and also arouses sympathy for Mesholem. This latter function is important, as otherwise the audience might see him—instead of his dead father—as the villain for abandoning Hadassah.

The third song is a duet by Solomon and Shifra about the hypocrisy of the world: how the rich succeed, how a faithless wife triumphs. Through their appearance in a duet, we are led to believe they will eventually be united and they are present as the humble folk (bakery boy and adopted child) who will be rewarded. The fifth number, a solo song by Solomon, carries this theme farther, as he satirizes various "Eves" (women), including one who succeeds by becoming a madam, before praising the virtuous, long-suffering working wife "such as you won't find among the rich folks." This sets up a rich-poor commentary based on song and satire that has a long pedigree stretching back at least to Shakespeare's comic singing servants. At the same time, it coincides exactly with a strong trend in Yiddish folklore, literature, and popular song towards didacticism on the one hand, and sympathy for the underdog on the other.

Hadassah and Shloyme Gorgel perform the fourth song in their role as street singers, for Gitele, the baker's widow, supported by a chorus of baker's apprentices. Here again Gorgel's noble side comes to the fore as he sings a plaintive religious song asking God to intercede on behalf of the Jews, who are in exile. Hadassah is given a solo part to sing, underlining the pathos of her personal situation. This song has a metadramatic function. It accurately symbolizes the social exile of Shloyme Gorgel and his daughter (and perhaps the bakery boys as well) vis-à-vis the rich Gitele. In other words, the preoccupations of the culture constantly intrude upon the presumably independent life of the melodrama, via music, a pattern characteristic of the popular drama of most ethnic groups. In short, the critics' harsh appraisal of Lateiner is valid with respect to "art" drama, but fails to recognize the audience's point of view.

The remaining musical numbers of *Shloyme Gorgel* echo most of the concerns already voiced. Thus, Hadassah is allowed an aria of joy when her name is cleared and her daughter is found alive, again letting music mark a highly expressive moment. Two more songs attack the rich and the faithless, followed by a closing congratulatory number to make a festive conclusion. Taken as a whole, all of the numbers contribute richly to the dramatic impact and cultural resonance of the play. Only one is strictly extrinsic, in a sense of being more a production number than a part of the action: Shifra's divertissement on the topic of the vileness of other nations as opposed to the Jews, a song theme found both in folklore and in other popular entertainment of the period. It is a sophisticated number, which moves from the French, who drink champagne and tell lies and dance (cue for the "Marseillaise") to the Germans, anti-Semites who guzzle and cavort to "Ach de lieber Augustin," and finally attacks the Russians, "Ivans" who "chew straw" and drink "strong rum" and dance to a *komarinskaia*. As for the Jews—they work hard all week, have lots of troubles, and get their satisfaction from going to the Yiddish theater; only a hot play will get them to dance; this bit of self-advertisement for the Yiddish stage ends the number.

The importance of this elaborate song-and-dance routine is that its music moves outside the in-group world. Eclecticism in repertoire marked the entire Eastern European Jewish folk and popular music culture and formed a basic component of the music of the Yiddith theater. The first datable item of stage music we have (1881, from Jassy, Rumania, birthplace in 1876 of the Yiddish Theater) consists of orchestrated salon music, and we have a score from 1889 that consists of "different national songs," including Russian, Rumanian, Tyrolean, Chinese, and "Negro."[3] What is crucial here is that this outward-looking and stereotyping impulse coincides exactly with the main thrust of mainstream American popular entertainment during the peak period of Jewish immigration. In other words, while for their own internal reasons (too complex to detail here) Eastern European Jews were conversant with and able to satirize varied ethnic musics, they were to find that they had a skill that was marketable in the theaters of the New World: among Irving Berlin's first hits were "Marie of Sunny

Italy" and "Yiddle on your Fiddle Play Some Ragtime." Even before Berlin's debut in 1909, Sadie Koninsky was publishing mock-black ragtime pieces (late 1890s).

However, mainstream American drama was slow to grasp the usefulness of the brash, electric Jewish entertainer as a subject for commentary. It was not until immigration had been slowed to a trickle that *The Jazz Singer* could be written. Prior to that time there appeared in 1908 a play of major importance, also centering on an immigrant Jewish musician: Israel Zangwill's *The Melting Pot*. This overripe vehicle for a simplistic social philosophy made a tremendous impact when it first appeared, helping the term "melting pot" to become part of our permanent national vocabulary. Zangwill was a flamboyant English Jewish writer and public figure whose sympathies fluctuated from one cause to another. Inspired by Theodore Roosevelt, to whom the play is dedicated in the most grandiloquent terms, Zangwill set about showing America its future, using as his mouthpiece David Quixano, immigrant violinist and composer from Russia.

Everything about the social situation portrayed rings false, beginning with the hero's very name. Quixano hardly sounds Russian-Jewish, but there is no doubt about David's rather quixotic nature. The house he lives in with his uncle is given as being in "the Richmond, or non-Jewish borough of New York;" the incongruity of this immigrant-based drama taking place on Staten Island needs little comment. As part of his program, Zangwill introduces a broguish Irish servant, Kathleen, who little by little takes on the ways of David's old Yiddish-speaking, Orthodox aunt, so that by Act IV she is busy keeping kosher. David falls in love with a non-Jewish Russian émigré settlement worker, Vera, with the rather odd surname Revendal, who despises her father, a baron. The latter turns out eventually to be the leader of the infamous Kishinev pogrom of 1903, an event that stirred great sympathy for Russian Jews worldwide; he is also the murderer of David's family. Yet this cold-hearted anti-Semite, when confronted with David, relinquishes his pistol to the Jew and asks to be shot. David merely walks off the stage mumbling, and the only dramatic moment of the play fizzles like a wet firecracker.

What makes the play of interest to us is the use of music as the agent for Zangwill's propaganda. David, who loves going to Ellis Island on visits because of his fondness for immigration (!) dreams of writing an American Symphony to express his passionate belief that America is the destined producer of a future super-race:

> *Vera.* So your music finds inspiration in America?
> *David.* Yes—in the seething of the Crucible.
> *Vera.* The Crucible? I don't understand!
> *David.* Not understand that America is God's Crucible, the great Melting-Pot where all the races of Europe are melting and reforming! . . . Germans and Frenchmen, Irishmen and Englishmen, Jews and Russians—into the Crucible with you all! God is making the American. . . . The real American has not yet arrived. . . . He will be the fusion of all races, perhaps the coming superman. Ah, what a glorious Finale for my symphony—if I can only write it.[4]

The last line hints at David's general inadequacy—his shoulder has been hurt in the pogrom, so that he cannot function as violinist, and his will is weak. He is seen as a necessary transition phase to the superman, but he is still too attached to the vision of the past, as symbolized by the pogrom. It is the orphans of the Settlement House, where his symphony is finally premiered, who can fully appreciate his work, and who provide the play's ending: "From below comes up the softened sound of voices and instruments joining in 'My Country 'Tis of Thee.' The curtain falls slowly."

In general, the play reads more like a work of socialist realism than like a Broadway production, even one of 1908. Cartoon characters representing American wealth, acculturating ethnics, and dastardly Europeans float by. How Zangwill succeeded in making a powerful statement out of David's effusive, rhetorical flights on the glories of the American Melting Pot is hard to understand at a distance of some seventy-five years. It is certainly one of the more curious intersections of the Jew, the musician, and American theater. Yet certain of its images seem to have struck a responsive chord. The idea of the American Symphony has echoed through the corridors of Hollywood. As late as the postwar Marx Brothers movie, *The Big Store*, a vapid department-store farce, much of the film was devoted to preparation for, and performance of, a work called "The Tenement Symphony." This turns out to be a piece with melting pot ideals subtly skewed toward the emerging liberal ideal of cultural pluralism; the ethnic groups are allowed to sing their traditional tunes before fusing in the Crucible.

But we anticipate. Returning to Zangwill, we can note that he was following a rather obscure tradition begun in the 1880s by the bizarre Henry Harland. Harland was apparently not Jewish, but under the pseudonym Sidney Luska he wrote fiction about New York Jews. He subsequently expatriated himself and ended up as the editor of the notorious English bohemian journal, *The Yellow Book*. In his novel, *As It Was Written: A Jewish Musician's Story*, the lurid melodrama of Luska/Harland's implausible plot is briefly interrupted by commentary on the Jews' invaluable contribution to American society: "It is the Jewish element that will leaven the whole lump," says a sympathetic non-Jewish character, adding that because of the Jews, the arts will flourish in America.

Zangwill's elaboration of this viewpoint, though weak in dramatic terms, evoked considerable admiration, but also some criticism. He felt compelled to write an afterword for later editions of *The Melting Pot* (reprinted still in 1930), which only exposes the unevenness of his thinking. He is forced into a racist position by asserting that somehow the Jew, though distinctive, will indeed melt positively, as opposed to the Afro-American: "Jews are, unlike Negroes, a 'recessive' type whose physical traits tend to disappear in the blended off-spring," whereas "justifiably America avoids physical intermarriage with the Negro." In short, only Euro-Americans can successfully dissolve. Zangwill observes that "the comic spirit cannot fail to note the spiritual miscegenation which . . . has given 'rag-time' and the sex-dances that go with it, first to white America and thence to the whole white world."[5] Though he has once again intuitively hit upon music as a key symbol for the evolution of multi-ethnic American culture, Zangwill was obliged, in 1908, to stick to the art traditions of a David Quixano rather than to the more far-reaching achievements of pop performer/artists like Irving Berlin and Al Jolson. Had he written his play a bit later, he might have had a different sort of hero to speak through, though it is doubtful that the genteel Zangwill would have seized such an opportunity.

A young man named Samson Raphaelson did undertand the inherent dramatic possibilities of the rise of the immigrant entertainer. While still in his twenties, Raphaelson wrote a short story called "The Day of Atonement," and then turned it into a highly successful Broadway production of 1925 called *The Jazz Singer*. It starred George Jessel, who apparently gave the performance of a lifetime. Indeed, some New York reviews concentrated on the remarkable dramatic skills of the vaudevillian and even presumed the play was put together as a vehicle for Jessel's crossover to legitimate theater. It was, however, a goal far from Raphaelson's mind. The author laid out his own agenda with extreme clarity in a preface to the published version of the play. So careful is his explanation that it deserves lengthy quotation, especially as the play itself is usually mentioned only as a footnote to the celebrated talkie film version of 1927, a landmark in cinema history:

> In seeking a symbol of the vital chaos of America's soul, I find no more adequate one than jazz. Here you have the rhythm of frenzy staggering against a symphonic background—a background composed of lewdness, heart's delight, soul-racked madness, monumental boldness, exquisite humility, but principally prayer. . . . Jazz is prayer. It is too passionate to be anything else. It is prayer distorted, sick, unconscious of its destination. The singer of jazz is what Matthew Arnold said of the Jew, "lost between two worlds, one dead, the other powerless to be born." In this, my first play, I have tried to crystallize the ironic truth that one of the Americas of 1925—that one which packs to overflowing our cabarets, musical revues and dance halls—is praying with a fervor as intense as that of the America which goes sedately to church and synagogue. The jazz American is different from the dancing dervish, from the Zulu medicine man, from the negro evangelist only in that he doesn't know he is praying.
>
> I have used a Jewish youth as my protagonist because the Jews are determining the nature and scope of jazz more than any other race—more than the negroes, from whom they have stolen jazz and given it a new color and meaning. Jazz is Irving Berlin, Al Jolson, George Gershwin, Sophie Tucker. These are Jews with their roots in the synagogue. And these are expressing in evangelical terms the nature of our chaos today.
>
> You find the soul of a people in the songs they sing. You find the meaning of the songs in the soul of the minstrels who create and interpret them. In "The Jazz Singer" I have attempted an exploration of the soul of one of these minstrels.[6]

Raphaelson's romanticization of the Jazz Age need not detain us; it is a fairly conventionalized sentiment of the day. What is interesting is his insight into the linkage of the Jew "with his roots in the synagogue" with the social ferment here loosely generalized as jazz. There are both literal and metaphoric truths lurking in his purple prose. Literally, he is correct: many of the main figures of Jewish-American, internal entertainment began their careers as choirboys; in addition, a figure like Irving Berlin had similar experiences, and Jolson himself really was the son of a cantor. Metaphorically, the sense of the star entertainer as being on a par with the ecstatic, shamanistic ritual of the evangelist and medicine man is an insight regarding American popular culture that was just beginning to emerge in 1925. Raphaelson had grasped the fact that the immigrants could wield power through entertainment, and that their power stemmed from an ability to channel their indigenous expressive systems into strategic, socially rewarding directions. It is no accident that he calls these entertainers "minstrels:" they literally were minstrels. Virtually every major entertainer—Jolson, Cantor, Jessel, Sophie Tucker, even the Yiddish comedienne Molly Picon—appeared in blackface early in their careers. Some of them explicitly state, in memoirs, the comfort they derived from putting on that all-American mask of burnt cork. In blackface, they were no longer the immigrant—they were one with the soul of America as represented by the grotesque co-optation of the slave's persona. As bizarre as such a phenomenon must have been for Eastern European Jews, so completely unfamiliar with the concept of black vs. white as cardinal principle of social organization, they quickly understood its value for them: the ritual mask of the powerless gave them, the underdogs, sacred strength in this strange and dangerous New World. Of course, for the Jolson generation, the strangeness had worn off a bit. We know that by 1900 the younger immigrants and first-generation American Jews were frequenting the haunts of the "coon shouters" and other purveyors of racial and ethnic entertainment. They were ready to move onto the stage at an early age, often at age ten or under.

Raphaelson's perception, then, is an accurate one, and also an unprecedented one. Earlier dramas on the topic of the immigrant entertainer widely missed the mark. We have already seen the Englishman Zangwill's American play. An even earlier vehicle was produced by none other than the Bishop of Broadway, David Belasco, in 1904—*The Music Master*. In it, Belasco starred David Warfield, who had made a career as a caricature Jew from low vaudeville through high vaudeville (Weber and Fields) all the way to Belasco's play *The Auctioneer*, in which he played a pawnbroker. *The Music Master*, then, was Warfield's first non-Jewish role, and was a great success. He played Anton von Barwig, a noble German composer, pianist, and conductor who has fallen on hard times in America and lives in a boarding house on Houston Street with an assortment of French, Italian, and German fellow musicians who are, precociously, straight out of the Marx Brothers. They have names like Poons, Pinac, and Fico, eat spaghetti, and play at the local café. Their entire world centers on becoming "legitimate" classical performers, but von Barwig himself must play at a "Museum" freak-show starring "Bosco, the armless wonder." For Belasco (or his house writer, Charles Klein, who is credited with the play), this immigrant musician froth is merely backdrop for von Barwig's pursuit of his lost daughter in America. We are given to understand that, if worse came to worse, he could always return to Leipzig and conduct the orchestra again. Von Barwig is an anachronism who more properly belongs to the mid-nineteenth century, when German musicians began to come to America to shape its classical music institutions. The upgrading of Warfield from pawnbroker to noble musician, then, represents a denial, rather than an affirmation of interest in the ethnic entertainer—the anachronistic von Barwig substitutes for the immigrant reality.

Thus, it is by comparison with the work of Zangwill and Belasco that we must measure Raphaelson's achievement, and that comparison only increases the stature of both author and character. The plot of *The Jazz Singer* is almost laughably simple. Jakie Rabinowitz, now Jack Robin, a cantor's son, is posed on the edge of great success—he needs only to appear at opening night in a lavish Broadway revue. This, however, coincides with Yom Kippur, holiest day of the Jewish year. His father dying, Jakie/Jack is implored by his mother and the community to sing the powerful Kol Nidre chant in the old cantor's place. After much soul-searching, the jazz singer acquiesces.

The first-night reviews for *The Jazz Singer* are interesting, demonstrating some ongoing aspects of ethnic-based entertainment. At first reading, the reviews of the *Times* and *Herald Tribune* seem contradictory:

> [The play is] so written that even the slowest of wits can understand it. *The Jazz Singer* takes no chances with its audiences; it strives always to be successful. *(Times)*

> It is a well-known fact that plays in which the principal characters are Jews, even in the broadest comedies, appeal particularly to Jewish audiences, and we believe that such will be the case with *The Jazz Singer*. We know of no play that requires so thorough an understanding of and sympathy with the Jew and his faith as does this one. Indeed, many of the lines of the play which were spoken in dialect, while wholly unintelligible to us, were received with enthusiasm by an audience almost entirely composed of those of the Jewish race. *(Herald Tribune)*

Both reviews are—partially—right. In fact, the play does depict some aspects of Lower East Side life in detail, and would particularly appeal to the in-group audience. This aspect of dramatic construction is one which marks popular drama in general, with its highly faithful reproduction of the outside world. It is necessary to gain an unsophisticated audience's approval of both the fantasy element of a play and of the underlying social message: reality must underlie illusion. Interestingly, the film version of *The Jazz Singer* was put together with equal care. Members of the cast studied East Side types, and those parts of the film that dealt with the Jewish quarter were filmed on location, including an actual synagogue. For a mainstream play like *The Jazz Singer*, there is little to lose and a good deal to gain by winning over the group being depicted. That has been obvious to New York dramatists since the days of the first important ethnic caricature, the stage Irishman, before the Civil War.

On the other hand the *Times* reviewer is certainly justified in describing the

portrayal as being done in broad brushstrokes. There is little subtlety in any of
the depictions of character, or in the plot, and the show is mainly a vehicle for
the ideas Raphaelson expresses in his preface; in this sense, he is the legitimate
heir to Zangwill. Perhaps the lack of dramatic excellence is one reason that
Jessel's performance was so central to the play's success (and later, Jolson's
contribution to the film). What is important about *The Jazz Singer* is not its
stature as a play, or its success as a ground-breaking talkie, but its myth-
making quality. This has two sides: one in the structure of the play itself, and
one in the nature of its screen adaptation. Internally, Raphaelson has so clearly
molded his drama around a character that almost looks like someone real—
Jolson— that once it was put on the screen, it was largely taken as being an
accurate biographical account of the great star. Indeed, one of the first-night
Broadway critics coyly suggested that there might be a reason for pictures of
Jolson to be seen hanging on the set wall in one scene. Yet the plot has scarcely
any documentary basis; indeed, it departs radically from the details of Jolson's
life in some key respects. While it is true that his father was a cantor, it was his
mother who died first, when the future star was quite young. It was the existence
of a none-too-benevolent stepmother that drove little Asya Yoelson out into the
streets with his older brother. The brother, who seems to have played a considerable role in Jolson's childhood, is completely absent from both the play and
the film. One of the interesting points about *The Jazz Singer* is the centrality of
the father-son rivalry, a topic by now buried in Jewish-American literature
under the staggering weight of the Jewish Mother Syndrome of recent years and
its critique. Raphaelson avoids such a stereotype of immigrant life to more
effectively place the locus of generational contention at the father-son interaction, particularly where the father represents a hereditary skill (sacred song)
and genealogy now in danger of abrupt disjuncture. In a sense, the doting
mother/hidebound father/rebellious son triangle is more truly American, and
shows Raphaelson to be a skillful manipulator of symbols.

Where Raphaelson departs from formula melodrama is at the very end. It is
rather unclear as to whether the hero will return to the stage or, moved by
singing Kol Nidre in his father's place, will stay in the ghetto as a cantor. That
there was a certain ambivalence to this open-ended conclusion is apparent from
the early reviews, which seem divided on the question of the outcome. In this
realm the screen adaptation makes the most telling shift. After we see Jolson
sing at the synagogue, we are immediately transferred to the vaudeville theater,
where he sings a mammy song for his sweet old mother, who now has no
compunctions at seeing him in blackface. This is a major change of focus for
The Jazz Singer, since a play's ending always illuminates the meaning of its
entire span. In the Broadway version, we are meant to be disturbed by the
internal tension of the hero and of the group to which he belongs—immigrant
entertainers. On the larger level, the story is meant to apply to immigrants in
general, who face the agonizing decision of throwing away their cultural birthright in the pursuit of successful assimilation. By suggesting that the decision
may be to reject success, Raphaelson has in fact flirted with a heretical state-

ment; neither the Jewish nor the mainstream audience of 1925 would be likely to find it palatable. One imagines Jessel to have implied, through his magnetism as vaudevillian, the inevitability of the hero's return to the stage.

The fact that the film version allows the hero to be both cantor and vaudevillian is somewhat more banal, but it is an ending which packs more mythic muscle. In effect, the film is an endorsement of the emerging doctrine of cultural pluralism in its early form. While the New Ethnicity of the 1970s proclaims the long-range possibility of being good Americans and colorful ethnics simultaneously, the earlier tendency of cultural pluralism was to imagine that ethnic heritages, valuable as they might be, would slowly pale as assimilation to mainstream culture took place. The acceptance by the Jolson figure's mother of blackface vaudeville is an embracing of America—for the first time, the Jewish mother and the black mammy are viewed as synonymous. In this sense, the screenplay goes a step farther than Zangwill's melting pot in asserting that even a black component can tinge the emerging New American. Yet the singer can officiate at "the church of his choice" on his off-time, and can promise his mother to move her uptown to "where all the —Bergs live," in a segregated ethnic neighborhood. It is significant that the passage about the move uptown comes from Jolson's own improvised dialogue and was not part of the screenplay. He surely would have liked to move his own mother uptown as, say, Milton Berle and the Marx Brothers did, had she not died young. One of my favorite comments on *The Jazz Singer* comes from a student paper, which characterized the film as being the kind of movie Jack Robin would have enjoyed taking his parents to see. Cheerfully acculturated, comfortably housed, the elder Rabinowitz/Robin might have had a good time watching a show depicting the rise of the immigrant entertainer. Essential to this cozy quality of the film is the fact that throughout, Jack Robin is a good guy. He has to be, of course, or we could not muster the sympathy sufficient to empathize, nor would he make good material for myth. Yet every account of Jolson's life makes it abundantly clear that he was a hard-driving, egotistical and incredibly ambitious showman who was not very kind to fellow entertainers. The very qualities which help define his intense striving for upward mobility and which might make the immigrants' struggle for success more believable had to wait for the later generation of *What Makes Sammy Run*. It is as if the seeds of a complex description of Jewish-American life had to germinate one by one as the cultural-ecological conditions allowed.

Space does not allow for a full survey of various trends in the intersection points of Jews, music, and theater in America from the 1930s through the 1960s. Mainstream entertainment's view of the Jews fluctuated considerably throughout, ranging from the persistence of Jewish-character comic strips through the success of *The Goldbergs*, an innocuous radio sitcom depicting slow acculturation, to the actual retouching of plays in the late 1940s to avoid offending post-Holocaust sensibilities. It seems useful to focus on one particular trend—the Jewish self-image as gleaned from two rather self-conscious works spanning the period under discussion: 1933 and 1964.

In 1933 one of the most extraordinary theatrical events in American history was produced—by the Jewish community. This was the grand pageant called *The Romance of a People*. Produced first at the Chicago World's Fair, it was re-staged in New York and then toured to various cities. Its first performance was seen by 200,000 people, resulting in a $60,000 profit, and the New York re-run was witnessed by nearly a million, with a $450,000 gross.[7] All funds were used to facilitate the emigration and resettlement—largely in Palestine—of European Jews who were feeling, already in 1933, the pressure of Nazi policies.

Romance was truly popular drama at its grandest, using a performance space 550 by 330 feet and a cast of thousands, drawn from Hebrew schools and communal organizations. Its action consisted of a set of scenes designed to cover the course of Jewish history, culminating in the colonization of Palestine. No energy was spared in creating the light and sound aspects of the production, and a separate musical component was assembled, based on the scholarly collections of the major researcher of Jewish music, A. Z. Idelsohn. The synopsis of the scenes and the music shows something of a hodgepodge of ideas, combined with extravagant claims, e.g. "many [melodies] were probably part of the services in the Temple at Jerusalem." Regarding Hasidic dance, we are told it is "the only dance in the world created out of humility." Despite the pretentiousness and propagandistic nature of the show, *The Romance of a People* was an important milestone in Jewish-American dramatic achievement. Exposing one's history to the full glare of non-Jewish secular scrutiny, daring to build the biggest production in American theater history to evoke sympathy for oppressed brethren—these are substantial goals that were successfully carried out. The self-confidence of the Jewish Americans who could boast the great civic and educational infrastructure capable of supplying *Romance* was formidable. That it was so ephemeral is not surprising; one need make such a point only once.

We have seen Jewish Americans evolve a set of complex responses to American life, using drama, the image of the entertainer, and music, and take their message to the mainstream audience in diverse ways. A full-length account of these processes would, of course, require a monograph. The purely internal reflections on life in Europe embodied in a melodrama such as *Shloyme Gorgel* was nicely complemented by the acculturated playwright Zangwill's insistence on the Jew's dissolving into the mainstream. By the time of *The Jazz Singer*, a Jewish-American playwright could depict the conflicts aroused by the end of mass immigration and the beginnings of cultural pluralism, still centering on the crucial personage of the Jewish musician. *The Romance of a People* showed a community capable of taking its internal feelings and aspirations and projecting them on a huge scale for all to see, a project that met with praise and financial success in the context of sympathy for the Jewish cause.

The 1960s brought about the reinterpretation of the European past through Jewish-American eyes, produced for the general world, not just for the American public. Reflected in the harsh light of the Holocaust, the New World experience sought re-definition through re-evaluation of the Old World in many literary, musical, and artistic genres after 1945. Nostalgia was the pleasantest road to follow, and the one most likely to open the doors to popular entertainment. Despite the success of *The Diary of Anne Frank*, it was only at the tail end of the 1970s, via television, that the saga of the destruction of European Jewry could be truly mass marketed through *Holocaust*. The 1960s demanded a lighter touch, and the fiddler, not the SS, was placed on the roof.

Of the many aspects of *Fiddler on the Roof* that merit analysis, one that is suited for our purposes is the re-shaping of the Old World via changes in the thrust of Sholom Aleichem's stories about Tevya the Dairyman, the fictional accounts of the Jews of the Southern Ukraine that form the basis for the musical's book.

The most obvious decision was to omit the fate of the remaining daughters of Tevya, Shprintse and Beilka, and concentrate on the first three (Khava, Hodel, and Tsaytl). Doubtless the format of a stage presentation is too short to contain five whole fates, and even Maurice Schwartz's elegant Yiddish film version of the stories doesn't attempt full coverage. Yet one might detect a certain pattern of treatment of the Old World theme that makes it logical that these particular daughters be omitted. Shprintse commits suicide after her romance with the son of a wealthy family humiliatingly falls through. Beilka succeeds where Shprintse failed; she catches a rich man, only to find herself alienated from her father in the city, and then her husband is ruined financially, and she has to emigrate.

These are tragic stories quite different from the material chosen for *Fiddler*. Tsaytl marries the sweet little tailor instead of the well-to-do but coarse butcher. Hodel sacrifices herself for the sake of secular idealism by linking her fate to that of the revolutionary Perchik. Khava commits the ultimate social crime of marriage to a non-Jew. The predicaments of Hodel and Khava are those of modernism vs. tradition. Tsaytl falls into the same category through rejecting an arranged marriage. Tsaytl's internally raised and resolved problem is of a fairly minor order; the major crises are those relating to the outside world of Christianity and revolution, specters that haunt the traditional Jewish world.

With Shprintse and Beilka, Sholom Aleichem was continuing an earlier type of in-group social commentary, one satirizing and condemning the class structure of the Eastern European Jews, for which these daughters pay more heavily than did Tsaytl. The repulsive game played by the rich folks, which kills Shprintse, and the unpleasantness of Beilka's foray into a foreign socioeconomic world are clearly not material for nostalgia, even the hard-headed nostalgia of *Fiddler* which admits of occasional (though bloodless) pogroms.

That this is not merely an accidental attitude of the Broadway show is underscored by two smaller, but significant, changes of the Sholom Aleichem original. *Fiddler* ends up being very unsure about Khava, the renegade. In the original, the reader is left poised on the agonizing knife-edge of the question of Tevya's indecision when faced with Khava's interest in reconciliation at the point of Tevya's forced departure from his village. Sholom Aleichem leaves the matter unresolved, though perhaps implies a "yes" answer to the question of whether the father should take the daughter back. In *Fiddler*, not only is the entire theme avoided, but the matter of Khava is drastically bleached out by having her appear with her Ukrainian husband Fedka and announce that they mean to "go to Cracow" out of indignation against the orders forcing Tevya and other Jewish villagers off their property. This wholesale avoidance of the social and domestic problems raised by the Tevya stories points toward the general weakening of thrust already indicated by the omission of two whole daughters.

The secondary extraordinary alteration of the stories is the assumption of America as Tevya's final destination. This is diametrically opposed to the sense of the original. There Beilka and her ruined husband have to go to America; Tevya means to proceed to Palestine. The unerring introduction of America is, of course, completely suited to the postwar Broadway audience, who would like to see all of the Yiddish heritage as prophetic of their successful rise to comfort in the New World. It is also an internationally acceptable way to end the show on a hopeful note, as musicals should end.

The music of *Fiddler* is rather like the show in general. Jerry Bock's score aims largely at being Broadway, with a soupçon of ethnic flavor. No systematic Jewish elements are introduced; one merely finds an occasional reference to the melodic turns and scale types that characterized Eastern European Jewish folk music. Many songs have no ethnic content whatsoever. This is a far cry from a recent opera based on Yiddish literature by David Schiff: *Gimpel the Fool*, adapted from I. B. Singer's short story of the same name. In his program notes, Schiff explains that he spent some time gathering authentic motives of Torah cantillation, which he then blended with the international idiom of twentieth-century music. Suitably, his libretto uses the original Yiddish. Even the hodgepodge of tunes assembled for *The Romance of a People* was based on Idelsohn's collection of folk tunes. *Fiddler* is a commercial, not a nationalistic, effort, and succeeded world-wide, using its own formula of ethnic local color.

The rewriting of Sholom Aleichem by the *Fiddler* crew is consonant with a general unstated policy of self-censorship of the past apparent in the Jewish-American community. Even *Fiddler*, when it first came out, was subject to the usual "what will *they* think" wonderings such as rose sharply to the surface with the publication of Roth's *Portnoy's Complaint* in the same era. With the rise of the New Ethnicity of the 1970s, however, a great deal more of the Jewish past is coming to light in dramatic works. The unsavoriness of the Americanizing Jake in the film *Hester Street* shows the exploiting of a new sensibility, and is part of the re-discovery of the Jewish-American community's immediate past, a process far removed from the concerns of both *Fiddler* and *Holocaust*. The Lower East Side has come increasingly to be "the Old Country" for younger Jewish artists, while Isaac Bashevis Singer's re-shaping of the myth of Europe implies a radical break with traditional notions of the Old World. It remains to be seen whether new examples of musical theater will develop that interpret the Jewish experience in innovative ways in the present period of conceptual ferment.

NOTES

1. Alfred Kazin, "The Jew as Modern American Writer," *Jewish-American Literature: An Anthology*, ed. A. Chapman (New York: Mentor, 1974), pp. 588–89.

2. Sholom Aleichem, *Wandering Star*, trans. F. Butwin (New York: Crown, 1952), p. 92.

3. The manuscripts cited are part of the Sholom Perlmutter Theatre Archive, housed at YIVO (Jewish Research Institute), New York. For a fuller description of the materials, see my summary in YIVO Annual of Jewish Social Science 18 (1983).

4. Israel Zangwill, *The Melting Pot*, rev. ed. (New York: Macmillan, 1930), pp. 33–34.

5. Ibid., p. 207.

6. Samson Raphaelson, *The Jazz Singer* (New York: Brentano's, 1927), Preface.

7. Quotations are from the programs for the play from the Chicago and New York performances, on file at the library of the Yale Drama Department. Other details are taken from David Garfield, "The Romance of a People," *Educational Theatre Journal* 24 (1972): 436–42.

Fanny Brice and Sophie Tucker: Blending the Particular with the Universal

June Sochen

THE BRILLIANT SUCCESS OF JEWISH-AMERICAN ENTERTAINERS RESULTS FROM A
fortunate blending of talent, opportunity, and cultural preparedness. Both
Fanny Brice and Sophie Tucker, the stars of this essay, possessed unique
talents that enabled them to identify and connect with their audiences in exciting and compelling ways. They both came of age when American burlesque and
vaudeville were prospering and when the immigrant audience, to whom they
especially appealed, crowded the halls for amusement. Their Jewishness, their
particular subcultural world, gave them a perspective on life, an angle of vision,
that enabled them to transcend their particularity and become one with large,
diverse audiences. Neither Brice nor Tucker ever forgot or abandoned their
connections with Judaism, but both transcended their Jewishness to connect
with Gentile as well as Jewish audiences. Their public personas spoke to all
peoples, while their message often had a particular poignancy for their Jewish
audiences.

Sophie Tucker came from a lower-middle-class Hartford, Connecticut, Jewish milieu. Her parents ran a restaurant in which Sophie served the food and
sang a few songs on the side. She was raised in a religiously observant and
Yiddish-speaking home. Her personality was such that she yearned to perform,
to be stage center. At an early age, she learned that she would have to remove
herself from Hartford to achieve her goal, but her Jewish environment made her
very sensitive to the immigrant and to the outsider. Fanny Brice, by contrast,
never spoke Yiddish, and although her mother sometimes spoke of her early
days as an immigrant girl in New York, there was no religious observance in the
home. Fanny watched the Jewish shop girls in her neighborhood and later noted
the differences between immigrants, daughters of immigrants, and the grand
American women who frequented Broadway. Neither woman ever erased her
particular culture from her professional style.

Timing, of course, is a crucial factor in show business as well as in all human
business. When Fanny Brice was born in 1891, burlesque was big business.
Jewish immigrants were coming to the United States in unprecedented numbers,
and New York City already claimed the title of America's entertainment capital.
Fanny's mother, Rosie Stern, had come from a village near Budapest. She often
told her daughter of the difficulties of life for a young Jewish woman in America
who worked in New York's garment industry sweatshops before marrying a
bartender named Charlie Borach. In later years, when Fanny sang "The Song of
the Sewing Machine," she described her mother's and countless other mothers'

44

early experience in America. Fanny's interest in telling tales, in singing, and in performing for anyone who would listen to her was already evident by the time she was ten years old.[1]

The fact that her mother left her father while she was still a child and took the four Borach children (Fanny had an older sister and two brothers, one older and one younger) to Brooklyn where she ran her own business was not lost on this spunky young woman. The delicate interweaving of many factors contributes to a woman entertainer's success. Surely one factor in Fanny Brice's case (and in Sophie Tucker's) was a strong mother and a weak, or absent, father. Young, talented women growing up in such a household witnessed strong mothers supporting a family, making decisions, and keeping the family together, roles that they would play when they grew up.

The working-class immigrant Jewish families struggled to survive in early twentieth-century America. Frequently, unmarried daughters worked in the garment industry while mothers took in boarders or sewed at home to make ends meet. The father's wages were rarely sufficient for the large families. For Fanny's mother to leave her husband and assume the support of her four children was a bold and atypical move. Charlie Borach tried, usually in vain, to see his children, but Rose Borach stubbornly kept him away from the family. Rose considered Charlie's gambling and drinking unsavory influences upon the children. Fanny Brice recalled in later life her ambivalent feelings about the warm but unpredictable father whom she rarely saw. Sophie Tucker remembered her father fondly in her autobiography. Though her mother was portrayed as the moral and financial anchor of the family, her father's pleasant nature warmed the family atmosphere.

Brooklyn's Keeney Theater was the place where fourteen-year-old Fanny Brice made per public debut. Her clear, melodious voice enchanted the audience, and she collected coins in great numbers. Owner Frank Keeney booked her into his two other theaters and she earned around sixty dollars a week from these amateur-night performances. From Brooklyn she moved to Manhattan and joined a burlesque show. Her singing style was already developing: Brice would sing a song straight the first time around, then follow up with a mugging, comic chorus. She frequently wore clothes too small for her and wiggled during her performance. In 1909, she was appearing in a show called "College Girls" singing a "coon song," "Lovey Joe." She received twelve encores. When impresario Florenz Ziegfeld saw her perform, he decided to buy out her long-term contract and put her in the Ziegfeld Follies. She first appeared in the Follies in 1910 and was a regular star until 1923.

"Coon songs" were a favorite kind of popular song; they were sung in Negro dialect by white entertainers in blackface. Brice, Sophie Tucker, Eddie Cantor, and Al Jolson are the most famous of the many performers who worked in this genre. Neither Brice nor Tucker remained coon singers; Sophie Tucker positively hated the four years she was billed as America's most prominent coon singer. But all of these Jewish-American entertainers adopted the popular American form and used it to display their particular talents. Not only did

America's entertainment cafeteria present a variety of specialty acts, it also required its performers to display versatility.

It is no accident that two minorities, blacks and Jews, became leaders in American show business. Not only was this new professional field a likely ladder for upward mobility, but the cultural history of black Americans and Jewish Americans prepared them for the role of commentator, satirist, and mimic. Constance Rourke has noted in her classic study of American humor how laughter democratized the heterogeneous population[2] and allowed people who were not yet comfortable with each other to get along through the medium of comedy. Blackface, practiced by black and Jewish entertainers, allowed for disguise, for masking one's true character. In a country made up of so many different immigrants, an assumed public face, albeit a black face, was easier to deal with than an unknown idiosyncratic 'other' face.

Jews and blacks also shared a history of oppression and of forced separation from the majority culture. They both had to learn the rules of the insiders' game as outsiders waiting to be admitted. They possessed the power of self-deprecation as well as the ability to satirize the majority because their social position demanded sensitivity and observation. Jews and blacks survived precisely because they watched their oppressors carefully. In entertainment, they could turn their watchfulness to good advantage. They could mock themselves and others without bitterness or rancor. They could invite the majority to witness and participate in the comedy and the music of human vulnerability.

Fanny Brice instinctively understood this position. Her comic strategy was based upon the woman as exposed creature. Her adoption of the Yiddish dialect put her in the position of the outsider announcing her linguistic difference from the majority. Though she never knew Yiddish, Irving Berlin suggested her use of dialect. In 1909, Berlin wrote "Sadie Salome Go Home," a song about a nice Jewish girl, Sadie Cohen, who left her family, became an actress, and did a striptease act as Salome. The refrain is sung by her boyfriend, Mose, who wishes she would return home. "Oy, oy," he cries, "how can a nice Jewish girl disgrace her family?" Berlin sat down at the piano and demonstrated the approach to her. Brice liked it and so developed one of her most effective stylistic techniques.

The following year, 1910, she sang her first song in the Ziegfeld Follies and demonstrated her new knowledge. The song, "I'm an Indian," was sung with a Yiddish accent while Brice wore the appropriate Indian costume. How, she sang, could she tell the Jews that little Rosie Rosenstein was a little Indian girl? Brice as American Indian/Yiddish girl captured two minorities in one characterization; she also displayed her sure comic instinct for incongruity, the meat of humor. She played a red-blooded American Indian with a Yiddish accent, a "klutzy" ballet dancer, an innocent ingénue who is pregnant, and a sweet girl who is always misused by men. Fanny Brice's genius for assuming a variety of poses, her inimitable sense of timing, and her humane satire enabled her to render most subjects farcically. The variety was in the material while the style became consistent and sure.

While Brice often capitalized upon the innocent woman as victim, Sophie Tucker developed the persona of the aggressive woman, the woman who initiates sexual encounters with men and never loses. Tucker, born in 1887, sang for her parents' restaurant customers, while her sweet father often gambled in the back and her mother dutifully cooked the food. At thirteen, Sophie was singing in amateur concerts in Riverside Park. She already weighed 145 pounds but conveyed an image of confidence in her singing. At sixteen, she married a local boy named Louis Tuck, had a baby boy, and separated from Tuck shortly thereafter. She returned to her parents' home, fearing that her life was going to be a duplicate of her mother's. In the fall of 1906, she left her son with her parents and went to New York, determined to become a successful performer.[3]

It was not easy, but in the best tradition of show business, she persisted. In November she got a job at the German Village for fifteen dollars a week; she sang fifty to one hundred songs a night, obliging customers by singing their requests as well. At Chris Brown's amateur nights, she was told to assume blackface for her act because, according to the owner, she was too big and ugly to just go out and sing. On the Park and the New England Circuits she was billed as "Sophie Tucker, Manipulator of Coon Melodies." Tucker disliked this persona but found the audiences pleased with her performance of black dialect songs. In fact, her accent was so convincing that audiences shrieked with surprise when she removed her gloves and displayed her white wrists and hands.

Sophie Tucker learned about show business, living alone, and being a woman on the road during her touring days. She found that her big, motherly presence encouraged the other male and female entertainers to confide in her but they offered her little social contact. Tucker reflected in later life how the forced independence of the solitary female entertainer, especially after she became successful, made it hard to have a true love relationship or any kind of solicitous male attention:

> Once you start carrying your own suitcase, paying your own bills, running your own show, you've done something to yourself that makes you one of those women men may like and call a "pal" and "a good sport," the kind of woman they tell their troubles to. But you've cut yourself off from the orchids and the diamond bracelets, except those you buy for yourself.[4]

Sophie Tucker learned how to vary her act to interest an audience. She was a good student and listened to the experienced entertainers discuss their routines. Comedian George Le Maire, for example, told her to open her act with a bright song, follow it with a dramatic one, then a novelty song designed to bring laughs, and end with a fast ragtime number. Once she abandoned blackface, she added Yiddish expressions to her act and found the audience responsive, especially the largely Jewish audiences who truly relished a sprinkling of Yiddish in her songs such as Irving Berlin's "All I Get Is Sympathy," and "Why Was I Ever Born Lazy?" Even in Jack Yellen's "red-hot mama" songs that were her trademark from 1925 through 1945, she retained her Yiddish sparks to heighten the glow. But in the early years she tried many show-business bits before she acquired her distinctive stage persona.

Tucker appeared in the 1909 Ziegfeld Follies, a year before Fanny Brice's fruitful association with the Follies began. However, Tucker's experience was not as favorable as Brice's. Nora Bayes, the star of the show, objected to another female singer doing a solo, and Tucker was unceremoniously dismissed. Around this time, she began including slightly off-color songs in her routine. As one reviewer said: "Some of her songs are red, white, and blue, and some of them omit the red and the white. But they are never quite dark navy blue."[5] Two examples of her pale blue songs of 1910 were "But He Only Stays Till Sunday" and "I Just Couldn't Make Ma Feelin's Behave." Sophie Tucker had found her métier. Her routines included a ragtime song, a ballad, a comedy song, a novelty number, and a hot song. The following year, black songwriter Shelton Brooks wrote "Some of These Days" for her and this became *her* song, requested by audiences for decades to come.

The pale blue songs of Sophie Tucker reflected a brilliant merging of maternal Jewish and sexy black themes. The one is always self-mockery. Jewish mothers take good care of their men and their families but, in a clever reversal of role and expectation, the mamas need taking care of too. Black blues singers like Bessie Smith, Ma Rainey, and Billie Holliday were exploring the very same themes. In the segregated nightclubs of America, Sophie Tucker sang "red-hot mama" songs for her Jewish audiences while black singers sang the same kind of material for their audiences. Tucker, however, was not the only Jewish woman entertainer to include slightly sexy song material. Belle Baker, a contemporary of Sophie Tucker's and a "red-hot mama," opened at the Bronx Theater in 1910, a vaudeville house, only to receive this negative review from *Variety's* critic:

> Vaudeville will accept just so much suggestion and no more. Miss Baker slightly oversteps the line. . . . This newcomer has the ability to deliver a "coon," "wop," or "Yiddish" song, but she will have to be coached as to where to begin and when to stop; also how far to go.[6]

In the same review, Tucker was compared favorably to Baker. As Tucker's material got bluer, however, she, too, found vaudeville less receptive to her performances than nightclubs. Baker, Tucker, and their imitators became the atypical Jewish woman, the defier of the traditional stereotype. If the Jewish young woman is generally portrayed as sexy before marriage but frigid afterwards, Sophie Tucker, who looked like the eternal mother, turned the maternal-frigid image on its head: the Jewish mother needed and wanted sexual attention just like the attractive, slim Jewish girl.

While this was not a message Jews wanted to hear in the synagogue, it was one they would laugh at in the newly emerging cabarets. Beginning in 1916, Tucker sang regularly at cabaret restaurants such as Reisenweber's, a new form of evening entertainment. In this nightclub format, her slightly off-color songs were more acceptable. While vaudeville houses were trying to attract family audiences, nightclubs were for adults only and permitted freer treatment of titillating material. She always sang Yiddish songs and ragtime ballads before inserting the "red-hot mama" songs. It was a testimony to her versatility as well as to her good humor that Sophie Tucker could laud the loyal, devoted Jewish mother in one song and follow it up with a lyric that emphasized the mama's need for constant sexual satisfaction.

Neither Fanny Brice nor Sophie Tucker found lasting happiness in their personal lives. Both were married three times and divorced three times. Both used their private woes as source material for their public performances. Women disappointed in love, of course, was the oldest of themes. Both women explored and exploited it to their advantage. Sophie Tucker made fun of her insatiable passion that could never be satisfied by men; she also portrayed men as faithless, unreliable, and difficult. Fanny Brice's much-publicized marriage to gambler Nicky Arnstein was well known by her fans. When Brice sang "My Man" on the stage of the Ziegfeld Follies in 1921, audiences screamed and cried with Fanny as she lamented her continued love for her faithless lover. "What can I do," she sang, "I love my man so, no matter what he does." With a fatalistic shrug and a single spotlight on her, Fanny Brice shared her personal misery with her adoring public. And they loved it. By all accounts, she stole the show. Sophie Tucker had one son by her first marriage, a son whom her parents raised and whom she only saw on occasional visits; Fanny Brice had a son and daughter with Arnstein.

> I always hoped I'd have a boy and a girl, and I had them. I always hoped the boy would have talent, and not the girl, and it worked out that way. Because, as I realize it, I didn't want my daughter to have a career. Because if a woman has a career, she misses an awful lot. And I knew it then, that if you have a career, then the career is your life.[7]

It is ironic that Brice, the consummate careerist, usually sounded like a traditionalist when speaking about her family and the role of women in society.

Fanny Brice's electric performances connected her with her audiences in an inimitable way. Even when she was making fun of people, she included herself in the spoof. It was her vulnerability, shared with the satirized group's, that she joked about. She was part of the humor's object, not the superior citic. Reviewers often commented on the humane way she had of making fun of ballet dancers, possessive mothers, or evangelists. No one or no theme was outside her purview. In the biography of Brice written by Norman Katkov, she was quoted as saying:

> In anything Jewish I ever did, I wasn't standing apart, making fun of the race. I *was* the race, and what happened to me on the stage is what could happen to them. They identified with me, and then it was all right to get a laugh, because they were laughing at me as well as at themselves.[8]

Critic Gilbert Seldes called Fanny Brice a farceur;[9] in a few simple words and gestures, she evoked a whole way of life and a total personality. Her sketches summarized both the humanity and the absurdity of a particular subject. Her magnetic attachment to her audience made her, according to Seldes, second only to Al Jolson as the greatest entertainer of her day.

From 1910 onwards into the twenties, Fanny Brice performed in many of the Ziegfeld Follies,[10] adding new routines and perfecting old ones. Her 1921 performance of "My Man" and "Second-Hand Rose" became very popular songs that audiences requested time and again. In many ways, these two songs capture two of Brice's most essential themes: the vulnerable woman, destined to love a faithless man, and the victim who gets everything secondhand. No wonder, she sings, I feel abused, everything I get has already been used. Sung with a Yiddish accent, her songs evoke the whole immigrant Jewish cultural life of the early twentieth century. All people, not only Jews and women, have felt misused, taken advantage of, at one time in their lives, so the particular experience Brice sings of becomes the universal experience of all peoples.

While "Second-Hand Rose" addresses both men and women, "My Man" and "Oy, How I Hate that Fellow Nathan" apply the theme of defenselessness particularly to women. Love, romance, and marriage, the essential facts of an adult woman's life, are responsible for the heroine's problems. She needed a man to give her life, identity, and a reason for being. Nathan was a "no-goodnik" who promised to marry her in December; though he told her the month, he never told her what year. Singing with a Yiddish accent, Fanny Brice mocked both herself for believing Nathan and Nathan for his unreliability. There is no rage or aggressivensss in her complaints. She assumes some of the responsibility for her problem. But what, she asks frequently, can a woman do? This question later generations would answer in an assertive, daring manner. To Fanny Brice, a woman's choices were limited. The test was how a woman dealt with her fate. Brice chose self-deprecation, satire, and farce, powerful weapons in all ages.

Fanny Brice did many singing-comedy routines that captured both self-censure and social commentary. "Becky is Back in the Ballet," a number she recorded in 1922, tells the story of a possessive mother who commands her Pavlova-like daughter to show off now that she's back dancing in the ballet (pronounced *belly*). Mocking first generation Jewish Americans, who viewed cultural pursuits as the means to assimilate, Brice made fun of motherly ambitions for untalented daughters. In "Mrs. Cohen at the Beach," Brice did a comic monologue about the Cohens in which Mrs. Cohen simultaneously supervises her children's bathing activities, gossips with a woman whom she has not seen for a long time, and tells her husband Abe what to do.[11] Brice's carping, her overzealousness, and her general bossiness made Mrs. Cohen an infuriating but funny Jewish busybody.

In a 1930 movie called "Be Yourself," Fanny Brice played a nightclub singer who supported a broken-down boxer. While he loafed, she sang another of her most popular hits, "Cooking Breakfast for the One I Love." Again, she makes fun of herself and her utter devotion to this worthless man. She is so thrilled that he's happy that she will gladly make "hoht' meal sprinkled mit lov." She'll make a "bees-cuit" delighted that he is willing to risk it. The mixture of humor and pathos contains the proper tension to give the song excitement and drama—and a laugh.

After Fanny Brice left the Ziegfeld Follies in 1923, she performed in a variety of Broadway musicals including some written and produced by Billy Rose, her third husband, whom she married in 1929. She also appeared in a few movies. It was not a great time for her, either professionally or personally. In 1920 the *New York Times* headlined the news that Nicky Arnstein was the mastermind in a plot to steal five million dollars worth of securities. In February of that year, Brice admitted marrying him. She was hounded by reporters who wanted to know Arnstein's whereabouts. Her finances were entangled with his and the ensuing four-year legal battle was an ugly and difficult time for her.[12] Arnstein finally went to prison in 1924 for over a year. In 1926 Brice did a serious play for David Belasco which failed. In 1927 she divorced Arnstein and opened at the Palace. In 1929 she appeared in her first movie, *My Man*, a Warner's talkie. The film was successful, but Brice preferred live stage appearances and returned to Broadway.

In 1934 she appeared in the Shubert Follies. Brooks Atkinson reported that she was in splendid form.

> Toward the end of the first act she is Countess Dubinsky, who right down to her skinsky is working for Minsky, whereupon she performs a hilarious travesty upon the sinful fan dance.[13]

Reviewers never tired of her great routines. Her imitations of "red-hot" singers, of "bewildered Jewish Juliets," as one critic called them,[14] and of zealots remained crisp and fresh over the years. But theaters were being converted to movie houses, and the number of variety shows was decreasing rapidly. Brice also seemed to tire of the routines though not finding a more satisfactory outlet for her considerable talent.

Like all the big entertainers, Brice was wooed by the new mass medium, radio. She appeared as a guest on shows like the *Rudy Vallee Show* as early as 1929 but did not become a regular radio performer until 1936. On February 29, 1936, on the *Ziegfeld Follies Show of the Air,* she introduced a character called Baby Snooks, an impish seven-year-old who outwitted adults. Though Brice had done a routine about a child as early as 1912 and another for Ziegfeld in 1921, the success of the radio performance of Baby Snooks assured its continuation. In December, 1937, Brice joined NBC in a musical comedy extravaganza called *Good News of 1938* and the Baby Snooks character became a regular feature of the hour-long program. In March, 1940, the program became the *Maxwell House Coffee Time* and was reduced to thirty minutes, divided evenly between a fifteen-minute routine for comedian Frank Morgan and fifteen minutes for Baby Snooks. In 1944, the *Baby Snooks Show* became a half-hour show on CBS; in 1949 it was transferred back to NBC. It was still going strong when Fanny Brice died in 1951.[15]

The Baby Snooks persona became Fanny Brice's public personality as well. She often gave interviews using her seven-year-old voice and referred to her character as "Schnooks." Gone was the wide range of the farceur, replaced by a single character, a devilish child. A whole radio generation grew up listening to Baby Snooks.[16] Snooks usually defied her father in a seemingly innocent way. When coached by "Daddy", Lancelot Higgins, to tell the bus driver that she's "not quite six," she says: "My Daddy says I'm not quite six." When acting as her father's witness in a trial concerning his fight with a neighbor, she says that her father is "evil-tempered," instead of the much rehearsed "even-tempered." Often Baby Snooks is spanked at the end of the episode allowing the audience the cathartic and assuring feeling that parental authority always wins. But the message conveyed throughout the sketch seriously questions this view.

At the same time that young Shirley Temple was the biggest star in movie history, Baby Snooks, a precocious radio child played by an adult woman, also became a hit. Americans embraced child stars during the Depression years and remained loyal to Baby Snooks long afterwards. Why Fanny Brice abandoned all other roles is not clear. Her attempts at dramatic acting in the 1930s proved unsuccessful, and the impetus to continue searching for new satiric material no longer existed. Baby Snooks gave Brice a public outlet, financial security, and a less taxing format for her talent.

In June, 1945, Fanny Brice suffered a mild heart attack. While continuing as Baby Snooks, she also collected art, a long-time passion, and pursued her interest in interior decoration. She died of a cerebral hemorrhage in May, 1951, at the age of fifty-nine. Her son had become an artist, which she had encouraged, while her daughter married producer Ray Stark. In 1964 Stark produced *Funny Girl*, the fictionalized Broadway musical based upon Fanny Brice's life and starring Barbra Streisand. Thirteen years after her death, Fanny Brice became famous again, thanks to Streisand's great performance. With new songs imitating the themes and style of Brice's greats such as "My Man" and "Second-Hand Rose," a new generation of theatergoing and moviegoing audiences became acquainted with one of America's greatest entertainers.

Sophie Tucker's bawdy songs had roots in the American tradition. Eva Tanguay, one of vaudeville's greatest stars, became famous with her sexy dances and her songs such as "I Want Some One to Go Wild With Me," "It's All Been Done Before but Not the Way I Do It," "Go As Far as You Like," "Nothing Bothers Me," and her theme song, "I Don't Care."[17] Belle Baker sang hot songs as well as comic songs such as Berlin's "Cohen Owes Me Ninety-Seven Dollars" in 1915, a song that could have easily been written for either Tucker or Brice. Tucker's four years as a coon singer followed in the tradition of May Irwin who, in 1893, created a sensation with the song "The Bully Song."[18] As already suggested, while Sophie Tucker was perfecting her "red-hot mama" songs for white, largely Jewish, audiences at Riesenweber's, black blues singer Bessie Smith was singing "Aggravatin' Papa," "T'aint Nobody's Biz-ness If I Do," and "Mamma's Got the Blues."[19] In the burlesque houses and in later movies, Mae

West developed a reputation as a no-nonsense woman who asked men to come up and see her sometime.

Many able performers shared Sophie Tucker's persona of a sexy, independent woman. True, within the Jewish culture, this pose was unconventional. Public discussions of sex and of women wishing sexual relations would offend traditional Jews. Further, the male chauvinism of Jewish men assumed that they were the proper, and only, initiators of sexual activity. Male Jewish entertainers could discuss "dirty" subjects, but Jewish Puritans frowned upon women doing this. Tucker walked a delicate tightrope. Initially she did not use vulgar words in her songs. Neither did she tell off-color jokes. In classic sex role reversal, her songs always poked fun at men. Men were tired or unwilling to be sexually attentive. Sometimes, of course, she good-naturedly called them cads, but rarely did she make scatological or pornographic references.

Tucker's "red-hot mama" songs seem tame next to Belle Barth's. But during the 'teens her frequent discussion of women as sexual initiators and as knowledgeable and insatiable sexual creatures delighted her audiences. "It's Never Too Late" and "Make Him Say Please" are only two of innumerable examples of this theme. Her 1923 recording of "You've Got to See Your Mama Ev'ry Night"[20] demands the constant sexual attention of her lover and assures him that she'll seek elsewhere for satisfaction if he does not perform every night. "You Can't Deep Freeze a Red Hot Mama" offers another sample of the same message. Tucker sings these songs with a certain amount of self-mockery while assuring the males that she means business.

Sophie Tucker's impressive girth (she weighed close to two hundred well-corseted pounds later in life) only added to the humorous touch of her message. "Nobody Loves a Fat Girl" does not mean what it says. Indeed, Tucker proudly asserted that a fat woman is a better lover, has more to give, and requires more than thinner women. Thus, there is a double edge to her songs: she shocks her audience with the bluntness of her message while making fun of her appearance, thereby taking the shock value out of the song. Her good-natured confession of need, her declaration of passion as a right, and her playful manner endeared her to audiences. Indeed, she developed a very loyal following in all of the major cities she played. At the beginning of her career, she began writing down the names of fans in each city and sent them postcards informing them of her next appearance there. Over the years, her faithful audience grew, and a Sophie Tucker appearance at, for example, the Chez Paree in Chicago was an assured sell-out.

Tucker's "red-hot mama" songs also displayed a woman independent and proud of it. "I'm Living Alone and I Like It." "I Ain't Takin' Orders From No One," "Vamping Sal," and "Some of These Days" all declare the independence of woman over erratic lovers, difficult circumstances, and changing times. There is no self-pity in Sophie Tucker's songs. Rather, in many, women are told to leave unfaithful men and search for new lovers. "No One Can Satisfy Any One Man All the Time" counsels women to seek other lovers. Women should amuse themselves, not cry over lost lovers. "Mamma Goes Where Pappa Goes," sung in both Yiddish and English, tells women to watch their husbands carefully if they want them to remain faithful. "Never Let the Same Dog Bite You Twice" and "No One Man is Ever Going to Worry Me" repeat the same message.[21]

Sophie Tucker only appeared occasionally on the radio. She once told an interviewer why she did not like radio:

> You can't do this, you can't do that. I couldn't even say "hell" or damn," and nothing, honey, is more expressive than the way I say "hell or damn".[22]

While Fanny Brice developed a new persona for radio, Sophie Tucker was content to continue her "red-hot mama" routine for her nightclub audiences.

As she grew older, Sophie Tucker's songs merely updated this theme. "I'm Starting All Over Again" and "I Am Having More Fun Since I Am Sixty" restated the same case with verve. Growing older was not a problem or a disability. One could cherish life, continue to be sexually active and interested, and preserve a sense of humor as long as the blood flowed through the veins. Tucker's appearances when she was in her sixties and early seventies surely buoyed audiences that had grown up with her and remembered her performing in the 1920s and 30s. When she died in 1966 at the age of 79, she left many admirers.

Both Fanny Brice and Sophie Tucker experimented with different song materials and styles before each found her respective forté. In the process, they collaborated with and borrowed from other famous American entertainers. Fanny Brice performed with black comic Bert Williams, W. C. Fields, Will Rogers, and Eddie Cantor on the stage of the Ziegfeld Follies. Indeed, this collection of performers represents a major sample of American entertainment forms. The storyteller and satirist Will Rogers is as American as the Yankee backwoodsman and the teller of tall tales. Bert Williams was the classic black minstrel player. W. C. Fields's antic humor, often done in skit form with Fanny Brice at the Follies, drew from the physical humor of the burlesque hall. Eddie Cantor, wearing blackface, and rolling his big brown eyes, while dancing around the stage, sang bouncy American tunes. In 1928, for example, Irving Berlin wrote a song for Cantor called "Shaking the Blues Away."

Show business absorbed and reinterpreted frontier American themes with black slave songs and Yiddish intonations. When Irving Berlin, a Jewish son of the ghetto, wrote "Yiddle on Your Fiddle, Play Some Ragtime" in 1909, he was successfully merging at least two genres. In the finished product, the various strains were still recognizable and could be singled out but the blending was eclectic American. Fanny Brice and Sophie Tucker always retained either the Yiddish accent or definable Jewish themes in their shows, but they also synthesized their materials so they had appeal beyond the Jewish audience. General American audiences knew that Brice was Jewish but they also knew that her words, her persona, and her style were primarily for them.

Fanny Brice made fun of herself, of Jewish mothers, and of Protestant evangelicals. Though her comedic material arose out of the Bronx and Jewish households, she found a ready audience beyond the Jews. She was not afraid to make herself look unattractive and awkward. She wore funny costumes and tripped over her own feet. Florenz Ziegfeld never liked comedy, surely a shortcoming of his, but he had to yield to the public's will and feature Fanny Brice, Eddie Cantor, and Will Rogers in his yearly Follies. Fanny Brice's versatility also appealed to her fans. Her effective rendering of blues songs like "My Man" and "I'd Rather Be Blue Over You" captured the hearts of her audiences. You could both laugh and cry with Fanny.

She had few imitators or successors in the theater. Because variety theater was declining by the 1930s, being replaced by radio and the movies as popular forms of entertainment, her style of comedy did not emerge again until Lucille Ball and Carol Burnett became the stars of television. Silent film comedy was dominated by men such as Chaplin and Keaton and allowed few women comedians. Silent screen comedy consisted of slapstick humor and the defenseless tramp image. Women were considered too delicate and dignified to have pies thrown in their faces and too protected to expose their vulnerability before the public. Sound movies, on the other hand, relied on verbal wit, clever talk, something women were supposed to be good at.

Television has allowed women comics to behave in the Brice style. The medium responds to Lucy imitating Chaplin and Brice. Similarly, television audiences witness Carol Burnett doing skits on a variety of characters that follows directly in the Brice tradition. The newspaper headlines offer Carol Burnett humorous characters and situations to make fun of, just as Fanny Brice satirized characters from the Lower East Side and the daily newspapers. Both Ball and Burnett, like Fanny Brice, have malleable, highly expressive faces and figures. Finally, all were good dancers as well as actresses willing to make themselves the butt of their humor. The medium of television, more intimate than the movies, allows women comics an opportunity to perform. Fanny Brice would have been a superb television comic.

"Red-hot mamas" like Sophie Tucker lost their audience by the 1960s. Nightclubs had become too expensive to operate efficiently, and live entertainment became rarer and rarer. Pornographic movies and books and open discussion of sex on television made the Sophie Tucker material appear tame and uncontroversial. Tucker's approach, innovative in the allegedly risqué twenties, seemed staid at best to modern audiences. Sophie Tucker, though, could be viewed as an early prophet of women's liberation. Her songs clearly told women to stop crying and start acting on their own behalf. She was a Jewish woman who said that Jewish men could be as unreliable as Christian men, thus making her message universal. She satisfied the Jewish preference for nostalgia by singing "My Yiddishe Mama" while her audiences knew that such a creature was a vanishing type.

Both Fanny Brice and Sophie Tucker were cultural Jews, the products of first-generation American life. Though Tucker had a traditional religious upbringing and spoke of Jewish holiday observances, her life as a travelling entertainer made it harder and harder for her to observe any of the ritual. In her autobiography, she noted with pride her attendance at one Passover Seder in her parents' home where her son read the Four Questions. She was a guest at a holiday celebration she understood but one which she rarely practiced. Fanny Brice's family upbringing did not include strict religious observance. Her Jewishness came from associating with Jewish people in Brooklyn and Manhattan, in observing Jewish shop girls and storekeepers, and in watching Jewish entertainers.

Fanny Brice and Sophie Tucker offer us two portraits of woman: the victim and the aggressor. While the Jew has traditionally portrayed himself as the hapless victim of Christian anti-Semitism, Czarist tyranny, and general Gentile oppression, Fanny Brice transposed that theme into that of the female victim, the woman whose sexual reliance upon men always got her into trouble. The woman's particular vulnerability makes her a victim. By contrast, Sophie Tucker turned the image and the behavior around: the victim became the initiator, the aggressive leader. The best defense is an offense appeared as her lyrical theme. Both Brice and Tucker ultimately used their femaleness rather than their Jewishness to make their enduring point but their Jewish heritage surely added a deep and subtle layer to the meaning of both vulnerability and the need to be assertive.

Fanny Brice and Sophie Tucker entertained thousands of twentieth-century Americans. They interpreted many important dimensions of modern life to Jewish immigrants, Catholic immigrants, and native American Portestants. They dealt publicly with private issues that concerned everyone: family conflicts, ambitious mothers, faithless husbands, and women's sexual yearning. By doing it with humor, they eased everyone's burden, bridged the gap between peoples, and showed how the particularity of their Jewish-American subculture was an essential part of the American whole.

NOTES

1. Much of the biographical information was obtained from *The Fabulous Fanny: The Story of Fanny Brice* by Norman Katkov (New York: Knopf, 1953).

2. Constance Rourke, *American Humor: A Study of the National Character* (New York: Harcourt, Brace and Company, 1931).

3. Biographical details were gained from *Some of These Days: The Autobiography of Sophie Tucker* (New York: Doubleday, 1945).

4. Ibid., p. 127.

5. Ibid., p. 91.

6. *Variety*, 29 October 1910, p. 17.

7. *The Fabulous Fanny*, p. 241.

8. Ibid., p. 205.

9. Gilbert Seldes, "The Daemonic in the American Theatre," in *The Seven Lively Arts* (New York: Harper & Bros., 1924), p. 179.

10. Contrary to some accounts, Brice did not appear in *every* Ziegfeld Follies from 1910 to 1923 but rather appeared in ten of the fourteen Follies of that period. See Roger

D. Kinkle, *The Complete Encyclopedia of Popular Music and Jazz 1900–1950* (Arlington House Publishers, 1974), p. 621.

11. "Fanny Brice/Helen Morgan" (RCA Victor Vintage series LPV-561, 1969).

12. From January through March, 1920, the *New York Times* had regular reports on Arnstein's legal troubles.

13. *The Fabulous Fanny*, p. 237.

14. Ibid., pp. 243–44.

15. John Dunning, *Tune In Yesterday: The Ultimate Encyclopedia of Old-Time Radio 1925–1976* (Englewood Cliffs, New Jersey: Prentice-Hall, 1976), pp. 51–54.

16. The selected radio broadcasts of the Baby Snooks show that I listened to include: "Cat Man's Revenge" (9/29/46); "Abnormal Psychology" (5/28/42); "Man Who Came to Dinner" (1/39); "The Trial" (11/4/43); "Patient Father" (6/15/44); "Doctor's Office" (6/19/38); and "Halloween" (11/1/46). I wish to thank my colleague Professor Fred MacDonald for loaning me these tapes as well as other tapes and records from his private collection.

17. Robert Toll, *On With the Show: The First Century of Show Business in America* (New York: Oxford University Press, 1976), pp. 225–26.

18. David Ewen, *Great Men of American Popular Song* (Englewood Cliffs, New Jersey: Prentice-Hall, 1970), p. 101.

19. Chris Albertson, *Bessie Smith* (New York: Stein and Day, 1973).

20. "Sophie Tucker: Some of These Days" (Pelican Records, LP133).

21. Some of Sophie Tucker's other records that included her most popular songs are: "Sophie Tucker: Cabaret Days" (Mercury, MG20046), "Sophie Tucker: Her Latest and Greatest Spicy Songs" (Mercury, MG20073), and "Sophie Tucker: The Spice of Life" (Mercury, MG20126).

22. Quoted in Lewis A. Erenberg, *Steppin' Out: New York Night-Life and the Transformation of American Culture, 1890–1930* (Westport, Connecticut: Greenwood Press, 1981), p. 196.

The Jew in Stand-up Comedy

Anthony Lewis

STAND-UP COMEDY IS FARING BETTER NOW THAN AT ANY TIME SINCE THE heyday of vaudeville in the early 1900s. Nightclubs devoted solely to the strange art of the stand-up comedian have sprung up all over the country, seemingly overnight. Each week audiences have the opportunity to see in person hundreds of comedians at the Comedy Store in Los Angeles, Catch a Rising Star and the Improv in New York, and at dozens of smaller clubs across the country. Comics are regulars on television talk shows, on the college entertainment circuit and, since Woody Allen's first film, in the movies as well. In the last two years alone, Steve Martin, Joan Rivers, Bill Murray, John Belushi, Richard Pryor, Gilda Radner, along with Monty Python and Woody Allen have brought us films which at least in part use stand-up comedy for some of their best effects.

This rebirth, both in audience interest in stand-up comedy and in the desire of large numbers of people to perform, is paralleled by a more significant change in taste; today's comedian uses material and has adopted a style which set him apart dramatically from the "monologist" of vaudeville. However, through all the changes in stand-up comedy in the last half-century, from the punch-line jokes of vaudeville, to the social satire of the "sick" comics of the early sixties, to the finely crafted routines of the "comedy stores" of the seventies, one ingredient has remained constant—the presence and influence of the Jewish comic.

While it is impossible to write a history of stand-up comedy in America without seeming to recite a who's who of Jewish entertainers, we need to remember that there are fewer Jewish comedians today than there were in vaudeville in 1900, but that even then the Jews were merely a small part of a diverse whole.[1] Fred Allen's description of the vaudeville population in his autobiography, *Much Ado about Me*, is a detailed picture of live entertainment in the early 1900s and puts Jewish participation in perspective:

> The elements that went to make up vaudeville were combed from the jungles, the four corners of the world, the intelligentsia and the subnormal. An endless, incongruous swarm crawled over the countryside dragging performing lions, bears, tigers, leopards, boxing kangaroos, horses, ponies, mules, dogs, cats, rats, seals, and monkeys in their wake. Others rode bicycles, did acrobatic and contortion tricks, walked wires, exhibited sharpshooting skills, played violins, trombones, cornets, pianos, concertinas, xylophones, harmonicas, and any other known instrument. There were hypnotists, iron-jawed ladies, one-legged dancers, one-armed cornetists, mind readers, female imper-sonators, male impersonators, Irish comedians, Jewish comedians, blackface, German, Swedish, Italian, and rube comedians, dramatic actors, Hindu con-jurors, ventriloquists, bag punchers, singers and dancers of every description, clay modelers, and educated geese: all traveling from hamlet to town to city,

presenting their shows. Vaudeville asked only that you own an animal or an instrument, or have a minimum of talent or a maximum of nerve. With these dubious assets vaudeville offered fame and riches. It was up to you.[2]

From this tradition Milton Berle, Henny Youngman, Jack Benny, George Burns, and Groucho Marx developed, as did Fred Allen, Bob Hope, Rose Marie, Gracie Allen, and Jimmy Durante. However, few would deny that in spite of their numbers Jews have influenced the direction and style of comedy profoundly during all of its phases, and that the Jewish comic is "the major force in modern American humor."[3]

The presence of Jews in entertainment, especially in comedy, is in some ways puzzling, going as it does against the grain of some time-honored Jewish stereotypes. Given Fred Allen's description of monkeys, one-legged dancers, and male impersonators, one wonders how circumstances could have conspired to allow Jewish boys, Milton Berle at five, Georgie Jessel at nine, to put studies second and entertaining first. Even more curious is the role played by their Jewish mothers who, tradition and Philip Roth tell us, dominate weak fathers and overprotect, even sissify, their sons in hopes of creating steady and serious "professionals." How, then, are we to account for Minnie Marx, who honed the Marx Brothers into a first-rate vaudeville act partly by making such unpleasant decisions as coercing the "expendable" Gummo into joining the Army during World War I to help support the troupe;[4] or the infamous Sarah Berlinger, Milton Berle's mother, who not only pushed him onto the stage but provided him women in his dressing room when he was a teenager ("You could accuse my mother of a lot of things, but being a typical Jewish mother wasn't one of them")?[5] Such problematic examples cease to trouble when we remember that a stereotype is by definition invalid, a caricature designed to distort. Jews went into vaudeville as singers, dancers, and monologists for much the same reason others did, "vaudeville offered fame and riches"; it is possible that the Jessels, living on West 118th Street in Harlem in 1908, had more in common with the Irish Allens in Boston than with a middle-class Jewish family in suburbia in 1980.

Today, aspiring comedians are rarely paid; they perform for the thrill of performing or on the slim chance that they will be picked up by an agent. Even for today's established professionals, the opportunities to perform for money are few; Jessel claimed in 1976 that "there's only about four weeks' work in all of America."[6] Sadly enough, Jessel himself by 1979 was reduced to performing for the first time in a burlesque house, "telling off-color jokes to a sparse audience between strip-tease acts."[7] But performers went into vaudeville precisely because even the humblest acts were paid, and because such a career could provide work fifty-two weeks a year. Minnie Marx used to ask her sons, "Where else can people who don't know anything make so much money?" Today the decision to perform is complicated, for not only is comedy unremunerative, but education is so much more readily available: the potential for earning a living onstage is less great, while the sacrifices are more apparent. Woody Allen did not turn to comedy until he had given college a try, but Milton Berle's family decided early on that education was a dead-end: "I could work or be educated, and my working was more needed at home. And the way I saw it, a kid in the spotlight was a lot better than a flop in a schoolroom."

Jews turned to show business because it was a thriving and paying profession and then developed into comedians in utterly unpremeditated ways. Then, as now, comedy was only infrequently a first choice, and the great Jewish comedians who were nurtured on vaudeville stages came into comedy by circuitous routes. Jack Benny only reluctantly left music, and Milton Berle as a child sang and danced and occasionally mimicked singers and dancers. Berle tried boxing for a while, as did Benny Rubin and Alan King (and Bob Hope, who boxed as "Packie East" when he was twenty-one). Henny Youngman worked in a print shop near 6th Avenue and on weekends played the violin in the Catskills, and Myron Cohen was a silk salesman in New York's garment center until he was forty-two. George Burns tried singing and dancing before teaming up with Gracie Allen (one of the dancing Allen sisters) and becoming her straight man, while Morey Amsterdam was an aspiring cellist. Of more recent comedians, Lenny Bruce worked on a chicken farm, joined the Navy in 1942, and turned to comedy only accidentally, filling in one night for the absent emcee of a show his mother was dancing in, and Rodney Dangerfield was a bored forty-year-old paint salesman who, he tells us, found his job "colorless." Several of today's best-known Jewish comics are the products of college and graduate school drama departments, for example, Shelley Berman, David Steinberg, and Robert Klein, all of whom began by doing sketch comedy with the Compass or Second City groups.

However they stumbled into it, Jews have found in stand-up comedy a career congenial to their tastes and abilities, largely because they *are* Jews. Many critics and comedians alike have suggested that Jews fare well in comedy partly because of their polyglot background. Like Feste, the clown in Shakespeare's *Twelfth Night*, who calls himself a "corrupter of words," all stand-up comics verbalize feelings and attitudes, relying most often on figures of speech, metaphors and similes, to draw analogies and uncover relationships. Joan Rivers's fur boa becomes Tony Newley's "eyebrow," Henny Youngman's wife is mistaken for the morning's garbage, and Milton Berle becomes an aging dowager. Leo Rosten believes that Jews use language with ease because so many grew up in a bilingual world; "nothing so sharpens the ear to the subtleties that differentiate words as constantly shuttling between two vocabularies."[8] Georgie Jessel, too, attributed success in comedy by Jews to the fact that "the Jews who came from Europe, or Russia, or East Asia or wherever they came from had to pick up all sorts of languages and dialects . . . 'cause they were moved from one part of the world to another."[9] In addition to their facility with words, Rosten posits for the Jews a kind of Mediterranean predisposition to talk, for "Jews think feelings are meant to be verbalized." In this regard, he sees a critical difference between Jews and Anglo-Saxons:

Jews may strike Anglo-Saxons as verbose and melodramatic because Jews are early taught (as I was) to feel an *obligation* to respond to the misfortunes of others with visible, audible sympathy—so that no one can possibly fail to recognize the depth and sensitivity of one's compassion. To Jews, emotions are not meant to be nursed in private: they are meant to be dramatized and displayed—so that they can be *shared*.

At the heart of stand-up comedy, of course, is the impulse to share one's feelings and attitudes, to communicate through words, to "dramatize and display."

The Jewish comic steps out onto the stage as a Jew, and this is as true of Woody Allen and Lenny Bruce as of Buddy Hackett and Shecky Greene. His Jewishness may embarrass, motivate, or anger him, but the connection between performance and cultural background is clear to him and, he assumes, to the audience as well. Milton Berle, for example, went as far as he could in denying his heritage; he changed his name from Berlinger, had his nosed "bobbed" ("I cut off my nose to spite my race"; "A thing of beauty and a goy forever"), and became a Christian Scientist ("for about twenty years"), but never hesitated to respond to anti-Semitism on or offstage. He jumped from the stage during a performance at the Palace in Chicago and was arrested for fighting with a man who had called him a "kike," and several years later joined a group of "cops and hoods" in a raid on a Nazi-sympathizer rally in the Yorkville Casino.

Jewish comedians bring their religion and culture into their act in explicit ways. Many comics tell stories in Yiddish or pepper their language with Yiddish expressions, and some have, or occasionally use, a Jewish accent (Jessel: "Nathan, Nathan, Tell Me for Vy You Are Vaitin'"). Jewish comedians tell jokes or stories about Jewish or Biblical history, such as David Steinberg (Bible routine) and Georgie Jessel (when Moses found out the Commandments were free, he said to God, "I'll take ten"), though curiously Steinberg sees no relation at all between himself and older-generation comedians. Mel Brook's 2000-Year-Old Man has a clear Borscht-belt, pseudo-Biblical flavor, and Yiddish, of course, is the language of several of his characters, the most notable being the Indian chief in *Blazing Saddles*. Several Jewish comics simply announce their religion to the audience, either as a confession or as an explanation or definition. Don Rickles refers to himself as "the Jew" or "the Jewish guy," and Mel Brooks often calls himself "'Your obedient Jew', as if to say, before anything else, this is what I am. Above all—Jewish, Jewish, Jewish."[10] Groucho Marx, who claimed not to be a "professional Jew" (and who said that "making love to a Jewish girl would be like making love to your sister"), nevertheless often reminisced about his *bar mitzvah* and sent his daughter, Melinda, on a trip to Israel. Being Jewish, he said, is "not something you can lose":

A Jew and a hunchback were passing a temple, and the Jew said, "I used to be a Jew." And the hunchback said, "I used to be a hunchback."

As we might expect, Jewish comedians as a group tend to be sensitive to, and articulate about, anti-Semitism; their biographies and autobiographies sooner or later categorize other acts on the basis of their attitude toward Jews. From sensitivity to anti-Semitism to concern for the public image of the Jews is no very great step, and sometimes Jewish comedians seem worried about how others see them. Groucho Marx called Jack Benny "a credit to the Jews," and Georgie Jessel praises Al Jolson for changing for the better "the whole portrait of the Jew onstage."[11] In *Annie Hall*, Woody Allen complains of an anti-Semite who purposely kept repeating "d' you" ("Jew"), and imagines himself in Hassidic garb at the Gentile home of his girlfriend. In one of his routines, Robert Klein tells us that during his freshman year at Alfred University, the student next door in his dormitory had a mobile made out of swastikas.[12]

Comedians have traditionally posed either as predator or prey (the metaphor is taken from Lenny Bruce), antagonistic or ingratiating. Jews found these postures not simply good performance attitudes, but two perfect vehicles through which they could comment, consciously or unconsciously, on their being Jews. Thus Jewish comedians frequenty appear to be not simply angry social critics or born losers, but angry Jewish critics and Jewish losers. Bob Hope is a perennial second-best, never winning the Oscar and always too frightened to fight, but his religious affiliation, a mystery to most Americans (Catholic), seems to have little to do with his onstage persona;[13] Lucille Ball often mentions her maiden name, McGillicuddy, but her Scotch-Irish background plays no part whatever in the audience's perception of her as a lovable bungler; similarly, Bob Newhart is weak and ineffective, always being put upon by those around him, but neither he nor the audience connects his actions with his nationality or religion. Except when John Byner and George Carlin explicitly mention their parochial school days and encounters with nuns, the audience is unaware of religion and makes no connection between their personalities, emotions, and attitudes, and their cultural heritage. But Woody Allen portrayed himself from the start as a Jewish loser, a *schlemiel* whose attributes as Jew make him a loser in contemporary American society. In *Play It Again, Sam*, when he is harassed by black-jacketed toughs, Allen confesses that he is a Jew, telling them that he has to leave in order to get up early and go to temple on "my people's sabbath." In his pose as victim, Allen harks back to the early days of vaudeville when a Jew onstage had a beard and "an ill-fitting suit, and his opening line was something like, 'We had a meeting of B'nai B'rith—three hundred of us—and one Irishman chased us out of the building'."[14] Though most commentators distinguish between "New Wave" comedians and earlier Borscht-belt comics on the basis of the former group's supposed dedication to presenting the truth about themselves rather than impersonal one-liners or punch-line jokes, the Jew as "loser" can be followed from vaudeville through Jerry Lewis, Buddy Hackett, Stanley Myron Handleman ("getting angrier and angrier by the minute" as the butcher hits his wife), Joan Rivers ("doctor looked at my face, looked at my tush, and said 'twins'; "gang-rejected in Central Park"), Woody Allen, and Rodney Dangerfield (who gets "no respect").

In a review of *Interiors* in the *New Yorker*, Pauline Kael wrote, "People like Woody Allen for a lot of good reasons, and for one that may be a bummer: he conforms to their idea of what a Jew should be."[15] Unfortunately, Miss Kael does not elaborate on this intriguing remark, though it is clear that she accuses Allen of being a kind of Jewish Uncle Tom. What she may not have considered is that the *schlemiel* is not simply one of the two main stereotypes used by stand-up comedy, but that it is also a natural response to the pressures of a social situation. As *schlemiel*, the comedian admits his Jewishness, ingratiates himself, disarms an alien and potentially hostile group, turns strangers into friends and ultimately wins their approval. Georgie Jessel, for example, who often complained of arthritis and who was the butt of his own stories, always tried to fit into mainstream America and to be accepted and loved by his audiences. Dubbed "Toastmaster General of the United States" by Harry Truman, Jessel took the role in dead earnest, hoping, in fact, during the Nixon administration, to become an ambassador. He proudly used a cane President Truman gave him and a watch given him by General Omar Bradley; he ended several post-Vietnam concert appearances by singing "God Bless America" while standing at attention, his jacket adorned with medals. The "loser," whom the audience has just laughed at, becomes a Jewish Uncle Sam, the "Toastmaster General."

By verbalizing his own anxieties, the comic tests them out and discovers that his admissions have reduced anxiety rather than created it. In performances on national television, in nightclubs, and on records, Jackie Mason uses a self-consciously exaggerated Brooklyn sing-song accent to identify himself as a Jew, to call attention, literally, to the question of his nationality and religion. Often it seems as though Mason purposely creates audience discomfort so that as comic he can relieve it, allowing them an excuse to laugh off their own anxiety about his blatant and stereotypical Jewishness. He opens one routine by asserting, correctly enough, that "people judge you from the way you talk."[16] "From the way I talk, people seem to think I come from Alabama"; "You'd be surprised how many people actually think I'm Jewish." The question of his nationality, religion, accent, and relation to Americans becomes much more meaningful in a routine entitled, "I Was Almost Drafted," in which he discusses why he tried to avoid fighting against the Germans in World War II. He begins in a Falstaffian way by relying on the audience's belief that cowardice is really common sense:

> I would have been proud to fight, but they called me at a ridiculous time. You know when they called me? In the middle of a war.

Like Falstaff, he too wants his "country to have the best, not guys like me." Though the routine appears to smack of the stereotype Jew-as-coward, it soon moves to higher ground as Mason discusses his anxiety about Germans and emerges as a survivor, smarter than American draftees or German soldiers:

> You think I'm a hit in this country? This is nothing. Germany—what a following . . . Storm Troopers. They all thought I was a Jew; I never opened my mouth. But I walk with an accent.

He turns cowardice into shrewdness by using compelling logic: "The Germans see me, are they gonna shoot at anybody else?" He finally ends by rising above global conflicts in an admission that as a Jew he has special needs that must come first:

> I said to myself, thank God they [the Germans] don't know where I am, I should go looking for them?

This is as close to Holocaust humor as Jewish-American comedians have ever come, though it seems at first merely to be the familiar routine of a "loser."

As the 2000-Year-Old-Man, Mel Brooks is asked by Carl Reiner about Paul Revere, whom Brooks calls "an anti-Semite bastard" who hated the Jews.[17] "He had fear that they were going to go in the neighborhood and move in." All night long he yelled, "They're coming, they're coming, the Yiddish are coming." When Reiner tells him that he is mistaken, that Paul Revere warned that "the British are coming," Brooks says, "Oh my God! The *British* are coming, *gottenyu!*" "What an error; I'm glad we spoke." Here we have a Jewish "error," no different from Woody Allen's mis-hearing "did you," though presumably Robert Klein did see a swastika mobile at Alfred University, and Jackie Mason did have good reason to stay far from Germany. The exchange between Brooks and Reiner is a classic wish-fulfillment for Jews: "What an error; I'm glad we spoke." If only the mobile were not made of swastikas, if only every "d' you" were "did you," if only Stern's wife, in Bruce Jay Friedman's novel, had not been knocked down by their Christian neighbor. The 2000-Year-Old Man mis-heard, "night after night," but the Jewish paranoid "spoke" and his anger melted into embarrassment: "I'm gonna have to send his wife a note." In stand-up comedy the Jewish *schlemiel* speaks and either relearns, or makes his experiences less threatening by reliving it before a friendly audience.

Miss Kael's description of Woody Allen's comic persona is useful because it suggests the differences between the losers and that large group of self-consciously Jewish comics who are angry and out to chastise the world. The fast-talking patter of the brash Jewish stand-up comedian varies from the low-brow ethnic jokes of Don Rickles, to the political insight of Mort Sahl, to the truly apocalyptic visions of Lenny Bruce. Once again, a clear line can be drawn, this time from Milton Berle on the vaudeville stage ("There may have been other child monologists more offensive offstage, but onstage Milton Berle . . . was without competition")[18], to the Marx Brothers, Morey Amsterdam, Lenny Bruce, Phil Silvers, Alan King, Mort Sahl, Robert Klein, Don Rickles, and Mel Brooks. Each is outspoken; many of them served as emcees in the Catskills where they soon learned to deal swiftly and effectively with hecklers or lose their jobs. Milton Berle's introductions of actors and singers were fearsome and he had several unpleasant encounters with Bea Lillie and Ethel Barrymore. On "You Bet Your Life" Groucho Marx was essentially doing a stand-up act, playing off the show's naive contestants, and Mort Sahl drew national attention by satirizing our political institutions and personalities (Shelley Berman said that Sahl had it easy—all his material was written for him by William Randolph Hearst, Jr.). Robert Klein, perhaps the preeminent Jewish stand-up comedian today, combines traditional targets in Borscht-Belt one-liners with political observations, routines on sports, television commercials, and Jewish family life. In "The Borscht Belt" Klein imitates the typical Catskill's emcee introducing the fictitious "Mickey Lee," a comic, who then proceeds to insult the audience with rapid-fire one-liners and longer jokes in English with Yiddish punch-lines. The emphasis, of course, is on the abrasiveness of the typical Jewish comic.

No comedian had a profounder impact on the course of stand-up comedy in the last quarter century than Lenny Bruce who, in some respects, epitomizes the varying ways in which Jewish comedians reacted antagonistically to American society and to their own background. If Woody Allen conforms to the Christian notion of what a Jew should be, Lenny Bruce embodies that community's worst fears of what a Jew could become. He was intelligent but no intellectual, physical if not indeed violent, radical in his politics, utterly free-thinking in his approach to sex and language, and often purposely contrary. Throughout his brief career, Lenny Bruce strove to clarify what he perceived as the opposition between Christians and Jews, though for most critics his attitudes and opinions remain a maze of contradictions. Bruce was obsessed with Christ and with Christianity, and this is curious, coming as it does from the comic who brought Yiddish out of the Catskills and into the jazz clubs. His autobiography, *How to Talk Dirty and Influence People*, is dedicated to "all the followers of Christ and his teachings, in particular to a true Christian—Jimmy Hoffa—because he hired ex-convicts as, I assume, Christ would have" (Milton Berle's autobiography concludes with praise from Archbishop Fulton J. Sheen).[19] As always with Lenny Bruce, the serious is confounded with the comic, indeed, the serious is the comic. He gives with one hand and takes with the other: the dedication to "all the followers of Christ" is genuine enough, as is the implication that there are few enough of them around today.

Lenny Bruce never did understand his own response to Christians and Christianity. It would appear that he appreciated Christianity fully and deeply; after all, time and again he mentions being "sort of swept up with the story of Christ—this big, beautiful man." When he spoke, the audience often felt they were listening to a sermon, and the appropriate verb for what Bruce did is "pontificate." He pretended not to be Jewish, he pretended to be religious in the truest sense of the word, above the parochial rites and obligations of any one religion. He was a preacher, a rabbi, he was Christ and Moses, but especially Christ. In the autobiography he tells of having become a priest (in habit only) and of having solicited money for the imaginary "Brother Mathias Fund." He quotes an article by Arthur Gelb in the *New York Times*, in which his act is called a "salvationist lecture"; he reprints a letter to him from the vicar of St. Clement's Church in New York City, in which his "honesty" on the stage is compared to that of a priest in a pulpit. A review for the *Los Angeles Times* said of Bruce in 1966, "I don't think he was a comedian, really, I think he was a preacher."[20]

Lenny Bruce's neutral posture, his attempt to rise above the sectarianism of either Judaism or Christianity, is most clear in his constant reference to Adolf Eichmann, and to the Jews' treatment of Eichmann in Israel:

> Eichmann really figured, you know, 'The Jews—the most liberal people in the world—they'll give me a fair shake.' Fair? *Certainly.* 'Rabbi' means lawyer. He'll get the best trial in the world, Eichmann. Ha! They were shaving his leg while he was giving his appeal! That's the last bit of insanity, man.

In another routine, Bruce quoted a poem on Eichmann by Thomas Merton, and told the audience, "it really says a lot to me." The poem suggests that we are no better than Eichmann, and concludes:

> I, Adolf Eichmann,
> vatched through the portholes.
> I saw every Jew burned
> und turned into soap.
> Do you people think yourselves better
> because you burned your enemies
> at long distances
> with missiles?
> Without ever seeing what you'd done to them?
> Hiroshima . . . *Auf Wiedersehen.* . . .

It is one thing to be against capital punishment (as Lenny Bruce always was) and another to argue for Eichmann's life, as Lenny Bruce does. The poem may be logically and perhaps morally unassailable but it is emotionally suspect, if not for Thomas Merton who, after all, was a devout Christian, at least for Bruce.

Lenny Bruce's ecumenism seems now to have been pretense and pose, though I do not mean to use these words in their pejorative sense. At best, Bruce's stand on religion was contradictory, and at worst hypocritical with regard to his Jewishness, for, side by side with his neutrality Bruce was fiercely Jewish. For him the world was indeed divided into "Us" and "Them," Jews and Christians:

> To me, if you live in New York or any other big city, you are Jewish. It doesn't matter even if you're Catholic: if you live in New York you're Jewish. If you live in Butte, Montana, you're going to be *goyish* even if you're Jewish.
>
> Evaported milk is *goyish* even if the Jews invented it. Chocolate is Jewish and fudge is *goyish*. Spam is *goyish* and rye bread is Jewish.
>
> Negroes are all Jews. Italians are all Jews. Irishmen who have rejected their religion are Jews. Mouths are very Jewish. And bosoms. Baton-twirling is very *goyish*.

He revealed different attitudes toward sex between Jews and Christians. He contends that "the Jews lost their god. Really." "Our god has no mother, no father, no manger in the five and ten, on cereal boxes and on television shows." While he seems to criticize Jews, the thrust of his comments is that no god at all is better than a dimestore version. Ostensibly indicating differences between Christians and Jews, he actually describes the secularization of contemporary Christianity, revealing an antagonism toward Christians that seems unexpected coming from a man who loved Christ. This same antagonism manifested itself clearly in his definition of "Jew," a definition which confronts the central myth of Jewish/Christian relations:

> Now, a Jew, in the dictionary, is one who is descended from the ancient tribes of Judea, or one who is regarded as descended from that tribe. That's what it says in the dictionary; but you and I know what a Jew is—*One Who Killed Our Lord*.

He complains that Jews are still paying for that crime, and finally confesses to it in order to "clear the air once and for all":

> Yes, we did it. I did it, my family. I found a note in my basement. It said:
> "We killed him.
>   signed,
>   Morty."

Like a kind of Christ, Lenny Bruce here confesses for all Jews, confesses to atone for all their sins as Jews, but only succeeds in trivializing Christianity's most serious charge against the Jews. As we might expect, the other shoe drops when, in the same bit, he goes on to state the point of his confession by predicting that if Christ returns, "he's going to get it. . . . definitely. He's going to get killed again because he made us [the Jews] pay so many dues." Again, as with the dedication to Jimmy Hoffa, Bruce attacks Christianity while most seeming to extol it.

Bruce's sense of "Us" versus "Them" pervades his routines and autobiography. Jack Ruby shot Lee Harvey Oswald because Ruby came from Texas where "They're really concerned with 'bawls,'" "and a Jew in Texas is a tailor."

> Well, if *I* kill the guy that killed the *president*, the Christians'll go:
> "*Whew!* What bawls he had, hey? we always thought the Jews were chickenshit, but look at that! See, a Jew at the end, saved everybody!"
> And the Christians'll kiss him and hug him and they'll lift him on high. A JEWISH BILLY THE KID RODE OUT OF THE WEST!

It is difficult to tell here if Lenny Bruce is putting his finger on prejudice in Texas or on his own sense of being different. Jack Ruby was Jewish, and for Bruce that was a fact of central importance. Is Bruce looking for a Jewish hero who will save us all from Christian stereotypes? As stand-up comic is he more sensitive than most and satirizing real Christian attitudes, or is he creating them out of his own anxieties, misunderstanding and mis-hearing like the 2000-Year-Old Man? Are they after Jews in New York, Boston, and Texas, in the 1700s and the 1900s? After all, he tells us the Jew, not the Christian, is concerned with, and aware of, the differences:

> So it's the same. The Jew is hung up with his shit and maybe the Christian—because, when the Christians say, like, "Oh, is he Jewish? I didn't know. I can't tell when somebody's Jewish."
> I always thought, "That's bullshit."
> But he can't. Cause he never got hung up with that shit, man. And Jews are very hung up with that, all the time.

Lenny Bruce did admire Christ and did think of himself as a kind of Christ figure. But his love of Christ served one important purpose: it allowed him to express his hatred of what he saw as the hypocrisy of the Christian community, professing love and truth, but behaving in ways antithetical to the teachings of Christ, especially by making Jews pay "so many dues." By posing as a lover of Christ, Bruce had the license he needed and could hardly be accused of being just another Jewish iconoclast. Indeed, while Bruce seems to contradict himself everywhere, there *is* a start and a finish to his ideas about Christians and Jews. He wanted reconciliation, a truce in the battle going on within himself between the two groups. He was "very hung up with" his own Jewishness and needed a rest, a "warm blanket"; perhaps, like George Burns, Lenny Bruce felt that "if the whole world were Jews, we'd have no problems."[21] He was tired as well of his own sniping at Christians, at the source of his anxiety, at the people who made him pay "so many dues," and he felt the additional burden of guilt, not for killing Christ, but for being antagonistic and for hating. His notion that the Jews control the motion-picture industry explained for him why there were so many apologetic movies about Christ:

> And you see a lot of pictures about Christ—a ton of religious pictures, in the most respectful position. And the reason that is, I'm sure, it's the way the Jew's saying, "I'm sorry." That's where it's at.

Bruce is angry at "Religions, Inc." for having divided up the world in the first place, and certainly sorry for the tension and guilt the division has spawned.

Theodore Reik, in *Jewish Wit*, sees in Jewish humor "two sides to every story," "an oscillation" between a masochistic and a paranoid attitude which forms a complex of "contradictions that characterize the Jewish situation in our civilization."[22] To a certain degree, Reik's observation is true of several Jewish comedians, for example, Georgie Jessel, Myron Cohen, Joey Bishop, Shecky Greene, Shelley Berman, and Gabriel Kaplan, all of whom alternate postures even in a single performance. However, even the brashest comics seem to "oscillate," or to find themselves with audiences who simply do not "know how to take a joke." Milton Berle was forever explaining away offensive public comments he had made (he was once stabbed in the throat with a fork after a performance in which he joked with an unsmiling couple). Mel Brooks had to explain in print to concerned special education groups that "Mongo" in *Blazing Saddles* was not a reference to the proverbial village idiot, but rather to the jazz musician, Mongo Santamaria; and Don Rickles is as generous with his blessings and apologies after a performance as with his insults during one. Such oscillation typifies many comedians' performances, though Reik's thesis is truest of Lenny Bruce, who addressed himself most directly to the issues and feelings troubling him.

As performance postures, being a loser or being angry, signs perhaps of "masochism" and "paranoia," are equally the result of complex emotions in the comedian, and both perform equally valuable functions for comic and for audience. After all, both attitudes point to a question beyond the purview of this paper, namely, why comedy needs a winner/loser relationship at all, for the angry comic simply attacks or belittles others, while the *schlemiel* directs his guns on himself. But predator or prey, in stand-up comedy the Jewish comedian is clearly acting out his own complicated and often contradictory response to personal conflicts and situations.

NOTES

1. See Larry Wilde, *The Great Comedians Talk about Comedy* (New York: Citadel Press, 1968), pp. 294–95.

2. Fred Allen, *Much Ado about Me* (Boston: Little, Brown, 1956), p. 241.

3. Albert Goldman, "Boy-Man Schlemiel: Jewish Humor," *Commonweal*, 29 September 1967, p. 606.

4. All references to Groucho Marx, the Marx Brothers, and the Marx family are to Charlotte Chandler, *Hello, I Must be Going: Groucho and His Friends* (New York: Penguin Books, 1978).

5. All references to Milton Berle are to *Milton Berle*, Milton Berle with Haskel Frankel (New York: Dell, 1974).

6. Bill Smith, *The Vaudevillians* (New York: Macmillan, 1976), p. 28.

7. "Comic's Indiscretion Cost Dignity of Waning Days," *Buffalo News*, 7 January 1979, p. 56.

8. All references to Leo Rosten are to *Leo Rosten's Treasury of Jewish Quotations* (New York: McGraw-Hill, 1972).

9. Wilde, p. 294.

10. Bill Adler and Jeffrey Feinman, *Mel Brooks: The Irreverent Funnyman* (New York: Playboy Press, 1976), p. 47. See also Kenneth Tynan, "Frolics and Detours of a Short Hebrew Man," *The New Yorker*, 30 October 1978, pp. 46–130.

11. Chandler, p. 531.

12. Robert Klein, *Mind over Matter* (Brut 6600, n.d.). See also Diane U. Eisenberg, "Mind over Matter: An Interview with Robert Klein," *American Humor* 4 (Fall 1977): 3–10.

13. All references to Bob Hope are to Timothy White, "Bob Hope without Laughter," *Rolling Stone*, 20 March 1980, pp. 46–52.

14. Jessel, quoted in Chandler, p. 532.

15. Pauline Kael, "Fear of Movies," *The New Yorker* 25 September 1978, p. 157.

16. All references to Jackie Mason are to *I Want to Leave You with the Words of a Great Comedian* (Verve V 15034, 1963).

17. Carl Reiner and Mel Brooks, *2000 and Thirteen* (Warner Bros., BS 2741, 1973).

18. Charles and Louise Samuels, *Once upon a Stage* (New York: Dodd, Mead, 1974), p. 162.

19. All references to Lenny Bruce are to his autobiography, *How to Talk Dirty and Influence People* (New York: Playboy Press, 1972); and to John Cohen, ed., *The Essential Lenny Bruce* (New York: Ballantine Books, 1967).

20. Enrico Banducci, quoted in Cohen, p. v.

21. Chandler, p. 500.

22. Theodore Reik, *Jewish Wit* (New York: Gamut Press, 1962), p. 229.

Elmer Rice, Liberation, and the Great Ethnic Question

Jules Chametzky

I

WRITING BACK IN 1932 ABOUT ELMER RICE, MEYER LEVIN—IN WHAT IS STILL THE best article on the once-celebrated playwright—quotes André Maurois, who said in *The Atlantic Monthly* that among dramatists who "ought to [be] read . . . [are] . . . Eugene O'Neill and Elmer Rice."[1] Maurois was a figure of great contemporary authority; moreover, he was not the only one to link those two names. In the twenties and thirties Rice and O'Neill were often cited as proof of the coming of age of American drama since 1914—that convenient date for marking the end of American innocence, which happens also to be the year that O'Neill published his first volume of one-act plays and Rice, at the age of twenty-one, achieved instant success and a modicum of financial independence with his first play, *On Trial*. Both won international attention because of their stage innovations, chiefly, though certainly not exclusively, for their experiments with expressionist techniques. At the time of Levin's article, O'Neill's *Hairy Ape* and *Emperor Jones* were, of course, well-known; Rice's *The Adding Machine* (1923) was still playing European art theaters; and Rice's Pulitzer Prize-winning *Street Scene* (1929) was widely regarded as "a superb documentation of American manners."[2]

From our contemporary perspective—O'Neill's reputation has never been higher than it is now—that the two dramatists were once considered equals by critics of the first rank makes one wonder why there is such a paucity of material about Elmer Rice.[3] The question almost answers itself. If O'Neill had remained the playwright he was between the wars, he would very likely still rank above even his most gifted contemporaries (Sidney Howard, Robert Sherwood, Maxwell Anderson, Elmer Rice), but some of his early work looks quaint and hollow today, only of historical interest (*vide* Groucho Marx's deflation of *Strange Interlude* in one of his films). That is, if O'Neill had not gone on to write, out of his age and his anguish, *The Iceman Cometh* and that authentic American masterpiece, *A Long Day's Journey Into Night*, he would be regarded as an interesting and worthy playwright, his work a measure of America's culture at a certain period, but not as one of the great dramatists on the world's stage. Elmer Rice, it must be said at once, never achieved that final breakthrough in his career. Mentioning O'Neill and Rice in the same breath both elevates and diminishes one's estimation of Elmer Rice and his achievement. It forces a generation to whom the name Rice is relatively unknown to pay attention; once we have read his plays, we find that we admire certain plays and certain intentions but are disappointed in others—some of his concerns and techniques seem dated and irrelevant. The causes of both reactions are worth exploring.

Today we ask who Elmer Rice is, or was, and why he should be remembered. At first glance, the rubric "Jewish-American dramatist" does not seem entirely germane—other approaches, the scholars' straight theatrical history, or a formal analysis of his themes and concerns seen in their various contexts certainly enable us to assess Rice relatively well.[1] But "the great ethnic question" (Henry James's phrase in *The American Scene*, framed when he regarded New York's new population at the beginning of the century) may not be, if approached humbly, entirely irrelevant. Put crudely, out of elements in his ethnic and family drama confronted directly, O'Neill achieved a major, tragic vision. Elmer Rice, born Elmer Leopold Reizenstein, the grandson of German-Jewish immigrants, usually ignored his own "Jewishness" and produced out of his energy and talent a fine body of work, much of it innovative and brave, that lacks the mark of ultimate greatness.

Lest the equation I have presented be taken too simplistically, let me acknowledge at once all qualifications—not the least of which is the need to maintain a proper historical sense. That is to say, had Rice, in his time, attempted to habitually "confront" his ethnic situation directly (even if he wanted to), he might well have driven himself from the competitive stage.

This is not the occasion to enter into a long discussion of anti-Semitism and American culture in the formative years of Rice's growth and early success, but some historical data are necessary. In those years—from the turn of the century into the thirties—the general climate in the dominant culture, responding to its own insecurities in the face of dimly understood but vast and visible changes in the American culture and economy, especially the increasingly obvious presence of millions of immigrants and ethnics, closed ranks against the "outsider" and advocated something called 100% Americanism. As John Higham has shown, much of this generalized unease and hostility began to focus on the Jew. American anti-Semitism crystallized in the early twentieth century, peaked in the twenties (the era of a renascent KKK and the 1924 Johnson-Reed Act that restricted immigration upon racist and nationalist grounds) and was unusually intense in the late thirties—although by that time a broad movement for "ethnic democracy" had emerged to fight Father Coughlin, the Silver Shirts, et al.[5]

During this time, the literary world was not free of the taint of anti-Semitism or unresolved ambivalences regarding the Jew, even in the work of major writers. Henry Adams's psychosis on the subject is well known, as is Dreiser's. Masterly works, the pride of American literature survey courses, like Wharton's *The House of Mirth*, Fitzgerald's *The Great Gatsby*, and Hemingway's *The Sun Also Rises*, are scarred by what the Jews in them are made to represent. On the stage, sentimentalized, stereotypic portrayals held sway—Lou Holtz, Dr. Kronkheit, Potash and Perlmutter may have been acceptable as funny vaudeville, but on the legitimate stage, the hit of the twenties had to be the kitsch of *Abie's Irish Rose*. In the face of all that, one is less surprised that a writer with Rice's skill at courtroom drama did not directly treat a subject like, say, the Leo Frank case (Frank was a northern Jew lynched in Atlanta in 1913, a year before

Rice wrote *On Trial*). When Rice did explore the potential for mindless violence in the average man frustrated by forces beyond his comprehension, he did so in the more oblique and stylized expressionist manner of *The Adding Machine*, written ten years after the Frank lynching. Mr. Zero in his defense to the jury talks about dirty "sheenies" always getting two to the other fellow's one, but Rice's target in the play is even broader and more generalized than anti-Semitism, which is only one of Zero's deficiencies. A similar pattern recurs in Rice's other plays that touch upon Jews.

The date and title of Michael Gold's *Jews Without Money* (1930) might be taken as a turning point of sorts. The title directly refutes the general lie behind much of American anti-Semitism, and throughout the Depression writers began to feel freer about using their ethnic origins as material—Odets's *Awake and Sing!* (1935) was among the first and best, as was Rice's even earlier and more commercial *Counsellor-at-Law* (1931). Broadway plays reached a small, relatively sophisticated audience—plays that were later made into mass-market films were often "de-ethnicized" in the process. Even as late as the forties, obviously Jewish material was deracinated, as the slightest reflection upon *Death of a Salesman* shows. We all *know* Miller's play is (or should be) about a Jewish salesman and his family, but in order to generalize its appeal, it seemed to be necessary to give the family no recognizable ethnic identity at all. This proved to be no impediment to its pop acceptance as an American classic. To be "American" was to remove the Jewishness—even as late as the postwar era. This obfuscation should not be surprising if we remember that according to Gallup, anti-Semitism was at its height in this country in the immediate postwar years and did not diminish significantly until after about 1947, when the full import of the Nuremberg Trials began to sink in.

But Jewish writers did begin to acknowledge their link to Jewish fate in the thirties under the increasing threat of German fascism. One thinks of the anti-fascist dramas of "non-identifying" Jewish writers like Edward Dahlberg, Lillian Hellman, and especially Elmer Rice. I daresay no Jew, however attenuated his or her connection with Judaism, could feel that those German troops photographed by Movietone News marching down the Champs Élysées in the spring of 1940 were not coming directly after him/her. Something like that must have been the impulse behind Rice's *Flight to the West*, produced in December, 1940. The protagonist, Charles Nathan, a serious young Jewish American, previously a pacifist (like Rice), tries to persuade his Gentile wife that personal participation in the fight against Nazi barbarity is necessary and proper. Interestingly enough, he is arguing not primarily as a Jew who feels he must combat anti-Semitism but as a human being who feels he must defend all civilized values. That is, the Jew is not the primary target of the brutes, he is only one of their many targets, which include not only all humane and right-thinking people but also such institutions of civilization as the library of Louvain (Rice resurrects the anti-Boche sentiments of the First World War).

After the war, Rice wrote few plays of specific social consequence although as a citizen he was enbroiled in defense of civil liberties causes. In the period of his major impact as a *writer*, therefore, it can be said that given the real alternatives available to him and who he was, where Rice did confront his ethnic situation, directly and indirectly, he made the most of it. In fact, those plays upon which his reputation as a serious dramatist may rest—*The Adding Machine, Street Scene, Counsellor-at-Law*— touch significantly issues that would lie at the heart of such a confrontation.

II

First of all, something of who Elmer Rice was and some of his achievements. Answering the charge that his changing his name (which he did sometime around 1918) was an attempt to hide his background, Rice said in his character-istically level way, "I have never paraded my origin, but I have never tried to deny it."[6] He changed it, he said, simply because it was so hard to spell and pronounce, and besides it was "foreign sounding" and he had no emotional ties with it. In his personal contacts he claims to have been influenced by race, nationality, religion; and although in his long career as a civil libertarian he fought anti-Semitism (as well as Jewish groups who tried to prevent the showing of *Oliver Twist*), he says he personally never suffered from it.[7] He was the only child of parents who maintained only a tenuous connection with Jewish religious observances (the last remnant was his mother's fasting on Yom Kippur) and who were all but assimilated. He was turned off by the hypocrisies of the religious life he saw around him on Manhattan's Upper West Side, where he grew up, and refused to be confirmed in the faith. He became a Shavian agnostic, by his own report, never turned back, and never regretted his position. He was in love with theater, ideas, the city.

This bare-bones version of his ethnic biography, if a little cool, would sound familiar to many another Jewish youth growing up in New York, despite the haze of nostalgia and fashion through which that experience is currently being filtered. The experience of being assimilated to a cosmopolitan image of enlight-ened values—rational, liberal and humane—is also a common one for the Jewish intellectual. It was a source of his liberated strength as well as, perhaps, a certain emotional thinness in some of his writing.

Rice was immersed in the theatrical and ideological concerns of his time. His first play was a tour-de-force of craft—a courtroom melodrama of no great significance except that it introduced the flash-back technique expertly to the stage, created a sensation, and made the young recent law graduate enough money that he could abandon a career he disliked for the life of a professional writer. His practical sense almost never deserted him, except that he frequently pushed against the safe and accepted modes of thought and substance as well as of craft and conventional modes of theatrical organization and financing— frequently against formidable resistance.[8] His great successes of the twenties, *The Adding Machine* and *Street Scene*, were produced and won their way only after considerable skepticism about their commercial or intellectual viability. In the thirties Rice played a heroic role that deserves an essay by itself. He was a key figure in the start of the Federal Theatre project, advising Harry Hopkins in a crucial way,[9] and became the first director of the New York section of it. He resigned in protest over the government's censorship of *Ethiopia*, one of the first *Living Newspapers*. In the late thirties he was one of the founders of The Playwrights Company (with Robert Sherwood, Maxwell Anderson, Sidney Howard, and others), which was short-lived but significant in its effort to elevate the country's commercial theater and its best writers. Throughout that period (and for the rest of his life) he was a mainstay of the American Civil Liberties Union, an important and active member of the Authors League, and a hard-working advocate of many liberal causes. He cites with pride his inclusion in Elizabeth Dilling's *The Red Network* (1934) and in *Red Channels*—both books were efforts to identify (some would say "smear") certain people in the media as reds, red sympathizers, or otherwise subversive types—although he was then and thereafter anti-communist and a pacifist.

It was a productive period, in which he attempted to broaden his range. He began the decade with a play that fizzled, *The Left Bank* (1931),a comedy about expatriates based on his sojourn in Paris in the twenties, followed in the same year by *Counsellor-at-Law*, after *Street Scene* his longest-running play. He closed the decade with a charming comedy—a love affair with Manhattan—that was a moderate success—*Two on an Island* (1940). In between, he experimented with ideological dramas, such as *We the People* (1933) and *American Landscape* (1938)—efforts to discern a positive American ethos during the Depression years—the anti-fascist (and in my view fatally melodramatic) *Judgment Day* (1934) based on the recent Reichstag Fire Trial, and *Between Two Worlds* (1934), an effort to mediate between the communist and capitalist world views. The later companion piece, *Flight to the West*, as already mentioned here, deals with the urgency of the Nazi threat. He was often lambasted for his ideological explorations—John Mason Brown thought (quite stupidly) that *Judgment Day* was as laughable as *The Drunkard*[10]—many bitter exchanges between Rice and his critics in the *New York Times* and elsewhere led to Rice's announcement in 1934 of his retirement from the theater. Of course it didn't stick (he returned four years later), though he made several trips abroad, writing books about them, and he wrote at least one successful novel (*Imperial City*, 1937) to prove to himself he didn't need the stage.

In 1945 he produced one of his slighter but most charming and successful plays, *Dream Girl*, as a comic vehicle for his second wife, Betty Field. His first wife, incidentally, to whom he had been married many years, was named Hazel Levy. It was a light treatment of a serious theme common to all his best works— the need to abandon moonshine and illusion, to come to grips with reality in a truly liberating way. He kept working through the fifties and sixties, writing more plays and books. At the time of his death in 1967 there were two plays left unproduced.[11] Even this brief outline shows that his was an extraordinary and interesting career—its relevance as cultural history cannot be doubted and awaits a full-scale treatment. What follows—a brief consideration of his three most significant plays—is a mere prolegomena, perhaps, to such a study.

III

Rice once wrote, in an apologia of sorts, that

> the dominant concern . . . of all of us . . . should be with the attainment of freedom of the body and of the mind through liberation from political autocracy, economic slavery, religious superstition, hereditary prejudice and herd psychology and the attainment of freedom of the soul through liberation from fear, jealousy, hatred, possessiveness and self-delusion. . . . Everything that I have ever written seriously has had in it no other idea than that. [12]

His own assessment of what is the most significant and consistent theme in his work cannot be faulted. Each of the plays I will consider examines and criticizes in its own way restraints upon human freedom and liberation.

In *The Adding Machine* the central character is Mr. Zero, whose name is meant to express his emotional, psychic, and social nothingness. [13] The stylized dialogue, rich in cliché and stereotype, between Mr. and Mrs. Zero—and their friends the Ones, Twos, Threes, Fours, Fives, and Sixes—reveals sexually repressed, bigoted, narrow lives. After twenty-five monotonous, robotizing years adding numbers in the office of a department store, Mr. Zero becomes a victim of technological advance and is fired. Shocked for once into significant action, in his rage he kills his employer. He is tried and convicted by a jury of his peers (the same Ones, Twos, etc.) and executed. In the Elysian Fields after death, he is vouchsafed a brief experience of sexual and emotional liberation with Daisy Devore, a fellow worker who has killed herself for love of Zero. Finally, he is offered the chance by the heavenly powers to return to earth as a more liberated person, but he rejects the opportunity and chooses to go back as the craven self he was before.

On its most profound level, in its portrayal of the timid little man fearful of freedom, the raw material of lynch mobs and fascism, Rice's *Adding Machine* anticipates the classic analyses of Wilhelm Reich in *The Mass Psychology of Fascism* and Erich Fromm's *Escape from Freedom*. But he does not probe as consistently as they do the social and psychological roots of this kind of behavior. At best Rice suggests obliquely that there may be such roots, but for the most part he is content to present as a given Zero's character structure, which he then exploits theatrically and ideologically. Why, when he has the opportunity to change at the end does Zero revert to slavish conformism once again? Well, says the heavenly functionary, "the mark of the slave was on [him] from the start." On the face of it, this judgment is too glib, too elitist, too despairing.

Such a judgment is strongly reinforced in the many long speeches in the play's last scene by this same heavenly emissary, who presumably provides out of his cosmic understanding the ultimate meaning of it all. He says,

You're a failure, Zero, a failure. A waste product. A slave to a contraption of steel and iron. The animal's instincts, but not his strength and skill. The animal's appetites, but not his unashamed indulgence of them. True, you move and eat and digest and excrete and reproduce. But any microscopic organism can do as much. Well—time's up! Back you go—back to your sunless groove—the raw material of slums and wars—the ready prey of the first jingo or demagogue or political adventurer who takes the trouble to play upon your ignorance and credulity and provincialism. You poor, spineless, brainless boob—I'm sorry for you! [p. 61]

Despite the mild expression of sympathy at the end, Zero stands indicted for his unchanging and slavish nature. But that is not quite all there is to it—as might be the case in a rigorously expressionistic drama of the twenties. To the two-dimensional portrait of an early Archie Bunker character, Rice adds many humanizing touches; more to the point, the play is fun to read, play, and see.

In support, one is tempted to quote extensively whole monologues, dialogue, scenes. Mrs. Zero's opening monologue in bed (a repressed and nasty Molly Bloom) and Zero's peroration to the jury as masterful evocations of a way of life, self-indicting but involving us as well ("Suppose you was me, now. Maybe you'd 'a' done the same thing. That's the way you oughta look at it, see? Suppose you was me—" [p. 24].) The jurors, of course, rise as one and venomously declare him "Guilty!" There are touching moments—Zero, enjoying his wife's ham and eggs as his last meal or Zero and Daisy in the Elysian Fields (and never out of character: Daisy says, "Look at the flowers! Ain't they just perfect! Why you'd think they was artificial, wouldn't you?"). Shrdlu, whom Zero meets after death, is a marvelous character (he was played in the original production by Edward G. Robinson). He is a mild-mannered murderer, surprised that one Sunday, at dinner with the minister, he stuck the carving knife into his mother's throat instead of the weekly leg of lamb. In heaven he is dismayed that the only ministers admired seem to be Dean Swift and Abbé Rabelais, for their indecent tales, and that the people there think of nothing but enjoyment and wasting their time in such profitless occupations as painting, sculpting, composing songs, and writing poems.

Rice is writing here out of his cosmopolitan urbanity. He reflects an American twenties' sensibility that owes as much to Mencken's attacks on the American "booboisie" and provincial philistinism as to German expressionism. There is a tension between the two modes: Rice may appear too facile in trying to accommodate both, but it assures the play life beyond its ideology. By manipulating our empathy with Zero—by humanizing him, making us complicit in his fate—the play becomes something more than a thesis-ridden cautionary tale. His background made it inevitable that Rice would be one of the enlightened anti-Puritans of his day. Out of that reality, Rice domesticated expressionism to his American language and assumptions, giving us, thereby, a continually relevant appeal to self-examination. The play is satiric and caustic, but its despair is only superficial, belied by Rice's witty, bedrock commitment to living and human values.

Street Scene is a lovely play, despite its dated, sensationalistic, and stereo-typic qualities.[14] For those unfamiliar with Samuel Goldwyn's faithful early thirties screen version or the operatic adaptation by Kurt Weill (lyrics by Langston Hughes), the play's chief elements can be briefly noted.

The entire action takes place during a summer evening and the following morning and afternoon on a one-set stage that represents the street before an ugly New York brownstone tenement whose stone steps, front door, first- and second-story apartment windows dominate the scene like the temple or royal entrance in Greek tragedy. The plot turns on a horrifying act that takes place in one of the apartments. A stagehand, Frank Maurrant, shoots and kills his wife and her lover, a milk-money collector. Maurrant is pursued, caught, arrested, and led off to a certain execution. Much of the play's interest focuses on the interplay among the various tenants, who comprise practically a cross-section of New York's white ethnics.

Street Scene was first produced in January, 1929, before the Crash and the Depression; at the time few professional theater people believed that a play dealing with such depressing fare and so mundane a milieu could succeed. In fact it did, phenomenally—and if we now decry what became the stereotypes and stock situations that were staples of drama and films for the next twenty years, we must acknowledge Rice's genius in originally creating them or at least realizing their dramatic potential. First of all, *Street Scene* was a superb piece of stagecraft. The set (designed by Jo Mielziner) was visually imposing; the use of only one set made for fluidity of pace; incorporating the city's sights (excava-tions, warehouses) and sounds (traffic, sirens, street games) was imaginative; and the variety of character types maneuvered gracefully through hundreds of difficult entrances and exits was simply breathtaking. It was Rice's first effort, almost against his will, as a director, and it was a triumph. More significant, the plunge into New York's ethnicity, for the purpose of a serious exploration of contemporary realities, and not just comic relief, gave the play much of the authenticity and power that it can still convey.

Rice was still caustic about the Zeroes of ordinary life—Mr. Zero's worst characteristics appear in both Maurrant (but with differences) and, especially, the Jones family. The Joneses, despite their name, are bigoted Irish and so unrelievedly awful they are wonderful. Father drinks and misses work; mother is the archetypal malicious busybody and gossip, doting on her two despicable children, Vincent (a coarse bully who drives a cab) and May (a drunken slat-tern). They have a dog named "Queenie." As their name suggests, they tran-scend ethnic stereotyping; they have no redeeming social value; they endure.

A cheerful Italian musician named Fillipo Fiorentino and his fat German wife Margharita (he is enormously affectionate toward her, although she regards her childlessness as a constant reproach) live on one side of the entrance hallway, a Jewish family on the other. Abraham Kaplan is an old radical writer for the Yiddish press; his sensitive son Sam, who quotes Whitman, is in his last year of college and on his way to law school; his daughter Shirley is described in the stage directions as "an unattractive Jewess"—she is a schoolteacher, supporting Sam through college. The janitors are Scandinavian (in the opera they are black—that way Hughes could write a blues song for them). It is unclear whether the Maurrants are Irish Catholic or Protestant, but the husband Frank is a "law and order" man, whose ideas are of the sort that used to be associated with the Hearst press. His wife Anna is sweet and touching, a gentle soul yearning for tenderness to grace her life. Their young son Willie is a kid growing up tough in the streets. Their daughter Rose (played in the original production by Erin O'Brien Moore, with what must have been unbearable beauty) is the play's strongest character. She speaks some of its best lines as she rejects crass suitors, feels for and advises Sam, comforts her mother (and ultimately her father), and assumes responsibility for Willie and a new life at the end.

Rice captures perfectly the New York period flavor in his scenes on the front "stoop" on a hot summer's night. The tenants come out to eat ice cream, cool off, and banter among themselves. Then suddenly serious issues are touched, raw nerves and the roots of character exposed. Discussing a recent eviction, in which the landlord had been a Jew, Mr. Kaplan offers his doctrinaire socialist analysis of the event (which has to do with capital and not ethnic issues), to which Maurrant takes exception: "Well, we don't want no revolutions in this country, see?" to which there is a "general chorus of assent." The Joneses jump in to denounce free love, Godlessness, the teaching of evolution. Shirley defends everyone's right to his own opinion. "Not if they're against law and order, they ain't," replies Maurrant. "We don't want no foreigners comin' in, tellin' us how to run things." At which Mrs. Fiorentino mildly demurs: "It's nothing wrong to be a foreigner. Many good people are foreigners." And so it goes.

Momentarily thrown off by the offense given by the foreigner remark, and a mock-serious discussion between Olsen and Fiorentino about who really discovered America, Maurrant and Jones get back on their track with a version of reality that all but the Kaplans can agree on: "Like I heard a feller sayin'," says Jones, "the Eye-talians built New York, the Irish run it an' the Jews own it." [Laughter] "Yeah," says Maurrant, "an' they're the ones that's doin' all the kickin'." Shirley responds with dignity, "It's no disgrace to be a Jew, Mr. Maurrant." To which he replies in Mr. Zero fashion—a mixture of right-wing platitudes and hysteria about freer sexuality—that seems to miss entirely the import of Shirley's remark:

> I'm not sayin' it is. All I'm sayin' is, what we need in this country is a little more respect for law an' order. Look at what's happenin' to people's homes, with all this divorce an' one thing an' another. Young girls goin' around smokin' cigarettes an' their skirts up around their necks. An' a lot o' long-haired guys talkin' about free love an' birth control an' breakin' up decent people's homes. I tell you it's time somethin' was done to put the fear o' God into people. [pp. 55–56]

Rice is deftly pointing to the irrational connection between these barely repressed anxieties and anti-Semitism. In response to her husband, Mrs. Maurrant quietly observes, "Sometimes I think maybe they're only trying to get something out of life." This innocuous observation elicits an emotionally brutal reaction from him that underscores his inability to understand or fulfill her needs and that shows again his own intense inner pressures. These pressures finally explode when Kaplan utters another doctrinaire line about the abolition of the family once private property is abolished.

> *Maurrant* [Belligerently]: Yeah? Is that so? No reason to exist, huh? Well, it's gonna exist, see. Children respectin' their parents an' doin' what they're told, get me. An' husbands an' wives, lovin' an honorin' each other, like they said they would, when they was spliced—an' any dirty sheeny that says different is li'ble to get his head busted open, see? [p. 57]

Indeed we see. The scene stops just short of its threatened violence, but its potential hovers in the air over Maurrant. Years before Adorno's famous study of the authoritarian personality, Rice explored its roots in frustration at the sense of things getting out of hand, the scapegoating that substitutes for real control of one's life, the fear and insecurities that underlie rigidity.

Rice does not idealize his non-Jewish ethnics, to whom anti-Semitism and its ugly epithets ("kike," "sheeny," "kike bastard") are pretty much taken for granted. They give ready assent to current notions of Jewish money-worship (along with their "bolshie" proclivities), but in the portrayal of Maurrant and beyond him, Rice sees their prejudice as only one of many undesirable results of a culture that supports rigid upbringing and demagogic indoctrination instead of reason, tolerance, and intelligence.

Significantly, the Jewish family stands out as a bastion of precisely those values that can humanize and transform the culture. The father seems doctrinaire in his unrelenting application of socialist analyses to every facet of the life around them—his own family is obviously so loving and supportive, could he really envision the demise of so bourgeois an institution "after the revolution?"—but he speaks out of Yiddish socialism's unwavering desire to see life constructed on more humane foundations than crass capitalism could provide to the spiritually and physically impoverished of America's ghettoes. Unlike the other tenement dwellers, Kaplan invariably speaks in the voice of reason and intelligence—to which his son Sam adds poetry and warmth, and a desire for transcendent love that is a bit moony but nevertheless touching. His sensitivity is in stark contrast to the emotional brutality of Olson, Maurrant, and Jones. His Irish Rose responds to him and mothers him, but she does not marry him. Both she and Shirley urge upon him the need to continue his studies and rise from the life they all are forced to live. Rose will sacrifice for her brother Willie, as Shirley does for Sam. Although a spinster, Shirley is a prototypical ghetto or immigrant mother. She finds fulfillment and dignity in holding the family together (which includes a strong injunction against intermarrying); she is sane, stable, self-sacrificing. Her virtues and strengths stand in sharp contrast to the other women in the play, even Rose, who is wonderful but must contend with forces disintegrating her family that simply do not arise in the Jewish family before us.

Finally, Rice extends sympathy even to the murderer Maurrant. Despite his monstrousness in the scenes quoted, one can feel pity for his general air of bafflement as he tries to affirm what he regards as eternal verities. His values, unlike Zero's, as well as his murderousness stem from his character and do not represent an ideological ploy of the playwright's. And his character is not wholly his own to shape. If that were not true, his final poignant scene with Rose, which is a tear-jerker, couldn't work:

> *Maurrant:* I ain't been a very good father, have I?
> *Rose:* Don't worry about that, pop.
> *Maurrant:* It ain't that I ain't meant to be. It's just the way things happened to turn out, that's all. Keep your eye on Willie, Rose. Don't let Willie grow up to be a murderer like his pop.
> *Rose:* I'm going to do all I can for him, pop.
> *Maurrant:* You're a good girl, Rose, You was always a good girl.
> *Rose* [Breaking down]: O pop!
> [She throws her arms about his neck and buries her head against him. Maurrant sobs hoarsely.]

Rose had earlier enjoined her father to be more warm and loving toward his wife ("There's a difference between loving and belonging"). In his final scene Maurrant admits he knew his wife had been a gentle and tender woman, but he had been drinking and "I must have been out of me head." Things just sort of happen—although not randomly. The implication is clear that background, training, environment, and social factors generally are more significant in shaping human conduct than morality or will power. This naturalist orientation, along with much else in the play, anticipates Odets, Kingsley, Shaw, and other dramatists of the thirties. The naturalist strain is emphasized further in the final scene between Rose and Sam following her father's removal.

Sam, in love with Rose, asks her to run off with him. She refuses, on the grounds that if she were to have a baby, they would end up trapped in their emotionally impoverished circumstances, like all the others around them. She agrees with his sister that he has a better future if he goes to law school (Shirley, interestingly enough, is also against marrying "out of one's kind"). The clincher, however, is that she and Willie will have a better chance if they leave the city—a motif that will become central in plays of the next decade. She aspires to have a house of her own in Queens or Staten Island. The slum, or rather the urban environment of the inner city itself, emerges as the enemy of the good life.

Somehow this is rather disappointing. I am reminded of Pare Lorentz's thirties documentary, *The City,* in which at the end of the film the order and cleanliness of the planned Greenbelt community is meant to be the desired antidote to the noise, congestion, and dirt of the city. Unfortunately, what emerges concretely in the film's images is the contrast between the vitality of city life and the sterility of the suburbs. In *Street Scene* no such contradiction arises—the image of the better life lies off-stage and in the future, as it were, while evidence of the vitality of the given is there before our eyes. The strength and beauty of Rose radiates even for contemporaries: what matters, she says early in the play to Sam is "not what you do but what you are." *Street Scene* deals, finally, with these archetypes of human desire, rather than with stereotypes, and will endure.

The "great ethnic question" looms larger and more explicitly in *Counsellor-at-Law* than in any other play by Rice.[15] The central character, George Simon, who came to America in steerage as a young child, is a self-conscious Jew who has risen to great success as a smart New York lawyer. His partner is an Italian, for whom he acquires a judgeship from his boyhood friend Peter J. Malone. Malone is an important Tammany politician, and shares a common bond of values with Simon against, as he says, "Those guys that came over on the Mayflower [who] don't like to see the boys from Second Avenue sittin' in the high places. We're just a lot of riffraff to them." The ethnics have a common cause in this play, produced two years after *Street Scene*, in 1931, the worst year of the Depression.

Rice subtly probes the contradictions apparent in the confrontation of ethnic outsider and dominant culture. Simon remembers and respects his past—he is generous to the poor, helps people of all kinds from his old East Side neighborhood, dotes on his mother (whose speech is sprinkled with Yiddish words). He is no angel, of course—he makes a killing on the market because of a leak from the Supreme Court and blackmails his WASP three-named rival who has the evidence to disbar him for malpractice. This shrewd, energetic highly capable man is utterly incapable, however, of seeing through and repudiating his shallow but indisputably upper-class WASP wife, Cora. She is snobbish and fatuously condescending (as are her snotty children from a previous marriage) to George, his work, staff, and mother. He disdains the enervated parasitism of one of his clients from her class (who will become her lover), and milks another (Schuyler Vandenbogen—the names and people of this group are caricatures) for some of his unearned millions in behalf of a show-girl client, but he requires the status of his marriage as a mark of his arrival and success.

This situation is not an unfamiliar one. Rice captures the historic moment and the myth well: a man from the lower classes, gifted with energy, know-how, and vitality, pits himself against a decadent dominant class but yearns for its marks of an assured civilization. On their part, the upper class—or, more accurately, the dominant Anglo parts of the culture—could see in the immigrants and their descendants the gravest threat to what they presumed was American civilization. It must be remembered that *Street Scene* and *Counsellor-at-Law* appeared within a very few years after passage of the racist (and to a considerable extent, anti-Semitically fueled) immigrant restriction act of 1924.

The cultural tensions and stakes were indeed high. What, after all, was America, and who would speak for it, control it? In the original production of *Counsellor-at-Law*, the past of George Simon was played to perfection by Paul Muni, who had a short time before transformed himself from the Yiddish actor Muni Weisenfreund and as Paul Muni went on from this play to fame and fortune in Hollywood. When the play made the same trip, it was similarly transformed and symbolically cleansed of its highly ethnic flavoring. In the film version George Simon was played by John Barrymore. Intermarriage between Jewish man and Christian woman was an emotionally charged issue then and was not often represented on the large screen. When it was, it was treated in the quasi-parodic style of Groucho Marx and Margaret Dumont.

Rice did the best he could with the materials at hand. He gave the public what it seemed to want, or what he could induce them to want—the illusion of real life in his set, lots of characters and human interest, plots and suspense culminating in the success of George Simon—which a contemporary will more often than not only groan at. To some extent, *Counsellor-at-Law* is a behemoth of a vehicle, an old-fashioned play that seems trapped in its sets and story. Even in that form, however, it should be seen as fixing an important moment in the evolving consciousness of Jew and ethnic in America. The heart of the play is Elmer Rice's characteristic plea for the liberation of human potentiality, and the freeing of self from dehumanizing illusions. Paradoxically, one is not always sure Rice is entirely free of the illusions of his own liberation—the hubris of rationalism, the trap of the contemporaneous.

Flight to the West showed that Rice could write a play in which a Jewish character close to his heart could prepare for heroic action, but not quite from the center of his Jewishness. Charles Nathan has to earn his moral authority by almost martyring himself, instinctively, leaping to the defense of a reprehensible Nazi. In this play and others written before the war, there are twists and paradoxes that Rice only half-confronted and explored. A few years later, if a serious social dramatist were to write about the fate of the Jews, knowledge of the Holocaust would call for a fuller confrontation—the result might be silence or a drama of towering rage and tragedy. In the years after the war, Rice obviously could not achieve such a dimension—his first postwar play was *Dream Girl*. And so, he is not the Jewish O'Neill, perhaps never could be, but he left an estimable legacy and, as Maurois observed many years ago, ought to be read. Even in oblique confrontations, Rice illuminates a part of America's cultural landscape we must increasingly come to know and appreciate.

NOTES

1. "Elmer Rice," *Theatre Arts*, January 1932, p. 54.

2. Ibid.

3. Jackson R. Bryer and Ruth M. Alvarez, "American Drama, 1918–1940: A Survey of Research and Criticism," *American Quarterly* 30, 3 (Bibliography Issue, 1978): 298–330. As the authors observe, "There is more material available about O'Neill than about all of the other playwrights of the 20s and 30s combined," (321) and "there is a need for good critical essays on Rice" (324).

4. The most notable studies in a lean field are Ralph L. Collins, "The Playwright and the Press: Elmer Rice and His Critics," *The Theatre Annual* (1948–49): 35–58, and the two books devoted to his work, Frank Durham, *Elmer Rice* (New York: Twayne, 1970) and Robert Hogan, *The Independence of Elmer Rice* (Carbondale: Southern Illinois University Press, 1965).

5. John Higham, *Send These to Me: Jews and Other Immigrants in Urban America* (New York: Atheneum, 1975), pp. 184–191.

6. *Minority Report: an Autobiography* (New York: Simon & Schuster, 1963). I have used the English edition of this enlightening book (London: Heinemann, 1963), p. 164.

7. Ibid., pp. 164–65.

8. *Vide*, Collins, "The Playwright and the Press."

9. Elmer Rice, *The Living Theatre* (New York: Harper & Brothers, 1959); See ch. 13, "The Federal Theatre Project," especially pp. 150–53, his letters to Hopkins.

10. Collins, p. 53.

11. Hogan offers a most interesting appraisal of these, as he does of most of Rice's voluminous output. He makes a good case for adding to my small list of plays representing major achievement. See also his "Elmer Rice: A Bibliography" (*Modern Drama*, February 1966) for a listing of Rice's work from 1913 to 1965.

12. In a *New York Times* piece (December 25, 1938), quoted in Hogan, p. 16.

13. The text cited is *Elmer Rice: Three Plays* (New York: Hill and Wang, 1965).

14. I use the Samuel French edition of *Street Scene* (New York, 1929), although it is conveniently available in *Three Plays*.

15. In *Seven Plays by Elmer Rice* (New York: Viking, 1950)—a useful collection that is unfortunately out-of-print. It includes *On Trial, The Adding Machine, Street Scene, Counsellor-at-Law, Judgment Day, Two on an Island* and *Dream Girl*. *Flight to the West* is available only in an out-of-print edition (New York: Coward-McCann, 1941).

Clifford Odets and the Jewish Context

R. Baird Shuman

SIGNIFICANT HAZARDS LURK IN ANY ATTEMPT TO CATEGORIZE A WRITER LIKE Clifford Odets in terms of ethnic identity. Certainly Odets was not a Jew in the sense that he was a participating member of a religious group that practiced the rituals of the Jewish faith. Organized religion never played a significant part in his life. Nevertheless, the ethnicity that surrounded him in his formative years imprinted itself upon his writing, much of which has strong Jewish overtones.

ODETS'S EXPOSURE TO THE JEWISH EXPERIENCE

The early Odets, it must be remembered, was essentially and above all a spokesman for the proletariat, a propagandist writing in the first half of the 1930s about the depressed economic and social conditions that threatened the very fiber of American society. Coincidentally, some of the themes directly related to proletarian writing also had legitimate historical archetypes in the Jewish experience.

Odets was born into a Jewish-American family in Philadelphia in 1906. Both his parents had come to the United States as small children; his mother, Pearl Geisinger, came from Austria, his father, Louis, from Russia.[1] For the first six years of Clifford's life, the Odets family lived in the so-called Northern Liberties area of Philadelphia, a section populated largely by German Jews, many of whom still spoke Yiddish, whose English was heavily accented, and whose speech patterns were primarily those of first- and second-generation Eastern European or German Jews.

The Odets family was essentially working class. However, the family was aspiring to the middle class, and in 1912 the Odetses moved to the Bronx, again settling in a largely Jewish neighborhood. They lived near Beck Street and Longwood Avenue in one of the better apartment buildings of the day. Louis Odets gradually advanced from his position as a feeder in a printery to become the owner of the shop. Soon he was able to buy a Maxwell automobile and to send his ailing wife to California to escape the cold of winter.

English was the only language spoken in the Odets household. Both of Clifford's parents were near-native speakers of the language. They neither read nor spoke Yiddish. However, Clifford's Aunt Esther and Uncle Israel Rosman, who were older when they immigrated to the United States than Odets's parents had been, spoke Yiddish and regularly read Yiddish newspapers. Odets recalls, ". . . while they were still my aunt and uncle, they were much more Jewish in their outlooks, and certainly in their language and customs, than my very American parents."[2]

Odets grew up hearing and speaking English at home, but the dialect of English used there and in the neighborhoods where he grew up probably had in it many of the melodies, intonations, and speech patterns of Eastern European immigrants with strong Jewish religious ties. Such patterns come through even in recorded interviews with Odets, where a sentence like, "I want to show in David, who is pursued by a psychotic Saul, a young poet,"[3] illustrates a basic structure and cadence of Jewish-American speech. This phrase structure of indirect object followed by direct object, while common in some instances in Network Standard English where the preposition of the indirect object is omitted (e.g. "He gave her a book"), is uncommon where the preposition is expressed and is a speech pattern characteristic of many Jewish Americans.

But Jewishness enters into the writing of an author with Odets's upbringing and background in more subtle and significant ways than are found solely in speech patterns and intonations. Some of the underlying themes of Jewish culture influenced his reactions to many of the social problems he treats in his plays, particularly the early ones, on both the literal and metaphoric levels. The very fabric of any writers' literary production is based upon the intricacies of his early, and in many cases, largely forgotten, experiences. For people raised in a Jewish family living in Jewish neighborhoods, whether the family appears acculturated or not, facets of the cultural heritage of the Jews come to be an ingrained part of their natures.

Guttmann, in answer to the question of how "Americans often assume that the folkways of *Mitteleuropa* and of the Russian *shtetl* are really the essentials of Jewishness," very rightly contends, "To answer such questions fully is to tell the story of the American Jews, but this much is certain: a minority that adopted many of the traits of its European neighbors is now distinguished in the eyes of its American neighbors by these adopted characteristics rather than by the fundamental differences that originally accounted for the minority status."[4] It is, as Guttmann suggests, all too easy to identify as Jewish some characteristics that are essentially European or Slavic. Many Jewish immigrants to this country came from Eastern Europe or from Russia, so that the traditions which they brought with them to the New World represent a melding of two cultures, their traditional Jewish culture and the European or Slavic culture that their forefathers had long since adopted.

Certainly Jacob in *Awake and Sing!* is typical of the kind of Jew Guttmann alludes to. Much of the political and social philosophy of Eastern European revolutionaries is reflected in Jacob's thinking. He is the somewhat confused and muddled revolutionary living with a much more conservative younger generation (Bessie and Myron Berger) whose ideas are considerably more down-to-earth and conventional than his. If Jacob can say, "If this life leads to a revolution it's a good life. Otherwise it's for nothing," Bessie can provide the put-down by responding, "Never mind, Pop! Pass me the salt."[5]

BIBLICAL INFLUENCES

In an interview with Michael Mendelsohn in 1961, two years before his death, Odets was asked about literary influences upon him and specifically about any influence the Bible might have had. He said,

> I like to read the Bible. I would like to read it more. I believe much that's in it. I want to write one more play—at least one more play that I know about—on a Biblical theme (that is after *The Flowering Peach*, which is about Noah and the Ark). I do want to write somewhere out of the two Books of Samuel, particularly the second book, I want to write about the life of Saul and David. I want to show in David, who is pursued by a psychotic Saul, a young poet.[6]

The extent to which Odets wished to use this Old Testament story for any of its specific and inherent Jewish qualities is, indeed, questionable. Rather, he seemed to find in the story a reflection of some of his own most personal feelings about the role of the artist in society. The interview continues:

> . . . I want to show how the young poet becomes a very successful man—indeed, the most successful in his realm, because he becomes the King. And I want to show the life of Man from the time he is a poet until he dies an old man, unhappy, but somehow still a poet gnawing at his soul. I want to turn the various facets of his nature around so that you see what happens to men of big success and how they meet the conflicting situations of their lives.[7]

The theme of what success does to an artist, which Odets had earlier dealt with in both *The Country Girl* (1950) and *The Big Knife* (1948), obviously fascinated him. Those two plays are certainly not prominently ethnic, nor is there any reason to suppose that in any dramatic verson he might have done of the Saul/David story, Odets would have set out to write a play which would have been essentially ethnic in its impact. Nevertheless, a number of Odets's early plays, as well as his last play to be produced, *The Flowering Peach* (1954), have a distinctly Jewish flavor and can legitimately be considered within the context of their Jewish ethnicity, as well as within a number of other contexts. Some of the less overtly Jewish plays can also be considered in terms of elements of the Jewish context that shaped Clifford Odets as a creative artist and as a person.

THE OVERTLY JEWISH PLAYS

Among Odets's early plays, both *Awake and Sing!* (1935) and *Paradise Lost* (1935) are about Jewish families. The Bergers in the former play are a lower-middle-class Jewish family struggling against the uncertainties of the economic depression of the 1930s. Three generations of the family live together and suffer the inevitable value confrontations that take place between people of different ages, backgrounds, and outlooks. The Gordons in *Paradise Lost* are an upper-middle-class Jewish family faced with economic and ethical problems growing out of the loss of the father's business through the dishonesty of his partner. The Gordons are more acculturated into American life, less obviously Jewish, than the Bergers. Indeed, they resemble Odets's own well-acculturated family.

Till the Day I Die (1935) focuses on the situation of a Communist in Nazi Germany. A tour de force in the *agitprop* tradition, it was written to accompany Odets's *Waiting for Lefty* (1935), which first played at the Civic Repertory Theatre on Fourteenth Street, then was moved uptown to the Longacre Theater where it and *Till the Day I Die* played together for 136 performances. The protagonist of *Till the Day I Die*, Ernst Tausig, is a Jew as well as a Communist, so is doubly a target for inhumane treatment by the German SS.

THE LESS JEWISH PLAYS

Waiting for Lefty, Odets's first successful production, deals with the economic issues of the Depression. The only direct allusion to Jews in this play is in Scene 5, which concerns Dr. Benjamin, a physician who is discharged from his hospital position, presumably because of anti-Semitism on the part of those who run the hospital.

Golden Boy (1937) has an Italian protagonist, Joe Bonaparte, and the play is without strong Jewish overtones, although Joe's manager, Mr. Carp, is clearly Jewish. Roxy Gottlieb in this play is also presented as being Jewish, particularly in certain of his speech patterns. Similarly, *Rocket to the Moon* (1938), *Night Music* (1940), and *Clash by Night* (1941), while they have Jewish characters in them, are not directly and primarily concerned with the Jewish experience, although numerous elements of Jewish life glimmer through them. Not until *The Flowering Peach* (1954) did Odets again deal with a subject as quintessentially Jewish as the depiction of the family in *Awake and Sing!*.

PROMINENT THEMES IN THE JEWISH CULTURAL HERITAGE

The Jewish cultural heritage is stronger than a number of other heritages which are basically religious in their origins. Even Jews who shun the faith of their progenitors remain in many ways Jews. Karl Shapiro addresses this point in *Poems of a Jew*: ". . . a Jew who becomes an atheist remains a Jew. A Jew who becomes a Catholic remains a Jew."[8] Harry Moore calls the Jewish heritage "environmental" and goes on to say "Granted, the environment of the Jews, usually clannish, sometimes produces physical characteristics that are fairly recognizable, yet these are intrinsically environmental. The young Jewish men often break with their community, leaving orthodoxy behind, yet many of them still marry Jewish girls, who understand their men's background, their early conditioning."[9] While Moore's comments perhaps represent a genetic oversimplification, a Jewishness appears to exist which is independent of religiosity and which is identifiable by certain patterns of behavior, philosophical stances, and value systems. Many of these hark back to the traditional religious faith and doctrine of earlier generations of Jews, of course, but they exist also quite noticeably and prominently in modern Jews who may, indeed, have denied the religion of their forefathers.

Irving Malin contends that many modern Jewish-American writers are engaged in "the search for new images of divinity in the absence of orthodox belief." He continues, "Our best [Jewish] writers are 'mad crusaders,' hoping for a transcendent ideal—art, potency?—to replace the tarnished ones they embraced in their youth."[10] He considers Jewish stories to be "those that witness, even in distorted or inverted ways, traditional religious and literary moments."[11] According to his definition, most of Odets's plays are not Jewish— the only ones that could be called Jewish are *The Flowering Peach*, most certainly, *Awake and Sing!*, somewhat less certainly, and possibly *Paradise Lost*.

However, Malin identifies themes common to the Jewish heritage, and many of them are prominent in Odets's work, as well as that of many other writers, some of them Gentiles. In *Jews and Americans*, Malin organizes his material into chapters that deal with individual elements common to the Jewish heritage: exile, fathers and sons, time, head and heart, transcendence, irony, fantasy, and parable. In *Contemporary American-Jewish Literature*, Malin posits that the creators of Jewish tales "seek to escape from exile, to break old covenants, and to embrace transcendent ideals" (p. 5).

A part of the Jewish cultural heritage is the dominant, often overly protective mother. She will often be counterbalanced by the acquiescent father[12] (like Myron in *Awake and Sing!*) and, in literature certainly, by the voluptuous, sexually tempting daughter (like Hennie, also in *Awake and Sing!*). The hope of the future is vested in Jewish children, particularly in boy children, who are viewed as the precious heirs and prospective leaders of what ideally was to be a patriarchal Jewish society.

The mother, while dominant, is also a sufferer. She often is, as Auchincloss might call her, an "injustice collector." She must sacrifice in order to feel fulfilled. Robert Warshow, writing of *Awake and Sing!*, capsulizes the values of middle-class American Jews: "be secure, be respected, be intelligent."[13] These are very much Bessie Berger's values in *Awake and Sing!*, Clara Gordon's in *Paradise Lost*, and Esther's in *The Flowering Peach*.

If Jewish society can be viewed as being ideally patriarchal, the Jewish family is in many ways matriarchal. The Jewish wife, when she becomes a mother, adopts a new role of dominance, particularly when she has sons whom she regards as the chief hope for the future. She becomes the beacon in an alien environment. She makes the home, which is because of her an impregnable fortress against all that might threaten it. With the birth of a son into a Jewish family, the father's dominance decreases and the mother's increases. In Odets's *Awake and Sing!* and *The Flowering Peach*, dominant women are the mortar that holds the family together in the most trying of times.

JEWISH MOTHERS

Some of Odets's plays have in them what might be called the conventional Jewish mother, the dominant female who suffers and serves, who is constantly urging food on her young, who assumes the responsibility for many of the necessary decisions within the family. Other of Odets's plays present in prominent roles women who, while they may be neither Jewish nor mothers, attempt to be surrogate mothers for weak husbands whom they treat as surrogate sons.

Among the former are Bessie Berger *(Awake and Sing!)* and Esther *(The Flowering Peach)*. Somewhat midway between the two polarities is Clara Gordon in *Paradise Lost*. The surrogate mother type is represented by Bertha Katz in *Paradise Lost*, in a much more fully developed way by Belle in *Rocket to the Moon*, and in a somewhat different way by Georgie Elgin in *The Country Girl*.

In the list of characters preceding *Awake and Sing!*, Bessie Berger is described in more than twice the detail accorded to either her husband, Myron, her daughter, Hennie, or her son, Ralph. The description presents, it would seem, Odets's conception of what the prototypical Jewish mother is, although it must be remembered that Bessie Berger lives in the strained economic context of the Depression and that many of her characteristics are heightened by the pressures this context imposes. Odets calls her "not only the mother in this home but also the father. She is constantly arranging and taking care of her family." He comments on her joy in living from day to day and on her resourcefulness.

Bessie is concerned with the here and now, with the day-to-day matters of human existence; her men, particularly Jacob, the grandfather, and Ralph, the son, are the dreamers, the philosophers in the family. Bessie deals with the mundane and revels in doing so. Odets writes of her, "She is a shrewd judge of realistic qualities in people in the sense of being able to gauge quickly their effectiveness. . . . She is naive and quick in emotional response. She is afraid of utter poverty. She is proper according to her own standards, which are fairly close to those of most middle-class families. She knows that when one lives in the jungle one must look out for the wild life" *(A&S*, p. 37). Bessie needs to be in control of things and she essentially is. The one threat to that control is the poverty she fears, because this could destroy her home and her family. Bessie alludes to this fear early in *Awake and Sing!*: "They threw out a family on Dawson Street today. All the furniture on the sidewalk. A fine old woman with gray hair" *(A&S*, p. 43). This concern is repeated toward the end of the play when Bessie warns, "A family needs for a rainy day. Times is getting worse. Prospect Avenue, Dawson, Beck Street—every day furniture's on the sidewalk" *(A&S*, p. 95).

Bessie's worst fears are the realities with which her counterpart, Clara Gordon, in *Paradise Lost* must contend; Clara and Leo's furniture actually is put out into the street. They lose their business, their home, and indeed their hope for the future, which has been vested in their children—one is shot during a robbery, one is dying of encephalitis, and one is rapidly becoming a recluse.

If Bessie seems to some to be "instinctively dedicated to emasculating the men in the family,"[14] she is equally devoted to keeping the family intact when it is threatened from without. She is also concerned with projecting an image of respectability for her family even when to do so involves an act such as deceiving the gullible Sam Feinschreiber into marrying her daughter, Hennie, who is pregnant by another man. Through this marriage, Odets implies that the whole family cycle will recur; Sam will become the emasculated husband, Hennie the dominant wife and controlling mother.

Both Clara Gordon and Bessie Berger tend to be shrill much of the time, hypercritical, opinionated. They bicker. Granted they sometimes emasculate their men, but at the base of all this are love and concern such as that reflected in Clara's line, "I found out many years ago I married a fool, but I love him" (*PL*, p. 160). Odets's Jewish mothers represent continuity and continuance. They are concerned with the survival of the Jewish tradition but equally, if not more so, with the economic and physical survival of the family. The Bergers in *Awake and Sing!* are under extreme financial pressures, but throughout the play they eat almost constantly. Bessie sees to that. The family survives and in Ralph's new beginning at the end of the play is the hope that both the Jewish tradition and the Berger family will continue.

The dramatic tensions in *Awake and Sing!*, *Paradise Lost*, *The Flowering Peach*, and to some extent in all of Odets's other plays, except perhaps his two agitprop dramas, *Waiting for Lefty* and *Till the Day I Die*, are part and parcel of the head-heart conflict which is developed through the interplay of practical, down-to-earth women who, in the last analysis, represent head, and impractical, idealistic men, who, in the last analysis, represent heart. Granted that Jacob, who reads books and listens to opera, is more the intellectual than Bessie; however, he functions according to emotion more than according to reason. Bessie, within her own value system, makes rational decisions that will preserve the family's appearance of respectability and improve its chances of survival. One must note that Odets, as his writing career progressed, came increasingly to side more often with the idealistic men than with the women.

As early as *Paradise Lost*, the play's last word is a long idealistic statement by Leo, whereas in *Awake and Sing!*, the idealistic Jacob commits suicide and there is less to suggest that Ralph is really going to be able to conquer new worlds despite his closing oratory. By the time of *The Flowering Peach*, written nearly two decades after *Awake and Sing!*, the Jewish mother, Esther, while somewhat carping and domineering, has mellowed a great deal. The idealism of Noah, her husband, who was commanded by God to build an Ark and did so despite the aspersions cast by others upon his judgment—indeed, upon his sanity—is, in the end, vindicated because his act saves the human race from total annihilation in the Flood. At the end of *The Flowering Peach*, Esther is dead, a victim of old age; but through Noah's idealistic following of God's word, future generations are saved and continuance is assured.

Toward the end of *Awake and Sing!*, Bessie has a speech that states very succinctly the head-heart conflict which exists in a Jewish mother like her:

" 'Mom, what does she know? She's old-fashioned!' But I'll tell you a big secret: My whole life I wanted to go away, too, but with children a woman stays home. A fire burned in *my* heart too, but now it's too late. I'm no spring chicken. The clock goes and Bessie goes" (*A&S*, p. 96). The theme of the worn-out mother recurs in *The Flowering Peach*. Esther says to Noah toward the end of the play, "Whatta you want from me, Noah? I'm a tired old woman . . . you're a young man."[15] As the action nears its resolution, Esther still fights for the family while Noah stands as the patriarch who will preserve the laws of God, laws much more abstract than those of the family:

> *Esther:* [to Noah] Marry the children . . . for the sake of happiness in the world. . .
> *Noah:* —Old friend, it hurts me to refuse you, but it stands in the books for a thousand years—
> *Esther:* —But all the books are in the water now. . . . Marry the children before I go.

Just before Esther dies, Noah having denied her wish that he marry the children, she proclaims, "The children, their happiness . . . is my last promised land" (*FP*, pp. 201–202).

This is a curious reversal and represents Odets's coming far afield from *Awake and Sing!*; in *The Flowering Peach*, which begins with Esther representing head and Noah representing heart, Esther, in the end, wants Noah to violate his conscience and to perform marriages among the children according to the dictates of *her* heart. Noah, by building the Ark, has assured the physical continuation of the human race; Esther now calls upon him to play God, as it were, and to help reestablish the conventions of the world which the Flood has destroyed. Esther, like Bessie Berger, remains concerned with the here and now; but Noah, with his more abstract philosophical concerns, really triumphs at the conclusion of *The Flowering Peach*.

SURROGATE MOTHERS

Some of the wives in Odets's plays are surrogate Jewish mothers. They are married to men of questionable strength and self-assurance. These men need strong women to tell them what to do (Ben Stark in *Rocket to the Moon*) or to keep them from vices that would destroy them (Frank Elgin in *The Country Girl*), wives who will suffer the abuse that stems from the husbands' own insecurities and inadequacies (Sam Katz in *Paradise Lost*). The first tentative step toward this kind of character is found in Tilly, Ernst Tausig's fiancée in *Till the Day I Die*. Tilly is the comforter, the one who understands and encourages Ernst after he has been interrogated, intimidated, and physically mutilated by the German SS. When Ernst returns to Tilly after the SS has crushed his hand, he is depicted as wincing in pain and Tilly tells him, "Sit down again. Don't be afraid of softness, of sorrow." She is the comforting mother type; but Ernst is not basically weak, as some male characters in other of Odets's plays have been. He has been victimized by a force much stronger than any man might be expected to resist.

Not until *Paradise Lost* did Odets develop to the utmost the surrogate mother type of character. Bertha Katz is childless, like Belle Stark in *Rocket to the Moon* and Georgie (a non-Jew) in *The Country Girl*. Being childless is particularly difficult for Jewish women, as Odets was well aware; they cannot obey the Biblical injunction, "Be fruitful and multiply." They are unfulfilled, and Odets turns their need for fulfillment toward their husbands. In *Paradise Lost*, where Odets really becomes concerned with this particular theme, it is Sam Katz, not his wife, who is responsible for their childlessness. Bertha tolerates Sam's abuse, both physical and verbal, dealing with him just as she might have with the children she has never had. He calls her "Momma," and she speaks the line, "Momma, he says, In the night he cried to God and no answer came. In my arms he cried, and no answer came." In the tense lines which follow, Bertha tells the Gordons of Sam's impotence, reveals to them that he has not slept with a girl in seven years, and then, like the good mother, she says, "He's a good boy—We'll go home Sam." The set directions here are especially revealing: "Goes up to Sam. Helps him up from the lower step. Wipes his face with handkerchief."[16]

Belle Stark in *Rocket to the Moon* is Odets's next depiction of the surrogate mother type. She is by no means so sympathetic a character as Bertha Katz. She has miscarried in her first pregnancy and can have no more children. Her internalized anger reveals itself in sarcasm and often in outright nastiness. Odets suggests that Belle's mother was temperamentally very like Belle. He also intimates that Ben once had promise, but that during his marriage to Belle, his promise has remained unfulfilled. Ben reveals some of his past potential in the lines, "I was a pioneer with Gladstone in orthodontia, once. Now I'm a dentist, good for sixty dollars a week, while men with half my brains and talents are making their twenty and thirty thousand a year!"[17] But Belle has now reduced him to the state where she does much of his thinking for him and says contemptuously, "Any day now I'm expecting to have to powder and diaper you" (*RM*, p. 330).

Belle presumably does not want Ben to advance professionally, because she would then have difficulty controlling him. As Odets had originally conceived the play, Ben's affair with his receptionist, Cleo Singer, was to have given him strength through love;[18] however, as the play finally appeared, the affair is fleeting, Ben is weak even in its midst, as is evidenced by his not even discouraging Cleo from going out with other men while it is going on; and when the affair is over, Ben presumably will return to the same trap in which he was before, except that Belle will have collected one more injustice to hold over him. Her longing for a child will continue, and she will use Ben as the child she cannot have, nagging him until the end of his days. There is a terrible irony in Ben's lines to Mr. Prince, his father-in-law, toward the end of the play: "For years I sat here, taking things for granted, my wife, everything. Then just for an hour my life was in a spotlight. I saw myself clearly, realized who and what I was. Isn't that a beginning? Isn't it?" (*RM*, p. 418). And with these words, with this plaintive questioning, he seals his fate. Even at the close of the original play, ending as it does with the word "Awake," which is an allusion to Ben's earlier line, "A man falls asleep in marriage,"[19] there is little hope that Ben will ever be anything but emasculated, mothered and smothered by a woman who must control him through diminishing him as a person.

The relationship between Georgie and Frank Elgin in *The Country Girl* is somewhat different. Frank, a gifted actor whose alcoholism has all but ruined his career, is offered a last chance, an important role in a play. His wife, Georgie, who has suffered with him through the decline in his career caused by his alcoholism, has become his protectress. Georgie does not resemble the Jewish mother quite so much as she does the deeply concerned wife. Her mothering grows out of her concern, and much of it seems necessary to her husband's professional survival as well as to her own survival, which is closely allied to her husband's success. She protects his interests, sees that his rights and privileges are duly accorded. She says of him, "He doesn't like to make the slightest remark that might lose him people's regard and affection. I've simply grown into the habit of doing it for him."[20] She then goes on to argue with Bernie Dodd, the play's director, about Frank's salary.

Georgie tells of having left Frank twice and of having twice returned to him, largely, it would seem from the dialogue, in a motherly role: "Twice left, twice returned. He's a helpless child" (*CG*, p. 107). Later she allows, "Yes, he has to be watched—he has to be nursed, guarded, and coddled." And she then adds the line, "But not by me, my very young friend [Bernie Dodd]!" (*CG*, p. 107)

However, despite this proclamation, Georgie, talking to Bernie backstage on opening night about the congratulatory telegrams Frank received, clearly shows that she cannot stop mothering her husband:

> *Georgie:* It was sweet of you to send him all those wires.
> *Bernie: impassively:* Who told you?
> *Georgie:* Guessed. How many did you send?
> *Bernie:* Nine or ten. And you?
> *Georgie:* Four or five.

> [*CG*, 123]

The husband-wife relationship in Odets's plays are often based upon sexual stereotypes current when he wrote. The Jewish mother and the surrogate mother present an interesting reversal of what was the usual role designation of Odets's era, i.e., the dominant male and the dependent female; but such role reversal is found in other plays which metaphorically presented the social and economic emasculation of their protagonists by a world which seems organized against them, characters like Willie Loman in *Death of a Salesman*.

EXILE AND ALIENATION

The story of the exodus as related in the Old Testament has long been with worldwide Jewry. As a cohesive ethnic group frequently in exile, Jews have been ghettoized throughout much of history. Those who have chosen to leave the ghetto have, nevertheless, been forced to bear all the kinds of discrimination visited upon Jews by many dominant cultures throughout history. Outbreaks of violent anti-Semitism through the history of the Western world have been sufficiently frequent and regular to remind Jews everywhere, particularly before the founding of the state of Israel, of their exile and to reinforce their feelings of alienation and homelessness. During Odets's early creative years, many Jews were exiling themselves from an insanely anti-Semitic Germany where, in many cases, they and their forefathers had lived for generations. Jews everywhere identified with these refugees, as today large numbers of Jews identify with their counterparts in the USSR.

Exiled and alienated as many Jews have been through the ages and were particularly during the Nazi era, there has always been a strong theme of redemption in their existence. Warshow writes,

> The adult immigrant had some advantages. Whatever it was that drove him to come [to the United States], he was able to carry with him a sense of his own dignity and importance. He had a kind of security, though it is a strange thing to say of a Jew. In Europe, with the club over his head, he had nevertheless lived in a community which was in important ways self-sufficient, and which permitted him to think of himself as a man of value: he was, a scholar, or a revolutionist; at the very least he knew himself to be a more serious man than his Gentile persecutors. To be a Jew was a continual burden, even a misfortune, but it could not have seemed to him a joke or a disgrace.[21]

A unique admixture of exile, alienation, and redemption exists among Jews and has so existed through much of their history.

It must be remembered that in Nazi German, anti-Semitism was directed against anyone with so-called "Jewish blood." Birth conferred the distinction of being Jewish in the Nazi view, and, as Ernest Van den Haag notes, "This was one part of the complicated truth which the Nazis grasped."[22] The Jewish Americans by whom Odets was surrounded in his youth, both in the neighborhoods in which his parents lived and among his associates in the Group Theatre, were well aware of the historic persecution of the Jews; the rise of the Nazi party in Germany during the thirties only intensified their awareness of this long and unhappy history.

Superimposed upon the situation of Jews in Nazi Germany was the complication of a worldwide economic depression which, within Odets's own immediate frame of reference, threatened the economic security of large numbers of people by whom he was surrounded and made them feel alienated from their society. The threat of homelessness loomed large for working-class Americans. In his interview with Michael Mendelsohn, Odets said, "Theatre in its profoundest sense—*all* literature in its profoundest sense—has come in periods when the plight or problem expressed by the actors was completely at one with the plight or problems and values or even moralities of the audience."[23]

During his interview with Arthur Wagner, Odets, in speaking about how one writes, asserted, "The question is really not one of knowing how to write so much as knowing how to connect with yourself so that the writing is, so to speak, born affiliated with yourself."[24] In the same monologue he acknowledges what he calls his "blood ties" with *Paradise Lost*, and indeed he could have established similar blood ties with most of his early plays.

Odets's immediate tie in a play like *Waiting for Lefty* was a tie with the working class caught up in the problems of the Depression. However, his blood ties to his material came out of his whole past, as they must in any author, and such ties reflect the way a Jewish-American writer reacts to the materials about which he is writing. Certainly Odets was not oblivious to the situation of Jews in Germany, as *Till the Day I Die* clearly illustrates. The "plights and problems" of which Odets speaks were the most legitimate plights and problems of his age and his Jewish background gave him a special competence to deal with them, "to connect with himself," as he put it.

Schaar suggests the pervasiveness of the exile motif and the attendant sense of alienation that accompanies it: "The motif of the eternal wanderer begins in the dawn of the Jewish tradition and weaves in and out of the whole subsequent history of Western religion. Abram is the prototype and universal symbol of alienated man."[25] Rosenberg and Bergen contend, "In becoming an object-self, part of an objective social history, the person can come to feel that he has lost control over his own being."[26] Many of Odets's characters, particularly those in *Waiting for Lefty* and *Till the Day I Die*, have lost control of their own destinies. Yet in both these early plays, the common Jewish motif of redemption is evident. Redemption for the cabbies in *Waiting for Lefty* comes after Lefty, who has been interpreted by some as being a Christ-like figure, [27] is murdered and the men gathered in the union hall call for a strike, moved to fever pitch by their indignation over the murder. The same motif occurs in a different way in *Till the Day I Die*. Ernst Tausig kills himself at the conclusion of the play, but Tillie is pregnant with his child, the prospective leader, the precious heir. Tillie emphasizes this: "Let us hope we will both live to see strange and wonderful things. Perhaps we will die before then. Our children will see it then."[28] Just before Ernst's suicide, his brother says to Tillie, "Let him die," but after the shot is heard, he utters the more redemptive, "Let him live" (*TDD*, p. 154).

Odets deals with the themes of exile (variations on the wandering Jew theme) and alienation throughout much of his writing. The concern is a central one for him. In *Waiting for Lefty*, the disparate group of people brought together by the economic uncertainties of their society are, for the most part, living unfulfilled lives—for example, the young hack and his girl cannot marry and Dr. Benjamin drives a taxicab rather than completing his hospital residency—and they are dealing with the "object-self." If they are to overcome the threat of complete alienation, they can do so only by joining together, and this is what they are forced into at the end of the play when they rally to strike after Lefty has been found dead behind the carbarns, a bullet in his head.

Odets, during the uncertain years of the Depression, was a member of the close-knit Group Theatre, and in the unity of this association he felt less alienated personally than he might otherwise have felt. Deeper alienation came later in his life, first when he left the Group Theatre to go to Hollywood, an act which was in his eyes a prostitution of his talents and ideals, largely so he could earn money to help the Group Theatre stay afloat; and later when he began to rankle under the artistic pressures of Hollywood, where he experienced a significant loss of identity and self-esteem.

In *Awake and Sing!*, the threat of economic disaster always impends, but the family unit remains together, as it does in the face of great crisis in *The Flowering Peach*. Some hope remains in the Berger household, despite all its tribulations and discontent: Bessie, after protesting at Myron's wish to buy a fifty-cent Irish Sweepstakes Ticket from Moe Axelrod, says, "I'll give you money. Buy a ticket in Hennie's name. Say, you can't tell—lightning never struck us yet. If they win on Beck Street, we could win on Longwood Avenue" (*A&S*, p. 43). Bessie, reflecting a mentality which keeps exiles alive, always holds on to the hope of a better future.

Jacob in *Awake and Sing!* is the philosophical center of the play; Bessie Berger is the practical center. Jacob is the idealist whose immediate world is not threatened in quite the same way that Bessie's is, partly because Jacob has not so long to live as Bessie and partly because Bessie's concerns about security are more specific, focusing as they do upon her family, than Jacob's, whose concerns focus upon mankind more broadly. Jacob has more philosophical detachment than Bessie, whose point of view is limited by the immediacy of assuring on a day-to-day basis her own survival and that of her family.

Bessie, struggling to preserve the family's respectability can pressure her pregnant daughter Hennie into marrying the unsuspecting Sam Feinschreiber, saying of him, "He's going to night school, Sam. For a boy only three years in the country he speaks very nice," followed by the crucial, "In three years he put enough money in the bank, a good living" (*A&S*, p. 55). She can first tell Moe Axelrod that Hennie is engaged to Sam, and then, upon hearing Moe, who is richer than Sam, say, ". . . maybe I'd marry her myself," can turn around and say, "Why don't you, Moe? An old family friend like you. It would be a blessing on us all" (*A&S*, pp. 57–58). Bessie is convinced that she is doing all this for the good and for the security of the family, which are her prime concerns; she can justify any deceit that will help her family to project an image of decency and respectability, to prevent an alienation of her family from its social milieu.

But Jacob's whole philosophical framework is different from Bessie's. He is sufficiently removed from the particulars of the immediate situation to be able to make a moral judgment about it and to be able to utter in disgust, "Marx said it—abolish such families" (*A&S*, p. 55). Their diverging viewpoints cause an estrangement between Bessie and Jacob, and the two are farthest apart when Hennie tells Sam that he is not the father of their child and Sam confronts Bessie with this information. Ralph tells his mother, "You trapped this guy" (*A&S*, p. 84), and Bessie's whole world is collapsing. Now, because of her efforts to keep up a respectable front, she is beginning to be alienated from her own family. At this point she turns to Jacob, venting her wrath upon him, saying, "You'll stand around with Caruso and make a bughouse. It ain't enough all day long. Fifty times I told you I'll break every record in the house" (*A&S*, pp. 84–85), and she thereupon breaks Jacob's cherished recordings, and in so doing probably precipitates his suicide.

Of this tense scene Warshow writes, "Bessie Berger reveals the whole pattern of psychological and moral conflict that dominates her and her family. . . . [She] turns upon her *father*, who has said nothing, and smashes the phonograph records that are his most loved possessions and the symbol of his superiority."[29]What remains to Bessie is the outer symbol of *her* superiority: respectability in the eyes of middle-class society, which probably scarcely knows she exists. In *Awake and Sing!*, redemption lies, albeit more facilely than artistically justifiable, not in Jacob's leaving Ralph three thousand dollars in insurance money—Ralph finally decides to "Let Mom have the dough" (*A&S*, p. 100)—but in Ralph's realization that Jacob's life and ultimately his death have perhaps given Ralph something on which to build a new beginning: "I'll get along. Did Jake die for us to fight about nickels? No! 'Awake and Sing,' he said. Right here he stood and said it. The night he died, I saw it like a thunderbolt! *I saw he was dead and I was born!*" (*A&S*, pp. 100–101. Italics mine). The cycle is repeated; Odets is suggesting that continuance is assured.

Noah, in *The Flowering Peach*, is alienated from his society for quite lofty reasons. God has come to him in a dream and told him that the earth will be destroyed in a flood. He orders him to build an ark and to take his family upon it along with seven pairs of clean, and one pair of unclean, animals. Noah's wife chides him for drinking too much and is, along with his sons, quite skeptical of the validity of Noah's dream, attributing it to his drinking. But when God sends signs and portents to Noah—first a gitka and then other animals arrive to be put on the Ark, and a tired old Noah becomes young and strong so that he can work at constructing the Ark—the family becomes more credulous. Yet even at this point, Noah is shunned. He is stoned out of town when he goes for supplies. He must refuse passage on the Ark to respected old friends, because God's command is that he shall take only his family on board. But Noah's oneness is with God, so his alienation is not complete nor will his exile during the flood be permanent.

Odets's Noah story ends on a note of affirmation. Noah's wife, Esther, has died on the Ark, but life will continue. Rather than drinking himself into drunkenness at the end of the story, as in the Biblical version, Odets's Noah asks God for a covenant: "You know what I want, Lord. Just like you guarantee each month, with a woman's blood, that men will be born . . . give such a sign that you won't destroy the world again" (*FP*, p. 204), and at that point a rainbow appears in the sky. Although the ending is again a bit facile, the theme of redemption is stronger in *The Flowering Peach* than in any of Odets's other plays. Noah's alienation and his exile—his forty days on the waters—have led him to be humble before God and obedient to Him. Life will go on thanks to Noah's heeding of God's command.

Night Music (1940) is a play about homelessness and alienation despite its bittersweet resolution. Writing of the theme of homelessness in the play, Harold Clurman, its director, says, "Odets does not state this [homelessness] as his theme in so many words; he does not have to, since he has made it part of every character, of every scene, almost of every prop. It is not a thesis, it is the 'melody' that permeates the play. The central character is made angry and adolescently belligerent by his inability to take hold in society."[30] This sort of alienation, this waste of human potential, had always angered Odets: "Nothing moves me so much as human aspirations blocked, nothing enrages me like waste. I am for use as opposed to abuse."[31] The wasted human potential of the Depression provided him with material for his early plays, but he was no less incensed by the waste and futility that he sometimes felt characterized his own endeavors in Hollywood.

In many ways his most acerbic play is *The Big Knife* (1949); in it he addresses directly the frustrations that had been gnawing away at him during his first decade in California and makes an open attack upon the motion picture industry. But these gnawings actually had been festering in the writer for quite a long time. *Golden Boy* (1937) addressed problems of unfulfillment that later came to be a major part of the substance of *The Big Knife*. Both plays can be viewed as escape-from-the-ghetto plays. Joe Bonaparte escapes through his boxing ability, but the price he pays is enormous; he is an accomplished violinist, but in becoming a boxer, he sacrifices his hands. In the end, he kills another boxer in the ring and then goes out in his new, expensive Duesenberg, a symbol of his success, and crashes it, killing himself and his female companion, Laura. Similarly, Charlie Castle moves from his humble background into a successful career as an actor, only to be destroyed by the threat of a disclosure that he has been involved in a fatal hit-and-run accident for which he has allowed someone else to accept the blame and be punished. The threat drives Castle to suicide.

The writing of both of these plays was a very self-searching activity for their author and each in its own period grew out of Odets's feelings of alienation and, in the case of *Golden Boy* particularly, out of the sense of self-imposed exile which he felt in deserting the Group Theatre for Hollywood, even though the desertion was done in the best interests of the Group. Cantor writes, "Indeed, it is difficult to disentangle the work and the man in Odets' career, for Odets' major plays on the subject of selling-out, *Golden Boy* and *The Big Knife*, are rooted in his personal experience."[32] The loss of identity with which Charlie Castle had to deal in *The Big Knife* raises again the object-self question; Charlie, like Joe Bonaparte in *Golden Boy*, becomes a commodity to be haggled over. A loss of identity, which begins with his having to change his name at the studio's command, progresses to the point that he has to sign a fourteen-year contract which he does not wish to sign, has to sign away fourteen years of his life, as it were, because the studio is blackmailing him. Well might he utter such lines as "I'll bet you don't know why we all wear these beautiful, expensive ties in Hollywood. . . . It's a military tactic—we hope you won't notice our faces,"[33] or "free speech is the highest-priced luxury in this country today" (*BK*, p. 16).

As Odets moved away from specifically Jewish settings for his plays, he nevertheless imbibed deeply from his Jewish heritage in their thematic development, and the intertwining concerns with alienation and homelessness appear to be outgrowths of the exile motif which is pervasive in the whole of Jewish history.

LANGUAGE

Reflecting on his early experience of seeing Odets's *Awake and Sing!*, Alfred Kazin remarks, "In Odets' play there was a lyric uplifting of blunt Jewish speech, boiling over and explosive, that did more to arouse the audience than the political catchwords that brought the curtain down."[34] Odets probably had a better ear for language than any other playwright of his period. His early plays surge with the vitality of an authentic Yiddish-American which, as employed by Odets, is neither exaggerated nor burlesqued. He made such speech a legitimate idiom of the theater at a time when dialects were used so exaggeratedly in some other plays *(Abie's Irish Rose)*, on the radio *(The Goldbergs* or *Amos and Andy)*, or in comic strips *(The Katzenjammer Kids)* that they really demeaned the people portrayed as using them.

The Goldbergs was one of the more popular radio shows of the thirties; Weales notes that the dialect in the Goldberg scripts ("For vat is your fadder slaving for vat I'm esking you?" or "Maybe he got himself runned over by a cabsitac.") uses "verbal humor at the expense of a real language, and it is used, perhaps unintentionally, to destroy any suggestion of validity in the characters and the situation." Weales continues, "Odets manages to find the humor in the language and retain the psychological truth of the family."[35] For the first time in American drama, Jews were represented, through an honest recording of their language, in something other than caricature.

At times Odets deliberately employed the dialect of older, less acculturated Jews, particularly for such characters as Jacob, Bessie, and Myron in *Awake and Sing!*. However, elements of Yiddish-American appear in all of his plays and, indeed, quite tellingly, in his responses to questions in interviews. Even in situations where Odets is not striving to project a Jewish image, as he is with a character like Bessie Berger, for example, Yiddish-American word order and phrasing still are evident. Sid in *Waiting for Lefty* quite unselfconsciously speaks lines like, "If we went off together I could maybe look the world straight in the eye" (p. 20), naturally selecting a locution which is Jewish-American in its placement of the adverb *maybe*.

Cantor, who writes in detail about Odets's use of language, says of it, "It is Yiddish in its inflections (sometimes even when he is writing about the *goyish milieux*), and contains Yiddish-English expressions."[36] Odets strove to establish a credible language for the people in his earlier plays and in so doing became the first American dramatist to use the Jewish-American dialect, with all of its humor, with all of its distinguishing cadences, for other than comic effects. Pochmann claims that while few Jews outside Palestine (and now Israel)

speak Hebrew, Judaeo-German (Yiddish) has become more or less the tongue of
the Jewish people throughout much of the world.[37] From this Judaeo-German
language Odets has borrowed so heavily.

One can open to any page of *Awake and Sing!* and find in it the most faithful
representations of the Yiddish-American dialect. A few follow:

> *Bessie:* Go to your room, Papa. Every job he ever had he lost because he's got a
> big mouth. He opens his mouth and the whole Bronx could fall in. [*A&S*,
> p. 55. Here one finds the object of the sentence in the primary position
> *(Every job)* and also finds the exaggerated humorous cliché, "the whole
> Bronx could fall in," so common to Yiddish-English. Note also the third
> person singular aside.]
>
> *Myron:* I was a little boy when it happened—the Great Blizzard. [*A&S*, p. 86,
> In this case the referent of the pronoun follows the pronoun.]
>
> *Bessie:* Myron, make tea. You'll have a glass tea. [*A&S*, p. 80. Characteristic
> of Yiddish-English is the omission of the qualifier *(some* tea) and of the
> preposition (glass *of* tea).]

Haslam, writing about Odets's use of language in *Awake and Sing!*, notes that
Odets used "four major types of lexical or grammatical aberrations in constructing a believable stage Yiddish: (1) prepositional differences; (2) sentence order;
(3) verb variations; and (4) Yiddish loans."[38]He notes that an authenticity of
dialect is achieved because Odets capitalizes on the difficulty that speakers like
Jacob or Bessie have in translating words like the Yiddish *foon,* which can mean
of or *from;* or *bei,* a more difficult preposition which can mean *at, by, among,
beside,* or *with.*

In order to achieve believable Yiddish-American sentence structure, Haslam
illustrates how Odets uses four specific techniques: (1) misplacement of
modifiers; (2) the running together of some independent clauses without punctu-
ation or conjunctions; (3) the misplacement of noun clusters used as objects;
and (4) the omission of the objects of prepositions from the end of sentences.[39]Haslam cites two types of verb variations that lend authenticity to
Odets's dialogue, one which he identifies as mistranslation ("I won't stand he
should make me insults" [*A&S*, p. 82] and the other as the frequent omission or
addition of auxiliaries in verb clusters ("Wait, when you'll get married you'll
know" [*A&S*, p. 56]).

Paradise Lost surges with the Yiddish-American idiom, despite the acculturation of the Gordons. Clara likes to begin speeches with "Do yourself a personal
favor;" "Take a piece of fruit" is another staple of her conversation throughout
the play, reminding one of the frequent allusions to fruit in *Awake and Sing!*.
The well-ordered Jewish household will have fruit to offer guests. In the same
play, one finds locutions like, "He's finished in ten minutes," rather than the
more American, "He will be."

Odets tried to move away from his earlier idiom in plays like *Golden Boy,
Night Music, Rocket to the Moon,* and *Clash by Night,* but one still finds bits of
the Jewish idiom creeping in: "Don't change the subject. Like my father-in-law

here—he's always changing the subject when I get a little practical on him" (*GB*, pp. 244–45) or a typical Jewish wisecrack, "You can't insult me, I'm too ignorant" (*GB*, p. 246) or a malapropism, "How do you like it with our boy for gratitude? He leaves us here standing in our brevities!" (*GB*, p. 279).

Odets has been accused of abandoning his natural dialect as he became more successful and, indeed, of losing "his ear for this idiom."[40] Cantor, however, points out that Odets's ear did not fail him when he was writing *The Country Girl* and *The Big Knife*, but that in these plays he "is dealing with success and failure in the upper echelons of Hollywood and Broadway."[41] *The Country Girl*, which Odets asserted "doesn't mean anything to me; it's just a theater piece,"[42] does not have the idiom of his other plays, nor is there any reason for this idiom. The cast of the play is not Jewish, nor does the play have overt ethnic characteristics. But Cantor makes a persuasive case for the idiom of *The Big Knife*, writing that in it "Yiddish-American dialect took a new turn when it went to Hollywood and incorporated a strain of what Charlie Castle called 'phony cathedral eloquence'; . . . Nat Danziger, Charlie Castle's agent, has 'all the qualities of the president of a synagogue' (Stage Direction, I), though he is still capable of inverted Yiddish sentences and verb variants, such as 'Her I'm gonna talk to again' and 'a million dollars is got an awful big mouth' (I)."[43]

If any doubt existed about Odets's ability to use the Yiddish-American idiom in his later productive years, *The Flowering Peach* should have erased it. In this play, Odets pulls out all the stops, borrowing Yiddish words like *tuchter*, the term Esther uses in addressing her daughter-in-law, using inverted word order, capitalizing on the comedy of Yiddish wisecracks and clichés much more than he ever had previously. *The Flowering Peach* is a comedy, and much of its comic character is found in its demotic language. When Noah tells a skeptical Esther that God has come to him in a dream and told of the impending flood, Esther replies, "And all this God told you in one single dream?" to which Noah responds, "Told it to me in one dream, yeh! So now you know" (*FP*, p. 182). When Esther wants Noah to urge their son Japheth to take himself a wife, Noah asks, "Such a boy, so strange, what could he offer a decent girl?" and Esther responds with the Yiddish humor of understatement "He could offer her a nice boat ride!" (*FP*, p. 186). This sort of cynical litotes, characteristic of much Yiddish humor, blossoms in *The Flowering Peach* and grounds it in reality. Also the scatological is mingled with the idealistic to produce a similar comic effect in, for example, the scene where Noah discovers Shem has been making briquettes from manure and storing them on the Ark so that he can sell them at the flood's end: "On the Holy Ark he's makin' business! manure! With manure you want to begin a new world? Everybody's life he put in danger!" (*FP*, p. 197).

Certainly in *Awake and Sing!* Odets strove most consciously to present the Yiddish-American dialect, using it as a means of building his characters and social setting. Cantor indicates how Odets manipulates the dialect: "That Yinglish in Odets' play involves a reciprocal relationship between young and old is evidenced by the fact that Hennie and Ralph, though for the most part they speak straight urban English, are influenced by the speech patterns of their parents and grandparents."[44] The gradations of dialect by generation is particularly interesting in *Awake and Sing!*. Jacob, the least acculturated member of the family, speaks a clearly identifiable sort of Yinglish, using borrowed words, mistranslated prepositions, misplaced objects, and verb clusters without the auxiliary. The next generation, as represented by Bessie, Myron, and Uncle Morty, still clearly speaks Yiddish-American, and at times Bessie's dialect is stronger than Jacob's. However, Ralph and Hennie speak essentially an urban American English with only an occasional injection of Jewish locutions here and there. Haslam notes two sorts of borrowings from Yiddish: words taken over in toto such as *knish* or *shtupped* or the *-chick* ending in *boychick*, or locutions which are translated directly into English from Yiddish such as the recurrent "by me," which comes from Yiddish *bei mir* or the frequent "already," which is translated from German and Yiddish *schon*.[45]

ODETS AS A JEWISH WRITER

Odets will be remembered historically more as a proletarian playwright than as a Jewish playwright. Nevertheless, his background and upbringing imposed a Jewishness upon his work, a *Hébrewtude*, as I have called it elsewhere,[46] in which were the roots of his depiction of characters (the dominant mother/wife, the acquiescent husband), his concern with the themes of homelessness and alienation which are outgrowths of the Jewish motif of the exile, his concern with redemption, and his use of language as found both in his depiction of Yiddish-American life and in his general use of a more conventional standard English.

Odets's social view in his early plays often suggested affirmation. Speaking of these plays, Odets said that they "undoubtedly came out of ascending values, out of positive values, out of the search of millions of American citizens for some way out of a horrifying dilemma—a dilemma which, by the way, I don't think is over."[47] These final words ring very true today as the United States faces problems which seem even more threatening than those of the Great Depression of the 1930s. By focusing on the plight of Jews during the Depression, Odets was able to write about characters whom he understood from the inside out and was also able to build the dramatic tensions which vivified his productions. It can certainly be said that the social and economic circumstances of the 1930s provided him with the perfect dramatic material to write about and that his early exposure to Jewish society provided him with themes, language, and folkways which lent themselves perfectly to the kind of writing that accounted for his meteoric rise as a playwright.

NOTES

1. Gerald Weales, *Clifford Odets: Playwright* (New York: Pegasus, 1971), p. 17. See also Margaret Brenman-Gibson, *Clifford Odets: American Playwright, The Years from 1906 to 1940* (New York: Atheneum, 1981), pp. 17–25.

2. See Mendelsohn's "Clifford Odets: A Critical Study" (Ph.D. dissertation, University of Colorado, 1962), p. 182, R. Baird Shuman's "Clifford Odets: A Playwright and His Jewish Background," *South Atlantic Quarterly* 71 (Spring 1972):228–29, and Brenman-Gibson, pp. 18–19.

3. Mendelsohn, "Odets at Center Stage," *Theatre Arts Monthly* 47 (May 1963):75. See also Brenman-Gibson, p. 187.

4. Allen Guttmann, *The Jewish Writer in America: Assimilation and the Crisis of Identity* (New York: Oxford University Press, 1971), p. 10.

5. *Awake and Sing!*, in Clifford Odets, ed., *Six Plays by Clifford Odets* (New York: Modern Library, 1939), p. 42.

6. Mendelsohn, "Center Stage," p. 75. See also Mendelsohn's "Clifford Odets: A Critical Study," p. 184. Odets drew his title *Awake and Sing!* from Isaiah 26:19, but the play itself is not a Biblical play. Little evidence exists to suggest that Odets was an avid student of the Bible in his early years. However, since the completion of this chapter, Margaret Brenman-Gibson's *Clifford Odets: American Playwright, The Years from 1906 to 1940* (New York: Atheneum, 1981) has appeared; and Brenman-Gibson, writing about Odets's search for answers to large philosophical questions shortly before his twentieth birthday, says, "Sophisticated friends, touched to pity, wonder, and laughter by Odets' genuine reliance on these methods [graphology, face-reading, etc.] of control in a variety of life crises, were also impressed by the fact that institutionalized religion, given much lip service by his father, appeared to play no real part in Odets' life. What is omitted from this observation is his close study of the Bible, especially of the Old Testament, from which themes for later work would emerge" (p. 96). Brenman-Gibson offers no documentation in support of her contention, nor has anyone else writing about Odets's early years presented incontrovertible evidence that Odets had any extended early exposure to the Bible.

7. Ibid.

8. *Poems of a Jew* (New York, Random House, 1958), p. ix.

9. Harry T. Moore in his Preface to Irving Malin's *Jews and Americans* (Carbondale: Southern Illinois University Press, 1965), p. vii.

10. Irving Malin, *Contemporary American-Jewish Literature* (Bloomington: Indiana University Press, 1973), p. 4.

11. Ibid., pp. 4–5.

12. In some literature about Jews, the ogre-father image is projected: Barabbas in Marlowe's *The Jew of Malta*, whose wife is dead and whose only child, Abigail, is an acquiescent creature in most respects, becomes a homicidal monster when she becomes a Christian and enters a convent. He poisons his daughter along with the rest of the sisters in the convent and is then himself killed.

13. Robert Warshow, *The Immediate Experience* (New York: Doubleday, 1962), p. 64.

14. This accusation is made by Morris Freedman in *American Drama in Social Context* (Carbondale: Southern Illinois University Press, 1971), p. 51.

15. *The Flowering Peach* in Louis Kronenberger, ed., *The Best Plays of 1954–1955* (New York: Dodd, Mead and Company, 1955), p. 196.

16. In *Six Plays by Clifford Odets*, p. 215.

17. Ibid., p. 330.

18. R. Baird Shuman, *Clifford Odets* (New York: Twayne Publishers, 1962), p. 92.

19. Weales, p. 136.

20. Clifford Odets, *The Country Girl* (New York: Viking Press, 1951), p. 67.

21. Warshow, p. 60.

22. *The Jewish Mystique* (New York: Stein and Day, 1969), p. 33. See also Brenman-Gibson, pp. 30, 115, 439–40, 582.

23. Mendelsohn, "Center Stage," p. 17.

24. Clifford Odets, "How a Playwright Triumphs," *Harpers*, September 1966, p. 64.

This article is a monologue based on Arthur Wagner's interview with Odets in September, 1961, two years before his death.

25. J. Schaar, *Escape from Authority* (New York: Basic Books, 1961), p. 174.

26. Stanley D. Rosenberg and Bernard J. Bergen, *The Cold Fire; Alienation and the Myth of Culture* (Hanover, New Hampshire: University Press of New England, 1976), p. 177.

27. See Harold Cantor, *Clifford Odets: Playwright-Poet* (Metuchen, New Jersey: Scarecrow Press, 1978), p. 131. Cantor writes, somewhat less than convincingly, "Christlike figures abound in Odets' early work: Lefty can be so regarded; after all, he is a martyr found in a kind of stable—the car barns—with a bullet in his head. It seems ironic that this God of radical action never appears, and his work must be done by disciples like Agate, who spread the new religion."

28. *Six Plays by Clifford Odets*, p. 139.

29. Warshow, p. 67. Warshow's italics.

30. Introduction to Clifford Odets, *Night Music* (New York: Random House, 1940), pp. viii-ix.

31. Eugene D. Gross, "A Study Based Upon the Plays of Clifford Odets," (master's thesis, Smith College, 1948), p. 1.

32. Cantor, p. 49.

33. *The Big Knife* (New York: Random House, 1949), p. 106.

34. *Starting Out in the Thirties* (Boston: Atlantic, Little, Brown, 1965), p. 81.

35. Weales, pp. 76–77.

36. Cantor, p. 149.

37. Harry A. Pochmann, "The Mingling of Tongues," in Robert E. Spiller et al., eds., *Literary History of the United States* (New York: Macmillan, 1953) pp. 690–93.

38. Gerald W. Haslam, "Odets' Use of Yiddish-English in *Awake and Sing!*," *Washington State Research Studies* 34 (September 1966):162.

39. Ibid.

40. Ruby Cohn, *Dialogue in American Drama* (Bloomington: Indiana University Press, 1971), p. 68.

41. Cantor, p. 161.

42. Odets, "How a Playwright Triumphs," p. 74.

43. Cantor, pp. 161–62.

44. Cantor, p. 155.

45. Haslam, p. 163.

46. Shuman, "Clifford Odets: A Playwright and His Jewish Background," p. 226.

47. Mendelsohn, "Center Stage," p. 16.

Lillian Hellman: "The First Jewish Nun on Prytania Street"

Bonnie Lyons

1

LILLIAN HELLMAN IS A SOUTHERNER, A WOMAN, AND A JEW. THE IMPORTANCE
of the first two is readily apparent in her work. Four (*The Little Foxes, Another
Part of the Forest, The Autumn Garden,* and *Toys in the Attic*) of her eight
original plays take place in the South; and major themes in these plays are
southern history, especially the Civil War, the decline of the old South, the rise
of the new South, and what it means to be a southerner. Likewise, virtually all
her plays are dominated by women, and she has drawn portraits of females of all
ages: children, young women, matrons, mothers, spinsters, grand dames,
widows. But there is no Jewish character in any of her original plays, and the
word Jew is almost never mentioned.

Nor is Jewishness, Judaism, or the question of what it means to be Jewish
directly addressed in her three volumes of memoirs, despite the fact that these
are the memoirs of a Jew who has lived in a time when these issues have been
particularly significant. In Hellman's two plays set in World War II, there are
no Jewish characters at all. Anti-Semitic violence (off-scene) is *referred* to in
The Searching Wind, but it serves chiefly as a sign of fascist excess and the
decay of Western civilization, rather than as an event that specifically concerns
Jews and their history. In *Watch on the Rhine* the word "Jew" is used only to
make explicit that the noble and idealistic Kurt Müller is *not* a Jew.

In spite of the paucity of Jewish material in her works, certain attitudes
toward her own Jewishness and toward Jews and Judaism in general are directly
connected to her central concerns and emerge as keys to the Hellman world
view. Does this make her a "Jewish writer" then? The vexed question of the
Jewishness of particular writers or literary works is finally unanswerable in any
absolute terms. While Leslie Fiedler insists that Nathanael West, for example,
"despite his disclaimers" is "in a real sense, a Jew,"[1] Allen Guttmann omits
West (along with Arthur Miller and J. D. Salinger) from his survey of American
Jewish literature, saying that all three are "nominally Jews, but they are in no
important sense Jewish writers."[2] Moreover, in their attempts to ascertain or
describe the Jewishness of a piece of literature critics often use as criteria
qualities that are not uniquely Jewish. As Robert Alter has insisted, "there has
been a tacit conspiracy afoot in recent years to foist on the American public as
peculiarly Jewish various admired characteristics which in fact belong to the
common humanity of us all. The Jewish folk is imagined as possessing a kind of
monopoly on vividness, compassion, humor, pathos and the like; Jewish critics

and novelists are thought to be unique in their preoccupation with questions of morality."[3]

Despite these pitfalls the question is worth pursuing in connection with Hellman's work, which I would say is not only un-Jewish in content (that is to say it does not portray Jewish life), but, more important, is distinctly un-Jewish, and ultimately anti-Jewish, in world view. Her interest in economic and social issues, her passion for social justice, and even her exhortatory and vehement tone can of course be seen as Jewish; indeed she often sounds like an angry Old Testament prophet. But Jews are not the only people concerned about social justice nor are the Old Testament prophets the only exemplars of righteous anger.

What is much more central to the Jewishness of American Jewish literature is the inheritance of *Yiddishkeit,* a particular way of experiencing and reflecting the world. For brevity, I will simply summarize key aspects of *Yiddishkeit* here.[1] First and perhaps central is the sense of a people, a group bound together by ties of memory and history, by outer limits and hostility and inner meaning and mutuality. Being a Jew means being part of a chosen people with a distinct sense of uniqueness, purpose, and calling. Because the covenant is between God and a people, because Jewish immortality is traditionally seen in terms of survival of the group rather than the individual, because in historical fact the survival of the Jews has been a *real* question, the Jewish world view is deeply and pervasively social rather than individual, oriented toward the group rather than any one soul. If the heart of the Protestant experience is the individual soul in relation to God and the heart of Catholicism is the church, then the heart of Judaism is the family—the biological family and the wider family of the Jewish people.

Jewish tradition and Jewish history, especially the group memory of centuries of dispersion, exile, victimization, homelessness, and powerlessness, gave rise to a distinct historical attitude toward humanity and heroes. Pervading Yiddish culture and literature is a questioning, in fact a downplaying of conventional heroism, even a distinctly anti-heroic bias, no doubt in part based on clear perception of the self-destruction resulting from usually vain gestures—and a powerless victim's knowledge that what passes for heroic can be egotistical, narcissistic, and brutal. Simply surviving decently and living to tell the tale are often sufficiently problematic. And if heroes are absent or found wanting, the common man is elevated, or at least evoked with love. *Dos kleine menschele,* the little man, with all his imperfections and foibles, is accepted and embraced. Likewise a wide range of human emotions, including ordinary, non-admirable feelings, is explored. The ordinary man struggling with his everyday problems is the core of Yiddish literature; the heroic individual and sharply climactic plot are conspicuously absent.

What is glorified in Yiddish life and literature is intellectual pursuit, not for its own sake but, ideally, as a route to God, a means of understanding. If the cultural ideal is a group of men deeply engaged in pursuing the precise nuance of a particular Talmudic passage, engaged in a spirit of love of Torah, then what is relatively devalued is the world of nature, manual labor, indeed all solitary or physical pursuits. While the intellect, the ability to understand, is honored, the *sine qua non* is compassion.

This brief sketch can only suggest the heritage of *Yiddishkeit*. To this, American Jewish literature adds certain "modern" and "American" elements. Major themes of American Jewish literature are the uneasy coming together of the American and the Jewish, the enormous problems of acculturation and assimilation, and the radical questioning of the traditions and values of both cultures. Economic and social change, the rapid, disorienting move from ghetto or *shtetl* to city to suburb, from street peddler and garment worker to doctor and professor—this is the external or social level of American Jewish literature. The psychological or spiritual side of these narratives portrays a search for meaning or authority, an attempt to fill the void that accompanied rapid change, the loss of traditional values and meaning. Whatever deprivations and parochialism *shtetl* life in Europe entailed, it was at least a world of values, order, and meaning. The breakup of that world gave rise to doubt, anxiety, questioning, and guilt—emotions and themes that dominate American Jewish literature and give rise to a tone of complexity, complaint, skepticism, and irony.

Nothing could be further from the Hellman world view. She sees the world in terms of individuals rather than groups, even when the individual is working for the presumed good of a group. And for her the ultimate value is neither intellect nor compassion, but courage, moral and physical courage, ultimately the courage to risk one's life, to confront death, to act bravely in the face of annihilation. This is the *dominant* theme of her memoirs; her own struggle to live courageously, her fear of fear, and the moving evocation of the courageous men and women who influenced her throughout her life, especially Sophronia, her black nurse; Julia, the rich socialist friend who died fighting fascism; and Dashiell Hammett, her "most beloved friend" and lover whom she remembers as "a man of simple honor and great bravery."

Hellman's vision is thus strikingly Hemingwayesque. In her memoirs she pokes fun at what Hemingway's vision could degenerate into—she pictures Hemingway drunk in a restaurant belligerently challenging Hammett to bend a spoon between his wrist and upper arm, and again, in Madrid, going out on a terrace to enjoy the "thrill" of the bombing. Hellman rejects Hemingway's theatricality and flamboyant gestures (although she reports many of her own), and unlike Hemingway she insists on courage as the essential virtue for *women* as well as men; nevertheless they share the same basic world view. Even though her portrait of Hemingway in *An Unfinished Woman* is hardly glorifying, she reports with evident satisfaction Hemingway's grudging admission to her, "So you have *cojones* after all." That praise, and spitting in Hammett's eye, are clearly cherished victories for her.

The months Hellman spent in Spain during the Civil War in 1937 were critical in the development of her vision. She extols the bravery of those who fought for the republic so fervidly that her praise approaches hagiography and contrasts them with those Jews a Czech companion describes as "liberal pigs"

who will "kill all the rest of us with their nothing-to-be-done-about-it stuff."
Calling the International Brigade *noble*, she says, "Because I had never used
that word before, it came hard to say it to myself even in the dark, and, as if I
had a vision of what I had missed in the world, I began to cry." And in her
chapter about her 1944 trip to Russia she again stresses the courage and heroism
of the Russians (whose other virtue is their lack of middle-class concern with
money) who fought the Nazis and ends by describing her encounter in a hospital
with a young soldier who had most of his face shot off: "He had one eye, the left
side of a piece of nose and no bottom lip. He tried to smile at me. It was in the
next few hours that I felt a kind of exaltation I had never known before."

The courageous, selfless few move her profoundly. For the rest of humanity
her memoirs and plays show what is basically disdain bordering on contempt.
Her remarks about Julian's character in *Toys in the Attic* provide an instructive
example. In an interview with Richard Stern she described Julian as a *schlemiel*
and later as "just a sort of nice slob—well, slob's not the word—pleasant, semi-
intelligent, good-natured, kindly, nothing one way or the other."[5] For most
American Jewish writers, with their legacy of *Yiddishkeit*, those are the marks of
a hero, or rather an anti-hero: the common man—flawed, complex, weak, and
very fallible, but worth affirmation and love. For Hellman that same *schlemiel* is
a slob.

Overall, Hellman divides the world into the noble and the ignoble, the
valuable Kurt Müllers and the worthless rest of the world. In this dichotomy,
Jews are consistently characterized as among the wanting—as weak, accom-
modating, self-serving, falsely sentimental. Her negative image of Jews coupled
with her Hemingwayesque world view suggest a flight from her own Jewishness:
she appears to have expended much of her life and work castigating—and thus
proving that she was not—a Robert Cohn.

2

Hellman's feelings and ideas about Jews, Christians, Christianity, and her
own Jewishness appear at key points in her memoirs. The early chapters of *An
Unfinished Woman* portray her as a product of a highly assimilated German
Jewish family. She claims Dashiell Hammett knew more about Judaism than she
did and writes that her encounter with National Socialism in Germany in 1929
when she was twenty-four was "the first time" she "thought about being a Jew."
Hers was a *southern* family, in which Judaism was only a religious affiliation; if
one was not an active synagogue-goer (which those in her family apparently
were not), then one was hardly a Jew.

In describing her mother, an eccentric, slightly dotty woman who brought
home lonely ladies she met on park benches, Hellman stresses three aspects: in
her attitudes she "skipped" the middle class; she had close personal relations
with simple black men and women (both traits Hellman approves of); and she
wandered indiscriminately in an unfocused religious fog, in and out of Baptist
churches, cathedrals, and, "less often," synagogues.

In her memoirs her mother's family, the Newhouses, are larger than life—vital, ruthless money-grubbers dominated by Hellman's maternal grandmother and great uncle Jake, who "was a man of great force, given to breaking the spirit of people for the pleasure of the exercise," totally unscrupulous in their "financial machinations." In *Scoundrel Time* she summarizes: "I had watched my mother's family increase their fortune on the borrowings of poor Negroes." Her father's family is pictured in contrast, as "free, generous, funny." What is striking, however, is that the memoirs about both sides of her family are full of incredible incidents of macabre violence, sensationalism, drug abuse, criminal connections, and miscegenation. Hellman did not identify deeply with either side of her family; instead her main childhood identification was with her black wet nurse Sophronia, whom she calls "the first and most certain love" of her life.

One of the earliest chapters of *An Unfinished Woman* describes an incident Hellman herself calls "of great importance." In this scene her father criticized the fourteen-year-old Hellman in front of strangers in her aunt's New Orleans boardinghouse, and she ran away from home. During the first night and next day she suffered from hunger, fear of rats and discovery, general terror, and she started her menstrual period for the first time. As the menstrual period signals decisive change, so does the fact that she sought refuge in a black rooming house and tried to pass herself off as "related to Sophronia Mason" and thus "part nigger." The chapter actually suggests two attempts at "symbolic conversion"—for when Sophronia and her father came to claim her, she mumbled a prayer asking forgiveness from her mother, father, aunts, Sophronia "and all others, through this time and that time, in life and in death." Overhearing her strange litany, her father responded, "Where do we start your training as the first Jewish nun on Prytania Street?"

In *Pentimento* Hellman relates another incident that supports the idea of an early "conversion" to identification with blacks and perforce, lack of identification with, if not hostility toward, Jews. When her father discovered through Sophronia's report that Lillian put money in the poor boxes of black Baptist churches, he asked why she did not give charity to the synagogue, and added, "Maybe we never told you that's where you belong." Her response was, "I said I couldn't do that because there was no synagogue for Negroes and my father said that was perfectly true, he'd never thought about that before."

In her memoirs Hellman describes the beloved Sophronia as a tough, proud, unsentimental, frequently harsh woman who "had contempt for the world she lived in and for almost everybody black or white, she ever met." According to Hellman, no white person being "liberal" or "kind" impressed Sophronia very much. Sophronia was also a religious Christian who believed that "when the black man's time comes around, it'll come from the people of the church."

Hellman's memoirs are totally devoid of mention of Jewish rituals or ceremonies at home or in a synagogue. What she does recall, however, is wandering into a New Orleans church at age seven or eight and being deeply moved and knowing that all of her life she would "be stirred and comforted, and discomforted, by people of strong belief."

Two of her major pieces of personal journalism outside of the three books of memoirs touch significantly on Christianity. "Sophronia's Grandson Goes to Washington" relates her deep pleasure at the emergence of the black civil rights movement and progress and her recognition of the church's positive role in these advances. In "The Land That Holds The Legend of Our Lives," she reports her reactions to the Pope's visit to the Holy Land. The article gives no evidence that it is written by a Jew except perhaps that one of the featured figures is a monk who (like Hellman's psychoanalyst Gregory Zilboorg) converted from Judaism to Catholicism. She describes thinking she "was seeing the land that held the legend" of her life, closing her eyes, and as she did in childhood, making faces for "Abraham and David and Solomon and John and Jesus." The barbed wire reminds her that "this land of the nobility of Christ" is a land haunted by massacres committed by religious fanatics. Seeing Israel as "the land of the nobility of Christ" is obviously a curious response for a Jew.

Hellman's reactions to her own Jewishness and to Jews in general are central to the events that are the heart of her adult life: the harassment of the McCarthy years and her letter to, and appearance before, the House UnAmerican Activities Committee. She herself considers that her finest moment. She refused to name others to the committee but expressed willingness to waive the privilege against self-incrimination. In her famous letter she says, "I cannot and will not cut my conscience to fit this year's fashions" and adds that she "was raised in an old-fashioned American tradition" and "respected these ideals of Christian honor." Apparently to her the "simple rules of human decency" and "honor" are identifiably Christian.

Scoundrel Time, her hotly debated political memoir of the McCarthy period, is itself obliquely anti-Jewish, and Jewishness there is associated with timidity, accommodation, and narrow personal ambition. Denouncing the Hollywood directors who did not stand up to the anti-Communist witch-hunters, she observes that "many of them had been born on foreign lands and inherited foreign fears" and thus timidly offered "a bowl of chicken soup" to the "Cossacks" in Washington. While overtly attacking all of the American intellectuals who did not fight McCarthy, she points her finger in particular at those who are the product of nineteenth-century immigration (which includes her own family): "The children of timid immigrants are often remarkable people: energetic, intelligent, hardworking; and often they make it so good that they are determined to keep it at any cost." She reduces any position except her own to "an excuse to join those who should have been their hereditary enemies."

Dashiell Hammett serves as her example of heroic behavior during the fifties, while the Jewish playwright Clifford Odets serves as her primary negative example. Earlier, after seeing *Awake and Sing!* Hammett had attacked the play saying, "I don't think writers who cry about not having had a bicycle when they were kiddies are ever going to amount to much." According to Hellman, Odets, despite his insistence to her that he would show the Committee "the face of a radical man and tell them to go fuck themselves," instead "apologized for his old beliefs and identified many of his old friends as Communists."

For her the political choice in the McCarthy era was a simple and absolute either/or. She allows no room for complexity, ambiguity, conflicting ideas. In her words, even those "who were right about Russia" misused their anti-Communism to "play ball with the wrong people." Her reaction to Arthur Miller's HUAC testimony and *After the Fall* reveals the same rigid severity: "I suppose, in the play, he was being tolerant: those who betrayed their friends had a point, those who didn't had a point. Two sides to every question and all that rot."[6]

In Hellman's eyes Jewishness often seems to be associated with weakness, flabby accommodation, and personal self-seeking. The only Old Testament story found twice in her plays (in both *Another Part of the Forest* and the adaptation, *My Mother, My Father and Me*) is the one about Abraham's self-protective weakness and slyness in pretending to Pharaoh that Sarah is his sister. What she seems to value in Christianity is the salvation/damnation dichotomy in which there is no middle position and the image of Jesus as the perfectly courageous, selfless, noble individual. Christian forgiveness, on the other hand, is anathema to her. Angry at the reception of a Soviet novelist in this country, she comments: "I heard those words of forgiveness about informers so often during the time of Joe McCarthy that I asked myself if Christian charity had not deprived us of heroes."[7] And since heroes are what Hellman loves, the radically democratic, God-loves-everybody aspects of the Christian vision are rejected by her.

Even the terms Hellman uses to describe herself and others are tellingly Christian in orientation: she is a "Puritan socialist," Tallulah Bankhead "an aging sinner," and Hammett a "Dostoevskian sinner-saint." Clearly one of the greatest compliments paid to her (in her estimation) was the description of her by her lawyer Joseph Rauh as "a Puritan lady."

3

Hellman has said of her own work, "I am a moral writer, often too moral a writer, and I cannot avoid, it seems, that last summing up." Defending this tendency, she concluded, "I think that it is only a mistake when it fails to achieve its purpose, and I would rather make the attempt and fail, than fail to make the attempt."[8] The self-conscious antithesis in the last sentence is unusual in Hellman's writing and underscores the defensiveness of her either/or position. All eight plays are obviously the work of a rigid moralist who divides the world into the noble and the ignoble, in exact contrast to the affectionate interest in the ordinary man in Yiddish literature. The plays separate into two groups in the way they embody and transmit the moral vision structurally.

The first group *(Children's Hour, Little Foxes, Another Part of the Forest*, and *Watch on the Rhine)* demonstrate the results of active evil (in the case of *Watch* the focus is on the results of active good, but the pattern is the same). In none of these plays are the characters probed in depth; nothing is discovered or revealed about their natures in the course of the play. Rather, their personalities are the given, and the plays explore the results. As shorthand, I will refer to these plays as the plot-unfolding plays. The major characters in these four plays are all prodigiously willful, whether for good or evil, single-minded, simple, monochromatic figures. Each play has a message, and the temptation to see certain lines as authorial keys, as the author's points mouthed by a convenient character, becomes unavoidable.

The second group of plays *(Days to Come, Searching Wind, Autumn Garden,* and *Toys in the Attic)* aim at a different kind of moralism: they unmask and expose (but do not develop) characters. These characters are less dramatic types, well-meaning but ineffective individuals whose crucial flaw is weakness, especially the inability and unwillingness to see themselves clearly.

At their best, Hellman's plays are theatrically lively, vivid, fast-paced, and tightly woven, but all of them lack memorable characters. This shortcoming is a direct outgrowth of her stance, her vision of the world—indeed, it is the price she pays for her insistence on making clear moral points rather than exploring human character and relationships. Two of her comments about Chekhov are more illuminating about her work than his. In praise of the Russian playwright, she observes that he "found out that the writer must not only find the truth, but he must wrap it up and take it somewhere."[9] This is a dubious observation about Chekhov's work; but true of Hellman's. All her plays are neatly tied packages of "moral truth." The characters themselves are only vessels for carrying this truth; there is little evidence of deep interest in them as complex, multidimensional beings. Either no psychological explanation for their behavior is discernible, or the psychology is reductive and simplistic.

A second Hellman comment about Chekhov is equally revealing: ". . . there is a lack of passion and power. Chekhov was without that final spiritual violence which the very great creative genius has always had."[10] Spiritual—more precisely, moral—violence is the heart of Hellman's work. Writing in judgment, she projects a world of simplified dichotomies. Many of her characters are unqualifiedly rapacious despoilers or selfless idealists. Toward the weak, the sentimental, the self-deluding, the all-too-human, well-meaning failures her attitude, as opposed to Chekhov's exquisite balance of irony and love, is often sneering and disdainful. When she has unmasked their weakness, judged them, and found them wanting, there is nothing more to be said about them.

The first structural pattern, the play as a plot-unfolding, is clear in her first drama, *The Children's Hour* (1934). Mary Tilford, a young boarding-school girl, because of the weakness of the other characters, is able to destroy her schoolmistresses, Martha and Karen, by accusing them of lesbianism. The dramatic center of the play is the girl herself, a "bad seed," whose evil is unmotivated, whose character is simply given, a *diabolus ex machina*. Hellman herself, unlike virtually every audience and every critic, does not see Mary as totally evil. In her words, "I thought of the child as neurotic, sly, but not the utterly malignant creature which playgoers see in her. I never see characters as monstrously as the audiences do."[11] This disparity between the playwright's intentions and audience reaction occurs with several of her plays, and a pattern emerges: in each case the audience sees the characters as more *extreme* than Hellman intended.

That Hellman provides no motivation for Mary's evil is particularly interesting in that Hellman's source, "Closed Doors; or The Great Drumsheugh Case," a crime case in William Roughead's *Bad Companions*, suggests plausible psychological background. The girl on whom Mary was modelled was half black, the illegitimate daughter of an upper-class Scotsman who died and left her to his aristocratic mother. Lacking "the advantage of legitimacy and a European complexion," as Roughead puts it, the girl was a troublesome scholar who was repeatedly punished for misdeeds. At first she tried to gain power by fawning on her teachers. When that failed, she denounced them to her aristocratic grandmother. Hellman may have eliminated the girl's blackness and illegitimacy in an attempt not to be racist or old-fashioned about sexual codes, but the result is that Mary seems unmotivated, inhuman, and the play lacks psychological complexity or credibility. Despite her unmotivated behavior, Mary is clearly the most compelling character in the first two acts, in part because of her acute cunning, powerful will, and brilliantly improvisational evil. When she disappears at the end of Act II, the play loses energy. The focus shifts to the accused teachers; Mary has served her plot function, destroying the teachers' livelihood and lives in the community.

Act III demonstrates the results of Mary's malignancy and community complicity. Mary's grandmother, Mrs. Tilford, is second only to Mary in guilt, because of her self-righteousness, credulity, and gossip-mongering; she virtually destroys the teachers' reputations before confronting them with the child's accusations. In Act III she is denounced and punished. A weaker character, Mrs. Mortar, Martha's aunt, who did not appear in court to defend the teachers and deny any homosexual activity between them, is presented as even more distasteful than the grandmother. Early in the play when Mrs. Tilford calls Mrs. Mortar a "silly harmless woman," Dr. Cardin to whom the schoolmistress Karen is engaged, insists that she is distinctly "not a harmless woman." Mrs. Mortar is the first of Hellman's weak characters whose timidity makes them dangerous and unreliable. Unlike the strong though erring grandmother, Mrs. Mortar is denied the dignity of recognizing and atoning for her sins.

The three "good" characters experience quite different fates. Dr. Cardin, who has stood loyally by the two women, shows a moment of weakness: he asks his fiancée if there is any truth in the charges. Because of this moment of doubt, the marriage is called off; Karen believes suspicion would forever taint their relationship. Martha suddenly announces that she did and does love Karen, that she feels guilty and "all dirty," and commits suicide offstage. Karen, the calm, clearly heterosexual woman, is thus alone at the end: her school is destroyed, her intended marriage is off, her best friend is dead, and she is emotionally drained; nonetheless, she is morally triumphant, as pure and untainted as Mary is utterly evil.

Although the charge is lesbianism, the play is essentially a denunciation of destructive scandal-mongering, the smear technique, and the big lie. In a 1952 revival, Hellman directed the play to point up the analogy with the activities of McCarthy and the HUAC. However, it is worth noting certain distinctions: for example, in the play the charges are simply false. In reality—including HUAC hearings—innocence is seldom so unequivocal. Secondly, our reaction to the "guilt" of homosexuality is likewise likely to be less unequivocal than to treason.

Hellman began *The Little Foxes* (1939), her best play of the first type, while in Spain during the Civil War. As those who fought for the Republic represent the nobility of courageous self-sacrifice to her, the Hubbards represent the exact opposite—almost disembodied selfish greed. The Hubbards are fictionalized Newhouses; some of her mother's family threatened to sue for libel after the play opened. Hellman has remarked that her family was divided between the tough, (and immoral) older generation and the "broken-spirited" younger generation of her mother, here seen as the hopelessly dreamy, sweet Birdie. Lillian herself appears as Alexandra, the only character moral and strong enough to defy the foxes successfully.

The Hubbards' religion is never indicated. Neither their name nor anything in their conversation or home suggests Jewishness. Their future Chicago business partner praises them for their professed "Christian" attitudes toward their town and admits his own motive is simply financial gain. The partner's remark is dryly sarcastic: he seems to recognize the Hubbards' oily hypocrisy. Whether the Hubbards are supposed to be Jewish and thus the remark meant to be doubly ironic—the Hubbards would then be unChristian in two ways—is unclear, although it seems unlikely.

By her own report, Hellman intended the audience to recognize some part of themselves in the Hubbards, to stand chastened rather than to view them as much worse and simpler than themselves. But on the page and on the stage, the characters seem inhuman, and the play is like an exemplum of one of the speeches in it: Addie, a black housemaid to the Hubbards, insists, "Well, there are people who eat the earth and eat all the people on it like in the Bible with the locusts. And other people who stand around and watch them eat it. Sometimes I think it ain't right to stand and watch them do it."

Almost all the vitality comes from the no-holds-barred greedy maneuvers of the Hubbards, especially Regina and Ben; the plot consists of the various moves each character makes to get the upper hand in a business deal with a Chicago factory owner. All the Hubbards are utterly ruthless: they will rape the town, use all its resources, turn the blacks and poor whites against each other to keep labor cheap, and fight each other to the death (as Regina does when she virtually kills Horace).

The play suggests two ways of responding to the Hubbards of the world: one is either a victim and gets devoured, like Birdie, or one learns to fight back. The two characters who do fight back are able to do so because they face death and use the confrontation with this ultimate fear to learn to live courageously. Previously, Regina's husband Horace has at least tacitly gone along with the Hubbards and not challenged them. When the play opens he is returning from a hospital where he has been told he is dying; now, for the first time, he tries to act. He refuses to invest in the Hubbard factory plan and tells Regina, "You wreck the town, you and your brothers, *you* wreck the town and live on it. Not me." When Regina's brothers steal some negotiable bonds from his bank safe to close the deal, he lets them get away with it to punish Regina but does nothing to thwart the destructive deal, or to save the town from being "eaten." So the only truly heroic stand is assumed by Alexandra: after her father's death she makes it clear that she will not fulfill Birdie's despairing prediction, ". . . in twenty years you'll be just like me." The battle lines are clearly drawn, and Alexandra's assertion, "I'll be fighting as hard as he'll [Ben] be fighting," is obviously the voice of the author.

The energy of the play once again emerges from the evil characters; we watch them with the rapt fascination of spectators at a cockfight. Ironically, the play does not serve Hellman's moral purpose: since we find the wicked Hubbards fascinating *and* much worse than we are, we never feel accused or have our own values deeply questioned. *The Little Foxes* reveals much of Hellman's pervasive anti-middle-class bias, which seems to derive from an animus toward her own family and the typical Jewish middle-class pattern. When Regina says, "I think you should either be a nigger or a millionaire. In between like us, what for?" she seems to express some of the playwright's spirit. Those who represent the old South in the play, including Birdie with her memoirs of culture, refinement, and benevolent slavery are seen as preferable to the new South and the emerging middle-class industrialism of the Hubbards.

The second Hubbard play, *Another Part of the Forest* (1946), is less successful than *The Little Foxes* because the Hubbards are such limited characters and because Hellman's dramatic aims were self-defeatingly mixed. Instead of simply enacting what *happens*, given the Hubbards, as in *Foxes*, here she also tried to explain them, or as Hellman herself says, to "look into their family background and to find out what it was that made them the nasty people they were."[12] So we go back in time twenty years and see Regina's and Ben's parents, Marcus and Lavinia. The play, which is dedicated to Hellman's analyst, Gregory Zilboorg, is Freudian and reductionist. Marcus is the primal father who keeps his sons weak and dependent and who loves his daughter Regina inordinately. Lavinia is a meek, sweet, dotty religious woman; but unlike Birdie whom she resembles in many ways, Lavinia, beneath her apparent subservience, has courage arising out of her facing mortality; "I'm not a woman meant to be afraid . . . I'm not afraid of anything." At the climax of the play, she defeats Marcus through blackmail: she threatens to reveal that during the Civil War he led Union troops to a southern training camp where the rebels were slaughtered.

Hellman's anti-middle-class animus pervades *Forest*; here both the dreamy, weak old southern aristocrat and the hopelessly vulgar, lower-class town whore are shown as superior to the *nouveau riche* Hubbards.

Children's Hour, *Foxes*, and *Forest* focus on characters of monomaniacal evil, larger-(and simpler)-than-life figures. *Watch on the Rhine* (1941) is the reverse. Here the characters, Kurt Müller, his wife and children, are paragons of virtue, embodiments of courageous self-sacrifice. Even though the play reveals the politicalization and radicalization of several more mundane figures, the dramatic interest is in the Müllers, who are *models* for the other, less perfect characters, and for the audience. The play is also a call to anti-fascism, with the reasons and appeal embodied in Kurt Müller. His central speech, recounting how he came to be an anti-fascist fighter, directly echoes Addie's remark about bystanders: "In the festival of August, 1931 . . . I see twenty-seven men murdered in the Nazi street fight. I cannot stand by now and watch. My time has come to move." Hellman's interest in *Watch* is totally in the depiction of the selfless, moral hero; the play reveals no interest in the Holocaust or the destruction of the Jewish people.

At the time *Watch* was written, Hellman was feeling "shame and sorrow at the Liberals' impotence in the face of the hurricane."[13] The play in a sense demonstrates the "conversion" of Sara Müller's mother and brother, who represent old money and social and political connections. The conversion is by example: Kurt shows what a true anti-fascist should do. The emphasis is on action, especially physical action; his face is bullet-scarred, his hands broken. Hellman's Hemingway ethic of physical confrontation and courage as the key to, and test of, the moral life is never clearer: as in Hemingway's work the heroes value action and distrust talk.[14]

The Müllers are the most idealistic of Hellman's characters, and Sara Müller is the most attractive of her women. Although Sara is not engaged in the physical fight against fascism, her commitment to the fight is total. Like Kurt, she values duty over love, the public interest over the private. She faces her husband's departure and probable death with noble stoicism. Kurt, who apparently was modelled on the same source as "Julia," is presented as equal to Christ or Socrates in his selflessness and unflinching attitude toward death. His commitment to anti-fascism justifies the ultimate physical action, murder. When he kills another character whose blackmail endangered the cause, we are expected to see the act as completely justified, unquestionably moral.

As the Hubbards and Mary seem inhumanly evil, the Müllers are unbelievably good. Even the children are noble; no sibling rivalry, pettiness, or childish weakness mar their stances. The audience may be awed by the Müllers but cannot identify with them: they are too perfect. Moreover, because we never see them struggle, never feel any conflict or any desire for personal happiness or safety, we cannot appreciate them or their acts deeply; it is as if they made a decision one fateful day and were unquestioning and undivided ever after.

Hellman's second play, *Days to Come* (1936), set the pattern for her plays of character unmasking. A conflict between strikers and strike-breakers in a small Ohio brush factory is the background, but the real dramatic focus is the owners' family, the Rodmans, and the play moves toward a series of unmaskings of them in the final act. Most of the characters are exaggerated types and simple and obvious foils or parallels to each other. For example, Firth, the sweet, simple, trusting worker who does not recognize the unavoidable conflict of interest between workers and owners, is the workers' equivalent of Andrew Rodman, who is also unbelievably naive, weak, well-intentioned, and outmaneuvered. Naturally both are denounced by the more willful and hard-headed.

The final act consists of the mutual unmasking of Andrew, his wife Julie, his sister Cora, and his best friend Ellicott. Andrew is revealed as a weak, self-deluding cuckold; Julie as a woman who refuses to see financial realities and tries to make up for the lack of focus in her life with sexual affairs, most recently with Ellicott: Ellicott as a sly manipulator who has gradually come to control Andrew's money as well as take his wife to bed; and Cora as a rigid, compulsive, hate-filled spinster.

Days closed after seven performances: the characters are hyperbolic, the explanations and revelations obvious, and the moral points too blatant and explicit. One aspect of the play worth noting is that the labor organizer Whalen, one of Hellman's unqualified moral heroes, expresses an opinion that seems to be Hellman's own: asked if he loves the poor for whom he labors, Whalen responds, "Love them? . . . the meanness and the cowardice that come with poverty? I hate the poor, Mrs. Rodman. But I love what they could be." Only nobility attained has value. Her viewpoint is a striking contrast to Saul Bellow's typically "Yiddish" description of humans as "not gods, not beasts, but savages of somewhat damaged but not extinguished nobility."

Unlike *Days to Come*, which only uses a social issue as a background, Hellman's second character unmasking play, *A Searching Wind* (1944), has a true dual focus: the rise of Nazism and the psychosexual analysis of individual characters. The play explores the three main characters' responses to Nazism and the love triangle of Alexander Hazen, his wife Emily, and Cassie, Alexander's mistress and Emily's best friend. Set against overwhelming world problems, the personal triangle ultimately comes to seem trivial, and the rendezvous, which coincides with the key political events, contrived.

Structurally, the play is overtly an unmasking: At the beginning it is 1944 and Emily invites Cassie over for dinner for a joint review of their lives. The plot entails three flashbacks: to Rome in 1922 at the time of Mussolini's takeover, to Berlin in 1923 during the early anti-Semitic riots, and to Paris in 1938 just before the Munich Agreement. In each of the three scenes, Alex reveals his vacillation, his lack of political foresight or understanding, his weak gestures of appeasement and compromise (he thus figures the spirit of appeasement which failed to react in time to stop fascism), and his unawareness of his true motives. Emily is seen as a rich, frivolous social butterfly who marries her friend's boyfriend on the rebound, knows about their affair after the marriage but does nothing about it, sees World War II in terms of her own financial investments and her son's safety. Of the three, Cassie has seen the political situations most clearly and ethically, but she has been weak and self-deluding in her personal life; in her final self-unmasking in the last scene she recognizes that her disguised motive all along has been "to punish Emily" and that because of her "small purposes" and bitterness, she has wasted her life. She concludes that she and the Hazens have been "frivolous people." Another character unmasked in the last scene is the reverse of Alex, the cynical, intellectual grandfather,

Moses. He has not agreed with Alex's political and personal compromises; rather, he has used his Tolstoyan belief that history is made by the masses to justify doing nothing—standing by in cynical, inactive judgment. The Hazens' son Sam emerges as the hero. Overtly anti-intellectual and activist (both populist and anti-Nazi), he denounces his parents' generation, saying he wants "no more mistakes for any reason," an adolescent ultimatum Hellman seems to take at face value. He then reveals that the next day doctors will amputate the leg he wounded fighting the war the older generation failed to prevent.

Hellman's two World War II plays are like inversions of each other. Kurt Müller is Hellman's great hero; Alex Hazen, a weak failure. Almost all the adults in *Watch* are either morally exemplary to begin with or rise majestically to the occasion; in *Searching Wind* all the adults are morally corrupt. Kurt saw what the Nazis were immediately and acted at once and for all time; Alex never saw and never acted decisively. The spirit of a courageous, moral grandfather pervades *Watch* just as his picture dominates the set; in *Searching Wind* the corresponding grandfather figure is an example of moral failure through lack of responsibility. The Müllers exude family closeness and mutual respect; the Hazens are distant and out of contact with each other. Despite Kurt's love for his children, he would sacrifice them for the public cause if need be; one of Emily's and Alex's reasons for not confronting Nazism directly was fear that Sam might have to fight.

Basically the World War II plays present the same either/or: either the nobility, courage, self-sacrifice, commitment, fulfilled love relationship, and family closeness of the Müllers, or the frivolousness, indirection, blindness, selfishness, failure to act, sexual infidelity, and shame of the Hazens. Which side are you on?

Hellman's other two plays of character unmasking, *Autumn Garden* and *Toys in the Attic*, are less schematic than *Days to Come* and *The Searching Wind*. Both are built up from biographical material (her father's family) found in *An Unfinished Woman* and *Pentimento*. Neither uses a background of large public social events. The tone in these later plays is more complex; there is a greater recognition of, and interest in, human personality and more emphasis on the role the unconscious plays in human activity. But in neither play are the characters' foibles forgiven; in both, the weak characters are unmasked, judged, and found wanting.

In *Autumn Garden* (1951) Hellman develops more characters than in any of her other plays. Most of them are middle-aged; the play is about the autumnal time of life when, according to Hellman, we have developed a serious self and built our character or we are face to face with their absence and the ensuing emptiness. Most of the characters are of the familiar weak and self-deluding type, but the damage they inflict is mostly on themselves.

The chief mover of the plot, the catalyst for all the revelations of the many characters, is Nick Denery, an artist who once showed promise but now does more philandering and meddling in others' lives than painting. Unlike Mary in *Children's Hour*, whose evil is simply given and unaccountable, Nick is a psychologically convincing character. At first his wife Nina appears to be the one who patches up Nick's mistakes, a blameless victim of his infidelity. Later we see that she needs to look down on Nick and "to be ashamed" and "demean" herself. Nick's pernicious meddling is the result of his failure as an artist and person: lazy, self-indulgent, and fearful, he has not finished a painting in years. In marrying the rich Nina, he has become a kept man, and money, not art, is the center of his life. So periodically, when they return from Europe and Nick "cannot manage to charm" Nina's family, he "inevitably" looks around for those he can. Nick, is Hellman's most psychologically convincing villain; Nina's and the other characters' complicity in his destructive meddling gives the play more emotional depth and resonance than any of her previous plays.

The play moves in a series of disclosures prompted by Nick's compulsive interference. The only character shown to be capable of decisive action is the young Sophie: when Nick ruins her reputation and spoils her chances of having a marriage of convenience with Frederick, she demands that Nick and Nina pay her for what she has lost. Refusing to be a charity case, she insists on calling her demand blackmail. We are prepared for Sophie's toughness because throughout the play she is given some of Hellman's favorite characteristics: she refuses to cry about her woes, warns against destroying relationships with too much talk, and suggests that worrying is an excuse not to think.

Sophie is the positive moral example; all the others are pathetic weaklings. Dashiell Hammett wrote the play's central speech which Hellman indicates is to be delivered "slowly, carefully." The line is clearly the final judgment on them all: "So at any given moment you're only the sum of your life up to then. There are no big moments you can reach unless you've a pile of smaller moments to stand on."

Autumn Garden is obviously Hellman's most Chekhovian play in subject matter, structure, and tone, but essentially the play is very unlike Chekhov's because Hellman lacks his ability to make us care deeply for the characters and his capacity to suggest complexity and depth through the characters' speeches, silences, pauses, and breaks in thought. Even in her most mellow play, the characters are too neatly defined, and the implicit attitude is one of *judgment*.

Toys in the Attic (1960), her last original play to date, is an unmasking of "love" to reveal dependence, control, victim-savior games, masochism, and incest. The play is full of eccentric characters (a rich middle-aged woman who sleeps all day and has a mulatto chauffeur for a lover) and bizarre events (a young bride trades her wedding ring to a dope dealer in exchange for a "knife of truth" with which she deliberately cuts herself). The play focuses on three women's diseased affection for a handsome ne'er-do-well, Julian. While both his sisters claim (and believe) they want him to succeed, both really want him to depend on and need them. When, through a wild financial deal involving a partially black former mistress, Julian comes into money and tries to assert himself and to give his sisters some of the things they presumably wanted all these years, the sisters are devastated. In addition to wanting to control Julian, Carrie, the younger sister, lusts after him. Out of her own desire not to lose

Julian, Carrie makes his pathetic, masochistic child-wife jealous, and together they bring about his downfall. When we last see him, he has been robbed of his new fortune and badly beaten. Although he has a dim recognition of Carrie's true nature (he asks why she "purrs" at him as if he'd "done something good"), the sisters and wife have him securely in their "loving" embrace.

The most "psychological" of all Hellman's plays, *Toys* rides its idiosyncratic sensationalism (violence, incestuous love, miscegenation, "secret" Negro blood, masochism) to no convincing portrayal of the human condition. Like Hellman's other plays, *Toys* is finally convincing only of its author's own idiosyncratic and distorted view of human character. It is certainly revealing that the only time "love" is at the center of a Hellman play, it is diseased and destructive. Except for the idealized family life of the Müllers (which seems a product of their nobility) there is no family closeness or positive sexual love in all her work. She seems to be saying that her characters do not *deserve* to be loved.

Hellman's best work is in her memoirs, rather than her plays. In part this is the result of the different, in fact antithetical demands of the two forms. In the kind of conventional, realistic plays she writes, the author's voice must be effaced and reality presented directly. In her plays, however, her highly moralistic, idiosyncratic, and often tendentious voice is all too apparent: too often we see the puppeteer jerking the strings. Paradoxically, the same quality—the powerful, highly individual vision and voice—is what gives the memoirs their distinctive, personal quality. In *An Unfinished Woman* and *Pentimento*, personal memoirs in which an easily discernible subjectivity is an attraction and virtue, Hellman writes brilliantly. *Scoundrel Time*, which attempts to be an objective historical essay as well as a memoir, is more problematic.

Hellman divides the world into the good and the bad and often seems to suggest that weakness is the fundamental human problem. And since she consistently depicts Jews as weak and self-serving, much of her work seems not only un-Jewish but ultimately anti-Jewish. Even her anti-middle-class bias (she evidently prefers the virtues of benevolent slave owners and lower-class whores) serves to make Jews unacceptable because of their typical class pattern and identification.

Her father's humorous gibe about Hellman being the "first Jewish nun on Prytania Street" finally comes to seem prescient in the way that it points to some of her traits that are (no doubt unfairly) attributed to the stereotypical nun—in particular, her rigid, excessively judgmental, unloving, and unforgiving nature. Like a stereotypical nun, she seems to insist on the extreme, undivided, absolute commitment and projects a world in which moral complexity is flattened into a simplified relief of good and evil.

Hellman writes in the realistic mode, but many of her characters are cartoons—monsters of depravity or secular saints. Ironically, her tendency toward hyperbolic characterization ultimately defeats her own moralizing intentions. Unlike the little man of Yiddish literature, her characters are too unlike us, too purely either good or bad, for us to identify with them and thus grow morally through imaginative participation in their struggles. Hellman's extraordinarily rigid moralism and her frequent either/or dichotomies make her plays into arguments and demonstrations rather than evocations and explorations. Melodrama is not a substitute for drama, and the requisite dramatic tensions are repeatedly defeated in her plays by her intrusive moralizing presence.

NOTES

1. Leslie Fiedler, *The Jew in the American Novel* (New York: Herzl Institute Pamphlet No. 10, 1959), pp. 35–36.

2. Allen Guttmann, *The Jewish Writer in America: Assimilation and the Crisis of Identity* (New York: Oxford University Press, 1971), p. 13.

3. Robert Alter, *After the Tradition: Essays on Modern Jewish Writing* (New York: Dutton, 1969), p. 22.

4. For a full description of *Yiddishkeit*, see the introduction to Irving Howe and Eliezer Greenberg, eds., *A Treasury of Yiddish Stories* (New York: Viking, 1954), pp. 1–71.

5. Richard G. Stern, "Lillian Hellman on Her Plays," *Contact* 3 (1959): 116.

6. John Phillips and Anne Hollander, "Lillian Hellman: An Interview," *The Paris Review* 33 (Winter–Spring 1965): 74.

7. Quoted in Richard Moody, *Lillian Hellman Playwright* (New York: Bobbs-Merrill, 1972), p. 345.

8. Quoted in Moody, p. 55.

9. Lillian Hellman, ed., *The Selected Letters of Anton Chekhov* (New York: Farrar, Straus, 1955), p. xxiii.

10. *Selected Letters of Anton Chekhov*, p. 207.

11. Quoted in Moody, p. 56.

12. Quoted in Doris V. Falk, *Lillian Hellman* (New York: Frederick Ungar, 1978), p. 58.

13. Quoted in Moody, p. 109.

14. Compare, for example, Robert Wilson's line to Francis Macomber, "Doesn't do to talk too much about all this. Talk the whole thing away. No pleasure in anything if you mouth it up too much" with Marthe's line in *Watch* at the moment she decides to leave her self-serving husband, ". . . when you know you can do it, you don't have to say anything; you can just go" or Sara Müller's line, "It's an indulgence to sit in a room and discuss your beliefs as if they were the afternoon's golf game."

Ethics and Ethnicity in the Plays of Arthur Miller

Enoch Brater

THE WORK OF ARTHUR MILLER OFFERS US A PRIME EXAMPLE OF A PLAYWRIGHT subsuming the particular flavor of his own ethnic background within the broader context of a pluralistic American culture. Miller's assimilation of his own Jewishness within the framework of universalism must be seen as part of the history of a nativist American theater he has helped to create, for such an approach goes a long way in explaining the originality of his accomplishment. The drama of the archetypal Jewish-American family, "struggling for life" amidst the "petty conditions" of the Depression, had already been captured on the New York stage by Clifford Odets.[1] Perhaps more than any other work of its time and place, *Awake and Sing!* exposed with raw honesty what it was like to grow up as an urban American Jew in the thirties. That way could not be taken again by an ambitious writer bent on establishing a voice of his own in the theater. Inspired rather than influenced by the achievement, Miller capitalized upon an entirely different dramatic solution, "Jewish in the sense that it is the Old Testament."[2] Turning away from his own immediate heritage, Miller returned to an even older one, finding in traditions more Judaic than Jewish the real conflicts he might still portray on stage.

Miller's own background, of course, had a great deal to do with the particular tone his work would take. The Depression, he wrote, "made me impatient with anything, including art, which pretends that it can exist for its own sake and still be of any prophetic importance."[3] But Miller's Depression years were spent in conditions unlike those of the Bronx-bound Berger family Odets had portrayed in *Awake and Sing!;* he grew up in the far less oppressive atmosphere of Brooklyn, a place of open spaces where trees might still grow.

> My mother was born in this country. My father came over when he was five years old. He grew up to be six feet two inches tall with blue eyes and red hair and everybody thought he was an Irishman. . . . My family's name has been Miller as far back as I know anything about. My mother thought one side was named Mahler in Europe, but wasn't sure. Miller happens to be a fairly common name for Jews and others in Europe. . . . I write what reflects my experience. I come from people who rarely, if ever, spoke Yiddish. I had no doubt that I was Jewish. . . . my struggle with nihilism may well express my Jewishness. . . . The roots of my aversion may well be Jewish, but my concern is for the country as a whole.[4]

Miller's neighbors had escaped from the tenements full of Eastern European Jewry to take up roots in more pastoral landscapes: he took the elevated Culver line to Abraham Lincoln High School and planted saplings in the yard of the house at Avenue M and 3rd Street—a pear tree still bears fruit today. In New York, local geography is important, for it frequently determines not only socio-economic class, but the quality of life itself. "This is Willy Loman territory," he said on a recent tour of the old neighborhood. "Places like this are the heart-land."[5] Miller's territory by no means escaped the reality of the Depression. The playwright's businessman father lost everything he had in the 1929 stock market crash, when Miller was still in his early teens. Today Miller's Brooklyn—hardly any open spaces—is an area of well-scrubbed, well-painted side-by-side houses, though in those years "nobody painted houses." This was a time when Brooklynites were "quietly desperate for a bowl of soup." Miller's mother was always taking them in. One man came for soup and stayed twelve years until Miller's grandfather threw him out for being drunk once too often. Despite the hard times, there was optimism and hope; things simply had to get better. This was the central impression Miller remembers from his formative years. In response to the question, "Do you feel whatever Jewish tradition you were brought up in influenced you at all?" Miller responded:

> I never used to, but I think now that, while I hadn't taken over an ideology, I did absorb a certain viewpoint. That there is tragedy in the world but that the world must continue: one is a condition for the other. Jews can't afford to revel too much in the tragic because it might overwhelm them. Consequently, in most Jewish writing there's always the caution, "Don't push it too far toward the abyss, because you're liable to fall in." I think it's part of that psychology and it's part of me, too. I have, so to speak, a psychic investment in the continuity of life.[6]

Fresh from Brooklyn, Miller began his experiments in playwriting at the University of Michigan in 1934. His first play, about a Jewish family, was produced in Ann Arbor by the Hillel Foundation. In 1936 he surprised himself by winning a prestigious Avery Hopwood Award for *No Villain*, the play written in haste (six days) during spring recess. A year later he did spadework in Professor Kenneth T. Rowe's playwriting course, struggling along with technical problems of exposition, plot development, scene change, and character motiva-tion. There he practiced how to give ideas dramatic shape and there he became convinced that the theater is *the* place for ideas:

> In all my plays and books I try to take settings and dramatic situations from life which involve real questions of right and wrong. Then I set out, rather implac-ably, and in the most realistic situations I can find, the moral dilemma and try to point a real, though hard, path out. I don't see how you can write anything decent without using the question of right and wrong as the basis.[7]

After Michigan Miller found his way back to New York. There he joined the ranks of other aspiring artists like Orson Welles, John Houseman, and Dale Wasserman, all of them hoping to come into their own—and keep themselves alive—under the umbrella of the Federal Theater Project, FDR's welfare plan for keeping show business in business. Here was a lucky break: the Manhattan unit of the Federal Theater Project was originally directed by Elmer Rice and its artistic core came from the Group Theatre Acting Company, that unique drama cooperative that nurtured such luminaries as Clifford Odets, Luther and Stella Adler, Morris Carnovsky, Lee Strasberg, Harold Clurman, Lee J. Cobb, Elia Kazan, and Mordecai Gorelik.[8] Miller read and evaluated plays submitted by other authors for production, but his real job was to become acquainted with the ideas and personalities dominating that side of the American theater whose main goal was the successful dramatization of the theme of social responsibility.

Ethics, not ethnicity, became Miller's special forte. "There is work to be done," he would observe later during the scoundrel time of McCarthyism, "This is no time to go to sleep."[9] He was a universalist from the very outset of his professional career, a writer interested not merely in the family, but in "the family of man."[10] Even in "I Don't Need You Anymore," the short story which deals most explicitly with the spirituality of being Jewish, Miller's accent is on a universalist God, not specifically the God of Abraham, Isaac, and Jacob. The young boy, Martin, walking along the hot beach in his uncomfortable High Holiday suit, remembers seeing the bearded face of God in the water at Far Rockaway, where the Miller family, not especially religious, sometimes found themselves on Tisha B'Av, Rosh Hashanah, or Yom Kippur. Frightened by the sight of praying men carrying Torahs outside of the synagogue, Martin only slowly understands that they have come to cast their sins upon the waters. Miller's vignette takes some liberties with religious practice: Torahs are not carried out of the Ark for the ceremony of Tashlich on Rosh Hashanah. The combination of fact and fiction, however, reflects the impressionable Martin's childhood fear, confusion, and blurred memory. But when the sensitive young boy finds himself alone once more on the shore, he has an elemental "religious" experience with the divinity of sun and sea and sky, those small parts of God we can see all around us. Judaism leads to a realm of human experience even greater than its own orthodoxy.

Social responsibility, man's behavior to man, becomes the universal theme Miller inherits from the Old Testament. In his theater he has always set about to dramatize this same story. Miller's first success, *All My Sons*, the play that took attention away from Eugene O'Neill's *Long Day's Journey Into Night* during the 1947 Broadway season, portrays the eternal conflict between a private morality and a public one. Miller deliberately distances the setting of this drama from the particulars of his own personal background in an act of self-restraint that lends breadth as well as depth to the moral implications of this work. Set in "August of our era," we move from biographical Brooklyn to the "back yard of the Keller home in the outskirts of an American town," a heartland quite different from the one Miller grow up in.

> The stage is hedged on right and left by tall, closely planted poplars which lend the yard a secluded atmosphere. Upstage is filled with the back of the house and its open, unroofed porch which extends into the yard some six feet. The house is two stories high and has seven rooms. It would have cost perhaps

fifteen thousand in the early twenties when it was built. Now it is nicely painted, looks tight and comfortable, and the yard is green with sod, here and there plants whose season is gone. . . . Downstage right is a small, trellised arbor, shaped like a sea-shell, with a decorative bulb hanging from its forward-curving roof. Garden chairs and a table scattered about.[11]

The "secluded atmosphere" of *All My Sons* allows us to study in some detail the currency of corruption that exists beneath the comfortable surface of bourgeois domesticity. This house is built on sand and this garden has been cultivated by sin. Miller's set foreshadows disaster, the transgression of a firm moral code, the crimes a man must pay for when he eats forbidden fruits: downstage "stands the four-foot high stump of a slender apple tree whose upper trunk and branches lie toppled beside it, fruit still clinging to its branches." What is important to notice about the set for this play is that all of its mythological paraphernalia is entirely integrated with a naturalistic set. Miller has designed a play whose allegory is dramatically compatible within the contours of fourth-wall realism. The forms Judaic morality takes in the present change, but the essence of man as his brother's keeper is sacred and universal. Joe Keller, manufacturer of defective airplane parts during World War II, defies this law and must pay the price for his transgression:

> *Mother:* Why are you going? You'll sleep, why are you going?
> *Keller:* I can't sleep here. I'll feel better if I go.
> *Mother:* You're so foolish. Larry was your son, too, wasn't he? You know he'd never tell you to do this.
> *Keller: (looking at a letter in his hand).* Then what is this if it isn't telling me? Sure, he was my son. But I think to him they were all my sons. And I guess they were, I guess they were. . . . (Exits into house.). . . .
> *Mother: (of Larry, the letter).* The war is over! Didn't you hear?—it's over!
> *Chris:* Then what was Larry to you? A stone that fell into water? It's not enough for him to be sorry. Larry didn't kill himself to make you and Dad sorry.
> *Mother:* What more can we be!
> *Chris:* You can be better! Once and for all you can know there's a universe of people outside and you're responsible to it, and unless you know that, you threw away your son because that's why he died.
> *(A shot is heard in the house. . . .)*[12]

All My Sons is the first of Miller's well-known plays to make its pact so directly with the law. Miller was himself surprised to see, when he looked recently at his work, how often he had made use of the law and the lawyer-like figure.[13] In *All My Sons*, however, the law is not merely legalistic, but Mosaic. It is all we have left of the memory of justice and man's moral obligations to his fellow man. Keller violates this law: he sins against something larger than himself, that intangible but civilizing force the Torah, perhaps for want of a better word, calls God.

But for all its popular appeal as a drama of identifiable moral imperatives—made all the more accessible in the screen version starring Burt Lancaster and

Edward G. Robinson—*All My Sons* is not a work without some conspicuous formal limitation. Miller's play suffers from the same contrivance as Lillian Hellman's first hit, *The Children's Hour*. Instead of integrating directly into the dramatic action the results of those tensions the play sets so vigorously in motion, the playwright falls back on a letter written by a character now dead to hasten the moral consequences of the tale. Unlike Hellman's curtain, however, Miller's curtain in *All My Sons* is not unnecessarily delayed: recognition follows quickly upon revelation, the gun goes off, mother and son embrace, the curtain falls. If Miller has made use in the play of one of Hellman's melodramatic little letters, he has at least attempted to disguise it in a swiftly paced scene coinciding dramatic impact with a moral one. Chris's closing remarks to his mother sound, however, a little too much like speechifying, and the whole business of ultimate Old Testament justice worked out in human terms is drawn just a little too tightly to make for a thoroughly convincing dramatic representation.

Miller will not make these same mistakes again. The structural weakness of *All My Sons* is the result, quite frankly, of Miller's lack of experience with the realistic technique. Before finishing this script, he had already completed a dozen plays, all unsuccessful, several in highly symbolic and expressionistic terms. "I wrote a verse, or near verse, tragedy of Montezuma and Cortez, for example, which had no relation whatsoever to any Ibsenesque theatre."[14] Only *The Man Who Had All the Luck* (1944) was a realistic play, "a family play." Determined to write a drama viable in popular performance, he wagered *All My Sons* as a last-ditch effort in playwriting. He was nearly thirty and the father of one son: his respectable novel about anti-Semitism, *Focus* (1945), had not exactly made his name a household word. *All My Sons* established Miller as a new force in the legitimate theater, but it had not yet shown him to be in complete control of the shape of his medium.

With *Death of a Salesman* Miller came into his own. "Wonder," he wrote in the introduction to the *Collected Plays*, "must have feet with which to walk the earth."[15] Integrating new theatrical mechanics into the set for this famous play, Miller made the past literally simultaneous with the present in a practical dramatic solution above and beyond formalism. The staging of Willy Loman's psyche, his frustrated hopes and his unfulfilled dreams, could then strike Miller's audience with some astonishing immediacy and clarity. Though the plot of *Death of a Salesman* is naturalistic, the tone is symbolic, as reality becomes the substance of myth. "Chasing all the things that rust," Willy Loman is the American Everyman somewhere between the pathetic and the tragic.[16] Ethnicity, then, is far less crucial to this work than universality. The question of whether or not Willy Loman is "Jewish" or "crypto-Jewish" is, in fact, entirely inappropriate, for it demonstrates a fundamental misunderstanding of the theatrical style of this work. *Death of a Salesman* is designed to show us life, not a slice-of-life. In this play—and on this set—any ethnic identification would severely undermine the entire basis of emblematic realism defining the tone of this work in performance. Though Jewish families—along with others—may have lived in the world of broken refrigerator fan belts, none of them lived in multilevel, partially transparent sets with imaginary walls where flutes played at strategic moments. In *Salesman* one cannot divorce staging from thematic implication. It is only because the play is structured in this particular way that the range of applicability is so large. Searching for ethnicity in *Death of a Salesman* limits Miller's "art of the present tense," "the unsingable heart song the ordinary man may feel but never utter."[17]

That *Death of a Salesman* is a work of symbolic realism is a point that seems to have eluded critics like Leslie Fiedler and, more recently, Joel Shatzky.[18] In *Waiting for the End* Fiedler complained that Miller, like Paddy Chayevsky, created "crypto-Jewish" heroes, "characters who are in habit, speech, and condition of life typically Jewish-American, but who are presented as something else—general-American say, as in *Death of a Salesman,* or Italo-American, as in *Marty.*" Calling this "a loss of artistic faith," Fiedler said this is "a failure to remember that the inhabitants of Dante's Hell or Joyce's Dublin are more universal as they are more Florentine or Irish." The same argument is sometimes made in slightly different terms about *A Raisin in the Sun:* Lorraine Hansberry had not written a black play at all, but a Jewish play with black characters. "This is Fiedler's problem, not mine," retorted Miller, expanding his argument as follows:

> Where the theme seems to require a Jew to act somehow in terms of his Jewishness, he does so. Where it seems to me irrelevant what the religious or cultural background of a character may be, it is treated as such. In *A View From the Bridge* they are Sicilians because the social code which kills Eddie Carbone is made in Sicily and it must be localized before it can be extended to all people. I see nothing in *Salesman, All My Sons, After the Fall,* or *The Crucible* which is of that nature. *Incident at Vichy* deals directly with the anti-Semitic problem so there are Jewish characters. Similarly, Gregory Soloman in *The Price* has to be Jewish, for one thing because the theme of survival, of a kind of acceptance of life, seemed to me to point directly to the Jewish experience through centuries of oppression. For me it is the theme that rules these choices.[19]

The theme of *Death of a Salesman,* however, is not nearly so easy to define as the theme of *All My Sons,* which can be attributed to the far greater maturity and complexity of this work. Nothing in *Salesman* so closely approximates Old Testament paradigms as the incorporation of fundamental as opposed to surface morality had done in the earlier play. Whatever Biblical typology there is in *Salesman* is the backdrop for a conflict of characters whose fate is social. And so the Jacob-Esau motif of Biff and Happy (or Willy and Ben), the whither-thou-goest-I-shall-go devotion of Linda, the responsibility of fathers to sons and sons to fathers, of community to individual and individual to community, are merely the archetypal strategies Miller employs to expand the scope of this requiem beyond the limits of this particular nuclear family. "How may a man make of the outside world a home?" is the universal question Miller ponders in this play— and he ponders it in typically universal terms.[20] When the curtain rises on this drama, "A melody is heard, played upon a flute. It is small and fine, telling of grass and trees and the horizon." Miller's set suggests rather than completes a realistic tableau. His stage makes highly selective use of the props of everyday life in order to liberate itself from the constraints of a too careful literalism which might threaten to dwarf the symbolic texture of the play. "The entire setting," we see, "is wholly or, in some places, partially transparent." Yet into this staged transparency Miller introduces those elements of tragedy which become in the course of this drama painfully real:

> Before us is the Salesman's house. We are aware of towering, angular shapes behind it, surrounding it on all sides. Only the blue light of the sky falls upon the house and forestage; the surrounding area shows an angry glow of orange. As more light appears, we see a solid vault of apartment houses around the small, fragile-seeming home. An air of dream clings to the place, a dream rising out of reality.[21]

In a very basic sense the set *is* Miller's play. The tiny frame house clings desperately to its frail life-line beneath the cold shadows of inhuman towers threatening to stifle so precarious an existence. This world has been passed by and somehow nobody noticed. Into this somber lyricism enters tired humanity in the person of Willy Loman, the Salesman, "carrying two large sample cases. The flute plays on. He hears but is not aware of it. He is past sixty years of age, dressed quietly. Even as he crosses the stage to the doorway of the house, his exhaustion is apparent."

The stark visual contrast between a highly symbolic set and the behavior of highly realistic characters is what adds such dramatic resonance to the universal themes Miller pursues in *Death of a Salesman*. What happens here on the level of everyday reality is performed on a set that has been delicately rendered in a rich symbolic texture. The actions and reactions of the Loman family, therefore, gain a density of meaning above and beyond what we normally expect from the conventions of theatrical realism. The play, in fact, carefully builds its conflicts from the interaction of its two separate levels of stage reality, the symbolic and the naturalistic. The careful orchestration of this scenic device prepares us for the thematic conflicts that will take place on this set and makes possible that conflict of ideas which, in Miller's own terms, "embraces both determinism and the paradox of will."[22] In light of this rare theatrical virtuosity, to wonder, as so many critics have done, whether names like Dave Singleton or Willy and Ben Loman signal Jewish characters in a watered-down ethnic situation, is to miss not only the significance of this drama, but the precise stage terms in which it has been conceived. From the moment the curtain rises on *Death of a Salesman*, the universal dimension has been established in concise and very conspicuous theatrical terms. "It isn't a question of reporting something," observed Miller about the construction of this play; "it's a question of creating a synthesis that has never existed before out of common materials that are otherwise chaotic and unrelated."[23]

"Most modern plays are concerned with the relation of man to man," wrote

Eugene O'Neill in a much-quoted letter to Joseph Wood Krutch, "but this does not concern me at all. I am interested only in the relation of man and God."[21] Miller takes his theater in the opposite direction: the center of this universe is man, changing and capable of change. In *Death of a Salesman* Miller's "ordinary man" is victimized and ultimately strangled by a system of values man, not God, has created. Willy Loman. "trying to write his name on ice on a hot July day," lives in a society portrayed as shifting, unstable, and undependable.[25] Moral choice and ethical behavior in a material culture are the subject of this dramatic inquiry. Society, not metaphysics or theology, occupies center stage. Responsibility, not guilt, is the major theme. Here, too, *Death of a Salesman* has firm roots in Judaic tradition. When one sins in the Old Testament sense, one begs forgiveness not only from God, but from the man one has sinned against. Judaic law is a system for moral interaction governing life as we know it in this world; the choice confronting Judaic man is necessarily an ethical one. Miller takes this inheritance and plants it firmly on socially identifiable ground, the social drama becoming, in this instance, "the drama of the whole man."[26]

Even when Miller uses specifically Jewish characters or historically Jewish tragedies, the emphasis is always on collective man with a capital M. *After the Fall*, for example, is really a play about defending man from himself, from his own destructive impulses. The title of this work refers not only to the Biblical expulsion from the Garden of Eden, but, as the playwright has admitted, to *The Fall* by Albert Camus: a juror walks home along an embankment, sees a Jew thrown into the canal, and does nothing to stop it.[27] The "fall" here is the Holocaust, man's modern banishment from innocence. "Unlike the professed Christian playwrights of our century, for example Eliot, Claudel, or Hofmannsthal, Miller finds the biblical version of the unblessed condition of man less useful to his inquest than the actual memory of the Fall of Man in the twentieth century."[28] The background for this play is, then, Auschwitz rather than Eden: "dominating the stage, is the blasted stone tower of a German concentration camp. Its wide lookout windows are like eyes which at the moment seem blind and dark."[29] In the face of such incomprehensible human misery, the sorrows of Quentin and the memories of his two failed marriages have a certain inevitable naiveté. Miller has been careful to note, however, that this action takes place in "the mind, thought, and memory of the central character. . . . The mind has no color but its memories are brilliant against the grayness of its landscape." Quentin places himself on trial, but standing alongside him in the dock is the Cain that lurks inside every man. The same destructive force that wreaks havoc with one's personal life causes wholesale slaughter when left unchecked in the community of which the individual is a small but representative part. "I think you see patterns finally," Miller observed in 1972:

> Earlier on in life the individual overwhelms your vision. But then when you see three, five, thirty variations of the individual there seems to be an archetype lurking in the background. Consciously, though, I'm still trying and I've always tried to put *people* up there on the stage. . . . But I don't think I could

ever generate the energy to do a whole play just to tell a story about some psychologically interesting folks. I mean, the most psychological of my characters was probably Willy Loman. And I've become aware now that I was dealing with something much more than Willy Loman, the tactile quality of the experience of that one particular character.[30]

In *After the Fall* the "tactile quality" of Quentin's memory is staged on a platform of "neolithic," "lava-like geography." Scenes emerge from small acting areas resembling the "pits and hollows found in lava." When characters sit on this stage, they do so on "abutments, ledges, or crevices," always in the shadow of a stone tower whose "bent reinforcing rods stick out of it like broken tentacles." Designed for an age of inhumanity, the set reaches out to embrace an historical landscape of nihilism, destruction, and death. "When you sell nihilism," Miller once said, "you are selling the grounds for nihilistic destruction, and the first one to get it is the Jew. . . . The Jew is always the one, or most of the time, who stands at the crack of the civilization, in geology it's the shearing point." Much of the struggle of *After the Fall*, he continued, comes from "some very old and imbedded sense that nihilism ends up with a club in its hand."[31] In his play Miller therefore uses the concentration camp not only as the ultimate metaphor for those "burning cities" Quentin refers to in his curtain speech, but more particularly as society's most painful example of "the death of love." In this play the stone tower reveals civilization at its most vulnerable. Yet, curiously enough, *After the Fall* is not a play *about* Jews or even about Auschwitz. It is, instead, a play about responsibility, the parts we all play in holocausts large and small.

Incident at Vichy explores the same theme, though Miller now abandons his strategy of dealing with the Holocaust in symbolic terms. A myth like the Fall of Man can no longer accommodate the brutal horror of human extermination. Even the existential perspective of Camus proves woefully inadequate in facing up to the fact of genocide. This heavily realistic play points its finger at complicity. Miller wastes no time here on depicting the enormity of this historical tragedy, for his subject is individual responsibility, how the actions of one man can make a difference. The scene for this human drama is a detention room where prisoners await the bureaucratic efficiency determining who shall live and who shall die, in this case according to racial lines. But the question of being Jewish is not the one Miller asks in this play; the question of being human is. The focus of attention in *Incident at Vichy* is not, then, on the religious old Jew who goes so "inevitably" to his death, but on the secularized figure of Leduc. Nazis, too, play minor roles in this confrontation of ethical opposites. The spokesman for the non-Jewish world is not a political fanatic, but the articulate and morally sensitive Austrian prince Von Berg. The scene, therefore, avoids any flirtation with absolute evil victimizing absolute innocence. History speaks for itself in this instance, and Miller has no inclination to trivialize its impact.

By centering his drama on the interaction of two non-extremist personalities, Miller is free to concentrate on those few options remaining in an extreme situation. This is why Miller was attracted to a Nazi detention center for this encounter with dehumanization: push liberal man against the wall and make him stare evil in the face. But if Leduc and Von Berg are alike in their horror of political absolutes, they are mighty opposites in that each represents a different moral system. Leduc must make Von Berg see, in the little time that he has left, that it is not the guilt an aristocrat feels that society wants, but his responsibility. Guilt is passive, responsibility active—the same message Chris delivers in the last act of *All My Sons*. Yet by the time of *Incident at Vichy* the situation of responsibility has become somewhat more problematical. Is Von Berg's "heroic" action prompted by a recognition of Leduc's social contract, or is it merely the only way out for a decadent aristocracy to expiate its guilt? Does an isolated act of heroism have any meaning at all in a world gone mad? Is Quentin right in *After the Fall* when he says that "no man lives who would not rather be the sole survivor of this place than all its finest victims"?

But if the prince's motives cannot be calibrated, his action certainly can. Compared to the "decent" army major, who hates the round-up but goes along with it for fear of alienating his superiors, Von Berg offers his "pass" so that Leduc, one Jew, can live. In the last moments of the play the moral aristocrat and the Nazi stand face to face "forever incomprehensible to one another, looking into each other's eyes." But before the curtain falls on this tableau, four more victims are brought into this cell of horror—and that is where guilt must end and responsibility begin. In light of the Jewish history Miller takes as the setting for this play, even the heroes are victims. Martyrdom has become an anachronism. *Incident at Vichy*, therefore, expands a Jewish crisis and makes of it a universal one. "I was not attempting to delineate psychological types," Miller said of this play. "In fact, I did everything to strip the characters of any such thing. The characters were functions of the society, and I wasn't interested in whether they had any itches or not."[32]

The Price, a dramatic confrontation between two estranged brothers at the sale of their dead father's furniture, makes use of another Jewish character, this one with the improbable name of Solomon Gregory Solomon, octogenarian junk dealer. Miller's Solomon is King Solomon in the guise of a comic seer. He has even been likened to the dybbuk of Yiddish folklore, the spirit who inhabits human bodies until he is exorcised.[33] But Miller uses symbolic structure primarily to make character imply social significance. Solomon is cast as a Jew in this play because he is a survivor, the only authentic role mankind can play at this late date in the twentieth century: "Solomon's laughter at the end is also the joy at being almost 90 and back in business again." Portrayed realistically, the two brothers have their being directly in this world. Walter is a prominent surgeon and Victor, who gave up his chance for success to care for the elderly father who lost everything in the Depression, is a lonely cop walking the beat. But something more is involved in this family conflict than the trappings of slice-of-life realism imply. Miller has said that if you extend the characteristics of Walter and Victor into society, "you see that neither one of them could run the world." They are little and local, and therefore painfully recognizable:

The things that can be done by Walter, full of daring, selfishness, power lust and inventiveness, are not the things the other one can do, which is to stick to a job that needs to be done, stay by the hearth and see to it that the fire doesn't go out. The price each pays for being what he is is what it is about.

As this workaday Jacob and Esau try to understand the multiple meanings their different versions of a common past have made on their lives, each struggles with moments of negation and clarity. That is the price they must pay, too. "They are the father's sons," the playwright said recently, "he's in them. That's another reason the old man is laughing at the end. All this human struggle isn't enough. They'll never rid themselves of their father." In selling old furniture the sons are engaged in a vain attempt to rid themselves of the baggage of the past. But what neither son sees is that what they are really selling is their own birthright. Solomon, the collector, preserves and cherishes the past, for he has long ago made his peace with it. In an uneasy present, he knows it paves the only road of survival. Unlike the brothers, whose psychological homecoming will always be an attempt to unburden themselves from a past that defines their existence, Solomon expresses "the welcoming of life" and "the overwhelming of fear." He's lived so long simply because "he's not afraid to live." In harmony with the past, Solomon-the-wise lives in harmony with his present. His future is assured. A domestic anecdote is suddenly charged with universal significance. It is Solomon's ethics, however, not his ethnicity, which enable Miller to elevate the tone of this work to "cast a shadow" on the human condition. In this sense Solomon becomes the playwright's *raisonneur*, the figure who comments on the dramatic action to set it in a social sphere. Solomon embodies the element we miss in a play like O'Neill's *Long Day's Journey into Night*. There the characters are similarly traumatized by a family history forever intruding on the present and threatening their future. "The past is the present, isn't it?" intones Mary Tyrone. "It's the future too. We all try to lie out of that but life won't let us."[34] In *The Price* Miller offers us Solomon's continuity in place of O'Neill's redemption. The family of man cannot be saved unless man preserves society for himself. In selling our inheritance, we sell ourselves short.

Soon after completing *The Creation of the World and Other Business*, Miller noticed something about his plays which should by now be readily apparent: they were becoming "more and more mythological."[35] Yet it is on the construction of Miller's myth that we should center our attention. In *The Creation of the World* . . . Miller's focus is really on the "other business," Cain's murder of his brother Abel. Destruction and creation are inextricably linked. The curtain falls here not on the expulsion from the Garden, but on the archetypal story of man's inhumanity to man. The accent of this play is strictly "after the fall," for the theme once again is one of moral behavior in a familial context—albeit in this case the specific family of man. Though this work shows a considerable weakening of Miller's dramatic power, his fable of social responsibility is as strong as ever. "Ask her pardon," Adam intones in the curtain speech, vainly pleading with his son to appeal to Eve, the *mater dolorosa* of this dramatic moment. As Cain turns away from his parents, Adam cries out:

Cain, we are surrounded by the beasts! And God's not coming any more—*Cain
starts away*. Boy, we are all that's left responsible!—ask her pardon!

The Creation of the World . . ., having abandoned scenic realism for a naked
encounter with the myth that has always been at the center of Miller's work,
takes us all the way back to the closing scene of *All My Sons*. Adam speaks here
in place of Chris Keller, but the moral imperative of his message is equally
unambiguous. "Mercy!," the "clear-eyed prayer" which ends not only Adam's
speech, but the play, is a call not so much to God as it is to mankind. "In God's
name cry mercy, Eve, there is no other!" Justice must be worked out in human,
which is to say familial, terms. We are all our brother's keeper.

The Creation of the World and Other Business, therefore, offers us a highly
ethical interpretation of the ancient Judaic myths. By reducing God to the comic
dimensions of his other dramatis personae in this play, Miller makes him an
actor on the stage, an agent of creation but not the exclusive power above all
others. Man, too, is a formidable protagonist in the action. How different from
Milton, where Christian perspectives like "grace" and "providence" are firmly
contracted in God's merciful hands. In Miller's rendering of the myth, man and
God still occupy center stage. But for Miller the act of creation is not yet
complete. Ethical man must place on it the finishing touches. Cain, however,
lurks somewhere within us, threatening destruction but always capable of something better. That something better is life itself. A play that begins on a whimsical tone has, therefore, become deadly serious by the time the curtain falls.

Yet even when not employing such Biblical figures as God and Lucifer and
Adam and Eve and Cain and Abel, Miller's work develops its tensions from
Judaic archetypes and a morality of justice drawn along Old Testament lines.
Less concerned with local color than with fundamental questions of right and
wrong, Miller recognized early on how a writer could faithfully recapture the
details of ethnic life while steering clear of any real confrontation with what
underlies and ultimately explains a human situation:

> I have stood squarely in conventional realism; I have tried to expand it with an
> imposition of various forms in order to speak more directly, even more abruptly
> and markedly of what has moved me behind the visible façades of life.[36]

Meaning—the meaning beneath the surface tinsel of life—therefore becomes in
Miller's hand "the ultimate reward for having lived." In a long series of totally
articulated works for the American theater, Miller builds "a structure which has
stood instead of collapsing" by incorporating a Jewishness that is not incidental,
but organic.[37] Pursuing his craft as a "serious business," he consistently avoids
the parochial in order to make man "more human, which is to say, less alone."[38]
Written to confront us not only with observations, but with options, his drama is
composed as a distillation of human experience in place of the provincialism of
local color. "The real person only supplies the surface," he mused, "the rest
comes from within."[39] If Miller's decisiveness as a playwright makes him turn

away from the universal in the ethnic particulars of his own background, it makes him celebrate instead the universal in all its human potentiality, not only what man is, but what he can become.

NOTES

1. Clifford Odets, *Awake and Sing!* in *Famous American Plays of the 1930s*, ed. Harold Clurman (New York: Dell, 1959), p. 21.

2. Josh Greenfield, "Writing Plays Is Absolutely Senseless, Arthur Miller Says, 'But I Love It. I Just Love It'," *New York Times Sunday Magazine*, 13 February 1972, p. 37.

3. Arthur Miller, "The Shadows of the Gods" in *The Theater Essays of Arthur Miller*, ed. Robert A. Martin (New York: Penguin, 1978), p. 179.

4. Robert A. Martin, "The Creative Experience of Arthur Miller: An Interview," *Educational Theatre Journal* 21, 3 (October 1969):315–17.

5. "Arthur Miller on Home Ground," Canadian Broadcasting Company documentary in the Spectrum Series, broadcast October 24, 1979.

6. "Arthur Miller: An Interview," *Theater Essays*, p. 292.

7. *Theater Essays*, p. xvii.

8. John O'Connor and Lorraine Brown, *Free, Adult, Uncensored: The Living History of the Federal Theatre Project* (Washington, D. C., 1978), pp. 5, 8.

9. "Many Writers: Few Plays," *Theater Essays*, p. 26.

10. "Arthur Miller on Home Ground."

11. *All My Sons*, in *Famous American Plays of the 1940s*, ed. Henry Hewes (New York: Dell, 1960), p. 201.

12. Ibid., pp. 287–88.

13. "Arthur Miller on Home Ground."

14. Martin, p. 310.

15. "Introduction to the Collected Plays," *Theater Essays*, p. 133.

16. "Arthur Miller on Home Ground."

17. "Introduction to the *Collected Plays*" and "The American Theater."

18. Leslie Fiedler, *Waiting for the End* (New York: Dell, 1965), p. 91; Joel Shatzky, "Is Willy Loman Jewish?" in *Studies in American Jewish Literature* 2 (Winter 1976):1–10.

19. Martin, pp. 314–15.

20. "The Family in Modern Drama," *Theater Essays*, p. 73.

21. *Death of a Salesman* (New York, 1949), p. 11.

22. "Introduction to the *Collected Plays*," p. 170.

23. Martin, p. 312.

24. Robert Brustein, *The Theatre of Revolt* (Boston and Toronto: Little, Brown and Co., 1962), p. 331.

25. "Arthur Miller on Home Ground."

26. *Theater Essays*, p. xix.

27. "Arthur Miller on Home Ground."

28. Alfred Schwarz, *From Büchner to Beckett: Dramatic Theory and the Modes of Tragic Drama* (Athens, Ohio University Press, 1978), p. 173.

29. *After the Fall* (New York: Bantam, 1964), p. 1.

30. Greenfield, p. 37.

31. Martin, pp. 316–17.

32. Greenfield, p. 37.

33. Ralph Tyler, "Arthur Miller Says The Time Is Right For 'The Price'," *The New York Times*, Sunday, June 17, 1979, sec. 2, pp. 1, 6. Miller's comments on *The Price* quoted in my text are taken from this interview.

34. Eugene O'Neill, *Long Day's Journey Into Night* (New Haven: Yale University Press, 1956), p. 87.

35. "Introduction to the *Collected Plays*," p. 167.

36. "On Social Plays," *Theater Essays*, p. 64.

37. "Arthur Miller on Home Ground"; Martin, p. 315.

38. *Theater Essays*, p. xvi.

39. "Arthur Miller on Home Ground."

Paddy Chayefsky's Jews and Jewish Dialogues

Leslie Field

ROBERT BRUSTEIN HAS CALLED PADDY CHAYEFSKY THE "KOHELETH OF KITSCH, the Benefactor of the Benefit Crowd, the Mahomet of Middle Seriousness."[1] A dismissal of this sort is akin to Alfred Kazin's rejection of Thomas Wolfe as a "cipher, a cartoon of the great American Effort, his features as smoothly heroic as Lil Abner's."[2] Brustein's first two epithets imply prostitution. But Chayefsky is no panderer or whore. "Middle Seriousness," however, is open to judgment. I believe the kicking season afflicts a Paddy Chayefsky because he is no Arthur Miller or Clifford Odets as much as it does Thomas Wolfe because he is no William Faulkner.

Faulkner's South is unique. His Yoknapatawpha is a universal county. Likewise Pulpit Hill is universal, although Wolfe's rendition falls short of Faulkner's genius. As seen through the eyes and emotions of Willy Loman, Miller's more lyrically perceived world is a powerful and universal American and Jewish world, even though Miller anglicized the Loman ambience. By contrast, Odets dramatized the American Jew in a starkly naturalistic manner. Chayefsky's Gideon and other Jewish characters are serious figures in American drama who also deserve serious consideration.

In his Jewish plays Chayefsky creates a dramatic medium I choose to call *a dialogue*. Sometimes the protagonist asks God a crucial Jewish question: "Why have you chosen us?" At other times Chayefsky probes the powerful Jewish folkloric motif of the dybbuk. But the dialogue usually focuses on an ongoing dialectic between the playwright and some "other," concerning the theological and ethical parameters of Jewishness.

But to view Paddy Chayefsky simply as a Jewish-American playwright would be reductive. Actually, his most successful dramas—Academy Award-winning film scripts—were *Marty* (1956), *The Hospital* (1971), and *Network* (1976). The earliest of these three has an Italian-American setting, but all three are powerful theater, not because of any focus on ethnicity, but because of Chayefsky's dramatic rendering of universal themes. In *Marty* we have Chayefsky's poignant concern with loneliness; in *The Hospital*, a Kafkaesque bureaucracy; and in his most recent movie, *Network*, a bureaucracy on a most awesome scale: nothing less than major institutions blocking our freedom to know, where information for all is trivialized, commercialized, and ultimately Nazified, a potent dramatization of modern urban man in a world becoming ever more dehumanized.

For about three decades Chayefsky has been analyzed by critics and scholars in a variety of ways. One has been to examine his Oscar films for their excellence, questioning why they are considered better than other films which did not receive awards. Another has been to study his many successful early television

137

dramas. In the 1950s, for example, he was one of the more successful television writers with a dozen or so original plays to his credit produced by various "playhouses" in vogue during the "golden age" of television.[3] Chayefsky had most success with the *Philco Television Playhouse*, under whose aegis *Marty* first appeared. (A published anthology of the television plays includes *The Mother, Holiday Song, The Big Deal, The Bachelor Party, Printer's Measure*, and *Marty*.)[4] Or one could focus on Chayefsky, "the dramatist of disillusionment." Plays that could fit into this category are *Middle of the Night, The Tenth Man, Gideon, The Passion of Joseph D.*, and *The Latent Heterosexual*.[5] Chayefsky the dramatist for the theater has not fared as well as Chayefsky the writer for the small and large screen. However, I have chosen to focus primarily on one aspect of his non-film drama because it reveals much about Chayefsky's craftsmanship and art, especially that which is close to his heart, and which offers clues about significant sources of his work.

In this area of his writing, Chayefsky is a Jewish playwright. Here he not only depicts Jews in a variety of familiar settings, but as he progresses in his craft dramatically and thematically, he creates the Jewish dialogues. In some ways these dialogues are concerned with the same universal problems of loneliness and love found in *Marty* or of success and sterility depicted in *The Goddess*, but in other ways the dialogues have special Jewish characteristics. For example, the early television play *Holiday Song* introduces a question about the existence of a monotheistic God which Jews have always asked about in times of crisis and sombre High Holy Days. The God may be the same one for Jews and non-Jews, but the nature of the questioning and the context in which it takes place is quintessentially Jewish. The special times are not Christian holy days but the most august Jewish holiday, Yom Kippur, the Day of Atonement. Moreover, the Jewish dialogues cannot be separated easily from the burden of Jewish history: the Holocaust, pogroms, Jewish customs, and Jews as a marginal people in a predominantly non-Jewish society.

If one concentrates on the Jewish milieu, *The Big Deal* and *Middle of the Night* are marginal in the Chayefsky canon because in these plays he does not dramatize the more significant Jewish concerns. In these "transitional" Jewish plays Chayefsky seems more interested in depicting assimilated or acculturated American Jews. In *The Tenth Man* and *Gideon*, however, he not only depicts Jews and uses familiar New and Old World Jewish settings, but finally perfects and creates dialogues that have been peculiarly Jewish for centuries. Here Chayefsky moves into the realm of myth, religion, eternal Jewish questioning. His use of *The Dybbuk's* subject matter in *The Tenth Man* and the theme of "chosenness" of the Jews in *Gideon* furnish the content for Chayefsky's most complex Jewish dialogues.

Chayefsky always seemed comfortable with his Jewish roots. Over the years he was an activist in the arts for his fellow Jews and others in the United States, the Soviet Union, and Israel. At the Academy Awards ceremony in 1978 he passionately reprimanded Oscar recipient Vanessa Redgrave for her propagandistic, intemperate, anti-Jewish, anti-Zionist diatribe. Chayefsky wore his Jewish identity with ease, and his work reflects his Jewish concerns. Concerning his early (1952) *Philco Television Playhouse* version of *Holiday Song*, Chayefsky said:

> I happen to be Jewish, and my understanding of the religious emotion is limited to the Jewish ritual, so my leading character automatically became Jewish. At the time I sat down to the adaptation, I was governed by an almost compulsive interest in Jewish folklore and humor. I had been wanting to write a show about synagogue life for years. I think it was beyond my conscious control to keep from imposing this long-repressed synagogue story onto this adaptation. [*T.V. Plays*, p. 37]

This early work, the first one-hour television drama Chayefsky wrote, was an adaptation based on a *Reader's Digest* article. But it was much more than adaptation. Chayefsky, with his unerring sense of theater and television drama, took the bare bones of the original and created his own conflict, tension, and drama in his script.

"I am not good at adaptations," Chayefsky has said, "and my final draft was only vaguely related to the original property" (*T.V. Plays*, p. 35). Moreover, Chayefsky feels that "a novel or a short story . . . do not lend themselves comfortably to dramatic exploitation" (*T.V. Plays*, p. 35). Nevertheless, he did with the article/story what he feels an adapter must do by "picking a kernel of a story from his material and improvising his own characters and insights" (*T.V. Plays*, p. 35).

The original *Reader's Digest* article was entitled "It Happened on the Brooklyn Subway." A photographer riding on the subway learns that the man beside him lost his wife in a concentration camp. Suddenly the photographer recalls a similar story told to him by a woman some time back. Putting two and two together, he soon reunites long-lost husband and wife. A wonderful coincidence has taken place, perhaps a miracle. But Chayefsky believed there was not enough "drama" in the original story despite its Holocaust connection. Suspense, yes, but not drama. For Chayefsky, the real drama of the story is that it illustrates "one dramatic meaning, and that is: there is a God" (*T.V. Plays*, p. 36).

The *Reader's Digest* plot involves solely a photographer who sees first a wife and then a husband who have been separated. He reunites them. The miracle is the reunification of two who have been at the abyss separately and are now together in comfort. God or faith engineers the miraculous reunion. In the Chayefsky play the subway episode is more or less incidental. Cantor Sternberger, the counterpart of the photographer, reunites the couple, and their reunion brings back his own faith miraculously so that he can once more act as a spiritual leader to his congregation at the time of the High Holy Days.

So Chayefsky the dramatist feels he must work out his own drama, which would focus on the "kernel" he has extracted from the original. He must create a character for whom the meaning, the kernel—"there is a God"—becomes all-important. Chayefsky, therefore, decides upon "a religious man who has lost his faith in God." This character must be put into a situation of "urgency," and once the circumstances and characters are created to convince us of the urgency, the Chayefsky drama or Jewish dialogue appears. This "kernel" of an idea, slight as it is, anticipates his important later plays—*The Tenth Man* and *Gideon*.

Chayefsky does not claim a great deal for this early work. In addition to the *Reader's Digest* source, Chayefsky "wanted to tell a charming folktale about a small Jewish community struck by the catastrophe of its cantor refusing to sing for the High Holidays. . . . In the first version . . . the concept of the community disappeared and the story was sliced down to the less involved story of an old man who had lost his faith in God" (*T.V. Plays*, p. 37). He concludes that although he meant "the show to be a comedy after the fashion of Sholom Aleichem, . . . it came out a rather ponderous spiritual message" (*T.V. Plays*, p. 37).

Chayefsky may be too hard on this television play. It has fast movement, clean conflict, and sharp resolution, and, above all, it shows Chayefsky's gift for dialogue. The Yiddish style and rhythms are omnipresent. Naomi, the cantor's niece, speaks the semi-educated Americanized English/Yiddish that later became so popular in the works of Bellow and Malamud:

> He's been lying in his bed for two days, looking at the ceiling. Like I told you over the phone, I bring him in his meals. He doesn't touch a thing. I ask him—are you fasting? What Holiday is it that you're fasting? [*T.V. Plays*, p. 4]

In response to Sexton Zucker's "But I don't see you laugh no more," Cantor Sternberger gives the obvious Yinglish retort: "What's to laugh?" (*T.V. Plays*, p. 6).

When the cantor says "Zucker, I . . . I . . . I believe I have lost my faith!" the sexton comes up with this plan: The cantor is to seek out "Rabbi Marcus of New York City, a Sage on earth!" (*T.V. Plays*, p. 9). On his way to see Rabbi Marcus, Cantor Sternberger gets lost on the subway. The subway confusion provides many comedic opportunities before the miracle takes place and the cantor resumes his rightful place, leading his congregation in song on the Jewish High Holy Days. All is resolved at the eleventh hour.

The television play was delightful popular comedy, especially for the New York Jewish audiences. John M. Clum argues that this early Chayefsky piece and his two other *Philco Television Playhouse* dramas of the early 1950s—*The Reluctant Citizen* (1952) and *Printer's Measure* (1953)—can be seen as a trilogy: "Their theme is the conflict between the traditional society of the Old World and the New World technology and the modern city."[6] *The Reluctant Citizen*, like *Holiday Song*, has an urban, Jewish setting. *Printer's Measure*, is about urban Irish-Americans. In all three plays, however, an older man is the protagonist, and "Chayefsky's three old men are transitional figures who are the products of a simpler age but who have to live in a post-war America."[7]

The Big Deal (1953) and *Middle of the Night* (1954) both appeared on the *Philco Television Playhouse*. *Middle of the Night* was made into a Broadway play and still later into a movie. Both dramas depict an assimilated American Jew who suffers. The protagonists, Joe Manx of *The Big Deal* and Jerry Kingsley of *Middle of the Night*, have, apparently, replaced their Jewish names with anglicized versions. They are not traditional figures transplanted from the Old World to the New like Cantor Sternberger and old Mr. Kimmer of *The Reluctant Citizen*. Manx and Kingsley have "arrived." They are very comfortable in their New World settings and take them for granted. Their problems are not unlike those of countless other "successful" urbanites of Greek, Italian, or even WASP origin. But "success" is a loaded word here. Joe Manx was once a success but is now a failure. He once had a contracting business in Toledo, Ohio, but things went bad and he lost his business. He has spent the last twelve years dwelling on the great yesterdays and thinking of grandiose schemes for the tomorrows while he and his wife live on his dutiful daughter's small income.

The Big Deal is aptly titled in that the climax of the play involves Joe Manx's realization that there may be more to life than "the big deal" he hungers for, especially if it means that he may have to gamble with his daughter's $5,000 dowry (inherited from an aunt) and destroy his loving wife in the bargain. In the end Joe realizes that he has overlooked a success in life that may be more important than a "pie-in-the-sky" contracting deal; that is, the love lavished on him by his daughter and wife.

The Big Deal is a very American urban/domestic realistic drama; it has strong parallels with Miller's *Death of a Salesman*. Neither Willy Loman nor Joe Manx has to be Jewish to suffer as he does. But they are tortured Jewish characters who feel somehow that they have not fulfilled themselves. (It has been frequently observed that despite Miller's attempt to "Americanize" his play, the rhythms are Jewish rhythms.) Whether Willy or Joe realize it or not, they are operating within the Jewish context of family, community, and Israel. Here Israel acts not as a modern nation, but as a social-historical-cultural-religious context. And in this context they have failed to provide, to educate, to enrich their wife and children. In both *Death of a Salesman* and *The Big Deal*, the aspiring businessman attempts to work out his personal destiny and execute his family responsibilities within the confines of urban America. Because he is unable to meet these two often conflicting demands, he suffers terrible guilt.

However, in Chayefsky's *Middle of the Night* Jerry Kingsley's suffering is somewhat different. Unlike Joe Manx, Kingsley *is* a successful manufacturer. But he is lonely in what seems to him an increasingly sterile work-society-family situation. He has made his place in the garment industry, but his wife is dead, his married daughter has her own life, and he now lives with his possessive sister. In the lives of his associates and former friends, Kingsley sees only sickness, death, and unhappy sexual adventuring. He is annoyed by the ministrations of his daughter and sister; life must have more meaning for him. He notices another lonely person who needs love and companionship—his employee, Betty Preiss, a pretty girl half Jerry's age. Her marriage is unhappy and she wants to be released from it. Betty and Jerry meet when they are both at low points in their lives, and they fall in love. One conflict involves their age and their positions. Another centers on the hostility of the respective families to the marriage. A third, but minor one, touches on the "Jewish question." Jerry is a Jew; Betty is not.

Both *The Big Deal* and *Middle of the Night* are the stuff of melodrama and soap opera. They are mixtures of realistic depiction of situation and character which the television and theater audiences could and did identify with, but in both there is also a strong thread of romanticism. Can Joe Manx give up his dream of becoming a millionaire once again? Can a middle-aged manufacturer find happiness with an attractive girl no older than his own daughter? For Chayefsky the answer to both questions is a resounding *yes!*

In both dramas ethnicity or Jewishness is more in setting, language, and rhythm than in something that can be labeled authentic Jewish dialogue. *The Big Deal* has been criticized because its locale is Toledo, Ohio, although the language smacks more of Jewish Brooklyn or the Bronx.[8] However, even today one finds pockets of transplanted New Yorkers in places like Mason City, Iowa, or Toledo, Ohio. At one point Joe's wife recalls the past to their daughter: "Before we were married, he used to take me to the Hippodrome in New York City. At that time, the Hippodrome was the big date of all dates" (*T.V. Plays*, p. 111). So in this speech and others one gets a sense of the New York Jewish urbanite who has resettled in the Midwest. Here and elsewhere syntax and context strongly suggest Jewish/Yinglish.

Similarly, in the *Middle of the Night* the little touches, the brief exchanges of dialogue give one a sense of the Jewish scene. Jerry lives in an apartment on West End Avenue, where Jews customarily congregated at the time; his sister plays matchmaker, a traditional Jewish role, which has been dramatized so well in *Fiddler on the Roof*. Dialogue often consists of inverted syntax, first names of characters are typically Jewish-American, the play's locale can readily be found on any Jewish map of the urban Eastern Seaboard, and the characters can be easily identified as affluent, assimilated Jewish New Yorkers.

Aside from these external Jewish trappings, both *The Big Deal* and *Middle of the Night* revolve around the more general themes of success, failure, loneliness, love. We almost hear Chayefsky saying that the characters he writes about are Jews only because he, Chayefsky, happens to be Jewish and that cultural milieu is the one he knows best. But this does not obligate him to write about exclusively Jewish matters. Moreover, when he wants to switch to Italian-American, he writes *Marty*, or to Irish-American, he writes *Printer's Measure*, and so on.

However, as Chayefsky's career developed, he became interested in the larger Jewish dialogues. Jews and Jewishness are not simply window dressing for his dramas. By the time Chayefsky wrote *The Tenth Man* (1959) and *Gideon* (1961), he was immersed in the crucial Jewish subject matter: chosenness, Jewish ritual, folklore, transplantation from the *shtetl* to America, faith and disbelief.

The Tenth Man, Chayefsky's most successful play (it ran on Broadway for eighteen months[9]), is about a figure often encountered in Yiddish folklore, the dybbuk, "the spirit of a dead person that enters the body of a living person and possesses it."[10] *The Tenth Man* draws on S. Ansky's classical Yiddish play, *The Dybbuk* (1920), whose enthusiastic reception through the years confirms the fact that the dybbuk story has captured the imagination of Jews much as the story of Faust has captivated the imagination of Christians.

Ansky's play is myth, ritual, pageant, melodrama, tragedy. Its subtitle, "Between Two Worlds," emphasizes dramatic force or tension between heaven and earth or hell and earth. Set in the *shtetl* of Eastern Europe, its atmosphere is suffused with old Hasidism,[11] which emphasized the heart and mysteries of man and the universe rather than man's intellect.

Ansky's play is in four acts. In the first a penniless student of the Talmud, Khonen, falls in love with Leah, daughter of a rich merchant, Sender, who wants a rich young man for his daughter. Meanwhile Khonen studies the mysterious work of the *Kabbalah*,[12] and as Sender fails time after time to find a suitor for his daughter, Khonen believes he has triumphed both in his unraveling of the *Kabbalah* and the winning of the bride of his choice. But Sender does find a wealthy man, Menassah, for Leah; Khonen then falls dead of grief in the synagogue.

In the second act Leah visits the grave of her mother and invites her to the forthcoming wedding, then visits Khonen's grave and invites him, too. When the groom visits Leah, she shouts at him and acts like one possessed; the voice of the dybbuk (Khonen) says that he is within her and she is Khonen's predestined bride.

In the third act a *minyan* of Jews and the Hasidic rabbi attempt to exorcise the dybbuk from Leah. There are complications. The chief rabbi has had a dream in which he has seen the fathers of Leah and Khonen. The fathers have had a dispute which has never been resolved. Years ago they vowed that if they (Sender and Nissen) should each father a child of the opposite sex, these children would be betrothed at birth. Nissen died, and Sender did not know that Khonen was Nissen's child. Justice demands that Sender make amends.

The rabbi recounts his dream, and it is agreed that a rabbinical court must decide upon Sender's punishment. But the spirit of Nissen will not accept the verdict. So the rabbi must use exorcism to force out the dybbuk which has inhabited Leah. Black candles, a *minyan*, incantations, the ram's horn are all used. Kohnen's spirit leaves Leah, but she dies and her spirit joins his in death, in the other world. The bargain struck years ago is consummated.[13]

Chayefsky's *The Tenth Man*, a modern version of *The Dybbuk*, also deals with two worlds: that of the Old World Jewish types transplanted to Mineola, Long Island, and that of young Jews born in America, who inhabit the same geographical place but have "new" ideas.

The storefront *shul* is a way of life for the old-timers. Some are religious in an Old World Hasidic sense. Most are not. The *shul* is simply a place for them to go, to meet, to pass the time of day. This small congregation shows the whole spectrum of religious feeling, from the faith of the resident *Kabbalist* to the unbelief of the militant socialist/atheist.

The action of the play takes place in the Mineola synagogue on a cold February day. The chief concern of the "regulars" is to get ten men for the *minyan* so that the ark can be opened and the prayers read. The "modern" rabbi, concerned with youth groups, fund raising, and adult education sessions, has no time for religious ritual. The few old-timers are the mainstay of the daily operation of the *shul*. Evelyn Foreman, the eighteen-year-old granddaughter of one of the old men, is thought to be possessed by a *Dybbuk*. Her grandfather brings her to the synagogue because he fears that she will soon be committed to a mental institution. Evelyn claims she is speaking as "the soul of Hannah Luchinsky," whom her grandfather "dishonored and weakened" in his youth so that "the gates of heaven are closed" to her.[14]

The grandfather explains that "Hannah was the handsome one who became pregnant, and they threw stones at her, called her harlot, and drove her out of the city" (*TM*, p. 17). Evelyn insists that she is "the whore of Kiev, the companion of sailors" (*TM*, p. 21). Foreman wants the advice of a renowned rabbi in New York in order to rid Evelyn of the *Dybbuk*.

Arthur Landau, divorced lawyer, freethinker, and drunk, comes on the scene. One of the elders asks him to fill out the *minyan*. He agrees but says he wants to get in and out of the synagogue in twenty minutes. He has been on a three-day binge; he is agitated and wants to see his psychiatrist. He meets the regulars and catches a glimpse of Evelyn, who has been hidden in the rabbi's office. Evelyn immediately falls in love with Arthur and wants him to marry her. Arthur is nonplussed by everything—the old men, the outlandish rituals in the synagogue, the proposed exorcism, and Evelyn's "love" for him.

Evelyn and Arthur talk in psychiatric jargon while the ritual proceeds. The juxtaposition of their talk and the ancient chants emphasizes the differences between the two modes, ancient and modern, of dealing with Evelyn's problem. Evelyn says:

> I'm being institutionalized again. Dr. Molinaux's Sanitarium in Long Island. I'm a little paranoid and hallucinate a great deal and have very little sense of reality, except for brief interludes like this . . . [*TM*, p. 66].

For Arthur, the problem is that he can no longer love: "Television . . . is a bore and ardent love is an immense drain on one's energy" (*TM*, p. 70). Later he says to Evelyn:

> I don't know what you mean by love! All it means to me is I shall buy you a dinner, take you to the theatre, and then straight to our tryst, where I shall reach under your blouse for the sake of tradition while you breathe hotly in my ear in a pretense of passion. [*TM*, p. 129]

Both Arthur and Evelyn parrot the dogmas learned from their respective psychiatrists. At first neither understands, or is even really listening to, the other. Then Evelyn grasps something in their soliloquies, an epiphany: "You are possessed," she says. "You are possessed by a dybbuk that does not allow you to love!" (*TM*, p. 129).

In Ansky's play there is a battle between reason and mysticism, the "other" world and the earth world, injustice and justice, materialism and love; Chayefsky shows us a battle between reason and emotion, between cynicism and love. In both plays the last act concentrates on the exorcism of the *dybbuk*. Chayefsky's scenes are also replete with the traditional *minyan* of men with prayer shawls, black candles, the blowing of the *Shofar*, and incantations. In *The Dybbuk* Leah dies and her spirit joins Khonen's; in *The Tenth Man* the cynic, the rationalist, the freethinker, is converted. He wants to live and love: "Dybbuk," he says, "hear me. I will cherish this girl, and give her a home. I will tend to her needs and hold her in my arms when she screams out with your voice. Her soul is mine now—her soul, her charm, her beauty—even you, her insanity, are mine" (*TM*, p. 153).

Although some of Chayefsky's critics have complained that the play is too simplistic, too pat, *The Tenth Man* does work well. True, Arthur's conversion is sudden. But taken in the context of the other elements of the play, it seems to stand up. The transplanted Old World types are alive. They show us what it is to be East European Jews in a New York community in the middle of the twentieth century. We see the second- and third-generation Jews adjusting to the New World and at the same time being recalled to the old, traditional, folkloristic world of the Jews. We sense the tension between Jewish superstition and trendy American patterns. Above all, we see the common denominator of love, which tends to homogenize the Old and New World settings.

Kenneth Tynan, reviewing the play for *The New Yorker*, wrote that Chayefsky reveals "his shortcomings as a thinker," but is a "wonderful creative listener."

> The best of his Jewish dialogue is as meaty as any I've heard since the heyday of Clifford Odets. Lou Jacobi as belligerent atheist who jettisons his principles in order to participate in the climactic ritual gets the funniest lines, and every word uttered by Arnold Marle, the ancient exorcist, shines and quivers with conviction.[15]

Tynan has equally enthusiastic observations about other members of the cast and of the dialogue, even though he admits he "failed to understand" all the Yiddishisms. Actually, Tynan was ambivalent about the play. On the one hand, he scored Chayefsky the thinker and the user of stereotypes; on the other, he liked the fast-moving, suspenseful, and charming ambience of the whole.[16]

In a longish essay in *Commentary*, Anatole Shub is much harsher. He labels the play "popular psychoanalysis," pop culture, and "murky."[17] "Arthur's mixed motives and Evelyn's mixed-up madness," he says, "show the irony with which Chayefsky treats both religion and psychiatry, permitting the spectator to believe what he pleases."[18] Then Shub asks:

> How are we to take the miracle we have just witnessed? Until the last few

seconds, Chayefsky seems to have covered all flanks. But the pretentious
sentimentality of the final moment reveals his condescending attitude toward
religion, psychiatry, thought generally, the Jews and his own creation.[19]

In effect, Shub feels that the theme of love and the dybbuk myth have been used
"cheaply." He believes that Ansky in his original play, and Singer in *Satan in
Goray* and other works with similar themes, have done much better.[20]

Robert Brustein's review is even harsher: the actors, he says, except for
Arnold Marle, "are concerned less with acting in depth than with ingratiating
themselves with the audience,"[21] and the play itself reveals that "Chayefsky
holds no traditional religious doctrine; instead he melts down all doctrines into
the gluey ooze of love."[22]

Despite such hostile criticism, in *The Tenth Man* I believe Chayefsky had
worked out his most comprehensive and sophisticated Jewish dialogue. And as
with his earlier Jewish plays the settings and characters are important. One is
immersed in the first- and second-generation Jewish types at the old synagogue:
socialist, *Kabbalist*, pragmatist, the "modern" rabbi, and others. The old men
who make up the daily *minyan* use the synagogue as a social place. But even
though most are disbelievers, they want to believe, and when the exorcism takes
place, they are given the opportunity to return to their roots—to a simpler time
in the old country when authentic religion permeated their everyday lives.

In *The Tenth Man* Chayefsky makes the Old World myth of the Jews work in a
modern setting. Arthur and Evelyn are Jews caught up in a chaotic universe, far
removed from their Jewish roots. The elders of the synagogue and even the
modern rabbi are adrift. But all can and do draw upon the folklore and faith of
their fathers. Even though the *Dybbuk* story differs from the original, the Chayefsky version dramatizes a crucial moment when Jews come together and are
sustained by ancient superstition, folklore, myth, faith.

There is also Chayefsky's compulsion to introduce slapstick, farce, and Yiddishisms which typify mid-twentieth century life in the Jewish sections of New
York—behavior that his New York audiences understood and loved. For example, he evokes laughter by showing one old-timer after another becoming befuddled and lost on subway rides (echoes of the earlier *Holiday Song*) while they
look for the wonder rabbi in New York. There are also the familiar curses voiced
by the retired and displaced old-country types as they put up with their modern
in-laws and children. Early on, Zitorsky says: "My daughter-in-law, may she
grow rich and buy a hotel with a thousand rooms and be found dead in every one
of them." And Schlissel, not to be outdone, adds: "My daughter-in-law, may
she invest heavily in General Motors, and the whole thing should go bankrupt"
(*TM*, p. 5).

John Clum sees *The Tenth Man* as "a turning point for Chayefsky: he added a
mythic dimension to his penchant for realistic setting and dialogue. No longer
satisfied with telling touching stories about average people, Chayefsky began to
dig deeper, to try to lay bare the spiritual malaise that cripples many modern
men."[23] That this was indeed a "turning point" becomes obvious when one
examines Chayefsky's probing of man and his institutions in the plays and

scripts that followed: *Gideon, The Passion of Josef D., The Latent Heterosexual, The Hospital,* and *Network*.

Gideon (1961) is his last thoroughly Jewish play. As with *The Tenth Man,* Chayefsky drew upon a myth or classical story of the Jews. His "kernel" is from the book of Judges.

Chayefsky focuses on that transitional period in Jewish history after Joshua— when the Jews were trying to establish themselves in the land of Canaan. God's emissary comes to a simple rural man, Gideon, much as he did to Moses earlier, and tells Gideon he will be the instrument for defeating the Midianites. In Judges Gideon accomplishes his task as God ordered and we simply have another episode in the centuries of movement toward the establishing of a Jewish presence in the Holy Land. *Judges* reveals much backsliding by the Jews, who early on had rejected monotheism. But then Gideon rallies his fellow Jews around him as he obeys God and triumphs.[24]

In both the original and Chayefsky's version we have a simple farmer, Gideon, who is called upon by God to act as leader and to defeat the enemies of the Jews. In both cases we are shown that God is to be considered the victor, not man. In Chayefsky's reworking of the story, however, we have a dialogue which has been compared to the great debates between God and Job in the biblical book of Job and in Archibald Macleish's *JB*.

In Chayefsky's play Gideon challenges God rather than the reverse. The play opens with the simple shepherd being chosen by the angel to represent God and lead his people against the Midianites. Gideon is a practical man. He wants proof that he is talking to a representative of God. (At times Chayefsky's Gideon sounds like Bill Cosby's Noah.) And he gets proof much as Moses did before him. During most of the play Gideon follows God's commandments, no matter how bizarre. He, therefore, routs the enemy and triumphs. Quickly Gideon, the common herdsman, becomes the great hero. And this is where the simple tale or "kernel" from *Judges* takes on a thematic significance and the Jewish dialogue emerges that is original to Chayefsky.

For God, the glory must be his; Gideon is only his instrument. But Gideon can't accept this subordinate position. He wants to assert his personhood. When the people acclaim him, Gideon becomes very human. He can't follow God's will simply because God insists: Gideon feels that his individuality is being threatened. And so in Chayefsky's *Gideon* we have the classic confrontation between Man and his God, betwen individualism and Judaic theology. Toward the end the angel says to Gideon: "You have given the life of men greater value than the work of God."[25] And Gideon says to the Lord: "Let me at least have some bogus value" (*Gideon,* p. 66). But the angel answers: "Hear me well, O Hebrew. I am a Jealous God and brook no other Gods, not even you. . . . Do not make a cult of man, not even in fancy" (*Gideon,* p. 66). Then Gideon counters once again by saying that being a servant of the Lord is not enough: "I must aspire, God." And later he says: "If you love me, let me believe at least in mine own self. If you love me, God!" (*Gideon,* p. 68).

Ultimately, the angel, the emissary of God, admits that he still loves Gideon.

He realizes, as God does, the weakness of man. Similarly, Melville in *Moby-Dick* had Father Mapple preach his version of the *Story of Jonah:* "If you accept God, you must deny yourself." This is a message in *Job* too. But Gideon seems to be saying in his dialogue that man cannot deny himself; he must be an individual too. He can accept God—but only within limits. He cannot permit God to make of man a cipher.

Gideon did not have as long a run in the theater as did *The Tenth Man*, and it opened to mixed reviews; some praised it highly. Susan M. Black, writing in *Theatre Arts Magazine*, notes that she was inspired to reread chapters six through eight of the *Book of Judges*. And her view is that Chayefsky transformed a rather perfunctory Biblical story into a dynamic drama.[26]

An anonymous reviewer in *Newsweek* divided his space between comments on the play and Chayefsky's own observations at an opening night party. The reviewer noted that in *Gideon* Chayefsky "is less concerned with violent ancient history than with creating a modern parable on the relationship between man and his God. . . . The major issues in *Gideon* are of the mind and the heart; they are clear-cut and explored with a clarity of thought and writing that turns Chayefsky's modest profundities into profoundly stimulating theater."[27]

Then the reviewer captures the mood and Chayefsky's own words after the play when those connected with it are celebrating at Sardi's. "My play," Chayefsky said, "is not about God testing Gideon, it's about Gideon testing God."[28]

Then Chayefsky commented about his "early struggles" with the play to render it *authentic:*

> The first time I wrote it I tried to keep the authentic archaic dialogue, but it was quite pretentious. It wouldn't work adjectiveless. It was terribly difficult to make it colloquial and yet keep it away from the modern idiom. Whenever possible I tried to keep to the straight Bible. . . . In the Bible God comes down frequently and chats. He chats away. . . . He's a very amiable sort of God. . . . What is God? That area of uncertainty that man can never know. Can't that uncertainty be dramatized? . . . *Gideon* . . . is pure existentialism. Not Sartre existentialism, but theological existentialism, Tillich and Buber existentialism.[29]

Such was the more or less favorable critical reception and Chayefsky's own revealing commentary. But one week after Chayefsky's remarks appeared in *Newsweek*, Robert Brustein in a long review in *The New Republic* damned Chayefsky as the playwright who "now leads all rivals as the Koheleth of Kitsch."[30] Brustein continued:

> It would not surprise me if Chayefsky, before writing *Gideon*, had made a sociological depth study of upward mobility among the newly rich, the growing religiosity in the suburbs, and just how much rebellion an audience is willing to tolerate before running for the exit.[31]

There is more, much more in this vein by Brustein. I believe it is safe to say that he was not enamored of Chayefsky's *Gideon*.

Gideon completes the circle of Paddy Chayefsky's most significant Jewish dialogues. He went on to write other dramas, most notably *Network*, the recent blockbuster for the movies. Were it not for his untimely death, he would continue to write vitally important religious and secular parables for the theater.

While Chayefsky was still living, John Clum summed up his achievement this way:

> Paddy Chayefsky is now at the height of his powers as a writer. He has
> moved from the area of sentimental, realistic comedy to satire; and he has, in
> the process, become one of the few living dramatists with the combination of
> perception and wit that is needed if a playwright is to follow the path of the
> great writers of comedies of manners.[32]

Clum goes on to say that Chayefsky, in his dramas, has shown man making a "chaos" of his world because he lacks "perception" or because he refuses to "accept social responsibility." Furthermore, says Chayefsky, our institutions ultimately rob us of our individuality.[33] This is a great evil, Chayefsky believes. Clum's overview of Chayefsky and Chayefsky's own insight into himself as a writer apply directly to his Jewish dramas. In addition, Chayefsky's methods of creating his dramas and his large questions within the plays cannot and should not be dissociated from Chayefsky as a Jewish writer.

When Henry James wrote *The Aspern Papers*, he plucked out incidents from his own past in Italy and from his reading of the English Romantic poets, primarily about Byron and his circle. James's use of his past and his reading supplied only a fraction of his final story. But his feel for Venice of bygone days, for the ambience of the Byron circle, for the "dustiness" of time eventually seeped into the pages of *The Aspern Papers* even though his final story departed drastically from the actual incestuous Byron situation and other "facts" that launched James into his story telling.[34]

Chayefsky's efforts and accomplishments in plays like *The Tenth Man* and *Gideon* are analogous. Chayefsky at his most realistic depicts Jews he has known and read about. Their strengths, weaknesses, and interactions have become a part of the dramatist's creative life. Thus the Jewish experience of the Holocaust impels Chayefsky to create concentration camp victims as characters. The awesome days of atonement (Yom Kippur) naturally provide a crisis situation for a Jew troubled about his own faith. How can a Jew confess his sins at this time if he doubts God's very existence? For Jews the *dybbuk* is as meaningful folklore as are the myths and stories of the folk that Hawthorne rendered imaginatively for his American Christian readers. Or one can take the Mosaic idea of God. The Jews are God's chosen people. But what does that mean to Gideon, a simple, Biblical representative of the Jews? To be a Jew one must accept God and his commandments. Simultaneously one must relinquish elements of an all-too-human individualism. Chayefsky's Gideon is a very human Jew; his God is ultimately a God of love and understanding.

Chayefsky, in dramatizing his Jews and creating his Jewish dialogues, has indeed built upon his "kernels." Whether or not the kernels or acorns grew into giant oaks may be debatable. But in a non-metaphoric way, one can say that in the best of his plays—*The Tenth Man* and *Gideon*—Chayefsky has produced Jewish drama as forthright, perceptive, and enjoyable as any written today in America.

NOTES

1. Robert Brustein, "All Hail, Mahomet of Middle Seriousness," *The New Republic*, 27 November 1961, p. 21.

2. Alfred Kazin's review of Andrew Turnbull's *Thomas Wolfe, Washington Post Book World*, 28 January 1968, p. 1.

3. To capture a feeling for this period, is has been very helpful to draw upon Marvin Newton Diskin, "A Description and Historical Analysis of the Live Television Anthology Drama Program: The United States Steel Hour, 1953–1963," Diss., University of Michigan, 1963.

4. Paddy Chayefsky, *Television Plays* (1954; rpt. New York: Simon and Schuster, 1971). Subsequent references to the plays in this collection and to Chayefsky's commentaries will appear parenthetically in the text as *T.V. Plays*.

5. See John M. Clum, *Paddy Chayefsky* (Boston: Twayne Publishers, 1976), chapter 3. This is the only book-length study of Chayefsky.

6. Clum, p. 40.

7. Ibid.

8. See Clum, p. 43.

9. Ibid.

10. *Dybbuk* definition, quoted from *Webster's New World Dictionary*, Second College Edition (New York: World Publishing Co., 1972), p. 436.

11. *Hassidism, Chassidism,* or *Hasidism* is "a popular religious movement giving rise to a pattern of communal life and leadership as well as a particular social outlook which emerged in Judaism and Jewry in the second half of the 18th Century. Ecstasy, mass enthusiasm, close-knit group cohesion, and charismatic leadership of one kind or another are the distinguishing socioreligious marks of *Hasidism.*" See *Encyclopedia Judaica*, Vol. 7, p. 1390; see also pp. 1390–1432.

12. *Kabbalah* "is a unique phenomenon, and should not generally be equated with what is known in the history of religion as 'mysticism.' It is mysticism in fact; but at the same time it is both esotericism and theosophy. In what sense it may be called mysticism depends on the definition of the term, a matter of dispute among scholars. If the term is restricted to the profound yearning for direct human communion with God through annihilation of individuality . . . , then only a few manifestations of *Kabbalah* can be designated as such, because few *Kabbalists* sought this goal, let alone formulated it openly as their final aim. However, *Kabbalah* may be considered mysticism in so far as it seeks an apprehension of God and creation whose intrinsic elements are beyond the grasp of the intellect, although this is seldom explicitly belittled or rejected by the *Kabbalah*." See *Encyclopedia Judaica*, Vol. 10, p. 490; see also pp. 490–653.

13. See S. Ansky, *The Dybbuk*, trans. and ed. S. Morris Engel, rev. third ed. (South Bend, Indiana: Regnery/Gateway, Inc., 1979); see also David S. Lifson, *The Yiddish Theatre in America* (New York: Thomas Yoseloff, 1965), pp. 103–16.

14. Paddy Chayefsky, *The Tenth Man* (New York: Random House, 1960), p. 16. Subsequent references will appear parenthetically in the text as *TM*.

15. Kenneth Tynan, rev. of *The Tenth Man, The New Yorker*, 14 November 1959, p. 121.

16. Tynan, p. 121. In a way, Gore Vidal echoed Tynan: "*The Tenth Man* is a clever and charming theater piece, well staged and well acted, and yet its conclusion is pat,

sentimental, and familiar." See "The Couch in the Shrine," *The Reporter*, 10 December 1959, p. 39.

17. Anatole Shub, "Paddy Chayefsky's Minyan: *The Tenth Man* on Broadway," *Commentary* 28 (December 1959): 523.

18. Shub, p. 525.

19. Ibid.

20. Ibid., p. 527.

21. Robert Brustein, "Love Does It Again," *The New Republic*, 23 November 1959, p. 21.

22. Ibid., p. 22.

23. Clum, p. 70.

24. See A. Cohen, ed., *Soncino Books of the Bible: Joshua/Judges* (London, Jerusalem, New York: The Soncino Press, 1976), pp. 203–232.

25. Paddy Chayefsky, *Gideon* (New York: Dramatists Play Service, Inc., 1962), p. 65. Subsequent references will appear parenthetically in the text as *Gideon*.

26. Susan M. Black, rev. of *Gideon*, *Theatre Arts Magazine*, January 1962, p. 11. She goes on to say that *Gideon*, "despite the weakness of its second act, is far more substantial than the runty comedies and mysteries currently on Broadway. This bold amplification of Judges 6–8 is intellectually provocative and commendably acted, staged, and directed."

27. "Man and His God," *Newsweek*, 20 November 1961, p. 69.

28. Ibid.

29. Ibid.

30. Brustein (1961), p. 21.

31. Ibid.

32. Clum, pp. 134–35.

33. Clum, p. 135.

34. See Henry James, *The Art of the Novel*, ed. R. P. Blackmur (New York: Charles Scribner's Sons, 1962), pp. 159–79.

Neil Simon's Jewish-style Comedies

Daniel Walden

MODERN AMERICAN JEWISH HUMOR HAS ITS ROOTS IN THE HUMOR OF THE
shtetlach, the Jewish ghettoes of Eastern Europe. Based on a recognition of the
power of the surrounding community and the helplessness of the Jews, it fused
sentiment with irony and self-satire with earthiness. Alienated from the mainstream, pressured to convert, lacerated by persecutions and pogroms, Jews in
the nineteenth century used religion, folklore, fantasy, mysticism, and humor to
survive and, almost miraculously, flourish.

From this cultural milieu, several generations of Jewish comics and writers
have emerged. Jack Benny, Eddie Cantor, Georgie Jessel, Smith and Dale and
so many more came out of the Lower East Side, one generation away from
Eastern Europe. Woody Allen, Jerry Lewis, Soupy Sales, Lenny Bruce, Joan
Rivers, David Steinberg, and Don Rickles are their heirs. Intellectually overdeveloped at the same time they are emotionally and sexually underdeveloped
(or sexually overdeveloped), these stand-up comics are urban, sharp, sophisticated, infantile, arrogant. So, too, are the Jewish-style comedies of Neil
Simon.

Lenny Bruce defined the symbolic significance of Jewishness as part of, or
equated with, urban sophistication, knowledgeability, and "hip-ness." He also
connected it with the problem of identity that all the ethnic and other minority
groups in America are faced with. "If you live in New York or any other big city,
you are Jewish. It doesn't matter even if you're Catholic; if you live in New
York, you're Jewish. If you live in Butte, Montana, you're going to be *goyish*
even if you're Jewish. Evaporated milk is *goyish* even if the Jews invented it.
Spam is *goyish* and rye bread is Jewish. Negroes are all Jews. Italians are all
Jews. Irishmen who have rejected their religion are Jews." The point is that the
style and content of Jewish humor strikes a deeply responsive chord in American culture, especially among aware, urbanized Americans. For Jews and members of other minorities the challenge of alienation and assimilation is central;
for the majority it is a question of personal versus mass-cultural identity.[1]

Neil Simon's characters are sometimes Jewish, but only nominally so, says
critic Edythe McGovern. In my view, Simon's points of reference are those
assimilated from the time before he consciously thought about himself; that is,
his points of reference are to an upwardly mobile Jewish lower- and middle-
class culture, politically and socially liberal. True, his concerns are not religious but since being Jewish involves a socio-historical-cultural definition,
Simon's concerns derive from his cultural affinities, vague as that may be, as
much as to his American-ness. As a Jewish American, one who is comfortable
being an American who has still retained his feeling of Jewishness, whether or

not he ever enters a synagogue, Simon writes out of the same mixed heritage that includes Saul Bellow, Bernard Malamud, and many other Jewish-American writers. Coming out of a long tradition forced to accommodate to an oppressive environment, the Jewish writer developed the capacity for smiling through tears. In Simon's case, as Tom Prideaux put it, "Another ingredient in Simon's success is his acute sense of comic strife, what some call Jewish irony and others the stories of the *shlemiel*, or the sainted fool."

Time after time, Simon is credited with the ability to write from the inside, from the heart, from the soul. But Neil Simon does not merely dash off semi-autobiographical comedies about middle-class New York, as some critics say. Not only is Neil Simon a careful writer, but he is a man proud of what he has created. To construct a play piece by piece so that a completed effort represents his best is what he's after. Of more importance here, he writes plays not about places but about people. As he put it in 1965, "I'll tell you when I'm funniest. It's when the situation is at its worst and I have my back up against the wall." Or as he explained more recently, my plays are "about conflict and that's around anywhere. My attitudes towards life have not changed." That is, "My view is 'how sad and funny life is.' I can't think of a humorous situation that does not involve some pain. I used to ask, 'What is a funny situation?' Now I ask, 'What is a sad situation and how can I tell it humorously?' "[2]

Marvin Neil Simon was born in the Bronx, New York, on July 4, 1927. Irving Simon, his father, was a garment salesman. When he was a child, he was nicknamed "Doc" because he was always playing "Doctor." His early feeling for comedy was shown in his constant attempts to sing and act like his brother Danny, and in his reaction to comedy films. His favorite comedian was Chaplin. "I was constantly being thrown out of theatres for laughing too loud," he recalled. His ultimate dream was to make a whole audience fall onto the floor, writhing and laughing so hard that some of them pass out. In 1946, after serving in the Army Air Force Reserve, he got a job in the mailroom at Warner Brothers in New York through his older brother Danny who worked there in publicity. Within a year or so he and Danny were writing for some of the best people in television. In 1956 after Danny became a director, Neil wrote for the Sid Caesar Show, the Phil Silvers Show, and the Garry Moore Show. The work was "tedious," done only to pay the rent. "It's degrading to try to be funny when you don't feel like it," he said. "They want you to write what you think a sponsor might like, or an advertising executive. That's death."[3]

In the late 1950s, in Hollywood with a few weeks on his hands, Neil Simon began writing *Come Blow Your Horn*, a play based on the experiences and feeling he and Danny had in trying to move away from their parental Jewish home. Reading many books on how to write a play, he decided to "do something about how my older brother Danny and I left home and took our first apartment, and what it was like in those days."[4] The play took eight weeks to write, three years to rewrite, and had at least eight producers before it appeared on stage. After a tryout at the Bucks County Playhouse in August, 1960, it opened in New York on February 22, 1961. Although it ran for two years, "without ever filling a house," it was only semi-successful. "That's when I started *Barefoot in the Park*, which turned out to be a smash," Simon remembered.[5] Since those days he has had at least eighteen shows produced, and has turned most of them into successful films. In 1978 he was said to be making $30,000 a week and he was worth $10,000,000. Not surprisingly, Simon has said that "Money is no longer a major factor of life. I work to keep busy and because I enjoy the work."[6]

In 1967 Neil Simon became the first playwright since Avery Hapgood in 1920 to have four plays running simultaneously on Broadway. *Barefoot in the Park*, *The Odd Couple*, and *Sweet Charity* were still running when *The Star-Spangled Girl* opened in December, 1966. There is little doubt that he is one of the most prolific and successful playwrights the United States has ever produced. At the same time, he has not forgotten his roots or his aspiration to be evaluated as a serious playwright. After *Barefoot in the Park* became a hit, he observed that "I was obsessed with proving that I could do better than that. I really wanted to be recognized as a writer." In the beginning, he wrote about himself, his family and friends, what he knew best. Later he took to writing about people he didn't know, about the human condition. At the same time, warring within himself was the necessity to confront his own past, his burden of guilt, together with his perception of the shoddiness of values that contrasts so strongly with the prettified exterior. In a revealing exchange he admitted, "I guess there is the whole business of Jewish guilt. You know the saying 'If you don't work, you don't deserve.' And I do want to pay my own way. The least respected people I know are those who are born rich and do very little with their lives." On the other hand, having pursued success and caught it, he's learned that up close the American Dream of Success is a vulgarity, that "people love you or hate you simply because you've made a lot of money." This conflict, between his sensitivity to pain and suffering and his extraordinary talent and success, is central to understanding Simon's plays and what makes Simon run.[7]

Simon's first plays were based on his family and his personal experiences. "In *Barefoot* and *Come Blow Your Horn*" he says, "at least one or two characters in each play resembled, perhaps in speech patterns, mannerisms or personal outlook, someone I've actually known."[8] *Barefoot* is a light play, a soufflé. *Come Blow Your Horn* is a play about Jewish family life, rich in humor and small tragedies, based in large part on the relationship of his father to his mother. "I grew up in a family that split up dozens of times," he recalled. "My father would leave home, be gone for a few months and then come back, and I felt that our life was like a yo-yo! We'd be spinning along pretty good, and then—zap, the string would break and he was gone."[9] But the horror of those years, he went on in a different context, was that he didn't come from one broken home, but five. "It got so bad at one point that we took in a couple of butchers who paid their rent in lamb chops." According to Danny, who tried to shield Doc from the brunt of it all, his brother "must have felt pain that he didn't show. He saved it for his writing." The result is that Neil often escaped to the movies. In retrospect, and this is central to understanding Neil Simon and his work, his childhood was funny, "but it wasn't funny when we were living through it."[10]

Come Blow Your Horn revolves about Alan Baker, his younger brother Buddy, twenty-one years old, and their parents. As in most good Jewish families, the parents are matchmakers and anxious for their sons to be achievers. In addition, there is great tension between Mr. Baker, who owns the largest artificial fruit manufacturing business in the East, and the boys, because of their inability to work as hard as he did. When Alan leaves home, Mr. Baker is angry but shifts his expectations to Buddy. But when Buddy leaves home, Dad explodes. I used to call Alan a "bum," he hollers, but now "I have a bum and a letter," just as his wife had predicted. When Buddy leaves, he explains to Alan: "It's different for you, Alan. You're hardly ever there. You're the salesman; you're outside all day. Meeting people. Human beings. But I'm inside, looking at petrified apples and plums. They never rot, they never turn brown, they never grow old. It's like the fruit version of *'The Picture of Dorian Grey.'*" Alan's response, predictably, in the tribal vein, is: "I'm proud of you. You walked out of Egypt, kid."

Mr. Baker's responses are within the Jewish tradition, laced with malapropisms and mixed metaphors. Was it "Alan put the bug in your mouth," he asks? He advises Buddy not to rush "into any decisions hell mell." In an agitated state he promised to throw himself "in front of an airplane" if Buddy joined Alan. But he also reacts to Connie, the girl Alan finds different, as well as the many transients Alan knows. Exasperated at last, he bursts out with what sounds like a direct translation from the Yiddish: "May you and your brother live and be well. God bless you, all the luck in the world, you should know nothing but happiness. If I ever speak to either of you again, my tongue should fall out!"

By the end of the play, although neither Alan nor Buddy have jobs, Alan misses Connie who has gone away to test his love for her. When he decides to become a responsible citizen, a *mensch*, he proposes to Connie. With two of the criteria for being a *mensch* satisfied, he moves up in the esteem of his parents. When Connie, trying very hard to make peace, suggests they all have dinner together, Mr. Baker reluctantly agrees, in an Eastern European way, "Maybe just a cup of coffee."

The point is that Mr. Baker, a Jewish father in the old sense, wanted to preside over a unified family in which his sons followed his lead, as it had always been. His reference points were the *shtetl* culture of Eastern Europe. To him a son should be well-motivated, work hard, and marry and have children. To Alan, who couldn't get to work on time, he said sarcastically: "If I was in the bum business, I would want ten like you." Alan protests that he came in early for three years, hoping to be listened to. "Only then I was 'too young' to have anything to say. And now that I've got my own apartment, I'm too much of a 'bum' to have anything to say. Admit it, Dad. You don't give me the same respect you give the night watchman." But Dad, an old-fashioned patriarch, can't understand the Americanizing process that has taken place. "Why am I a bum?" is Alan's question. Dad's answer, a non sequitur, is "Are you married?" followed by: "But now that you're over thirty and you're still not married, so you're a bum, and that's all there is to it."

The concerns of the parents for the children are characteristically Jewish, although not restricted to Jewish families. Mr. Baker, working all his life to build a business for his sons, is in the cultural milieu. Similarly, when his wife intercedes, it is because of the strife between her husband and her sons. Because of his constant reiteration of the descriptive accusation, "Your bums, your two bums," she leaves home, intending to move in with the boys. In her words, she's now a "bachelor" with two grown sons. Only when harmony prevails does she patch up her marital relationship. At the end, conceding that Buddy is not a baby any longer, in an invitation as old as Judaism in Eastern Europe and before, she says she expects Buddy for dinner Friday night, for the Sabbath. And bring your laundry, she adds.[11]

The Odd Couple also came from Simon's life. After Danny Simon's divorce, he wanted to write a play about his experience but after writing fourteen pages he couldn't go on. It was the germ of a play "about two divorced men living together, and the same problems they had with their wives repeat with each other." When Neil took over the idea, he wrote a play about two guys he knew; he thought he was writing a black comedy about two men who were basically unhappy. However, Neil Simon's genius, says Mike Nichols, is for "comedy and reality; extremely distorted but recognizable, not zany behavior." The question is whether art was imitating life or vice versa. As Neil Simon has admitted, "I suppose you could practically trace my life through my plays. . . . they always come out of what I'm thinking about and what I am as a person."[12]

Between 1961 and 1970 Neil Simon had a succession of hits. *Come Blow Your Horn* opened in 1961; *Barefoot in the Park,* 1963; *The Odd Couple,* 1965; *The Star-Spangled Girl,* 1966; *Plaza Suite,* 1968; and *The Last of the Red Hot Lovers,* 1969. Paralleling these successes, however, an undercurrent of criticism was suggesting that Simon take more chances than he previously had. Of *Plaza Suite,* Brendan Gill wrote that he regretted that "the greater Mr. Simon's success in the world, the fewer the chances he seems willing to take with his considerable talent." Of *The Last of the Red Hot Lovers,* Gill said that "Simon's so-called seriousness has a banality of insight not easily to be distinguished from that of soap opera." The reviewer for *Time* magazine wrote that "Simon ought to risk more seriousness. The wine of wisdom is in him, and he ought to let it breathe longer between the gags."[13]

The problem with the criticism Simon was receiving is that Simon was whipsawed between those who wanted him to take a risk, and those who wanted him to continue doing what they thought he had been doing. Known as a sure-fire gagwriter, as a manufacturer of machine-gun humor, he had created a kind of monster. There was always the question whether a serious play, unleavened by humor, would be accorded fair treatment. It was just as reasonable to suppose that a departure from the customary would garner brickbats rather than kudos. At the same time, Simon, quite naturally wanting to be accorded serious consideration, kept trying for that mix which would represent him at his best as well as lead to commercial success and general approbation. With *The Last of the Red Hot Lovers* he began moving in that direction. Having searched for decency and beauty, Barney Cashman, trying hard to be "the last of the red hot lovers," ends up, first, disillusioned, and then certain that decent and beautiful people do exist. Along the way, Simon commented on the values of our society and the problems married couples have.

The Gingerbread Lady, in rehearsal during October, 1970, for a pre-Broadway run in New Haven, promised to be Simon's first completely serious and success-ful play. On the day before the first reading, Simon had been exhilarated by what he had heard, in spite of the theme and the treatment. The characters are Evy Meara, a middle-aged alcoholic, ex-supper club singer, who is involved with Lou Tanner, a macho nontalent; Jimmy Perry, an unsuccessful actor who is homosexual; Toby Landau, a forty-year-old narcissistic fading beauty; and her daughter Polly, a bright seventeen-year-old. Evy is a compulsively filthy talker who finds love almost anywhere she can but is determined to destroy herself. In Toby's words, "We all hold each other up because none of us has strength to do it alone." With no reinforcement from outside, they use substitutes—alcohol, sex, makeup, homosexuality. At the end, goaded by her daughter to try once again to relate to her, Evy sends her away; having been beaten up by Lou, she can no longer struggle against the odds. Evy is alone, drinking, on the road to tragedy, as the curtain falls.

Very early on, it was apparent to the play company that something was wrong. After the first preview Maureen Stapleton, who played Evy, said: "I thought everybody out front had taken a suicide pact." Neil Simon, the next night, just before the New Haven opening, said: "There's a crisis." He was right. The *New Haven Register* called it "an uncomfortable play." After the Boston opening, Simon summarized the reviews with the words, "They just felt I didn't write a very good play. . . . It's very simple. When people leave the theater they are filled with despair—despite the fact that they were filled with truth. They say 'I paid $9 and I don't want to be filled with despair.'" That is, "People want to be told to fight on; you can win. I'm telling them if you fight on, there's nothing but crap."[14] The point is, as Simon read the audiences and the critics, the people wanted hope, affirmation. He decided to rewrite the play. Now, instead of emphasizing the tragic, he tried to find out how he could lighten the play, but without compromising his standards. He made Evy a more sympathetic woman, he cut down even more on the vulgarity, he allowed Toby to see a brighter future before her, and he changed the ending so that the audience would feel Evy might possibly gain strength and improve.

After the revised play opened on Broadway, Simon carefully weighed the reviews. *The New York Post* spoke of his "distinction as a playwright." *The New York Times* dwelt on "the dialogue between a great actress and a playwright who has suddenly discovered the way to express the emptiness beneath the smart remark and the shy compassion that can be smothered by a wisecrack." But *The Post* also pointed out that the contrast between the sadness and the humor weakened the play, while Walter Kerr of the New York *Times* lamented the weakness of Evy as a character. Even Mel Brooks, with whom he worked years before as a writer, commented that "Doc is going to have a long, hard road. He's got to have his papers stamped. He doesn't have his credentials and he will not be allowed into Serious Land. I think it is very important that he launch this deeper side of his talent. The best thing Doc could do to make that transition would be to dig his pen in the blood of his heart and write for an Off-Broadway 199-seat house a total tragedy. The easiest thing Doc could do is just obliquely to insinuate there's more to life than one laugh after another." But for Simon, in many ways it was "the most satisfactory play I've ever written"[15]

Simon was right. He had given his all. He had taken an enormous risk. Was he right in rewriting the play? In twenty or thirty years we will know with more certainty than we do today. All we can do now is try to probe the reasons for the writing of the play and Doc's reactions. That he was guilt-ridden is probably true. Simon admits that his guilt stems from his past. Carol Matthau believes that there is a whole well of grief in him. Lester Colodny, Neil's former agent, rhetorically asks "you know part of his guilt? He's a Jew." That is, it seems true that what made Doc a comedy writer, by his own admission, was the blocking out of some of the really ugly, painful things in his childhood. To live with the pain it was necessary to relate to it in terms of humor. Which is why to Simon the ideal play is one where the audience laughs all night except for the last few minutes when they get touched by a sense of tragedy. Which is why Colodny believes that Simon is destined to go down in history as one of our greatest playwrights—"but he has yet to write from the very pit of his gut." And until he does that, says Colodny, "he will not be able to write the really great drama he's capable of."[16]

Whether the criticism is correct or not is not an issue. The real question that remains is whether Simon is doing the best he can do. Similarly, in recent years Woody Allen has been applauded time and again for his struggle to develop technique, a greater sense of cinema, a closer relationship to serious intent. With *Annie Hall*, Allen took one giant step forward; with *Manhattan* he is said to have blended the drama and high concerns of *Interiors* with the comedy of *Annie Hall*. He has presented the human condition in such a way that laughter is felt through the tears, as in Chaplin's films or in the writings of Mendele, Sholem Aleichem, and Peretz.

Neil Simon, too, has been growing and progressing, but in a more subtle way. After *The Odd Couple*, convinced that he could make people laugh, he no longer felt compelled to. He learned to protect the serious moments of his plays. *The Sunshine Boys*, for instance, is a very serious play that deals with old age and its problems. It is also a very funny play whose humor helps the playwright to convey his message.[17]

Smith and Dale are among the most famous vaudeville teams in the history of the American stage. Their Dr. Krankheit sketch, at the beginning of the century, still draws laughs on records and in its disguised version in *The Sunshine Boys*. There is no doubt that Al Lewis and Willie Clark are patterned after Smith and Dale, but it also possible that Lewis and Clark (their name recalls the early nineteenth-century explorers) are meant to remind us of the great performers of the past and the way they carried on through thick and thin, often beyond the time when they should have quit.

The Sunshine Boys concerns the attempts of Ben Silverman, Willie Clark's nephew, to get the pair to perform again, on television, in a comedy retrospective. Willie, living in a one-room apartment, hasn't talked to Al Lewis for years. A crotchety old man, he accuses Al of having poked him in the chest for years, and of having spit in his face everytime he spoke. Still, as a professional, Willie had to admit that Al was terrific and they worked wonderfully together. "One person that's what we were. No, no. Al Lewis was the best, the *best*." On the other hand, Willie hated Al as a human being. Eleven years earlier, Al had suddenly retired without asking Willie's permission, thus retiring the team. "When he retired himself, he retired me too . . . and God damn it, I wasn't ready yet."

But Ben maneuvers them into rehearsal. Unfortunately, the rehearsal degenerates into a personal fight, a name-calling contest. Their sketch, "The Doctor and the Tax Collector," done in Yiddish inflections and using Jewish humor, depends on mispronunciations and misused words, and many references to the size of the nurse's anatomy, fore and aft. In addition, because Willie believes that some sounds are funny, a "K" occurs in almost all the names: Willie plays Dr. Klockmeyer, Al plays Kornheiser, the patient is Mrs. Kolodny, and the nurse is Miss MacKintosh. Of all Simon's plays, *The Sunshine Boys* is probably the earthiest, the one closest to Yiddish theater. In the heyday of vaudeville, the Jewish comedy teams were often crude, even bawdy, but they were always in tune with the audience, and involved them in the problems of the performers.

Neil Simon, with his eyes on the reality of the past, has given us the talent of the older generation, especially reminiscent of the flavor of the Second Avenue theaters. Historically, Jews maintained unitary households, but in the New World, with success and affluence, it became easier for some young people to farm out their parents, aunts, and uncles to old-age homes. In this case, the Actors Home in New Jersey, was the alternative for Willie and Al. Joe Smith, the model for Willie, has lived there for many years. Of course, in the plot, the nephew Ben said that he was willing to take Willie in, but Willie knew that that meant moving in with Ben's family, and Willie detested kids. Willie also resented being an unwelcome guest, or at least an unlooked-for guest, in Ben's home. In any case, Simon mixes humor and tragedy. The two old performers hated each other but secretly admired and loved each other. They also needed attention, they needed people to fuss over them, they needed to be made to feel that they were still human beings. The title suggests warmth and energy, given freely by all in the way the sun has sustained us all. But behind the title is Simon's feeling for the situational conflict, the irony in the plight of the talented elderly who are to be honored and admired for what they gave to their era. In Eastern Europe the extended family was common, old people were organic parts of the household because the family was essential to Judaism. America broke down the old ways. The conflict was plain to see. Indeed this was a humorous situation in which pain was involved. *The Sunshine Boys*, embedded in the Jewish experience, is a sad tale told humorously.

Flirting with danger, doing the difficult and unpredictable, or using conventional themes in an unconventional way, has its costs. That *God's Favorite* (1974) was not a huge success artistically is no secret. But the attempt to rework the story of Job was a test for Simon at a difficult period of his life as well as a testing of Job's faith in God. In *God's Favorite*, wealthy businessman Joe Benjamin, living on the North Shore of Long Island Sound, is married to Rose, a "walking Harry Winston's." Their twins, Ben and Sarah, twenty-four-years old, have an IQ of 160, "between them." The eldest son, David, is a hedonist who deliberately baits his father. The servants, Mady and Morris, remind us of the stereotypical "Negroes" we used to see in movies like *Gone With the Wind*. Reminiscent of the Baker family in *Come Blow Your Horn*, father Joe has to remind his son, David, of all he has accomplished. The house, the business, the jewelry, the furniture, the swimming pools, are all resented by David, partly because Joe, sounding like a Jewish Horatio Alger, keeps reminding his family of his bootstrap background. He began with "I grew up in a tenement in New York," and ended with "All I wanted for my wife and children was not to suffer the way I did as a child, not to be deprived of life's barest necessities." To his own question, why this success? he answered, "It's God's will."

At this point a messenger enters. Sidney Lipton, a not very impressive person in khaki slacks, a tweed cap, a thin raincoat, white sweat socks, and Hush Puppies, is crawling around the floor looking for his glasses. In a Talmudic way he answers every question with another. When he asks "What is this, the living room?" Joe says "Certainly it's the living room. What does it look like?" To which Sidney responds: "Do I know? Was I ever invited before?" Sidney quibbles over definitions. What does ambiguity mean? What does anything mean? Then, all in capitals, he asks: "What business do we, strangers till not five minutes ago, have unto each other?" Joe, a bit slow, finally understands that Sidney is not God, but a messenger. Thus when Joe asks if Sidney ever saw God, Sidney answers I heard him. "I sneezed and God blessed me," that is, he said *"Gesundheit."* Sidney says he has been sent *"To test your faith, that's why,"* because the Devil said there's not one man on earth who would would not renounce his God once the Devil put enough heat on, and God volunteered Joe Benjamin.

Joe affirms his faith. Then the testing begins. First, his factory burns down; he had no insurance. Next the paintings and furniture are gone; soon there is no heat or hot water; the house is freezing. Still Joe says to question God is not to love God. When David taunts God, Joe asks God for forgiveness for his son. When Sidney threatens him with "humidity," he repeats his faith. Even when he itches unbearably and his family begs him to give in so they can go to bed and watch television, he continues to love God. But, when his son David is blinded, Joe yells at God: "I'm angry at you, God . . . And still I don't renounce you." Only after David is given back his sight does Joe realize that the test is over. David's response, as a renewed David, is to thank God for sparing his father's life.

God's Favorite is a didactic play. Like his characters, Simon was sitting in the corner observing everything that went on. But, as a lesson play, as the most biblical of Simon's plays, it is also the play that is most directly involved with the Jewish past. Joe, of course, is an example of the kind of nouveau riche person who too ostentatiously displays his success, who is too permissive, who too eagerly embraces the American success ethic. At the same time he says he's a "plain, simple man," when in fact he isn't. But Sidney, who is a nine-to-fiver in Queens, is an ordinary man called on to do a king-size job. Unfortunately, with all the Jewish flavor, the characterizations are not up to the best of Simon; *God's Favorite* does not display Neil Simon's strengths! But it is a serious attempt to deal with a serious subject, in a humorous way, all part of Simon's mode of working.[17]

After *The Good Doctor*, Simon's adaptation of some of Chekhov's short stories, opened, a woman in the opening night audience said, "It's not Neil Simon." To Simon's question whether the play was good or bad, she repeated, "I don't know. It's just not Neil Simon." The point is that even when Simon writes or adapts serious drama, it is difficult to be accepted for what it is. On the other hand it must be said that Simon does not want to write a strictly serious drama, that is, he can't write a play totally without humor. Because of his childhood, he sees humor in even the grimmest of situations. In the "Visitor from London," the third of the four one-act plays in *California Suite*, we meet a woman who is married to a man who turns out to be a practicing homosexual. That they love each other and love will somehow continue is apparent. To Simon, it's a serious piece, but the laughs throw the audience off. Still and all, in Simon's view, the laughs are necessary. "It's like a political speech—when you hear one filled with bromides that you've heard over and over again, you turn off. But if there's a bit of humor injected into it, you might listen, and you still get the point."[18]

In spite of having written for the screen, television and the musical theater, Neil Simon's heart is still with the stage. Playwriting is still the most important aspect of his life because when he's writing a play, what he visualizes is exactly what the audience sees. Given that his life is in his plays, that the plays come out of what he's thinking and what he is as a person, it's easy to understand his dedication to playwriting above all. It also helps explain why he doesn't direct plays. Not only does he not have the energy and talent for doing both at the same time, he believes that he could not direct anyone else's play because he'd be sure to bend it to his view. He turned down directing the stage version of Woody Allen's *Play It Again, Sam*, "because I'd have made him change it due to my own point of view. I don't think I'd ever be good for someone else's work."[19] Neil Simon's penchant for originality is very strong. He goes into new territories to keep interested in the work, which is one of the reasons he wrote the book for his first original musical, *They're Playing Our Song*, with music and words by Marvin Hamlisch and Carol Bayer Sager. According to Walter Kerr, the music was "irrepressible," but "it's as though someone went to Simon with a non-

existent plot," wrote Kerr, "two agreeably efficient principals, and some baggage cars full of beautiful scenery and asked him to give the principals
something, *anything*, to say. Which is what he has done . . . ." But, Kerr
added, Simon never was a mere manufacturer of one- or two-line gags. "He's
always needed a situation to suggest what the laugh's going to be about, needed
a character idiosyncrasy to prod him into phrasing responses that will explode."
In short, "Middle-of-the-road tepid it is, with Mr. Simon uncharacteristically
boxed in. Next time let's hope they'll play *his* song."[20] Significantly, Gordon
Rogoff for the *Village Voice* agreed in most respects, adding that Simon appeared to think that Hamlisch's music was as good as that of Mozart and
Beethoven, saying he was "as important to our time as they were to theirs." He
asked: "Wouldn't the show be better off if the author didn't compare himself
with Aristophanes, Molière or Chekhov? Why mix genres and ambitions so
vengefully? It is one thing to tell jokes all the way to the bank, quite another to
believe that the bank confers distinction or immortality."

After almost two decades of criticism, it appears that the critics only partly
understand Neil Simon. Kerr is surely right in noting that Simon needs character and is not just a gagman. And Rogoff is surely right in pointing out that
telling jokes does not confer distinction or immortality. But it might be stressed
that what fascinated Simon, what made up the challenge, was the relationship
between the two principals, Vernon and Sonia. What cried out for analysis,
dissection, explanation, enlargement, humor, whatever, was the way in which a
male composer and a female lyricist related to each other. Whether the result
was successful or not is a separate question. What, it seems to me, is important,
is that apples and oranges not be confused. It is possible that Marvin Hamlisch's music, along with that of Richard Rodgers, Irving Berlin, Stephen Sondheim, et al., may be as important in our times as Mozart's and Beethoven's were
in theirs. The imprimatur of history is still to be heard. But where, in what play,
in what interview, has Simon pretended to equality with Aristophanes, Molière,
and Chekhov? True, he was happy when someone once referred to him as a
"distinguished" playwright, and another called him a playwright of distinction.
But he has never forgotten that it is history that confers distinction and immortality. Part of an age-old tradition, he has never given up thinking of himself as
a kid who grew up in the Bronx, as a Jewish kid whose childhood was traumatic,
as one of those buffeted by external forces for so long, as he was reminded
recently when he read Irving Howe's *World of Our Fathers*.

Neil Simon, seemingly at the height of his fame and success, is going through
a difficult period in his life. Having moved from New York to California, he is in
the process of trying to find a middle ground, trying to find his roots again. As he
explained, everything in his New York house reminded him and his second
wife, Marsha Mason, of his first wife, Joan, who died of cancer in 1973. Moving
to Los Angeles seemed reasonable. Doc and Marsha both had many friends in
California and the warm weather seemed ideal for Neil's mania for tennis. But
he missed "the vibrations and the almost electrical input" he got from New

York. He knew that he couldn't write a New York play there. He also knew that he could live in California another fifty years and never be a Californian. As he saw it, in Southern California people were very concerned about making their life comfortable, while in New York people were concerned with making their life interesting. He knew at least "two million interesting people in New York— and only 78 in Los Angeles."[21] In *Chapter Two* Neil Simon has tried to deal with Joan's death and his marriage to Marsha Mason.[22] To George Schneider, in *Chapter Two*, Neil Simon has entrusted his past and his present. Married to Barbara for twelve years, George is crushed by her death. When he is given the name of Jennie Malone, recently divorced, he is at first not very interested. Like any good New Yorker, he has his friends, the Knicks, the Giants, the Mets, his jogging, and his watercolors. But he is pushed by his brother, Leo, as Jennie is pushed by her friend Faye. They talk, look each other over and like what they hear and see. Within two weeks they have decided to get married. As George explains to Leo, "It's Monday morning, ten o'clock, Judge Ira Markovitz's chambers," the kind of Jewishly neutral ground usually chosen by secular and Reformed Jews for marriages. Characteristically, Leo, who loves his brother and has his best interests in mind, tries to get George and Jennie to delay the marriage for a few weeks. After a long talk with Jennie, during which time he explains to Jennie how George went to pieces after Barbara's death, he winds up charmed by Jennie, saying he doesn't know why George waited so long. "I don't know what the hell I'm doing in publicity," he groans. "I was born to be a Jewish mother."

There is an undercurrent of Jewishness that runs through the play. George and Leo are obviously Jewish. Jennie and Faye are just as obviously not. In fact, Jennie has a Catholic upbringing that is responsible for her sense of order and discipline. Thus, George's mother calls him from Florida, the haven for many retired, well-off Jews, wanting to know who Jennie is, what does her father do, and so on. She is a stereotypically Jewish mother. Similarly, when George cuts himself shaving, the morning of the ceremony, he asks Leo "Was there any royalty in our family?" and, predictably, hears Leo answer: "Yeah. King Irving from White Plains."

What was an undercurrent becomes a rushing stream late in the second act when George and Jennie return from their honeymoon. It had been a beautiful five days and a terrible last two days. George has not been able to forget Barbara; he hasn't been ready for a full commitment. In fact, in a truth-telling outburst, he tells Jennie that he resents her for everything, mostly because he couldn't tell her that he missed Barbara so much. Jennie, trying desperately to understand, is at first confused. But after George packs his bags and announces that he's off to Los Angeles, presumably for business, she finally gets angry. In a moment of justifiable rage she tells him of her love and devotion, and she criticizes him for his guilt complex. "You know what you want better than me, George," she begins. "I don't know what you expect to find out there," she goes on, accusingly, "except a larger audience for your two shows a day of suffering."

If Jennie knows anything, she knows how to feel. She also is able to tell George directly that what ails him is George, and his inability to break with certain aspects of his tradition, no longer compatible or appropriate to the American present.

Jennie's outburst, her insightful remarks, are the medicine George needs. He was wearing his heart on his sleeve, indulging in suffering, in the way many Russian Jews did in the *shtetlach*. Breaking through, he can now concede that she's one of the healthiest people he knows. At last, he understands that he's been holding on to "self-pity." Though he's committed to going to Los Angeles, he almost immediately decided to return. He now sees that he was afraid of being happy. He now finishes his book. Significantly the title of the book, *Falling Into Place*, describes what has happened with the pieces of their lives. George, of course, is still Jewish, but he has traded the archaic reliance on suffering that marred his health for the refreshing outlook of a metropolitan-oriented Jennie Malone who, as Lenny Bruce insisted, is Jewish even if she's *goyish*. After all, it is not only George Schneider's way, it is Neil Simon's way. As Simon said, in his Introduction to *The Comedy of Neil Simon*: "May I make a suggestion? How about a blending of the two?"

In interview after interview over the years, Neil Simon has reminded himself and his readers that he and his brother Danny came from the Bronx, and that his childhood experiences were very important. As a result, defining his style of humor, he said: "The humor itself is often self-deprecating and usually sees life from the grimmest point of view. Much of that, I think, comes from my childhood."[23] What was unsaid, however, was that this style of humor comes right out of the Lower East Side (and Brooklyn and the Bronx) experience, and is consistent with the humor and pathos in the tradition that includes Abraham Cahan, Saul Bellow, Bernard Malamud, and Philip Roth. For Simon, writing plays rather than short stories is the best form of self-expression. It is the healthiest outlet he can find for his neuroses and frustrations. It is the best way he knows to share his joys.

In the only book on Neil Simon, Edythe McGovern argues that among Neil Simon's strengths are his great compassion for his fellow human beings which precludes his soliciting laughter in direct proportion to the hurt suffered by his "people;" his basic regard for the family; his awareness of human limitation; his sensitivity to language; and his theory of plots—he never relies on subplots but stays with the story line as the characters live out their scenes naturally. In addition, Simon, respecting conventional and moral behavior, allows his characters great latitude in mortal fallibility. Above all, "his plays, which may appear simple to those who never look beyond the fact that they are amusing are, in fact, frequently more perceptive and revealing of the human condition than many plays labeled complex dramas."[24] Perhaps as Barney Cashman put it, in *The Last of the Red Hot Lovers*, speaking for Simon, "We're not indecent, we're not unloving, we're human. That's what we are, human."

In his human concerns, smiling through the tears, Simon deals with people he has usually known. His characters are often but not always Jewish. On the other hand, coming from a Jewish and metropolitan background, like Woody Allen, he understands Lenny Bruce's words that "if you live in New York, or any other big city, you are Jewish," and he realizes that Leopold Bloom, James Joyce's hero in *Ulysses*, the Jew with his hang-ups, his self-doubt, his self-hate, and his awkward alienated stance, is a twentieth-century symbol for Everyman. The style and content of Jewish humor strike a deep responsive chord in post-World War II America. Alienation, acculturation, and assimilation, allegedly Jewish diseases, belong to all, just as the humor that emanates from the tensions is universal. For the Jew the conflict is real. For the others, the conflict is more difficult but powerful, nonetheless, for most Americans are caught between the nostalgic yearning for a safe, comfortable, well-defined past and a difficult challenge of adapting to an increasingly and frighteningly depersonalized society.[25] This conflict is also at the heart of Neil Simon's plays. Being Jewish, being very human, he understands Horace Walpole's admonition: "Life is a comedy to the man who thinks, a tragedy to the man who feels."[26] In Edythe McGovern's words, "To Neil Simon, who thinks and feels, the comic form provides a means to present serious subjects so that audiences may laugh to avoid weeping."[27]

NOTES

1. The introductory, background materials are drawn from Daniel Walden, ed., *On Being Jewish* (New York: Fawcett, 1974), pp. 11–29. For Lenny Bruce and an excellent chapter on Jewish humor, see Albert Goldman, *Freakshow* (New York: Atheneum, 1971), pp. 169–82.

2. Simon quoted in Edythe McGovern, *Not-So-Simple-Neil Simon: A Critical Study* (Van Nuys: Perivale Press, 1977), p. 17. I am much indebted to this pioneering work. Also see Thomas Meehan, "The Unreal, Hilarious World of Neil Simon." *Horizon*, January 1978, p. 72; interview with Gerald Nachman, *New York Post*, 17 March 1965; Harry Waters and Martin Kasindorf, "Sunshine," *Newsweek*, 26 April 1976, p. 75; and Paul Zimmerman, "Neil Simon: Up from Success," *Newsweek*, 2 February 1970, p. 55.

3. "Neil Simon," in *Current Biography Yearbook 1968* (New York: H. W. Wilson, 1969), p. 360, and Roberta B. Gratz, *New York Post*, 5 January 1967, interview.

4. Interview with Lawrence Linderman, *Playboy*, February 1979, p. 68.

5. Interview with Alan Levy, *Sunday New York Times Magazine*, 7 March 1965, pp. 42–43, and Linderman *Playboy* interview, p. 68.

6. Estimates of Simon's attitudes and wealth are in many sources. See especially Meehan, p. 71; "Neil Simon: Hilarity All the Way to the Bank," *Time* 12 January 1970, p. 65; and "Keep 'Em Laughing," *Forbes* 15 July 1976, p. 42.

7. Zimmerman, p. 56. In spite of strong criticisms, Martin Gottfried, in James Vinson, ed., *Contemporary Dramatists* (New York: St. Martin's, 1973), p. 23, agrees that Simon is "aware of the inhumanity of the middle-class ethic and realizes that it is observed at the price of frustration and hypocrisy, but he cannot bring himself to dismiss it."

8. Neil Simon, "Prescription for Comedy," *The Writer* Winter 1979, p. 23.

9. *Playboy*, p. 75.

10. Zimmerman, p. 54.

11. *Come Blow Your Horn* (New York: Samuel French, 1961).

12. Tom Prideaux, "He Loves to Kill Them," *Life* 9 April 1975, p. 39; *Current Biography Yearbook 1968*, pp. 361–63; *Contemporary Authors* (Detroit: Gale Research,

1977), p. 802, ed., Christine Nasso; *Playboy*, p. 74; and Richard Meryman, "When the Funniest Writer in America Tried to be Serious," *Life* 7 May 1971, p. 68.

13. *Contemporary Authors*, pp. 802–3.

14. Simon's struggle to save *The Gingerbread Lady* is in Meryman, pp. 60–81, an exceedingly valuable, illuminating story.

15. Meryman, p. 81. Mel Brooks's advice came immediately after saying that he was thrilled by *The Gingerbread Lady*, and "I thought I was suddenly able to see some light at the end of the tunnel of privacy. The play is his first tentative groping for true exchange with the world." In Meryman, p. 73.

16. Meryman, pp. 64–67.

17. For *The Sunshine Boys* and *God's Favorite*, see Neil Simon, *The Sunshine Boys: A New Comedy* (New York: Random House, 1973), and Edythe McGovern, pp. 143–59 and pp. 179–94.

18. *Playboy*, pp.57–58, and "Comedy," a multi-interview, in *Vogue* 1 October 1968, p. 255.

19. *Playboy*, pp. 73–74.

20. Walter Kerr, "Too Many Weak Notes in Neil Simon's Song," *Sunday New York Times, Theatre Arts Section*, 18 February 1979, p. D3; Gordon Rogoff, *Village Voice*, 26 February 1979, pp. 77–78.

21. *Playboy*, pp. 73–74.

22. *Chapter Two*, by Neil Simon (New York: Random House, 1979).

23. Among the best sources for material on Simon's childhood, found in almost every interview and mini-biography, are Meryman, Zimmerman, *Contemporary Authors*, and *Playboy*.

24. Edythe McGovern, pp. 223–28.

25. Goldman, p. 172.

26. Hugh Walpole, *Fortitude* (New York: George Doran, 1913), p. 470.

27. Edythe McGovern, p. 228.

Jules Feiffer and the Comedy of Disenchantment

Stephen J. Whitfield

NO STUDENT OF AMERICAN POPULAR CULTURE GETS EXTRA POINTS FOR OBSERV-
ing that, for most of the twentieth century, Jews have contributed disproportionately to the national treasury of humor. They have been ubiquitous, and
conspicuous, and too humorous to mention. Yet the intense involvement of Jews
in the mass production not just of ready-to-wear apparel and cosmetics but also
of laughter should not obliterate critical distinctions. In the creation of comedy,
those whose work is marked by freshness of style and resonance of vision are
uncommon. The authentically talented are, as in all the arts, as rare as aurochs.
Jules Feiffer, therefore, deserves to be judged a singular figure. Few creative
figures approach him in the exactness of his view of life, in the virtuosity of his
art, and in the consistently high standards his work has attained. He is not quite
a comic strip creator, although his syndicated cartoons look more or less like
comic strips. Though he is politically savvy, he is not a political cartoonist like
Herblock. Though our national leaders are instantly recognizable in his work,
he is not, like David Levine, a caricaturist. His cartoons probably constitute
"the primary stylistic inspiration" of *Doonesbury*, and they have influenced
others.[1] Moreover, Feiffer's one animated cartoon, *Munro*, won an Academy
Award in 1961.

He is, of course, more than a pictorial artist, and is indeed even more than a
triple threat. For Feiffer is also a novelist, a movie scenarist, and above all a
dramatist who, according to John Lahr, "has all the assets to become one of
American theater's major craftsmen." For over three decades, many Americans
have been heard to call themselves and one another Feiffer characters; he has
given us images of ourselves. In transferring such arresting figures from page to
stage, Jules Feiffer has become "one of those artists who compel life to conform
to their visions."[2]

A few contemporary comic artists have gained greater prominence and influence than Feiffer, especially as performers in films. But very few have
matched Feiffer's versatility; perhaps his only counterpart is James Thurber,
whose exquisite and often haunting fables appeared in the *New Yorker*. It is no
disparagement of Thurber's stature to note that, of his two plays, one was with a
collaborator and the other adapted from his own work. And when another *New
Yorker* cartoonist complained to Harold Ross, "Why do you reject drawings of
mine, and print stuff by that fifth-rate artist Thurber?", the editor promptly
corrected him: "Third-rate."[3] Satire was largely outside of Thurber's range, but
it has been Feiffer's specialty; and if he is to be categorized at all, it may as well
be with the nightclub and cabaret artists who had emerged from the underground by the end of the 1950s. Speaking at the 1964 obscenity trial of one of

167

them, defense witness Feiffer paid tribute not only to Lenny Bruce but also to Mort Sahl and Mike Nichols and Elaine May, who "came along at a time in America when they were desperately needed. . . . They were making human and political commentaries that could not be published in this country." The satire that had been flourishing by 1964, including *Catch-22* and *Dr. Strangelove*, "has grown out of the atmosphere . . . in these little clubs."[4]

The confrontation with that cabaret world invigorated Feiffer's own sense of artistic promise and possibility and stimulated him to graft a second career onto his first. As cartoonist and dramatist, he has sought to press the language and logic of his characters so far that both the shock of recognition and the release of laughter are effected. He is still in mid-passage in both careers, but he can already be identified as an important and representative figure in the history of Jewish-American drama and in the social context of the popular arts.

Feiffer's work exemplifies the dissolution of minority culture and the absorption of ethnic creativity within the mass culture of American society. In less than two generations, the artistic power and appeal of *Yiddishkeit* waned, with a suddenness that therefore lent special nobility to the recent gesture of a Nobel Prize to Isaac Bashevis Singer. "What does it mean to be a poet of an abandoned culture?" Singer's compatriot Jacob Glatstein once wondered. "It means that I have to be aware of Auden but Auden need never have heard of me."[5] What the immigrants had created and sustained was abandoned by most of their children and grandchildren, who were often raised on the *dreck* of radio serials, comic books, Saturday matinees, Tin Pan Alley songs, and sports lore. For many talented and ambitious Jews of the second and third generations, the claims of a minority culture held little or no interest compared to the lure of the popular arts. The generalization holds as much for New York and other metropolitan areas as for smaller places like Hibbing, Minnesota, the hometown of Bob Dylan (whom Auden, in 1965, professed not to have heard of either).

It is noteworthy that the first significant American novelist of Jewish origin, Nathanael West, described his *Miss Lonelyhearts* (1931) as "a novel in the form of a comic strip."[6] But West was ahead of his time in synthesizing high art from elements of mass culture. It was perhaps not until the 1950s that the lines that once separated the vulgate arts from what had been considered their opposite blurred. (Here was one symbolic meaning to the 1956 marriage of Marilyn Monroe to Arthur Miller; with his horn-rimmed glasses and pipe, his Jewish liberalism and calls for moral responsibility, he seemed to personify the idea of the high-brow.) In that decade several Jews who rose to prominence had been nourished—heavily if not exclusively—on the aesthetic equivalent of junk food, which was then made the butt of mockery.

For example, those Feiffer had praised—Bruce, Sahl, Nichols and May—and, later on, Woody Allen turned the material of popular culture into parody and often into a kind of social criticism. Others shifted back and forth, like Philip Roth, who claimed to admire not only the *ouevre* of Henry James but also the one-liners of Henny Youngman, or like Leonard Bernstein, who composed symphonies and an opera and had also worked in Tin Pan Alley using the pseudonym Lennie Amber. Milton Babbitt, perhaps the most cerebral of serious contemporary composers, was once a prolific writer of pop songs. Another giant of American composition, Aaron Copland, the Brooklyn-born student of Nadia Boulanger, also wrote movie scores. When Copland told Groucho Marx of his consequent "split personality," the comedian replied: "It's O.K., as long as you split it with Mr. Goldwyn." Erich Segal lectured on Roman comedy at Yale while co-authoring the script for the Beatles' animated *Yellow Submarine*. Mordecai Richler's grandfather had translated the Zohar into modern Hebrew, but he himself wrote novels about pushy Canadians bereft of Judaic learning—one of them observes that his generation learned of mortality when Lou Gehrig was benched, and learned of evil from the Wicked Witch in *The Wizard of Oz*. Wallace Markfield's first novel followed a gang of four New York intellectuals who remember everything about radio shows and comic strips. One of these characters will be giving a course in the fall on popular culture "from Little Nemo to L'il Abner."[7] Long before 1968, when French radical students led by Daniel Cohn-Bendit were repeating slogans like "*Je suis Marxiste, tendance Groucho,*" American Jews had fashioned dissidence out of dross. That alchemy is what makes Feiffer's career so emblematic.

His parents immigrated from Poland when they were teenagers. He was born in 1929 and spent most of his life, until the age of 22, in the East Bronx. The economic system was not at its most benign, and it was not difficult to discover that "nice guys finish last: landlords, first." He "observed, registered things, but commented as little as possible." It was, in other words, an intellectual's childhood. Feiffer was unathletic ("one of my great desires to grow up was that, as I understood it, adults did not have to take gym") and bored by school, except for art classes. He loved comic books—especially Will Eisner's *The Spirit* and Milton Caniff's *Terry and the Pirates*. For theirs was "a believable world on the comic page. What was important to me from the beginning was telling a story and creating characters." Just shy of the necessary credits for N.Y.U., Feiffer went to work for Eisner, himself a Jew, and attended the Pratt Institute of Art. After two dreadful years in the army (1951–53), he returned to New York and entered psychoanalysis. In 1956 he took a batch of cartoons to the office of *The Village Voice*, which Dan Wolf, Ed Fancher, and Norman Mailer had founded a year earlier. Only three years later Stephen Becker's standard *Comic Art in America* was already willing to crown Jules an innovative figure in the history of graphic humor.[8]

By then the vivisector of Greenwich Village had become syndicated, even in the London *Observer*. Leslie Fiedler, before he himself admitted his own fascination with pulp comics, reported from Montana that "everyone everywhere digs Jules Feiffer. . . ." Indeed his cartoons won the admiration of Flannery O'Connor, a Catholic southerner, and the British critic Kenneth Tynan, who praised Feiffer as a "profoundly funny" artist who had wrought "a minor revolution . . . in the art of drawing for newspapers."[9]

Although an *Art News* critic considered Feiffer "surely one of the best artists we have," his place in the pantheon is not incontrovertible.[10] Here a compari-

son may be instructive. Feiffer is not alone in his appreciation of Saul Steinberg, who has referred to himself as a "writer who draws." But that description
is far more applicable to Feiffer himself, who illustrates his ideas. Steinberg's
ideas, by contrast, are fully incorporated in the drawings themselves.[11] Feiffer's
faces generally undergo very minute changes of expression; his art calibrates
only slight shifts of gesture and emotion. For he gets his effects less as a
draftsman than as a dramatist. Through their spoken and private idiom and their
rituals of self-deception, his characters betray themselves and indicate the
meaning of their own identities. It is as though the comic-strip characters on
which he grew up had been rendered vulnerable to the psychologizing of others,
though the armor of their own self-delusion is rarely pierced. *Feiffer's Marriage
Manual* (1967) for example, is truly adult entertainment, the sophisticate's
Blondie; and indeed in one series the husband turns into Dagwood Bumstead. In
Feiffer's Album a woman whom Superman saves from a mugging evaluates with
such devastating effect his compulsive derring-do, his exhibitionism, and his
flair for prancing about in "skin-tight, effeminate leotards" that Superman suffers an anxiety attack, his omnicompetence diminishing and Krafft-Ebing.[12]
Feiffer's characters are, as the title of another collection aptly labels them,
explainers—to each other but mostly to themselves. They are not, to be precise,
conversationalists, since they tend to talk past, rather than to, one another.

Tynan, among others, recognized the primacy of Feiffer's ear—"an odd tribute to pay to a cartoonist." Others, too, stressed the acuteness of Feiffer's
dialogue, though one of his readers, Vladimir Nabokov, voiced a minority
opinion: "Too many words."[13] (Given the compressed force of Feiffer's language
when he needs to be and the fidelity with which he has recorded the loopiness of
the vernacular, the novelist's objection is unconvincing, especially since the
narrator of *Lolita* asserts that for the pain of existence there is only "the melancholy and very local palliative of articulate art.")[14] As the apolitical concern
with "interpersonal relations" in the 1950s yielded to the open conflicts and
range of the 1960s, Feiffer's art increasingly focused on the duplicity of official
speech and the rhetorical camouflage of reality. In a decade in which
"pacification" did not mean peace and racism required code-words, Feiffer
became increasingly devoted to exposing the corruption of language. He claims
to have been the first cartoonist to oppose the American intervention in Vietnam
(in 1963). As his opposition to the Johnson administration deepened, the New
York *Post,* for example, shifted his cartoons from the editorial page to the comic
section, and then dropped him entirely. Feiffer found Johnson himself "a glori-
ous subject" for caricature; and eventually so many other cartoonists were
drawing and quartering the President that Feiffer gleefully announced that
"these are the best times since Boss Tweed."[15] He also published a savage
series of cartoons about Johnson's successor, and showed as much animus
toward Nixon antagonistes as Herblock achieved. But by then Feiffer's satiric
instincts could no longer be confined to about half a dozen panels in a weekly
cartoon.

He had been lured down the enchanted aisles of the American theater. As a cartoonist limning the daffiness of contemporary life, Feiffer had observed a symmetry of approach in the skits of Nichols and May—and he was hooked. His first play, the one-act *Crawling Arnold*, was included in a revue that Nichols himself staged in 1961. Nichols also directed a Feiffer skit, "Passionella," in *The Apple Tree* on Broadway in 1966. Feiffer wrote the original screenplay for Nichols's *Carnal Knowledge* (1971); Kenneth Tynan had staged another Feiffer exploration of sexual relations, "Dick and Jane," in *Oh! Calcutta!* two years earlier. Alan Arkin, one of the improvisers who had worked with Nichols and May in The Second City, directed Feiffer's first full-length play, *Little Murders* (1967), as well as the film version, which Feiffer adapted. The play won the Obie (for best Off-Broadway work), the Outer Circle Drama Critics Award and the London critics' prize for best foreign play. Arkin also directed *The White House Murder Case* in 1970. Feiffer has written four other works for the stage: *God Bless* (1968), which bombed in New Haven and London; *Knock Knock* (1976), which ended up on Broadway to critical enthusiasm; *Hold Me* (1977), a revue; and *Grownups*, a comic melodrama first staged in Cambridge, Massachusetts, in 1981.

It was inevitable that his plays would be accused of resembling cartoons, and that he would be dismissed in some quarters as not fundamentally a writer for the theater at all. It is hard to resist the suspicion that his dramaturgical credentials would not have been questioned had he spent formative years in sailors' dives and before the mast. To Feiffer himself such criticism has meant only "that there's a continuity [with the cartoons], that I write like me."[16] His plea of *nolo contendere* means, in effect, that Feiffer writes like no one else. In some instances the continuity has been deliberate. An early cartoon strip about fallout shelters and rioting at the United Nations was expanded into *Crawling Arnold*, and the revue *Hold Me* was also transferred in part from strips to skits. Such transitions are so feasible because Feiffer conceives his cartoons in such dramatic terms, and he has claimed to enjoy the challenge of working within the limitations imposed in each medium—whether of space or time. His targets have been similar, and the characters in his cartoons have long been on the verge of going to pieces before he put them *in* pieces for audiences to laugh at so anxiously.

On both page and stage, Feiffer is a miniaturist, relying on economy of means for his effects. He writes about a very limited number of characters in a land-scape devoid of detail. There is little upholstery, or incorporation of a wider world. Only the psychological states are thick with implication, as the charac-ters try desperately to convey impulses they themselves may not understand and to pick up the signals of others. Since there is nothing monumental or ambitious about his plays, they are not obliged to be brilliant but, as was once said of early Hemingway, "merely perfect." Though Feiffer's lines have the snap of comic authority, he is not notably original in theme or technique; and his debts to the anti-naturalism and the antic terror of the theater of the absurd are obvious. He has left large assertions about the human estate to other playwrights, however. Instead Feiffer has been satisfied to comment upon subtle changes in the atmospherics of American life. With the weird exception of Joan of Arc and her voices (in *Knock Knock*), all of the characters in his plays have been contemporary Americans.

The scale of his work, which emerges naturally from his experience as a cartoonist, has rendered his dramatic enterprises especially suitable for small or cabaret theater. That is also why there is something unsatisfactory about his two movies. The grisly humor of *Little Murders* depends upon the claustrophobia and paranoia packed within the walls of the Newquist family's apartment. Little is gained by moving the camera into the streets, where the menace is somewhat abated when the imagination of the audience has less work of its own to do. The apparent clarity and precision of the cinema's powers of observation diminish the terror by distorting the pressure of the violence inflicted upon the beleaguered New Yorkers. The problem with *Carnal Knowledge* is somewhat different. Despite the standard length of the film and its frequent close-ups, the characters are so one-dimensional and reductive that they lack credibility and verisimilitude. The two male characters are more illustrations of an idea (like depersonalization), rather than recognizable types who assume a life of their own independent of the thesis they are supposed to embody. Jonathan and Sandy are conceived so exclusively in terms of their sexual attitudes that the camera is restrained from showing anything else in their lives—neither money nor politics (as Mort Sahl pointed out), nor work or family feeling or sports. The film's characters, Pauline Kael complained, lack "even eroticism, even simple warmth"; and she even defended the acting honor of Candice Bergen, who was "given scenes of emotional stress that are probably unplayable (since they don't make sense)."[17] At such close range and with such relentless immediacy, the camera simply demands more than Feiffer's characterizations managed to provide.

Within the limitations he has imposed on himself, he has chosen to record the ruling obsessions and fashions of his time. Having noted the ambiguity of the triumph of "psychological man" in the 1950s, he depicted the political and social turmoil of the 1960s from an independently radical perspective and then, in the 1970s, reflected the receding importance of public conflict. He works within the groove of history in order to comment upon it. For all his sensitivity to the *Zeitgeist*, a corrosively skeptical temperament has kept him disenthralled, detached, and nonpartisan. His plays have little to affirm and usually no message to communicate. If they are united by a common theme, it is a familiar one: truth must be distinguished from fantasy, rationalization, mendacity, and delusion. Buried within the mockery of modern conventions, the deflation of language, the surreal leaps of logic, and the quick stabs of wit is a warning about the treachery of social reality—and, perhaps, an invitation as old as the Delphic injunction.

Crawling Arnold documents the transition from the age of private anxieties to the political preoccupations of the 1960s. Its cast of characters includes Barry and Grace Enterprise, who descend into the family fallout shelter and cower before authority as much as they fear the bomb itself; Millie, the maid, who spends part of her time denouncing "white imperialism" before the U.N.; and Miss Sympathy, a social worker who whispers to Millie her support of "the aspirations of your people." But the central character, the Enterprises' 35-year-old son Arnold, engages in apolitical protest: he regresses.[18] Like the protagonist of Joseph Heller's *Something Happened* (1974), who announced, "When I grow up I want to be a little boy," Arnold has chosen to repudiate the responsibilities of adulthood. Growing up in *Crawling Arnold* means acceptance of the normality of atomic terror, submission to irrational authority, conformity to the pieties of middle-class liberalism, the suppression of natural emotions in favor of the banalities of social convention, and commitment to the stability of the nuclear family (the pun is unavoidable). The imperatives of satire have, therefore, stacked the deck in favor of Arnold, whose withdrawal represents a deeper kind of sanity (though not necessarily of wisdom).

Arnold's parents cannot accommodate themselves to his apparent perversity and irrationality, though their own grasp of reality is far from perfect. What that really consists of, beneath the surface of "togetherness" and submissiveness, makes *Crawling Arnold* the farcical analogue of Freud's *Civilization and Its Discontents*. For Arnold has smashed the sound system that will announce that the civil defense drill is over; and he is about to extract sexual favors from Miss Sympathy, who reveals to him that he falls "into my spectrum of attractiveness." The play thus hints at the aggressive and libidinal forces lurking in the subterranean recesses of society. Since the play is a farce, no genuine evil is evoked or analyzed. Arnold describes his own destructiveness as "naughty" behavior; and his conflict with social convention is snap, crackle and pop, not *Sturm und Drang*. The protagonist's escapism may be viewed as a wacky extension of Feiffer's own experience of maturation. Having worked in the comic-book "shlock houses" of Manhattan during World War II, he came to realize that his bosses, "who had been in charge of our childhood fantasies, had become archetypes of the grownups who made us need to have fantasies in the first place."[19]

Disenchantment has deepened with his next—and still best—play, *Little Murders*. Staged in 1968, it was written against the backdrop of violence that is likely to be long associated with the 1960s. Within a five-year period, the assassinated had included a President and his brother, civil rights leaders Medger Evers and Martin Luther King, and Malcolm X (murdered during National Brotherhood Week). The national murder rate doubled between 1963 and 1971. Had that 1971 rate remained constant, anyone born and remaining in a major city would be more likely to meet an untimely end than an American soldier was likely to die in combat in the Second World War. Violence was, however, no urban monopoly. In 1967, one year after Truman Capote had published his account of the extinction of a Kansas family, Charles Whitman climbed to the top of a tower at the University of Texas and murdered fourteen people. Whitman, whom his psychiatrist had labelled "an all-American boy," was also a product of the age of anxiety—besides his several guns and snack food, he brought with him to the tower a spray deodorant.[20]

The extravagance and grotesquerie of American violence threatened to out-strip the most gallant efforts of black humorists to imagine something more nightmarish. Feiffer's response was to chart the decomposition of the bourgeois family amid relentless beatings and random snipings on city streets. The New-quists are "an Andy Hardy family" that has already lost one son to an unknown assassin before Act One. The father tries to get through each day "in planned segments"—mornings without getting shot, afternoon without a knife in the ribs, a return home without finding the apartment burglarized or the rest of his family slain. At the end of the day, he can report to the other Newquists, "It's murder out there." His wife is batty and dim-witted, his remaining son a simpering absentee from the family constellation. The daughter, Patty, is de-scribed by Feiffer as "an All-American girl, Doris Day of ten years ago." Through strength of will she hopes to prevail over the madness and mayhem around her. Though her previous boyfriends were homosexuals, she finally latches onto Alfred Chamberlain, a self-proclaimed "apathist." With his para-lyzed energies, Alfred is the stock Feiffer cartoon figure of the 1950s, suddenly dropped into the turmoil of the 1960s. He responds to his weekly sidewalk beatings by daydreaming during them. After their wedding Patty is killed by a bullet through the Newquists' window. As the play ends, the surviving members of the family, including Alfred, are inspired to pick up the gun themselves, and take turns shooting at pedestrians outside.[21]

The surreal dimensions of *Little Murders* are ghoulish extensions of the ap-prehensions of the audience. Feiffer has heightened such fears by punctuating his play with the introduction of characters whose lapsed authority testifies to the utter helplessness of the middle class. A magistrate, Judge Stern, garru-lously reminisces about the immigrants' pursuit of the American Dream; but such earnest expectations of improvement, which are daily undermined by the evidence of urban anarchy, turn Alfred off entirely. (Alfred's intimacy with his own father was so minimal that he never called him Dad, or any other name: "The occasion never came up.")[22] The minister who marries Alfred and Patty, Reverend Dupas of the First Existential Church, is no spiritual leader at all but a hip, mindless defender of every form of behavior and belief. He embodies the anomie and moral inadequacy of institutions that once compelled allegiance, and the monologue he delivers—with its short-circuiting of sense and its loopy flights of self-delusion—is the funniest episode in the play. Finally there is Lieutenant Practice, a police officer who maniacally concludes that all the violence must reflect a vast conspiracy to extinguish authority. Paranoids can have enemies too, and the policeman (played by Arkin in the film) is shot down by the surviving Newquist child as an arbitrary act of vengeance for Patty's death.[23] Rev. Dupas has already been slain, and there is every sign that the slaughter will continue. Contemporary fears have thus been pushed almost to their logical limits, with the playwright combining merriment and dread in equally effective doses.

The White House Murder Case was staged a year before the publication of the Pentagon Papers. Both document the discrepancy between the official explanation and the actual justification, between the public pronouncement and the private motive. In Feiffer's play, the war in Vietnam is history; the United States is currently fighting guerrillas in Brazil. Instead of "Charlie," the enemy is "Chico." The Pentagon's Operation Total Win has failed. When American counter-insurgency forces are accidentally killed by their own illegal nerve gas, the administration of President Hale decides that "The American people must be told the truth." That means it will lie, and blame the Brazilians themselves for the American deaths. The President's wife, a peacenik opposed to her husband's policies, threatens to leak the actual facts to the *New York Times*, whereupon she is stabbed to death with a sign pleading, "Make Love Not War." Eventually the assassin confesses: it is the Postmaster General, a political operator concerned about the forthcoming election. That truth also cannot be revealed, so her death is blamed on food poisoning.[24]

Though part of the action takes place in Brazil, *The White House Murder Case* is not strictly speaking an anti-war play. Feiffer's real subject is duplicity—the political definition of truth as whatever is most useful and convenient, whatever "works." That definition undermines the very basis of classical democratic theory, which requires a citizenry enlightened enough to judge the policies of its elected representatives. Our first president supposedly could not tell a lie; less than two hundred years later we found ourselves with a president who apparently could not tell the truth. But Feiffer's play made no attempt to account for the mendacity of Nixon and others or to present the causes and consequences of widespread and willful deceit. Evelyn Hale decries the insertion of advertising values into democratic politics, but this clue is undeveloped and unrelated to the possible vulnerability of the political process to manipulation and deception.[25] Instead the play shrinks the motives of politicians to the crassest sort of self-interest, cloaked in lies. Henry Adams once wrote of President Monroe that his character "was transparent; no one could mistake his motives, except by supposing them to be complex."[26] That, however, is the theatrical problem with Feiffer's comedy, at least once the melodramatic shock of Mrs. Hale's impalement is assimilated. All the characters are replicates of Adams's image of Monroe, which means that they are too reductive, too lacking in nuance, too illustrative of a single insight to sustain dramatic interest.

The cynicism and moral outrage that found artistic expression in *The White House Murder Case* found complete legal protection as well. Feiffer had helped to demonstrate that by 1970 freedom of political criticism was almost entirely complete. "For the first time in almost twenty-five hundred years," Robert Brustein concluded, "it is possible to satirize the highest leaders of government on the stage without fear of physical harm or legal retribution." But the very indulgence of audiences and of authorities robbed satire of much of its sting. A typically clever Feiffer cartoon had showed President Johnson including a bigot in his special commission designed to promote consensus. "The White House requested [the honor of owning] the original," the cartoonist recalled. "Talk about effectiveness." Under such conditions the possibilities of saying no in thunder or in jest were rapidly becoming exhausted. "Everybody knew everything anyway," Feiffer added. "Everybody knew how bad it was. You couldn't disturb or shock or create new discontent because there was so much old discontent that still hadn't been absorbed."[27]

Instead of silencing or repeating himself, he chose to explore sexual politics. It is sometimes hard to recall that in *The Naked and the Dead* (1948), Mailer could not fully record the profanity of infantrymen, or that ten years later Congressional interest had been aroused by Al Capp's fondness for using the number 69 in the home addresses and license plates in *L'il Abner*.[28] By the end of the 1960s, however, words could be used on stage and in print with a freedom perhaps never before imagined. The word "obscenity" itself, whose Latin root means "off-scene," what could not be shown on stage, lost its meaning almost entirely. Feiffer, who had testified in Bruce's trial in 1964, participated in this enlargement of expression as well. In 1971 the manager of a movie theater in Albany, Georgia, was convicted under a state obscenity statute for showing *Carnal Knowledge*. Two years later the Supreme Court, after viewing the film, overturned the conviction. Speaking for the majority, Justice Rehnquist held in part that the depiction of nudity is not in itself grounds for nullifying the guarantees of the First and Fourteenth Amendments. Nor did the film exhibit "the actors' genitals, lewd or otherwise," and the depiction of sexual conduct was not "patently offensive." Censorship alone is hardly proof of artistic merit (because her *ouevre* "incites to incest," South Africa banned the fiction of Jacqueline Susann).[29] But the Court's decision in *Jenkins* v. *Georgia* made it less likely that artistic issues would be confused with police powers.

There are indeed cinematic problems with *Carnal Knowledge*, arising largely from the obsessiveness enforced on Sandy and especially Jonathan. They are prisoners of sex, spending much of their life sentence in what amounts to solitary confinement, because of a failure to integrate sexuality with the rest of experience. In the summation of the philosopher Ernest Becker, both the sensualist (played by Jack Nicholson) and the romantic (played by Art Garfunkel) are "pitifully immersed in the blind groping of the human condition." The cruelty and hollowness of their attitudes toward women have resulted in disillusionment and emptiness; but the bleak moral of the film—its implacable seriousness—was lost on feminist critics in particular, who accused Feiffer and Nichols of sharing the very attitudes that *Carnal Knowledge* seemed to mock. "No contemporary film," Joan Mellen claimed, "offers as vicious a portrait of female sexuality. . . . All the women in this film are shallow, crass or stupid." She added that Feiffer and Nichols' "tone and the absence from their film of women at least as articulate as the men amounts to a smug assent, a silent endorsement." Although Molly Haskell found "one intelligent-romantic woman of that film, Candice Bergen, [she] cannot be envisioned beyond the moment she outlives her romantic usefulness to the men, and so disappears from the movie." The Ann-Margret character "is presented as a harridan so that Nicholson can emerge with more dignity and sympathy than he deserves. We get an image that purports to indict the men," Haskell concluded, "but that insidiously defends them, not least through the satisfaction they take in degrading the women."[30]

What these criticisms miss is that Feiffer, as a satirist, hardly exempts women from the humanity he habitually prosecutes. The misogyny of the characters makes them quite unsympathetic, and should not obscure the misanthropy of their creator, since the film has no affirmative images of humans of either gender. *Carnal Knowledge* comprises the fullest statement Feiffer has presented of the sexual comedy of self-deception and disenchantment, a subject that he has treated in the entire course of his career as a cartoonist as well. The opening bull session between Jonathan and Sandy, on whether it is better to love or be loved (a dialogue as old as Plato's *Phaedrus*), is the echo of countless panels depicting the uncertainties and ambivalences linked with desire. In transferring such cartoons to the screen, Feiffer and Nichols failed to produce an unqualified artistic success. But they touched an important nerve in a generation whose conscientious objection to the ongoing war between the sexes still reverberates.

After *Carnal Knowledge* the author apparently realized that his pessimism was at wit's end. He professed to be "worn out by evangelizing," with rounding up the usual suspects. The point was "to start working out ways of living a life." His writing had always vibrated with intelligence—but not with whatever consolations and satisfactions the world might surrender. So Feiffer's next play marked a new phase—if not quite from alienation to accommodation, then at least toward allowing room for fantasy rather than requiring reason of human beings. James Thurber once did a famous cartoon of a seal above a bed, with the wife finishing the argument with her husband: "All right, have it your way—you heard a seal bark!" *Knock Knock* is the dramatic equivalent of the seal in the bedroom. As with the screenplay for Nichols, the primary characters are two men. But its subject, as Feiffer once explained, is "the absolute collapse of logic. . . . how two particular people deal with the irrationality of order and, finally, the collapse of order."[31]

The two people are Abe, a former broker, and Cohn, an unemployed musician, who have been living in a cabin in the woods. Abe is willing to grant some powers to the imagination; Cohn trusts only his senses. Havoc enters their lives with the arrival of Joan of Arc, who is seeking a sort of Noah's ark that will soon ascend to heaven. She offers the only glimmer of affirmation in a Feiffer play that is not meant to be risible, telling Abe and Cohn that they "should be self-sufficient, but not alienated, not despairing, not sneering, not cynical, not clinical, not dead unless you are dead, and even then make the most of it."[32] Her plea for the avoidance of extremes is as bromidic as Judge Stern's paean to the American Dream in *Little Murders*, but this time some credence is to be placed amid the absurdity. There is mugging in *Knock Knock*, but it is the vaudeville version, not what happens on mean streets. *Knock Knock*, which reaped the best reviews of Feiffer's theatrical career, is more silly than slashing; and its humor is rather pointless, indeed deliberately childish. During the run of a musical in which she was appearing, Mary Martin once commented: "I told Lady Bird—she came to see us—that I wanted the President to see *I Do, I Do* because it's not against anything."[33] That is precisely the trouble with Feiffer's latest play. It in fact knocks nothing, and, therefore, amounts to an abandonment of the playwright's distinctive resources.

In praising the play, *Time*'s reviewer located it within the context of Jewish humor—"skeptical, self-deprecating, fatalistic and with an underlying sadness that suggests that all the mirth is a self-protective mask hiding imminent lamentation."[34] Those terms may stretch *Knock Knock* a little beyond recognition, but it would be hard to deny that there is a Jewish dimension to Feiffer's interpretation of life. There is admittedly little in his topics or his language that betrays ethnic consciousness. Given the satiric possibilities inherent in North American Jewish life, which Roth, Richler, Markfield, Heller, and others have exploited with fiendish delight, it is noteworthy that Feiffer has avoided this topic. Occasionally he creates characters who are clearly Jewish, like Abe and Cohn and Judge Stern, and he uses Yiddish words (like *schlepp*) that have entered the American idiom. The cartoons have occasionally included Jewish mothers, smothering with love and aggression, as well as a figure named Bernard Mergendeiler, the sort of victim who might be called a *schlemiel* if that term had not replaced Christ-figure as the most overused term in the critical lexicon. But otherwise there is not much else overt and explicit for the student of Jewish-American expression to identify.

The only exception is *Grownups*, a three-act play that Feiffer first wrote in 1974 and which, with revisions, opened at the American Repertory Theatre at Harvard in 1981. The word "Jew" does not appear in it. All the characters are members of one family—the parents, sister, wife, and daughter of a *New York Times* reporter named Jake; and all are manifestly Jewish. All these relatives make demands upon Jake that he finds exorbitant. All his problems stem from his failure to function like an autonomous adult when he is in the bosom of his family which, according to one estimate, is about a 42D. When Jake's sister Marilyn, who shares his frustration and helplessness, has the inspired notion that they should kill their parents, he dismisses the proposal as "a short-range solution." Set in Marilyn's New Rochelle kitchen and in Jake's Manhattan apartment, *Grownups* shifts rather jerkily from tense satire of suburban banality to the acrid atmosphere of generational and marital warfare; and the play lacks the formal resolution found in its antecedents, the Jewish domestic dramas of the 1930s and 1940s. But not only does *Grownups* offer welcome moments of comic insight, it also shows a remorseless flair for picking at the scabs of familial resentment and indignities that is compelling in its urgency and even its savagery.

To assert that Feiffer lacks the ethnic involvement of, say, Odets or even Neil Simon is not to dismiss the pertinence of Jewishness entirely. Feiffer's life—from the East Bronx to the *Village Voice* and the theater—has been spent primarily in settings and institutions in which the presence of other Jews has been noticeable. By 1930 a popular history textbook was informing public school children that the Jews were "conspicuously successful in the various forms of theatrical enterprise."[35] The creators of the first of the great comic-book heroes, Superman, were, like the three founders of the *Voice* itself, Jews. They were among those who shaped the institutions and values within which an artist like Feiffer operated, and therefore, must have exerted some influence on his vision of the Americans who populate his cartoons and plays. True, it is possible to exaggerate the importance of locale to an author's development. (Kipling wrote *Kim* in Vermont, which is also where Solzhenitsyn completed *The Gulag Archipelago*.) But it would be impossible to divorce Feiffer's stance and style from his lifelong residence in New York, from the pungent wit, nervous energy, open anxieties, quickness and rancor that so many other New Yorkers have defined as sophistication. The city's inhabitants accepted the thrusts of psychoanalysis more easily than the Viennese or Middle Americans have, and this appropriation of the Freudian vocabulary in daily life is also reflected in Feiffer's work. The ambience that he has absorbed has been largely devoid of deliberate incorporation of Jewish religious culture and themes, and is entirely secular in orientation. Nevertheless, the flavor and spirit of that ambience has been heavily and unmistakably Jewish, as though amplifying the jocular definition of an assimilationist as one who only associates with Jews who refuse to associate with Jews.

The artistic and commercial energies of New York Jews have mostly been without politically radical implications. Those who have gravitated toward the theater and other popular arts rarely sought fundamental changes in the social order. But those writers and artists who have been the most dissident and daring have come disproportionately from one ethnic group, and satire itself may be as strikingly a Jewish instrument as the violin. What President Nixon once told H. R. Halderman about the arts—"They're Jews, they're left wing—in other words, stay away"—is sound sociology, even if it is bad advice. For the existence of Jewish conservatives—and philistines—does not negate the fact that, wherever attacks have been mounted against elites and established values, Jews are likely to be found.

One episode, while hardly conclusive, may be suggestive. During the 1969 Chicago conspiracy trial, Judge Julius Hoffman continued to dine at the Standard Club, established by wealthy and successful Jews. One day his luncheon calm was violated when myrmidons of the counter-culture decided to eat at the Standard Club too. They included: defendants Jerry Rubin and Abbie Hoffman; radical organizer Saul Alinsky; publisher Jason Epstein, who was writing a book critical of the judge's conduct of the trial; Norman Mailer; and Jules Feiffer, who had attended the Democratic party convention the previous year as a Eugene McCarthy delegate. Judge Hoffman rearranged his seat to avoid seeing them, but the incident serves as a reminder that the connection between Jewish background and political and cultural rebelliousness can be as close as hand-cuffs.[36] From the status of outsiders, from the distancing or maginality, many Jews have indeed developed a combative stance toward the rest of society, even after allegiance to Judaism itself has evaporated. "To the degree that there is anti-Semitism in the world, I acknowledge being Jewish," David Levine has proclaimed. "In the same sense, when cartooning is ridiculed, I confess to being a cartoonist."[37] Feiffer's actual relationship to his ethnic origins may not be much more positive than that; but his satiric animus, his leftist perspective, his urban irony, and his psychoanalytic spirit help give his work a Jewish component in the sense that a Jew is most likely to have created it.

Whether that work is of enduring significance is, of course, another question. Satire, in George S. Kaufman's *bon mot*, "is what closes Saturday night"; and posterity rarely revises such quick and devastating judgments. The targets of satire may suffer from familiarity, given the constancy of human affairs; and its humor may leave audiences wondering whether it seemed funny at the time. Feiffer may have realized these dangers and may be trying to get beyond satire. Yet to do so may be too subversive of his own talent, which has been to serve as a touchstone of the fashions and follies of his time. It is true that his plays tend to be subjugated to a thesis, which may limit their appeal, even as delusiveness, political chicanery, and sexual stereotyping persist. It is true that Feiffer's capacity for breathing the semblance of life into his characters is undeveloped; but if that were the test of mature art, Damon Runyon would be considered a better writer than Samuel Beckett. It is also true that Feiffer's range is restricted, for he cannot find quite as much dignity and value in life as others have managed to do. As the narrator of his novel *Ackroyd* puts it, "I see like a cop; I see prejudicially; I collect evidence; what can't be included as evidence is not seen; doesn't exist."[38] What Feiffer has seen, however, has been reported with gem-cutting precision; and the requirement to be uplifting as well is demeaning and antagonistic to the imperatives of art, Feiffer's included.

It might also be recalled that what helps make life bearable is the exposition of its incongruities in comic modes. Few of Feiffer's contemporaries have been as unerring and as unsparing in the representation of folly. Few have shown such clarity in the perforation of the confusions, the rationalizations, the deceptions behind which we hide. Few contemporary artists have drawn healthier laughter from pumping irony into the solitude and sadness that may be intrinsic to life. Such claims are not always susceptible to proof, though social scientists have reportedly devised a measurement for enjoyment, broken down into units known as benthams. By enlisting both the cartoon and the drama in the case against humanity, Feiffer has generated more benthams than we have any right to expect.

NOTES

1. John Culhane, "The Cartoon Killers Thrive Again," *New York Times Magazine*, 9 November 1975, p. 38.

2. John Lahr, *Up Against the Fourth Wall: Essays on Modern Theater* (New York: Grove, 1970), p. 94; Robert Hatch, *Little Murders*, Nation, 20 January 1969, p. 95.

3. James Thurber, *The Years with Ross* (1959; rpt. New York: Ballantine, 1972), p. 56.

4. Feiffer quoted in Martin Garbus, *Ready for the Defense* (New York: Farrar, Straus and Giroux, 1971), pp. 112–13; Robert Brustein, *Seasons of Discontent: Dramatic Opin-*

ions, 1959–1965 (New York: Simon and Schuster, 1965), p. 112, and *The Culture Watch: Essays on Theatre and Society, 1969–1974* (New York: Knopf, 1975), p. 36; Arthur M. Schlesinger, Jr., *A Thousand Days: John F. Kennedy in the White House* (1965; rpt. New York: Fawcett, 1967), pp. 667–68.

5. Glatstein quoted in Irving Howe, *World of Our Fathers* (New York: Harcourt Brace Jovanovich, 1976), p. 452.

6. Nathanael West, "Some Notes on Miss L," *Contempo* 3, No. 9 (15 May 1933): 1–2.

7. Philip Roth, *Reading Myself and Others* (New York: Farrar, Straus and Giroux, 1975), pp. 80–82; Richard Kostelanetz, *Master Minds* (New York: Macmillan, 1969), p. 216; Edward Rothstein, "Fanfares for Aaron Copland at 80," *New York Times*, 1980 November 9, p. 21; Mordecai Richler, *St. Urbain's Horseman* (New York: Knopf, 1971), pp. 87–88; Wallace Markfield, *To an Early Grave* (New York: Simon and Schuster, 1964), pp. 110–13, 183–86.

8. Feiffer quoted in Robin Brantley, "Knock, Knock: Who's There? Feiffer," *New York Times Magazine*, 16 May 1976, p. 48, and in Julius Novick, "Jules Feiffer and the Almost-In-Group," *Harper's*, September 1961, p. 60; Kevin Michael McAuliffe, *The Great American Newspaper: The Rise and Fall of the Village Voice* (New York: Scribner's, 1978), pp. 83–91; Feiffer, ed., *The Great Comic Book Heroes* (New York: Dial, 1965), pp. 17, 34–36, 49–52; Stephen Becker, *Comic Art in America* (New York: Simon and Schuster, 1959), p. 378.

9. Leslie A. Fiedler, *Waiting for the End* (1964; rpt. London: Penguin, 1967), p. 74; Flannery O'Connor, *The Habit of Being: Letters*, ed. Sally Fitzgerald (New York: Farrar, Straus and Giroux, 1979), pp. 349, 371; Kenneth Tynan, Introduction to Jules Feiffer, *Sick Sick Sick* (London: Collins, 1959).

10. Elizabeth Frank, "Jules Feiffer: Articulate Rage," *Art News*, 73 (February 1974): 80.

11. Steinberg quoted in Hilton Kramer, "Getting a Line on Steinberg," *New York Times Magazine*, 16 April 1978, p. 40; David Segal, "Feiffer, Steinberg and Others," *Commentary* 32 (November 1961): 433–34.

12. Novick, p. 59; Feiffer, "Superman," in *Feiffer's Album* (New York: Random House, 1963), pp. 66–69.

13. Tynan; Novick, p. 59; Segal, p. 432; Nabokov quoted in Alfred Appel, Jr., *Nabokov's Dark Cinema* (New York: Oxford University Press, 1974), p. 83.

14. Vladimir Nabokov, *Lolita* (New York: Putnam's, 1955), p. 285.

15. Brantley, p. 50; Feiffer, Introduction to *LBJ Lampooned: Cartoon Criticism of Lyndon B. Johnson*, eds. Sig Rosenblum and Charles Antin (New York: Cobble Hill Press, 1968), p. 10.

16. Feiffer quoted in Brantley, p. 60.

17. Mort Sahl, *Heartland* (New York: Harcourt Brace Jovanovich, 1976), p. 54; Pauline Kael, *Deeper into Movies* (Boston: Atlantic-Little, Brown, 1973), p. 284.

18. Feiffer, "Crawling Arnold," in *Feiffer's Album*, pp. 108–10.

19. Ibid., pp. 119-20, and *Comic Book Heroes*, pp. 50–53.

20. James Q. Wilson, *Thinking About Crime* (1975; rpt. New York: Vintage, 1977), p. 19; Robert Sherrill, *The Saturday Night Special* (New York: Charterhouse, 1973), pp. 126-27.

21. Feiffer quoted in Lahr, p. 83; Feiffer, *Little Murders* (New York: Random House, 1968), pp. 23, 83, 88, 102–4, 106.

22. Ibid., pp. 52–55, 63.

23. Ibid., pp. 64–67, 97–98.

24. Feiffer, *The White House Murder Case* (New York: Grove, 1970), pp. 46–48, 106–07.

25. Ibid., p. 48

26. Henry Adams, *History of the United States of America* (New York: Scribner's, 1921), VII, 35.

27. Brustein, *Culture Watch*, p. 32; Feiffer, Introduction to *LBJ Lampooned*, p. 14; Feiffer quoted in Brantley, p. 50.

28. Hamlin Hill, "Black Humor: Its Cause and Cure," *Colorado Quarterly* 17 (Summer 1968): 63.

29. *Jenkins* v. *Georgia*, 418 U.S. 153, 160–61 (1974); Clarence Petersen, *The Bantam Story* (New York: Bantam, 1970), p. 126.

30. Ernest Becker, *The Denial of Death* (New York: Free Press, 1973), p. 169; Joan Mellen, *Women and Their Sexuality in the New Film* (New York: Dell, 1973), pp. 63, 68–70; Molly Haskell, *From Reverence to Rape: The Treatment of Women in the Movies* (New York: Holt, Rinehart and Winston, 1974), pp. 360–61.

31. Feiffer quoted in Brantley, p. 50, and in Tom Buckley, "Feiffer Fills Play with Food and Thought," *New York Times*, 10 February 1976, p. 42.

32. Feiffer, *Knock Knock* (New York: Hill and Wang, 1976), pp. 29, 116–17.

33. *New York Times*, 21 November 1967, p. 54.

34. T. E. Kalem, "Kooky Miracle," *Time*, 2 February 1976, p. 55.

35. Charles Garrett Vannest and Henry Lester Smith quoted in Frances FitzGerald, "Rewriting American History: II," *New Yorker*, 55 (5 March 1979), 42; William Goldman, *The Season: A Candid Look at Broadway* (New York: Harcourt, Brace and World, 1969), pp. 148–51.

36. Nixon quoted in Staff of *The Washington Post*, *The Fall of a President* (New York: Delacorte, 1974), p. 222; J. Anthony Lukas, *The Barnyard Epithet and Other Obscenities: Notes on the Chicago Conspiracy Trial* (New York: Harper Perennial, 1970), p. 103.

37. Levine quoted in Thomas S. Buechner, Foreword to *The Arts of David Levine* (New York: Knopf, 1978), p. x.

38. Feiffer, *Ackroyd* (1977; rpt. New York: Avon, 1978), p. 308.

The "Mental Comedies" of Saul Bellow

Keith Opdahl

SAUL BELLOW HAS ALWAYS BEEN INTERESTED IN THE THEATER. HE WROTE A survey of Broadway for the *Partisan Review* in 1954, and published his first one-act play, *The Wrecker*, that same year. His novels are filled with references to the theater, from the actor Alf Steidler in *Dangling Man* to the pervasive allusions to acting in *Herzog*.[1] Citrine in *Humboldt's Gift* is a playwright, Allbee in *The Victim* takes up with a movie actress, and Tommy Wilhelm in *Seize the Day* quits college to become an actor. Bellow often uses theater imagery to suggest something false, pretentious, inauthentic, as he does in the play *The Last Analysis* or in the climactic scene of *Herzog*; but at other times he uses it to suggest something real and moving, perhaps the spectacle of our human life or the mystery of our social place (our "seat"), as at the end of *The Victim*.

Thus when Lillian Hellman suggested, in the late 1950s, that Bellow write a play, he didn't need to have his arm twisted. "In a short time, my play was ready," Bellow wrote in *The New York Times*. "Miss Hellman found it amusing and estimated it would run about eight hours without Wagnerian orchestration."[2] He let the manuscript sit for a few years, read it to a group known as the "Theatre of Living Ideas," and then in 1965 saw the play produced on Broadway, with Sam Levene in the major role. Bellow has said privately that he suspected in this period that *Herzog* might flop and that *The Last Analysis* (with Zero Mostel in the lead) might succeed. Instead the novel was a best seller and the play folded in three weeks. Walter Kerr gave it a bad review, but it was praised by several reviewers who felt the production failed the play. John Simon summed up this last viewpoint when he charged that "there is still no excuse for reviewers and audiences not to have come to the rescue of *The Last Analysis*. It was, in the last analysis, far more provocative than anything else around."[3]

Bellow wasn't done with Broadway, however. After publishing a refurbished version of *The Last Analysis* in 1965, he wrote two one-act farces, *A Wen* and *Orange Soufflé*, which he gathered together with an unpublished one-act farce, *Out From Under*, to form the entertainment *Under the Weather*, so named because all three protagonists are not quite themselves. It was produced in 1966 and was praised in Spoleto and London, but it failed on Broadway, where Walter Kerr felt both the play and the production were frivolous.

By the end of 1966, then, Bellow had written a total of five plays, four of them one-act farces, and had seen two Broadway productions fail. And that (as of 1982) is the extent of his career in the theater, although his work is still produced on occasion in such places as Philadelphia or the Saul Bellow Conference in Brussels in 1978. None of the five plays is considered a masterpiece, although critics cite Bellow as the best of those contemporary novelists attempt-

ing drama, and at least two of the plays, *A Wen* and *The Last Analysis*, are
delightful. We might even say that Bellow has done very well, given the essentially untheatrical cast of his imagination. His fiction consists largely of observation and meditation, and the driving force of his story is less often a
suspenseful action than a description—a scene, an image, an emotion, precisely that texture which a play leaves up to the director and actors. And yet
Bellow's gifts *do* lend themselves to the theater, too, as Bellow achieves not only
some of the most dramatic characters around, but the kind of large, complete
image or situation that will play—the human situation that can penetrate the
footlights and yet retain its subtlety.

Bellow's problems, such as they are, seem due rather to what the theater
means to him. In his review of *Under the Weather*, Walter Kerr objected to
Bellow's writing "with what seemed more a giggle than an accepted obligation,
[for] he gave the impression of toying with the stage, of idly building sandcastles
that were bound to be swept away."[1] Kerr defines this "giggle" in terms of a lack
of narrative drive, which is fair enough, but his impression is also that of a
writer at play, which is precisely how Bellow regards the stage. "I wrote a play
. . . because I thought it would be easier than a novel," Bellow confessed to an
interviewer. "You have to worry less about moods and details, and one is freer
to come to the point."[5] To Bellow the theater means freedom, which is reflected,
too, in his choice of the farce, which he saw as liberation. The farce would
permit him to mix the high and the low, as he puts it, or a sexy obsession with a
metaphysical speculation, all in a play that, like the Yiddish theater, is swept
along by its energy and emotion rather than any careful structure, mixing the
earthy and the sublime, the passionate and the sentimental, the insightful and
the grand. Bellow also remembered the joy of vaudeville (in which Jews were
prominent) and thought that a string of sketches, if acted broadly and energeti-
cally, could be a lot of fun.

In this desire for liberation one hears, of course, echoes of *Augie March*. One
could do worse than define Bellow's history as a writer in terms of his struggle to
free himself, for his desire to be free cuts across not only his work and his
attitude toward the theater, but also his attitude toward his Jewishness. How
many of the novels begin with the energetic rush of an uncertain or forced
liberation? One thinks not only of *Augie March*, but *Henderson* (freed from WASP
conventions, which is very much to the point) and *Herzog*, who doesn't care if
people think he's mad, and then *Dangling Man*, which shows its own strain. All
of these novels announce a rejection of shackles. And what are the shackles?
They are the formal restrictions of a WASP art and a WASP society. Bellow is very
much like Walt Whitman in paralleling aesthetic forms with political ones—and
in seeking liberation in both areas. "A writer should be able to express himself
easily, naturally, copiously," Bellow has said,

> in a form which frees his mind, his energies. Why should he hobble himself
> with formalities? With a borrowed sensibility? With the desire to be "correct"?
> . . . I should add that for a young man in my position there were social

inhibitions, too. I had a good reason to fear that I would be put down as a foreigner, an interloper. It was made clear to me when I studied literature in the university that as a Jew and the son of Russian Jews I would probably never have the right *feeling* for Anglo-Saxon traditions, for English words.[6]

Bellow's use of his Jewish heritage in his writing is, of course, complex. Even as he's struggled with religious prejudice—and his interviews reveal how painful it has been—Bellow has resisted the label of "Jewish novelist," describing himself instead as a Jew who writes fiction, a description that does justice to both his citizenship in the larger European-American culture and his experience as a Jew, which ranges from that of a child of Russian-Jewish immigrants who has experienced the pain and pleasure of assimilation into America to that of the immigrant himself, coming to Chicago at the age of nine. One is struck in fact by how unselfconscious Bellow's characters are of their Jewishness. With the obvious exception of Asa Leventhal in *The Victim*, the protagonists are so absorbed by personal and metaphysical issues that they pay only occasional mind to their cultural and religious identity. And in the plays it is notable that Bellow deals most directly with Jewish experience when the characters are not identified as Jews—in the *Orange Soufflé*, which dramatizes the relations of an East Chicago Pole and a millionaire WASP, and in *The Wrecker* in which only an allusion to Samson among the Philistines implies a Jewish identity, as the middle-aged husband seems to express the frustration of immigrants cramped in small apartments and of Jews forced to swallow resentment in an alien culture. In the other two plays, Bummidge in *The Last Analysis* is a Jew who suffers from "humanitis," which is actually a personal malady, and Ithimar in *A Wen* is alienated not from a society (though that plays a part) but from a birthmark.

Bellow uses Jewish character, then, but not necessarily as Jews. They are characters who happen to be Jews, and whose Jewish experience is important but not dominant in the story. Believing that "it is impossible for men to be rejected in great literature,"[7] which by definition recognizes our common humanity, Bellow fulfills David Daiches's observation that "the American Jewish writer has been liberated to use his Jewishness in a great variety of ways, to use it not aggressively or apologetically, but imaginatively as a writer probing the human condition. . . ."[8]

And yet we can't really understand Bellow's plays without recognizing the profound and often unconscious effect on him of his Jewish background. One of the most interesting definitions of the Jewish writer is that of Alfred Kazin, who refers to the intermingling in the *shtetl* of the spiritual and material worlds: "The so-called Jewish novel (there really is one, though only a few Jews have written it, and those who write it are not always Jews) takes place in a world that is unreal, never *our* world." Kazin thus fuses alienation and transcendence: Bellow's fiction, he wrote in 1971, "tells, as the best Jewish stories always do, of the unreality of this world as opposed to God's."[9] If many critics have rather curiously overlooked this quality of Bellow's work, it nonetheless suggests Bellow's deep kinship with the culture that provided the West with its concept of God. From Joseph in Bellow's first novel, whose story climaxes in a personal sense of the "strangeness" of existence, to Charles Citrine's rather desperate search for a form for his transcendental intuitions, Bellow has written about the sense of the transcendent in the midst of a materialistic and distractingly gaudy society.

As one reads Irving Howe's *World of Our Fathers*, moreover, one is struck by how many of Bellow's attitudes belong to the Jewish immigrant experience. The protagonist's deep suspicion of the street outside his window, for example, epitomized by Asa Leventhal's feeling that "he really did not know what went on about him, what strange things, savage things,"[10] might be related to the Jewish immigrants' suspicion of a strange culture, in which, as Howe says, "the street enclosed dangers and lusts, shapeless enemies threatening all their plans for the young."[11] Bellow's fiction is filled not only with the famous Jewish literary types, the *schlemiel* and the *schlimazel*, but with the lesser known.[12] When Earl Rovit describes the character "generally known in the old Catskill Borscht Belt as the *meshuggah*—the wild irresponsible, disconnected buffoon who oscillates between the frenetic edges of obscenity and tearful sentimentality," he could be describing Bummidge.[13]

And then Bellow's prose is deeply influenced by Yiddish, ranging from the very specific qualities of repetition, question, inversion, allusion, and inflection—giving to a populace starved by the dry Hemingway manner a strongly human voice—to the more general and profound strategies of "verbal retrieval," in which the beset and overpowered Jew wins a victory by virtue of wit or language.[14] Bellow himself in the introduction to *Great Jewish Short Stories* describes language as a refuge for the oppressed as they right wrongs and express pain. And some critics have claimed that the mixture of the realistic and the fantastic, so often characteristic of Bellow's style, even in subtle ways, is characteristically Jewish. Indeed, Bellow theorizes that storytelling itself is especially important to the Jew.

Thus Bellow reflects a typically Jewish love of language when he says that a writer would feel the American stage has "no language" and "lacks rhetoric or gesture" and that he wanted "to bring rhetoric back to the theater."[15] For the most striking influence of Jewish culture on a writer such as Bellow must be the emotional openness of his style, the ease and directness with which he negotiates the distance not just between the object and the feeling, but between the objective and subjective worlds, the external and the internal. To some extent the key here is energy, for the enthusiasm in a typically Jewish-American style picks up all, sweeping objective and subjective together in a rich mixture of motive and setting, present and history, quotidian and mythic, action and feeling. The grandiloquence of Yiddish explains quite a bit of this, of course, as does the emotional openness which, "ranging from a rich abundance to a wanton excess," in Irving Howe's words, "permeated the whole of Jewish immigrant life."[16]

I am not talking about sentimentality, of course, nor excessive emotion, but rather inwardness, the interior experience which involves will and desire and sensation and thought—all of which we mean by "our feelings." To note that a Jewish story tends to revolve around the feeling of the character is to say that it gives the human being his due, recognizing the importance of human reactions. How many Jewish-American writers give the interior of their subject, writing with the ease of a writer at home with feeling? To a non-Jew this is the most striking similarity among the Jewish-American writers, accounting for their warmth and perhaps even for their great appeal to the general American public. Just as Jewish prose sweeps up allusions to the creation and to the daily wash, so it moves from action to feeling, assuming remarkably in our Cartesian world that both the object and the human attitude are crucial, and equal.

Thus Bellow can worry that "the Jewish imagination has sometimes been found guilty of overhumanizing everything, of making too much of a case for us, for mankind, and of investing externals with too many meanings."[17] And thus, too, Bellow has defined his identity as a writer, a Jewish writer, in terms of human emotion. Joseph begins *Dangling Man* by attacking the emotional reticence associated with Hemingway. "Do you have feelings? There are correct and incorrect ways of indicating them. Do you have an inner life? It is nobody's business but your own. Do you have emotions? Strangle them."[18] Joseph will give in his book his "inward transactions," which is exactly what Bellow ten years later calls for in "The Pleasures and Pains of Theater-Going." Reviewing the year's plays, Bellow charged that audiences attend the theater "to test their powers of resistance to emotion. . . . to find whether they can eat without tasting, view without suffering, make love without feeling and exist between winning and losing." What Bellow would prefer is an audience seeking to "be diverted, delighted, awed, and in search of opportunities to laugh and to cry."[19]

What can we make of this recurrent theme? Bellow began to write in an era when reticence, among other stiff-upper-lip WASP attitudes, was prized and practiced by the likes of Hemingway, Eliot, and John Crowe Ransom. A tight, careful form tended to parallel a tight, careful—and exclusive—social order, so that Bellow's plea for energy and sensation in the face of correctness was a demand for an open society. It also involved a new model for the American, for Hemingway and Eliot spawned an ideal of the unemotional and the understated, perhaps as a reaction to the "wasteland" they portrayed. To the WASP who'd had things pretty much his way for a while, the response to chaos was a buttoned lip. A thing doesn't exist if you don't acknowledge it, and at any rate, the situation was dire. But the Jews over the centuries had learned to live with chaos, and so could offer a more open kind of model, a type well-worn, harassed, and suffering, but large and dignified and persevering, finding his ideal in the human being itself. Such a character is Schlossberg in *The Victim*, a drama critic in the Yiddish press who calls for emotion, for liveliness, for a sense of the magnificence of the character—sexual and otherwise. "She had a mouth, she had flesh on her, she carried herself," he says of an ideal actress. "When she whispered tears came in your eyes, and when she said a word your legs melted."[20] She was simply a handsome, open human being.

Such was the dialectic in which Bellow engaged in the late forties. David

Daiches has suggested a shift in American literature at this time and in these terms from what I will call an aesthetic of distance, involving precisely the emotional reticence of Hemingway, Eliot, and the New Critics (based on irony, control, and paradox) to an aesthetic of empathy or passion that stressed emotion, story, and a renewed interest in the human experience.[21] If such a shift occurred—and the plethora of writers who are now at home with feeling (John Updike, for instance) suggest that it did, evolving into a new, enriched realism—it was led and nurtured by such Jewish writers as Bernard Malamud and Saul Bellow.

But whatever its effect on literary history, the expression of feeling is absolutely central to Bellow's drama. The four plays[22] we have in print are almost uncannily alike in the themes they share—different though they are in character and setting—and in their celebration of emotion against the background of a middle class unable to deal with it. Bellow's plays tell us a great deal about his novels, in fact, as though the long, tricky passage across the footlights (or into dialogue) filtered out the subtlety and diversion that complicate his novels. The protagonists in the plays are cruder than those of the novels, and more naked in their needs and emotions, which is, of course, both the challenge of drama for a novelist and the liberation, as Bellow is free to indulge his love of the broad, farcical stroke.

The most striking fact about these four plays is that the protagonist is in every case an enthusiast. He has a vision, a dream that excites him, much to the discomfort of the more literal-minded, less emotional types about him. What is more, the protagonist gives up worldly concerns, money, position, power, for this dream—a sacrifice based upon a biting criticism of the American middle class. Bellow clearly feels the enthusiast is funny, often because he deals with ideas that are beyond him, but Bellow sympathizes with him too, and even champions him, giving the victory in both plays and novels to the imaginatively liberated.

We can see this theme in Bellow's first play, *The Wrecker*, in which the dream is that of tearing down an apartment which has been condemned by the city and from which the protagonist, "The Husband," refuses to move until the end of his lease. "The Husband" wants to vent with his axe the reservoir of resentment he's built up in fifteen years of married, middle-class life. "I'm getting rid of a lot of past life, dangerous to the soul," he says. "The past, you understand, is very dangerous if you don't deal with it" (p. 203).

The Wrecker is a decent play in spite of the fact that Bellow is not quite sure where to take his idea. The concept is at once striking and familiar, revealing human emotions in a form that is dramatic and visible. One of its most attractive qualities is the good humor of the characters, as "the Husband" does not turn against "the Wife" in his disappointment—he's too active here, too much the happy maniac for any nastiness—and the wife for her part handles the implied insult of his frustration with patience. The play finds its true story, in fact, in the wife's struggle with what the wrecking implies about her marriage, even though the husband clearly means something general ("I learned my own limitations"), so that when she joins the husband, confessing that she, too, has stored up some resentments in the bedroom, we are delighted—and he's not sure this wrecking is a good idea.

Bellow has fun with this small, unconventional visionary; we laugh at the husband's obsession even as we nod in agreement with its content, the need to vent the accumulated emotions of an ordinary life. Bellow plays the man-woman relationship off the rigidity of an idealist. And he does the same thing in the next one-act play he published, *A Wen*. The protagonist, a scientist, does not so much attempt to destroy the resentments of his life as to leap beyond them, back to the moment of childhood ecstasy when the girl next door favored him with a glimpse of the birthmark on her inner thigh. At the time of the play, the scientist (Ithimar, or Iggy) has found nothing to compare with the beauty and delight of that feminine favor. Though powerful and famous, he tells Marcella (when he finds her in a flea-bitten Miami hotel) that his life is empty. To fill it, he desperately wants another look.

Bellow suggests a certain inevitable process of aging in this, perhaps reminiscent of Wordsworth's concern over the loss of childhood radiance. Bellow also means to criticize our middle-class American life, for Marcella's chiropodist husband is, she says, "typically American. . . . He acts cheerful but feels gloomy. . . . And you have to call him Doc, or he blows up. It's an ordinary life" (p. 73). Ithimar is so familiar with such emptiness that when Marcella insists, he willingly risks his position and power for her favor.

A Wen is good theater for several reasons. Since Iggy wants only a look, Bellow enjoys the comedy of female modesty. A middle-aged Hadassah matron, Marcella worries that Ithimar is not interested in her as a *person*. Isn't it just the birthmark he's after? We laugh at Iggy's obsession even as we like him—he refuses to lie down and die. And in calling his obsession grotesque, Iggy is really too apologetic, for his desire catches not only the immense and innocent pleasure of intimacy as a gift, together with the sense in which things were larger and purer in our youth, but something real about the importance and impersonality of sex.

We can see in fact how much Bellow had grown in the ten years since *The Wrecker*, for Bellow offers not only a complete, sustaining situation and psychology, he has the playful pleasure of explaining the meaning of the wen. Its meaning is immeasurable to Iggy, of course, and so the small apricot-colored mark expands in its symbolic significance: it suggests the female favor, and then the central importance of small beauties and then, as Iggy makes like Henry Adams, the correlation of human emotion and physical power. The small mark becomes the occasion of a religious ecstasy that is at once great fun and convincing. Ithimar recalls to Marcella (as a hurricane develops outside) his first glimpse, "the secret moment of intimacy which silenced the whole world. When you disclosed that personal object, you and I were sealed in stillness. Then my soul took form, a distinct form. I experienced all the richness and glory for the first time consciously. I recognized beauty" (p. 74). He later tells her that the wen contains the "secret of life" and is "the same diameter as the sun."

When he thought of it, he says, he felt "explosions within me like whole novae, scattering my matter through sidereal space. . ." (p. 74).

If the hurricane striking just as Iggy gets his wish seems pat, it is not because Bellow has not prepared us for it; the power of the storm comically parallels the power of his emotion—and of the social taboos they are breaking. At bottom, *A Wen* is about the power of the imagination, but it's playful, mixing in a way we can call Jewish the earthy and the grand, the sad and the comic, the psychologically real and the farcically fantastic. Bellow gets some of his best comic effects in this potpourri, for in all of these plays he mixes—with comic inappropriateness—the sexual with something as solemn as urban renewal or Henry Adams. In *Orange Soufflé*, as light as its title promises, Bellow combines sex and sociology in a rather disturbing way. The visionary here is Hilda, a Polish whore who entertains Pennington, the WASP millionaire, once a month. After ten years, she'd like a little recognition ("If I were one of your employees I'd have plenty of seniority by now" [p. 130]), but even more, she foresees a deadly existence when her sister moves in. Like Iggy and "The Husband," she is desperate to escape her middle-class life, and Pennington, so feeble he can't even don his own trousers, is her answer. She, too, has a vision: wouldn't it be grand if he set her up in Palm Beach as his hostess? She's learned to be a gourmet cook and has actually been out of the trade for years. The play begins as a light, sexy farce but becomes more serious as the desperate Hilda begs. Pennington does not want anything as complicated as a human being around, and so, in the one play with a downbeat ending, Hilda's soufflé fails to rise.

Thus the plays have the same kind of unity as Bellow's novels, returning within their different stories to similar themes. All three plays are about sex, about the emptiness of middle-class life, and about the imaginative individual attempting to persuade his more literal-minded and cautious associates to adopt an exciting and original idea. The three visionaries seek to break out of their seclusion, even though they are surrounded by a middle class that is narrow and even antithetical to the imagination. And as all three seek a new life—involving always the persuasion of another—they attempt to deal in their separate ways with the past, to break it up like "The Husband" or to recover it like Iggy or to build upon it, like Hilda—who would erase it, too.

This emphasis upon confronting the past is at the center of Bellow's work, for Bellow not only champions the emotional and the imaginative; he discovers the deepest function of his art in catharsis, which is one of the keys to the nostalgia that informs his work.[23] Almost all of the novels explore the past in some way, and by the time of *Humboldt's Gift*, reminiscence has become the central activity. Herzog portrays a man in the past remembering a man in the past remembering his childhood. Joseph reviews his many memories, past and present. Allbee is the living embodiment (he says) of a past wrong, while Tommy Wilhelm remembers vividly the moments of his life-destroying error. More important, in each of the works the protagonist comes in contact with violence or death, whether in a dream, as in *Dangling Man*, or in a suicide or murder attempt, as in *The Victim* and the Basteshaw chapter in *Augie March*, or in a corpse, as in *Seize the Day* and *Henderson the Rain King*. Herzog almost commits murder, almost kills himself in an accident, and is almost incarcerated in a penitentiary. Mr. Sammler witnesses the corpse of Elya as well as the near murder of the black pickpocket, and *Humboldt's Gift* involves direct messages from a dead man about whom the protagonist broods.

What can we make of these patterns? It is clear that the play or novel works for the reader (and no doubt the author) in much the same way as the protagonist's memories work for him, offering an opportunity to vicariously rehearse an event (often violent or fatal) and thus discharge the emotion connected with it. Bellow's art drives to discover the hidden emotions of protagonist and reader. Its point is less theme than experience, a fact we have been slow to recognize: our modern realists like Bellow and Updike offer their readers (and audience) a vicarious experience that is *necessary* to them, purging as it does the accumulated emotions of daily life.

But in *The Last Analysis* Bellow uses this mechanism openly and for the purposes of comedy. He makes fun of his own art, presenting a comedian who has slipped because of his seriousness and who now, in his New York warehouse studio, seeks to combine laughter and homestyle psychoanalysis. Bummidge seeks a cure for "humanitis," and his technique he says is to act out "the main events of my life, dragging repressed material into the open by sheer force of drama" (p. 74). In the first act he struggles to get enough money to go on closed-circuit TV before a gathering of psychoanalysts, and talks about his performance with his associates and relatives—his agent Winkleman, his mistress Pamela, his sexy but platonic secretary Imogen, his sister, his wife, his son—many of whom resent the money he is squandering. He rehearses his method, remembering a few minor traumas such as getting caught fondling his sister's step-ins. In the second and last act, Bummidge gives his lecture-demonstration, taking himself through the birth trauma, conflicts with his father, sexual adolescence, marriage and then death, the experience of the last triggering an ecstatic state in which he disposes of all those who had obstructed him and determines to proceed with an institute to advance his new therapy.

One of Bummy's chief motives is his rebellion against our shallow culture, for he sees that as an entertainer he had distracted people from the truth that lies beneath the surface confusion of our lives. He will now drive deep, as Bellow has always done, engaging in what is no less than a metaphysical quest. Bummy tells us that he is "on an expedition to recover the forgotten truth . . . . It's fantastic, intricate, complicated, hidden. How can you live without knowing? Madge, look deep! Infinite and deep!" (p. 18). The "truth" is psychological too, for Bummy, like all the protagonists, fears something is wrong with him. Having pandered to his audiences, he now seeks an independent, dignified manhood—this, too, to be discovered by means of the Bummidge method. Bellow finds his climax in Bummy's reliving of his own birth, a play within a play, which Bummy entitles "The Birth of Philip Bomovitch" and plays lying on a sofa behind which, heads sticking through holes in a black cloth, his associates declaim. As the chorus talks, he is born, undergoes an unplanned attack of humanitis

("Farce follows horror into darkness. Deeper, deeper" [p. 96]) and then undergoes his own death, too, from which to the "Hallelujah Chorus" he is reborn.

The result is a witty and imaginative play that ought to work quite well as theater, especially since the published play is a reworking of the version that flopped. Bellow reduced the number of characters, he tells us, and emphasized the *"mental* comedy" of Bummidge, making for greater consistency. For the truth is that Bellow did not find in farce the freedom he had sought. Although some have worried about the ending, it is clear that Bellow did too: the revised play makes good formal sense. Why does Bummy now cure himself, on camera as it were, having used this technique for years? The answer is that the actual performance was necessary to heighten the emotion, creating the pressure that drives the repressed material into the open. Bummy does not discover any insights into himself, moreover, because the point is less insight than catharsis—or say that the imagined experience of his own death offers insights that cannot be articulated. Psychoanalysis slides into religion, self-analysis becoming epiphany, but then psychoanalysis has always had a kind of religiosity, and Bellow prepares us for Bummy's revelation by Bummy's comic assumption, at the end of Act I, of Christ's position on the cross.

Bummy does die, comically, and his ghostly, abstracted demeanor at the end of the play combines serenity, rebirth, and high humor. Theater professionals tell me *The Last Analysis* not only plays well, but that Bellow knows a great deal about the theater.[24] The first act reminds us of *Volpone*, for example, as a series of rapacious characters visit the protagonist. Bellow also gets high marks for daring—the concept of a character dredging up repressed material is inventive, offering risks the playwright accepted. Bellow has typically conceived of a grand idea within which he can present a more or less chaotic potpourri of characters, events, and comic bits. As character after character comes on stage, the influence of vaudeville is clear: each encounter could be viewed almost as a sketch.

We like Bummy then, and we enjoy Bellow's wit, as he develops a series of punchy, aphoristic lines, parodying academic research and professional meetings, self-help and deep theories, existentialists and back-room messiahs. And yet the play is flawed, or offers dangers to the unwary director. For what Bummy has repressed and must now purge—what he recalls throughout the bulk of the play—is family friction, bad feeling, resentment. His obstacle in the present, the real antagonist in the play, is once again family and friends. If the main business of the play is Bummy's obsession with an idea, as Bellow has said, its basic conflict is between Bummidge and the people around him. What does he do when he is reborn, strength discovered? He tells them off, one by one—wife, mistress, agent, son—and then orders them hauled away.

> Beat it, the whole gang of you.
> . . .
> *A device appears above. Bella, Pamela, Winkleman, Mott, Madge, Fiddleman*
> *and Max stare up.*

Winkleman: A net! Duck! Look out!
All are caught in the net. Bertam runs up like the ratcatcher he is to see what he has trapped. [pp. 116–17]

The farce often sweeps away the hangers-on in a catharsis of hostility and justice, but in this play the high spirits are marred by a certain misanthropy, as though the farcical form permitted Bellow's own personal feelings to come to the fore. And indeed, Bellow defines "humanitis" in precisely such terms. In a version of the play published in *Partisan Review* in 1962, Bellow had Bummidge say that "Humanitis means that you begin to come on with another person, but all of a sudden you can't bear him anymore. Take the sonofabitch away!"[25] He softens this in the final version, but "humanitis" remains other people. The reborn Bummidge, having relived some very unpleasant experiences, confesses a revulsion:

"Please—please don't crowd. Oh, don't touch! It makes me cold in the bowels. I feel you breathing on me. See how my skin is wincing" (p. 109).

Such lines give the lie to a more or less accepted view of Bellow as the champion of community. Certainly the protagonist desires community, but he desires the opposite too, for the people around him are distracting. He can triumph only by escaping them—and by surmounting an unclean world too, rendered here not in the description of the novel, but in dialogue, characters, attitudes. Bummidge has stopped making people laugh, he says, because "I can't stand the sound they make. And I feel hit by the blast of sickness from their lungs" (p. 8). Bummy's colleague is a ratcatcher who offers chopped liver prepared with his own hands. Bummidge exhorts his colleagues, "Onwards to the Tilby. We have to clean up the floors and purge the smell of blood" (p. 118).

Bummy's rejection of his associates makes *The Last Analysis* a notably non-Jewish play. Bummy is himself a Jewish character, as we have seen, but he ends up alone, like the American cowboy with a sidekick or two. So, too, do the protagonists in the novels, so that we must confess that the Bellow hero defines his final victory in terms of solitude. Or is the truth about us to be found in such solitude, since we fantasize about it so much? Bellow seems to tell us that we are not nearly as gregarious as we think we are, and after such novels as *Portnoy's Complaint* and *Good As Gold*, not to mention Bellow's own stories, "The Old System" and "The Silver Dish," we might want to argue that discomfort with a close family is indeed Jewish. Perhaps it is now the tension between the self and the relatives that captures the imagination of Jewish writers.

Or is such ambivalence very Jewish indeed? We might well argue that "humanitis" is a personal or emotional equivalent to the very real Jewish ambivalence about assimilation. To join the larger community is to end a painful alienation, obviously, but it is also to risk losing one's identity. No wonder characters such as Augie March first join and then resist the smothering community of their fellows. And then, perhaps deeper than the problem of assimilation, is a Jew's knowledge of the world's treachery: in a very personal way,

Bellow's protagonists live out the conflicts of a people who have been persecuted.

Is there any doubt that many of the other themes and situations in this play are Jewish? The emphasis on purity certainly is, though not many cultural historians comment on it. God's demand that the Jews be holy and righteous requires—as orthodox law suggests—a life of physical purity, including diet. Like the other protagonists, moreover, Bummidge is a visionary, and is surrounded by unbelieving companions, living a personal form of Jewish alienation. Bummy's concern with the past is obviously Jewish, for, as Irving Howe puts it, "nothing is more deeply ingrained in the Jewish experience than the idea of the past," and the problem of dealing with it in some way "forms the major burden of their art."[26] Psychoanalysis has been called the "Jewish science," since it was invented and widely practiced by Jews, and we have already commented on the Jewish emphasis on ideas, on talking, on language. Alfred Kazin describes Bummy with precision when he cites "the age-old Jewish belief that salvation is in thinking well—to go to the root of things, to become a kind of scientist of morals, to seek the ultimate forces that rule us."[27]

And the Yiddish theater? Certainly it stressed energy and spectacle and emotion over form or coherence, but I think it influenced Bellow in an even stronger, though more subtle, way. For in the Yiddish theater actors sought to be larger than life, as Schlossberg tells us in *The Victim*, to act in the open and sweeping Russian manner, indulging their emotions and projecting their nobility. Part of Bummy's need for a new self derives from his sense of having fallen away from a richer, deeper humanity, of being somehow smaller than his ancestors. Though the delightful Bummidge seems large enough, the fact remains that he is driven by an image of humanity that owes something to the large, full, exuberant character of the Yiddish theater.

But even more important than that, in terms of Bellow's Jewishness, is the play's striking internality. In *Great Jewish Short Stories* Bellow cites the old man who in his despair at lightening a burden, summons death. But when the Angel of Death appears, he changes his mind: "I can't get these sticks upon my back and wonder if you'd mind giving me a hand."[28] We find the old man funny and lovable in his will to live, his wit (as he retrieves the situation verbally) and his sass. But most importantly, we find him vivid because of the flash of the internal; as we stand outside of him, watching the old man talk to the Angel of Death, we get a glimpse of his inner self, a change of feeling that makes him at just that moment blossom into life.

Such it seems to me is the Jewish genius. And certainly it is Bellow's, at least in these plays, since they, too, are based on feeling, gaining their power from the pleasure of a middle-class verisimilitude: we are delighted by our surprised recognition of the emotions portrayed. What is important perhaps is the fact that Bellow finds an external way of expressing those feelings—the point of his use of farce. For Bellow can give us in farce the character turned inside out, a character revealing his inner life in an imaginary external world. The plays thus bring forth to public view emotions that would otherwise remain unarticulated.

They make us recognize our community, really, since we share those feelings, or many of them, and thus are in on the secret. And they make us laugh, providing comedies that are the world writ funny—comedies that permit Bellow to say what he really thinks (as Bummy's method makes a kind of sense) and to express what he must.

NOTES

1. For an interesting discussion of this point, see James M. Mellard, "Consciousness Fills the Void: Herzog, History, and The Hero in the Modern World," *Modern Fiction Studies* 25 (Spring 1979): 81–85.

2. Saul Bellow, "My Man Bummidge," *New York Times*, 27 September 1964, Section 2, p. 1. In the late 1950s Bellow also collaborated with Mary Otis on an adaptation of "Seize the Day" for the stage. This manuscript, which is in The University of Chicago collection, received only a reading (with Mike Nichols playing Tommy Wilhelm). See Richard Gilman, *Commonweal*, 29 March 1963, p. 21. Another Bellow novel, *The Victim*, was adapted to the stage by Leonard Lesley in 1952. See Wolcott Gibbs, *The New Yorker*, 10 May 1952, p. 54.

3. John Simon, "Theater Chronicle," review of *The Last Analysis*, *Hudson Review* 17 (1964–65): 557.

4. Walter Kerr, "Three Writers New to the Theatre," *New York Times*, 25 December 1965, Section 2, p. 3.

5. Gerald Nachman, "A Talk with Saul Bellow," *New York Post Magazine*, 1964, October 4, p. 6.

6. Saul Bellow, *Writers at Work*, Third Series, ed. George Plimpton (New York: Viking Compass, 1967), p. 183.

7. Saul Bellow, "The Jewish Writer and The English Literary Tradition," *Commentary* 8 (1949): 366.

8. David Daiches, "Breakthrough?" in *Contemporary American Jewish Literature: Critical Essays*, ed. Irving Malin (Bloomington: Indiana University Press, 1973), pp. 37, 38.

9. Alfred Kazin, *Bright Book of Life* (Boston: Little, Brown, 1973), pp. 132, 133.

10. Saul Bellow, *The Victim* (New York: Viking Compass, 1956), p. 94.

11. Irving Howe, *World of Our Fathers* (New York: Harcourt Brace Jovanovich, 1976), p. 261.

12. Sanford Pinsker, *The Schlemiel as Metaphor* (Carbondale: Southern Illinois University Press, 1971).

13. Earl Rovit, "Jewish Humor and American Life," in *Herzog*, ed. Irving Howe (New York: Viking Press, 1976), p. 515.

14. Sarah Blacher Cohen, *Saul Bellow's Enigmatic Laughter* (Urbana: University of Illinois Press, 1970), p. 20.

15. Bellow, "Bummidge," p. 5, and Robert Gutwillig, "Talk with Saul Bellow," *New York Times Book Review* 20 September 1964, p. 40.

16. Howe, p. 222.

17. Saul Bellow, "Introduction," *Great Jewish Short Stories* (New York: Dell, 1963), p. 10.

18. Saul Bellow, *Dangling Man* (New York: Meridian Fiction, 1960), p. 9.

19. Saul Bellow, "Pleasures and Pains of Playgoing," *Partisan Review* 21 (1954): 312, 313.

20. Bellow, *The Victim*, p. 126.

21. Daiches, p. 33.

22. Pages in parentheses are to the following editions: *The Wrecker*, in *Seize the Day* (New York: Viking Press, 1956), pp. 193–211. *A Wen, Esquire*, January 1965, pp. 72–74, 111. *Orange Soufflé, Esquire* October 1965, pp. 130–31, 134, 136. *The Last Analysis* (New York: The Viking Press, 1965).

23. For an extended discussion of this, see Keith Opdahl, " 'Stillness in the Midst of Chaos': Plot in the Novels of Saul Bellow," *Modern Fiction Studies* 25 (Spring 1979): 15–28.

24. I am indebted here to Fred Nelson, director, playwright, and teacher.

25. Saul Bellow, "Humanitis," *Partisan Review* 29 (1962): 345.

26. Irving Howe, "Introduction," *Jewish-American Stories* (New York: National American Library, 1977), p. 4.

27. Kazin, *Bright Book*, p. 134.

28. *Great Jewish Stories*, p. 11.

The Jewish Folk Drama of
Isaac Bashevis Singer

Sarah Blacher Cohen

ISAAC BASHEVIS SINGER WAS AWARDED THE NOBEL PRIZE FOR HIS "IMPASSIONED
narrative art"[1] with roots in the Eastern European Yiddish cultural tradition,
but his plays differ in important and interesting ways from those representative
of that tradition. The plays of Avrom Goldfadn combined melodrama and music
to dramatize stirring Biblical events and inspirational stories from Jewish history. Those of Jacob Gordin sought to elevate the Yiddish language and enlight-
en the Jewish masses with their realism and moralizing. Sholem Asch made the
theater his soapbox and wrote social protest plays denouncing the ills of the
Jewish community. Singer's plays, however, veer off in their own direction. At
the age of sixty-eight, he created his own special brand of Jewish folk drama,
while retaining many of the conventions of the standard form. Through decep-
tively simple writing, he has artfully fashioned a naive world, where wonder and
superstition prevail over skepticism and reason. The structure of his plays is
also uncomplicated; a leisurely beginning, an accelerated middle, and a star-
tling end recur in the customary two acts, each with many short scenes. The
plots are simple; each has a central action in which improbable events occur
suddenly and swiftly. Most of the protagonists are distraught females in the grip
of powerful obsessions who act recklessly and defiantly. Their language is of a
feverish intensity, but the dialogue of the minor characters resembles the cute
prattling of children or the cryptic utterances of old crones.

Singer's plays, however, depart from the traditional folk drama in one crucial
way. "The folk play centered thematically on the response of the characters to
the land on which they lived. Close to the soil, their identities and destinies
were shaped by a force they sensed moving in the earth."[2] The Jews Singer
writes about were excluded from having vital connections with the land; they did
not experience the hardship of its sterility or the joy of its fertility. Nor, for that
matter, were they permitted to survive at all in their landless ghettos. Deprived
of the sustaining theme of folk drama, Singer mobilizes greater forces of his
imagination to invent an alternate theme and related setting for his folk plays.
He pretends the Holocaust did not exist and writes about these Jews as they live
in his memory and imagination. Believing that "literature must have an address,
that it just cannot be in a vacuum,"[3] Singer constructs his version of the *shtetl*
and converts it into an appropriate backdrop for his resurrected Jews to act out
their parts. In place of the idyllic or malevolent land of the typical folk drama,
he creates idyllic or malevolent *shtetls* to shape the destiny of his characters.
Just as the land became more symbol than fact, so Singer's *shtetl*, stripped of
historical verisimilitude, is more a stylized creation of his imagination than a
realistically specified place. In this alternately charming and grotesque realm of

his fancy, the world is finally "but lure and appearance, a locale between heaven and hell, the shadow of larger possibilities."¹ And the quaint Jewish folk, the temporary inhabitants of this insubstantial sphere, are intent not on cultivating a piece of land but on purifying their souls. The greatest deterrent to their doing so is the temptation of illicit sexuality, either adultery or homosexuality. Though they yield to temptation, the primary evil lies not in their forbidden indulgence in the carnal but in their surrender to the secular hedonism which the carnal represents. Their struggle on earth and in the world beyond is to forsake this hedonism and embrace the austere life of piety. The spiritual territory recedes before them, but still they journey toward it.

At their best, Singer's dramas are authentic expressions of a folk culture whose speech, emotions and thought he intimately knows. They are also products of his idiosyncratic imagination, which freely consorts with the improper and the farfetched. But Singer's plays have not emerged full-blown from his head as plays. They are adaptations of his short stories made with the assistance of literary collaborators and theatrical advisers.

The Hebrew poet Chaim Bialik observed that reading an author's work in translation is like "kissing the bride through a veil," but in the transit between story and play, one can miss seeing the bride altogether. To make the bride conform to the public's notion of beauty and make the spectacle a more commercial success, those in charge can so alter her appearance that she loses much of her charm and distinction. When Singer is not directly involved in the wedding, as, for example, in the movie version of his novel, *The Magician of Lublin*, adapted by a Hollywood screenwriter, the bride is so distorted that she is scarcely recognizable. When Singer is the principal adapter, she fares much better. But Singer does not have total control. Given the communal nature of theater with its disparate standards and tastes, the bride is unavoidably robbed of her pristine loveliness. So it would seem that Singer's plays are commercial as well as spiritual folk dramas. Not only do his characters struggle to purge themselves of corruption, he, too, has undoubtedly struggled to keep his work unsullied. Of his participation in the theater he states, "I like art to be pure. A book is written by one man. In the theater you have too many partners—the director, the producer, the actors, the writers. In a way it is already a collective."⁵ Though Singer's imagination as a fiction writer has been linked to the "pagan animism of the European Middle Ages,"⁶ his dramas are necessarily tied to the capitalism of the contemporary American theater.

Singer's first boyhood association with the theater was as a place of evil. From a sermon his rabbi father preached, he learned that "the wicked sit day and night in the theater, eat pork and sin with loose women."⁷ Many years later, therefore, *The Mirror*,⁸ the first play Singer adapted from his similarly titled short story, concerned the seduction of a loose woman by a demon. In "The Mirror,"⁹ one of several demon-infested stories Singer wrote for a projected volume, *Memoirs of the Spirit of Evil*,¹⁰ the first-person demon narrator performs different functions than he does in Singer's play. As a witty teller of the tale, who seems more like a puckish wedding jester than a grim fiend, he causes us to take a lighthearted view of Zirel, the beautiful but bored *shtetl* woman who succumbs to temptation. By emphasizing his maverick origins and wily stratagems to ensnare her more than her anguish at being ensnared, he distances us from her plight. He takes the sting out of evil by showing its charming irresistibility and infects us with his cavalier attitude toward it. Because he is the demonic master of ceremonies, he determines the pace and length of the story. He serves, according to Irving Howe, as a "wonderful device for structural economy: [he] replaces the need to enter the 'inner life' of the characters, the whole plaguing business of the psychology of motives, for [he embodies those] symbolic equivalents and coordinates to human conduct, what Singer calls a 'spiritual stenography'."[11] The English translation of the story, with its rapid narration of events and snatches of dialogue at only the most crucial junctures, is only eleven pages long. Little is revealed about Zirel's life before the demon's arrival, what actually prompted her capitulation, or the full extent of her remorse in Sodom. The story's larger questions are left unanswered. "Is there a God? Is he all merciful? Will Zirel ever find salvation? Or is creation a snake primeval crawling with evil?" (pp. 87–88). The demon pleads ignorance. Since he is a "minor devil" who is unlikely to get promoted, he is deprived of a larger omniscience.

Singer expands our understanding of Zirel's plight and the philosophical issues connected with it in the two-act play he wrote for the Yale Repertory Theater in 1973. He leaves behind the demon's limited point of view and focuses on Zirel's behavior before, during, and after her fall. Zirel is another of Singer's educated women, who, denied access to the study of sacred writings, has no function in the *shtetl*'s male-dominated world of traditional Judaism. Nor is she blessed with children to absorb her energies and give her status as a worthy Jewish wife. At the play's beginning, Singer treats her dilemma more whimsically than tragically. Unlike the angry heroines in Singer's stories, Zirel does not grievously lament her fate and castigate a patriarchal society for its gross injustice. Rather she acts like a wayward fairy-tale creature who resorts to subversive means to obtain compensating pleasures. She stealthily reads erotic supernatural tales and, like the wicked stepmother in "Snow White and the Seven Dwarfs," continually gazes at her mirror to confirm she is the fairest of them all. Zirel is not totally to blame for her profane reading and idle vanity since in the play, unlike the story, her cabalist husband, Shloime, is so engrossed in his messianism that he wears his breeches to bed to be ready for the Messiah's coming. Zirel, for her part, is so sexually frustrated that she can only jest at her own expense: "All I have is a marriage contract. He's either praying, studying, or just murmuring" (I, 1, 5). Indeed a measure of the first act's humor concerns the burlesqued clash of values between the puritanical husband and the sensual wife, which for Singer symbolizes the irreconcilable conflict between religious asceticism and carnal delight. The more extreme each character's behavior becomes, that is, the more each renounces the body for the soul and the soul for the body, the more desperately comic Zirel and Shloime become.

Since Zirel cannot wait for Shloime's love in the world to come, she practices self-love in this world. In Singer's value system, worship of self replacing worship of God is a sign of demonic possession. Drawing upon the Jewish folk tradition, Singer, therefore, has the mirror become the devil's hiding place. The demon in the mirror distorts reality and points up the void at the heart of existence. Or as Zirel's father admonishes: "A mirror lies. You see things and they have no substance. You see a person and it's not a person" (I, 1, 4). At the same time the demon-inhabited mirror becomes a magnifying glass that expands Zirel's imagination. It contributes to her erroneous sense of a double identity: the dutiful wife and the wild harlot. Projecting an illusion of a titillating worldly realm, the mirror also offers her an escape from provincial Krashnik, the stultifying Polish village she lives in. Adam, she claims, wouldn't even stop there to urinate. Above all, the mirror confuses Zirel's aesthetic and ethical judgment. She finds the ugly demon beautiful and infinitely preferable to a pious Jew, for she would rather have "one measure of debauchery than ten of modesty."[12]

In the short story no one tries to prevent Zirel from succumbing to the demon. To lengthen the play and broaden its scope, Singer mocks the Jewish community's futile attempts to save its errant daughter. The servant Yente tries to protect Zirel but is a caricature of her, since she has the same lewd fantasies. Her husband, Shloime, prays for Zirel's soul but performs ablutions to cleanse his own dirty thoughts. Her father, offering no constructive advice, can only lecture Zirel on the impropriety of divorcing her abstinent mate. Reb Yoetz, the old exorcist from Babylon, cannot free Zirel from evil and tries to seduce her himself, justifying his behavior by saying: "the respected ones have the same desires as the rascals and the lechers" (I, 3, 63) and "the old need it more than the young" (I, 3, 64). In Singer's temporal world, then, people of all classes, ages, and persuasions clandestinely or openly court the devil, and no mortal can rescue a fellow mortal from his powerful embrace.

The first act of *The Mirror* belongs to the morally flawed but humorously quaint world of Krashnik. Its characters, resembling the stock figures of Plautine comedy and the commedia dell'arte, are the familiar types of Singer's folk parables: the rascally servant, the religiously fanatic husband, the sexually spurned wife, the demon lover, and the specious sorcerer. The situations are sparse and sketchily developed. The seduction scene, which is the focal point, is economically and wittily drawn, but the exorcism is but a hackneyed version of the one in Ansky's *Dybbuk*. The dialogue in the remainder of the play is, for the most part, original. The demon, whose power resides in words, has the most arresting lines, by turns lyrical, antic, and exotic. Reb Yoetz is a master of Singer's folk aphorisms, a blend of the ribald and the religious, cast in the rural idiom. Zirel's language has verve when she is the comic ironist ridiculing her unconsummated marriage. The minor characters, however, could be directly imported from *Fiddler on the Roof*, for they speak in the same Yiddishized primer language of predictable simpletons.

The second act is anything but predictable. Just as Zirel takes a leap of faith, or more appropriately faithlessness, to follow her demon Hurmizah to the *sitra achra*, the other side of the mirror, so Singer takes an imaginative leap by depicting the supernatural realm beyond the mirror, the surreal world of Sodom, his equivalent of Hell. While Singer's Hell contains the requisite amount of tortures and perversions, it is more a caricature of both Hell and earth. The only sin in Sodom is not to sin. Desiring "all good things now," the demons, like contemporary Americans, are constantly rushing to indulge in as many pleasures as possible. The king of Sodom wants "natural love in five minutes" and takes a pill to awaken such love. But he and the demon, Hurmizah, who turns out to be a eunuch and pimp, are incapable of any individualized love. Even though they are "so clever and refined in the science of lechery" (II, 2, 85), they can only analyze sex, not indulge in it.

Zirel soon realizes that she has been lured to Sodom under false pretenses. She is not to have her lust sated by the demons, but is to arouse their lust. Sodom, she ruefully discovers, is not the delightful haven of the damned. Its desperate hedonism proves ultimately as confining as her life in Krashnik. At this point, the play's allegorical implications are obvious. It is impossible for the person with a rarefied imagination to survive in a tedious ritual-bound society or in its obverse equivalent: a compulsorily exciting, aimless existence. It is far more satisfying to remain inside the mirror, the realm of possibility, removed from the fixed position of either sphere. Singer, however, advances a more religious interpretation of the play. *The Mirror*, he claims, is about "a person who cannot be happy with God and cannot be happy with the Devil. God—the way the Jews understand God—is too boring, too dogmatic, too stagnant. So Zirel thought the Devil—let's call it the secular life—would be good. But the play shows that the secular life is also full of dogmas, also full of silly duties, also full of checks, not of assets—and a lot of cruelty in addition."[13]

For Singer, the way back from Hell is impossible. In the *Gilgamesh*, the Babylonian creation epic, once the individual has coupled with animals, he cannot return to the world of men. Similarly, once Zirel has consorted with demons, she cannot begin life over again with ordinary mortals. Subscribing to the doctrine of the irreversibility of sinful actions, Singer consigns Zirel to the interior of the mirror, his form of limbo, where she suffers for her own misdeeds and assumes the guilt of all former Zirels. She thus joins the ranks of the penitents in Singer's novels who immure themselves to painfully work out their own and the world's salvation.

Singer's idea of having a person who cannot live with either the religious or the worldly remain within a mirror is ingenious. However, in Act Two it takes Singer too long to get Zirel into her mirror. A good deal of extraneous happenings impede the resolution of the principal action: The orgiastic dance numbers are too excessive and lengthy; a gratuitous civil war breaks out between Sodom and Gomorrah; a precipitous love affair occurs between Zirel and a sodomite Reb Yoetz. But above all, the cryptic philosophizing most retards the pace. Moreover, all these distractions prevent Singer from fully developing Zirel's character. Devoid of the vitality she had in the first act, she is not as convincing as the pathetic object of demonic torture and mental anguish. The vibrant folk character of the first act becomes an enervated figure of allegory. Singer's circumscribed world of Krashnik thus proves more interesting than the orgiastic revels of Sodom and the solemn truths from the mirror's interior.

In *Teibele and Her Demon*,[14] Singer's most recent play, which he, with collaborator Eve Friedman, adapted from his short story by the same name, there is no danger of getting lost in *The Mirror*'s phantasmagorical netherworld or being detained in its murky realm of abstraction. The setting in *Teibele and Her Demon* is the palpable world of Frampol, Poland, in the 1880s, which, like Krashnik, is another of Singer's self-contained *shtetls* ruled by its own set of orthodox laws and unorthodox superstitions. Frampol, like Krashnik, is untouched by the shifting trends of secular thought or of the convolutions of history. The only current events that interest these villages are the moral rise and decline of their inhabitants and the swift administration of just rewards and punishments.

Since a deserted Jewish wife and her demon lover are the central characters of both *The Mirror* and *Teibele and Her Demon*, it would seem Singer is as much obsessed with depicting this incongruous couple as they are obsessed with each other. But the couples are not identical. Though the male lovers are both named Hurmizah and both employ the same lurid, exotic language in their seductions, the one in *The Mirror* is an actual demon but an impotent one. He is not smitten with Zirel but is only performing his duty of enticing her to Sodom. He gloats over his triumph and her weakness which for him is symptomatic of the weakness of all women. Hurmizah in *Teibele* is an ordinary mortal, the lackluster teacher's helper, Alchonon, who masquerades as a very potent demon much devoted to Teibele. Indeed, in the original short story Alchonon as demon risks his life for Teibele, dying of pneumonia from his winter visits to her. His true identity and self-sacrifice are never revealed even at his funeral which Teibele by chance attends.

Obviously, Singer and Friedman did not feel that the death of a selfless male would be the most compelling subject for their play. Following the advice of Poe, one of Singer's favorite authors, they dramatized instead the death of a beautiful woman. Before Teibele's death, however, they involve her in a very lively bedroom farce, where the sexual organs, according to Singer, "are even more *meshuga* [crazy] than the brain."[15] In the first act, six wry elliptical scenes reveal the origin and intensity of Teibele's and Alchonon's sexual craziness. The convoluted rising action produces the hilarity of preposterous gullibility and farfetched deception. It captures the antic hypocrisy of daily respectability and nightly licentiousness. The dialogue conveys the inflated lyricism of new-found love and the deflating bawdy language of unabandoned mating. The characters are endearing folktale types, but their unlikely union makes for improbable transformations. Every Wednesday and Saturday night, the bedraggled Alchonon ceases being the village *schlemiel* and disguises himself as the demon Hurmizah, the genital superman who overwhelms Teibele with his sexual prowess and his sensual cabalistic lore. She, in turn, leaves off being the pious Jewish wife to become the uninhibited lover of her demon, though his breath smells of garlic and his nose sniffles in winter.

Sex, as in Singer's short stories, immediately becomes a leveler, removing distinctions between class, body, and mind. It also becomes an anesthesia numbing those in its power to any of its injurious effects. Teibele especially is so caught up in her passions that she sees nothing wrong with the affair. Alchonon, however, grows to dislike the relationship.

In a comic reversal of the typical male-female conflict, he resents being viewed as a sexual object and wants to be valued for his mind as well as his body. He objects to playing a role, to pretending to be someone he is not. He wants Teibele to cherish him as a mortal not a demon. He, therefore, resorts to further deceit by having Teibele's absent husband declared legally dead and in his guise as Hurmizah orders her to marry Alchonon, the man he actually is. By refusing to remain a supernatural creature and settle for a supernatural love, Alchonon transforms the play from a light-hearted romantic comedy to a serious drama with tragic overtones. For in Singer's moral universe, once an individual commits a falsehood and does not confess it, he is compelled to practice more and more damaging forms of deception until the accumulated weight of his subterfuge crushes him and those he implicates.

While Alchonon painfully complicates his life by relinquishing fantasy for reality, Teibele in Act Two suffers from clinging to fantasy and not accepting reality. Enthralled by the fiery raptures of her demon lover, she cannot tolerate the lukewarm connubial pleasures of her prosaic husband. Her nocturnal transports of joy with Hurmizah degenerate into daily marital strife with Alchonon just because her faulty imagination cannot discern that they are the same person. Teibele is thus Singer's embodiment of the perennially dissatisfied mortal who craves magic over the mundane, the exotic over the ordinary. For her these qualities are mutually exclusive categories which she cannot envision existing in the same individual. Longing for the rare excitement of the unknown, she fails to recognize the rare excitement of the familiar which, in this case, is the earthbound yet mystical Alchonon, the source of both spiritual exultation and fleshly ecstasy. Yet the deluded Teibele demands the return of the demon, thus forcing Alchonon to cuckold himself. And when his version of the demon no longer arouses her, he has his friend act as a more titillating substitute. Here the play shows that even the exotic can grow tedious and needs constant injections of depravity to keep it provocative.

Teibele's failure to recognize Alchonon's dual identity has been criticized not only as a flaw in her character, but as a flaw in the play itself. Since Alchonon's appearance and language are not significantly altered between his demonic and human state, the question arises: how could she not be aware of the tricks played on her? Walter Kerr claims that our credulity, if not hers, has been taxed, that the play's "compounded sleight-of-hand," its "improvised twists and turns" defy the "bothersome laws of human logic."[16] But what Kerr overlooks is that *Teibele and Her Demon* is not meant to be either a realistic problem play or a convincing psychological case study. It is another of Singer's erotic fables with its own idiosyncratic logic, its intentionally obvious mistaken identities, its outrageous improbabilities. As a fable, it adopts the childlike view that anything can happen in the world of adults and does not offer elaborate explanations for these happenings. It simply presents the implausible as plausible and asks us, in the name of make-believe, to accept the conversion.

Teibele and Her Demon is also a spiritual fable in which the characters struggle to atone for their mistaken moral identities. In an epilogue several years after the demonic orgy, Alchonon is an emaciated penitent, still punishing himself for his former transgressions. Teibele, mortally ill, still cannot accept the fact that the demon was Alchonon, for "she knows that had it been a demon, not a man, she lay with, her sin would not be as grave as adultery" (II, 6, 43). But given the happy resolutions of Singer's benign fables, Teibele is not the victim of harsh retribution. The rabbi, invoking the compassionate Jewish doctrine of calming the agony of the dying even with deception, bids Alchonon lie one last time by informing Teibele that he was not the demon after all. Because such a lie will grant Teibele (whose name means "little dove") peace in her journey to the afterworld, Alchonon will be committing a *mitzvah*, a good deed, and will be aiding his own salvation.

The ending of the play precipitously shifts from the somber realism of a deathbed confessional to the expressionistic treatment of Teibele's embrace of a new consort, the Angel of Death. Showing her the composite nature of seemingly disparate entities, he enables her to see that her husband, her demon lover, and he are united as one. This dreamlike intrusion of the otherworldly into the worldly is not merely a sensational *deus* or angel *ex machina* device. It economically and movingly resolves what could not be accomplished by conventional staging.

The excellence of *Teibele and Her Demon*, however, does not rest on the novelty of its staging. Largely relying on Singer's familiar brand of stylized realism, it is most innovative in the kind of love story it tells. The erotic is not merely trivial foreplay for a moralistic climax as in *The Mirror*. Nor is its magic dispelled by weighty philosophizing. In *Teibele* the erotic becomes the primary focus where it is accorded the highest reverence and the most intricate development. Teibele and Hurmizah do not, like Zirel and her demon, fantasize about love; they are its active celebrants. Their sexual union becomes a holy sacrament which, according to Singer's cabalistic view, is directly patterned after "God's love for the Schechinah" (II, 1, 7), the female spirit of the universe. Through the first half of the play, the couple's love is, therefore, more divine than demonic, more soaring in mystical heights than plummeting into naturalistic depths. But no matter how uplifting ecstatic consummations are, they are not long-lasting so that in the remainder of the play their love becomes more human than divine. Its lack of fulfillment, however, proves just as moving as their earlier requited love. Tormentingly real are their anguished separations, their cruel rejections, their bitter disappointments. Yet these deterrents do not destroy their perpetual longing; they only heighten its intensity. Alchonon's love for Teibele is so consuming that he panders for her and perjures himself to allow her to die happily. So powerful is Teibele's love for Hurmizah that she forsakes earthly tranquillity to remain true to him. In the end both are rewarded for their fidelity and treated compassionately. Though they are separated in this world, they will be reunited in Singer's eternal realm of "lust and mercy." From carnal to divine, from mortal to immortal, their love story transcends the ordinary.

When the spotlight is on the two principals caught up in the turbulent course of their love, *Teibele and Her Demon* is an absorbing play. But when Singer and Friedman introduce subsidiary characters whose only function is to provide exposition or tone down the eroticism with irrelevant levity, the results are disappointing. The couple's two friends, Genendel and Menasha, not only bore us with their broadly comic equivalent of demonic seduction but distract us from the more significant action. At their worst they are extra bodies who take up stage space and, with their superfluous antics, mechanically stretch the delicate fable into a two-act play. The same holds true for the adapters' inclusion of quaint bits of Jewish ritual: a partial exorcism, a few lines of a *Purimshpil*, an abbreviated wedding ceremony. When these are an integral part of the play, reinforcing characterization and theme, they greatly enhance the work. But many of these ethnic scraps of local color serve only as kosher-style forms of parochialism to satisfy the commercial taste for things Jewish. Some of the dialogue is also the source of artificial Jewish seasoning. When the secondary characters imitate Catskill comedians straining for laughs, they are both anachronistic and cloying. Fortunately, the mercurial wit and poetic eloquence of Teibele and her demon drown out these voices.

This is not to suggest that Singer is incapable of creating authentically funny ethnic stereotypes who, in their own right, assume center stage. In *Shlemiel the First*,[17] a play I have worked on with Isaac Bashevis Singer, the entire town is populated with dwarfed intellects whose sole excuse for being is to amuse. The amusement we devise for them makes no pretense at profundity. It consists of adolescent ruses, moronic credulity, domestic slapstick. The scantily developed characters suffer mounting escalations of confusion, but their humor of verbal retrieval enables them to make light of their mishaps. Their dialogue is filled with risible nonsequiturs, foolish aphorisms, and silly travesties of Talmudic logic.

In many ways *Shlemiel the First* burlesques the serious concerns of Singer's spiritual dramas. The questioning of values, the sexual misdeeds, the *shtetl* puritanism, and the misapprehensions of reality so earnestly discussed in *Teibele* and *The Mirror* are drolly treated in *Shlemiel the First*, which more resembles the classic numbskull tale than Singer's philosophical fantasies. The play, like the numbskull tale in which "misunderstanding results in inappropriate and absurd actions,"[18] deals with the compounded misunderstanding of Shlemiel, the docile town fool who agrees to spread the wisdom of Gronam Ox, the self-proclaimed sage of Chelm. Ox's wisdom consists of such gastronomic idiocy as: "The Tree of knowledge . . . was a Blintze Tree" (2, 6, 186) and "Cain killed Abel because he thought blood was borscht" (2, 6, 186), yet the addlepated Shlemiel, inspired by these truths, volunteers to go to the ends of the earth to convey this knowledge.

Fortunately, Shlemiel does not travel far, since the local vagabond, Chaim Rascal, tricks him into believing that he is heading toward the world when he is actually returning to Chelm. Thus upon his arrival home, Shlemiel mistakenly thinks he has discovered Chelm Two and convinces everyone, including his dubious wife, that he is a visitor from another Chelm. Gronam Ox validates Shlemiel's misjudgment with the humorously specious argument: "If God could arrange it that man has two hands, two feet, two eyes and two ears, why couldn't he have created two Chelms, two Shlemiels" (1, 5, 58)?

What follows is a ludicrous imitation of *Teibele and Her Demon*, whereby the power of illusion transforms the same man into a sexually more appealing one so that he ends up cuckolding himself. Mr. and Mrs. Shlemiel, like Singer's marriage violators, are guilt-ridden over what they believe is an adulterous union and are convinced they will be punished in Hell. However, in *Shlemiel the First*, they undergo a mock penance and are granted a mock salvation. Chaim Rascal, not the Angel of Death, confesses his deception and frees them of their delusion. Gronam Ox, the caricature of the merciful rabbi, pardons them for their unintentional sins and reunites them in lawful marriage. The final wisdom he dispenses is not another of his ridiculous pronouncements but a well-worn truth which serves as the real wisdom of this numbskull tale: while waiting for Paradise, "enjoy life" in this world.

Since *Shlemiel the First* is based on episodes from Singer's children's book, *The Fools of Chelm and Their History*, and his children's story, "When Shlemiel Went to Warsaw,"[19] itself derived from Yiddish folklore, the enjoyment of life in the play is not defined abstractly and complexly, but concretely and simply. In Chelm, which is the microcosm of the human condition, the numbskull characters long for a time when they can daily eat kreplach with cheese and blintzes with sour cream and indulge in all their whims. But until then, they settle for the imperfections of their life: cookies that don't satisfy hunger, telescopes without magnifying lenses, trumpets that don't put out fires. They temporarily give up the idea of moving to Dalfonka, the city of paupers where the rich never die, but happily endure their ephemeral existence in impoverished Chelm. Since they are comic characters without total self-awareness, they are sure to repeat the same mistakes. Gronam Ox and his elders will continue to be pompous idiots who, with their skewed logic, will again twist rationality into absurdity. Their wives will remain the founts of common sense, exasperatingly at a loss to clean up the mess around them. And the Shlemiels will still be the engineers of their own misfortune, ready to be duped by the next rogue. Singer and I, however, do not examine their fallibility in any great depth. Like his children's literature, we have written this play for people "who don't read to find their identity," but who "love interesting stories, not commentary. . . ."[20]

Of Singer's strictly adult plays, the most mature and substantial of them is *Yentl*,[21] which absorbed viewers primarily because it deals with problems of identity confronting Jewish women in the late-nineteenth-century Polish *shtetls*, problems that have not been resolved in our own century. In *The Mirror* and *Teibele and Her Demon*, the heroines' craving for otherworldly sensuality suppresses any desire they have for intellectual fulfillment in this world. In *Yentl*, however, the heroine's love for Torah vies forcefully with her love for a man. Her yearning for mental and spiritual liberation is strongly at odds with her need for physical and emotional union. Singer's play explores the religious context that gives rise to Yentl's conflict, subtly analyzes the complex dimensions of it, and compassionately depicts the painful consequences of the need to choose one alternative.

In the original short story, "Yentl the Yeshiva Boy,"[22] Singer endows Yentl with some biologically masculine features. She is "tall, thin, bony, with small breasts and narrow hips. . . . There was even a slight down on her upper lip" (p. 122). Her desire to explicate the holy texts, a privilege reserved only for men in nineteenth-century orthodox Judaism, is thus partially attributed to her hormonally determined masculinity. In the 1975 Broadway play which Singer wrote with Leah Napolin, Yentl's gender is not in question. Actress Tovah Feldshuh's eighteen-year-old Yentl is very much a comely girl whose formidable knowledge of Torah and Talmud derives not only from the secret instruction of her father, Reb Todrus, but from her own rare intelligence and high-spirited, rebellious nature. The play differs from the story, then, in depicting a less genetically programmed Yentl, who exercises free will to enrich and complicate her life. It reveals her plight in greater detail and probes more deeply into her feelings. To accomplish this, the play dramatizes many more scenes of Judaism's discrimination against women in which Yentl actively combats and covertly undermines this discrimination.

The most obvious interpretation of the play is, therefore, a feminist one. Yentl is a victim of a patriarchal society which believes that "he who teaches his daughter Talmud is corrupting her" (p. 8). It is a religious society that regards women not as juridical adults but as biological creatures, since it exempts and thereby excludes them from performing those highly esteemed liturgical and communal responsibilities designated for a particular time. The assumption is that they will be so busy rearing their children and caring for their households that they will be unable to pray at the synagogue and study at the academy. The Jewish community makes no allowance for a woman like Yentl who rejects the stereotypical feminine role, who refuses to rejoice when her sons and not she are permitted to study Torah or objects to being her husband's eternal footstool in Heaven. Because Yentl is so bright, she is barred from equal participation in Judaism's higher intellectual and spiritual realms for yet another reason besides her sex, a reason embodied in the Hebrew phrase—*kavod ha-tsibur*—which translated means "the honor [or self-respect] of the community." In other words, Yentl is such a brilliant student of Torah and Talmud that her flawless mastery of the subject would demean the community (of men), since none could rival her achievement. As the highly educated woman, she is such a threat to their supremacy that the men of the play choose a male half-wit rather than the precocious Yentl for the ritual quorum at her own father's funeral. In their eyes "a learned woman is a monstrosity" (p. 38) who must be excluded from the group. Such an exclusion is very painful for Yentl, since she is deprived of the most enlightening and holy aspects of Judaism. But what the play also makes clear is that Yentl's exclusion is a great loss to Judaism as well. By cutting women off from the primary sources of learning, the Jewish community "amputates half of its potential scholarship, that is akin to cultural self-destruction."[23] With women excised, there can only be what Cynthia Ozick calls "the Jewish half-genius."[24]

Yentl is complex enough to warrant a modern psychological interpretation as well as a traditionally religious one. According to Singer, one of the principal reasons he wrote the drama was to show that "the human soul is full of contradictions."[25] Just as a thief steals a prayer shawl to worship the Lord, "so Yentl breaks the law in order to be able to study the law."[26] Yentl errs by trespassing in the male's learned domain, and by dressing in men's clothes to do so, she also damages her own God-given femininity. She is contravening the Torah's prohibition against men and women switching apparel, for "when the body dresses in strange garments the soul will be perplexed" (p. 19). Appropriate clothing, according to this view, prescribes correct behavior and preserves rightful identity, or as Singer states, "clothes guard a person just as words do."[27] By donning alien apparel and being possessed by it, Yentl assumes an alien sexuality and acts in unpredictably illicit ways. What starts out as a pragmatic disguise for the purest of motives ends up as a major transgression in which Yentl perverts her own desires and harmfully deceives those closest to her. Her male disguise as Anshel prevents her from consummating her natural love for her study partner, Avigdor, and leads her into an unnatural marriage with Hadass, to reclaim her for Avigdor. What results is a sinful homosexual union, since it blurs the "distinctions between the sexes,"[28] distinctions that traditional Judaism believes are as important as those between the weekday and the Sabbath, the Gentile and the Jew. Moreover, the union is sinful because it not only thwarts Hadass's personal need for maternity, but it makes impossible the Biblical injunction: "Be fruitful and multiply." Thus Singer implies that if the world were made up of only Yentls who devoted their lives to being Torah scholars, there would be no Jews born to study the Torah. To stress the need for perpetuating the Jewish people, he ends the play with the lawful heterosexual marriage of Hadass and Avigdor and the birth of their son, Anshel. There is no room for Yentl the Yeshiva student in this society whose survival depends upon reproducing itself. She must depart as a male to attend another seminary where as a female, Singer leads us to believe, she will secretly atone for her sacrilegious study of sacred texts. But there is a final reason Singer, the traditionalist, must rout Yentl from the community: she is not dependent on a man to define her identity and, therefore, does not provide a model for man's dependence on God.[29] Viewing herself the accomplished rival of any man, she encourages man to view himself the accomplished rival of God.

However, Singer, the modernist, sees some worth in Yentl's depravity. Because she possesses the "divine androgyny of the soul" (p. 7), she is able to combine the strength of both sexes in her pursuit of wisdom. Her intellectual understanding of the Torah and Talmud is augmented by her enriched powers of perception. Her spiritual involvement with these holy writings is enhanced by her added religious fervor. Similarly, her ability to love both Hadass and Avigdor in ways which please each is due to her special sensitivity. Her decision to leave both of them is a reflection of her high degree of altruism. Though Heaven may have made a mistake in giving Yentl "the soul of a man" (p. 10) and creating her a woman, the mistake has its compensations. Thus for Singer *Yentl* has a "kind of cabalistic meaning" in that sins can serve to "lift up the soul."[30]

The blending of the traditional and the modern pertains not only to *Yentl*'s thematic concerns, but to many other features of the play. Of all of Singer's dramas, *Yentl* contains the most resemblances to the traditional Yiddish theater. They both include ingenious female disguise to enrich characterization and heighten romantic complications. Molly Picon, in a Yiddish drama by her husband, played a mischievous Yeshiva boy named Yankl, and in the Yiddish film, *Yidl mitn Fidel*, she masqueraded as a young male fiddler temporarily prevented from marrying the man she loves. However, Molly Picon's comedies emphasized the farcical not the psychological, the musical not the meditative. Jewish rituals, on the other hand, serve the same function in *Yentl* as they did in the Yiddish theater. They are not only colorful spectacles in their own right, but they lend Jewish authenticity to the works. Their cultural and religious import convey ready-made profundity to commonplace scenes. The emotions they evoke increase the audience's involvement with the dramatic action and intensify their identification with the characters. Unlike Singer's other plays, *Yentl* has compelling full-length rituals performed in the original Hebrew and quaint *shtetl* customs celebrated exactly as they were in the past. The only difference is that Singer and Napolin have taken certain liberties with them. The *Kaddish* for Yentl's father is the familiar prayer for the dead, but it is made even more moving by Yentl's forbidden recital of it. The wedding ceremony is the legitimate orthodox one, but it consecrates the illegitimate union of two women. Consequently, the bride's premarital rite of purification, while correct in form, does not have kosher results. Conversely, the wedding jester's chastisement of the bride and groom for their former sins is not just the standard speech, but it is unwittingly appropriate. Aside from these ironic variations, Singer and Napolin tried to make *Yentl*'s orthodox world as genuine as possible. The actors had an orthodox rabbi to advise them; they "visited several Boro Park Hasidic communities; they went to Jewish weddings; the women went to a real *Mikvah* [ritual bath]; and Tovah and her understudy both passed as boys and got into a Yeshiva to observe."[31] The resulting duplication of this world is so accurate that *Yentl*, of all of Singer's plays, is most steeped in the kind of literal realism prevalent in the Yiddish theater. Yet Singer occasionally yielded to the temptation of modernizing this world. Here he parts company with the more puritanical Yiddish theater, for he introduces such shockingly implausible *shtetl* behavior as male and female frontal nudity, latent pederasty, and gratuitous transvestitism.

The structure of *Yentl* is also not in keeping with strict realism. Its two acts consist of a series of essential and nonessential short scenes that are not always cohesively linked to each other. The first act is split between a dramatized feminist polemic and a subtle parody of it, while the second act is more symbolic and tragic. Disguise and the unmasking of disguise constitute the rising and falling action, but there is no clear-cut resolution. The play ends with no successful explanation of "the mystery of appearances, the deceptions of the heart" (p. 7).

The dramatic mode of *Yentl* is equally unrealistic. It is a mixture of the presentational and the representational. Yentl and Avigdor are both characters within the play and outside commentators on it. They frequently interrupt a scene to give the audience necessary background information and important narrative transitions. Their animated preview of what is to come gives the play added excitement, just as their confidential soliloquies and asides make for a greater sense of intimacy. Some have claimed, however, that their chatty intrusions give the play an unnecessary rambling quality and an undramatic linear development. But I would argue that their engaging anecdotal skills help retain the charming folktale quality of the play which is, after all, the most winning feature of Singer's drama.

Isaac Bashevis Singer considers himself a novice at playwriting. "Playwriting is the most difficult art," he says, "the greatest challenge to a writer. A great play should be from the beginning written as a play. But since there are very few great plays, and many people who want to go to the theater, it becomes the custom to make from a story a play. So, I, too, try my hand at it."[32] Clearly, Singer's most deft and original hand is that of a storyteller. As a dramatist he does not always have full artistic control of his hand which sometimes lacks agility through inexperience and is sometimes pushed in the wrong direction by the commercial demands of the theater. Yet given American audiences' hunger for plays of authentic Jewish content, Singer's folk dramas, with their substantial roots in the life and spirit of Eastern European Jewry, more than satisfy this hunger. Like Yiddish theater, Singer's plays are an entertaining substitute religion that revives the dead past and evokes communal solidarity in the present.

NOTES

1. Excerpt from Isaac Bashevis Singer's Nobel Prize Award quoted in Paul Kresh, *Isaac Bashevis Singer: The Magician of West 86th Street* (New York: The Dial Press, 1979), p. 395.

2. Travis Bogard, *Contour in Time, The Plays of Eugene O'Neill* (New York: Oxford University Press, 1972), p. 206.

3. Quoted in Marshall Breger and Bob Barnhart, "A Conversation with Isaac Bashevis Singer," *Critical Views of Isaac Bashevis Singer*, ed. Irving Malin (New York University Press, 1969), p. 35.

4. Irving Howe, "I. B. Singer," *Critical Views of Isaac Bashevis Singer*, ed. Irving Malin, p. 109.

5. Quoted in Paul Kresh, *Isaac Bashevis Singer: The Magician of West 86th Street*, p. 308.

6. Mark Shechner, "Jewish Writers," *Harvard Guide to Contemporary American Writing*, ed. Daniel Hoffman (Cambridge, Mass.: Harvard University Press, 1979), p. 218.

7. Quoted in Elenore Lester, "At 71, Isaac Bashevis Singer Makes His Broadway Debut," *New York Times*, 26 October 1975, p. 1.

8. *The Mirror*, based on Singer's short story by the same name, was given its world premiere on January 19, 1973, by the Yale Repertory Theater. It was directed by Michael Posnick, with music by Yehudi Wyner; scenery and costumes, Steven Rubin; lighting, Nathan L. Drucker; choreography, Carmen de Lavallade. Marcia Jean Kurtz played Zirel, with Richard Venture as Hurmizah and Eugene Troobnick as Reb Yoetz.

I am indebted to the Yale Repertory Theater for sending me a copy of the unpublished script. Further citations to this play will be placed in parentheses in the text of the essay.

9. "The Mirror" was first published in English in the 1955 edition of *New World Writing*. It subsequently appeared in Isaac Bashevis Singer's short story collection, *Gimpel the Fool and Other Stories*, translated by Saul Bellow, Isaac Rosenfeld, and others (New York: Farrar, Straus and Giroux, 1957), pp. 77–88. Further citations to this story will be placed in parentheses in the text of the essay.

10. A most insightful discussion of these first person demonic narrators is found in Chone Shmeruk, "The Use of Monologue as a Narrative Technique in the Stories of Isaac Bashevis Singer," translated into English by J. Taglicht for the Yiddish collection of Singer's stories, entitled *The Mirror and Other Stories* (Jerusalem: Shamgar Press, 1975), pp. v–xxxv.

11. Irving Howe, "I. B. Singer," p. 115.

12. A Talmudic saying quoted not from the play but from the short story, "The Mirror," p. 82.

13. Quoted in Paul Kresh, *Isaac Bashevis Singer: The Magician of West 86th Street*, p. 314.

14. *Teibele and Her Demon*, which Isaac Bashevis Singer and collaborator Eve Friedman adapted from his short story by the same name, first opened at Minneapolis's Guthrie Theater on June 3, 1978. With a slightly revised ending, it opened on Broadway on December 16, 1979. For both productions Stephen Kanee was the director; Richard Peaslee wrote the incidental music, Desmond Heeley was in charge of costumes and Duane Schuler created the lighting. Laura Esterman and F. Murray Abraham were the principals in both performances.

I am extremely grateful to Isaac Bashevis Singer for giving me an unpublished copy of the script. Further citations to this play will be placed in parentheses in the text of the essay.

15. Quoted in Richard Burgin, "Isaac Bashevis Singer Talks . . . About Everything," *The New York Times Magazine*, 26 November 1978, p. 26.

16. Walter Kerr, "The Theater: *Teibele and Her Demon*," *The New York Times*, 17 December 1979, p. 64.

17. A rudimentary early version of *Shlemiel the First* was performed by the Yale Repertory Theater on April 12, 1974. It was a collection of quaint episodes from Singer's favorite children's tales rather than the cohesive, intricately developed children's comedy for adults which the Singer-Cohen *Shlemiel the First* strives to be.

18. Stith Thompson, *The Folktale* (New York: The Dryden Press, 1951), p. 190.

19. *Shlemiel the First* is based on the following children's fiction of Isaac Bashevis Singer: *The Fools of Chelm and Their History*, translated by Isaac Bashevis Singer and Elizabeth Shub (New York: Farrar, Straus and Giroux, 1973); "When Shlemiel Went to Warsaw," a story in the collection *When Shlemiel Went to Warsaw & Other Stories*, translated by Isaac Bashevis Singer and Elizabeth Shub (New York: Farrar, Straus and Giroux, 1968), pp. 99–116.

20. Quoted from Isaac Bashevis Singer's acceptance speech for the National Book Award for his children's work, *A Day of Pleasure*, in Paul Kresh, *Isaac Bashevis Singer: The Magician of West 86th Street*, p. 381.

21. *Yentl*, which Isaac Bashevis Singer and Leah Napolin adapted from his short story, "Yentl, the Yeshiva Boy," was first performed by the Chelsea Theater at the Academy of Music in Brooklyn on December 17, 1974. This production opened on Broadway on October 23, 1975. It was directed by Robert Kalfin with scenery designed by Karl Eigsti; costumes by Carrie Robbins; lighting by William Mintzer; and music composed by Mel Marvin. Tovah Feldshuh starred as Yentl with John V. Shea as Avigdor and Lynn Ann Leveridge as Hadass.

The copy of the play I am using is the one published by Samuel French in 1977. Further citations to this play will be placed in parentheses in the text of the essay.

22. Isaac Bashevis Singer, "Yentl the Yeshiva Boy," translated by Marion Magid and Elizabeth Pollet, appears in Singer's collection, *Short Friday and Other Stories* (New York: Farrar, Straus and Giroux, 1965), pp. 131–159.

23. Cynthia Ozick, "The Jewish Half-Genius," *The Jerusalem Post*, 8 August 1978, p. 11.

24. Ibid.

25. Quoted in Paul Kresh, *Isaac Bashevis Singer: The Magician of West 86th Street*, p. 10.

26. Ibid., p. 11.

27. Isaac Bashevis Singer, "The Extreme Jews," *Harper's*, April 1967, p. 57.

28. Edward Alexander, *Isaac Bashevis Singer* (Boston: G. K. Hall & Co., 1980), p. 138.

29. Irving Buchen intricately develops this idea in his book, *Isaac Bashevis Singer and the Eternal past* (New York: New York University Press, 1968), p. 128.

30. Quoted in Paul Kresh, *Isaac Bashevis Singer: The Magician of West 86th Street*, p. 69.

31. Quoted in Letty Cottin Pogrebin, "Yentl—Better a Fool Than a Woman," *Ms. Magazine* (February, 1976): 38.

32. Quoted in Elenore Lester, p. 1.

The Americanization of the Holocaust on Stage and Screen

Lawrence L. Langer

WE BRING TO THE IMAGINATIVE EXPERIENCE OF THE HOLOCAUST A FOREKNOW-
ledge of man's doom. Not his fate, but his doom. The Greeks sat spellbound in
their arenas in Athens and witnessed the unfolding of what they already knew:
proud and defiant men and women submitting to an insurrection in their spirit
that rebelled against limitations. Oedipus and Phaedra, Orestes and Antigone
hurl their own natures against laws human or divine, suffer the intrusions of
chance and coincidence, but *make their fate* by pursuing or being driven by
weaknesses or strengths that are expressions of the human will. Whether they
survive or die, they affirm the painful, exultant feeling of being human; they
declare that man, in the moral world at least, is an agent in the fate we call his
death.

But the doom we call extermination is another matter. The Athenians could
identify the death of their heroes on the stage with a ritual for renewal, ally
tragedy with comedy, and make both a cause for celebration. The human drama
allowed it. But the Holocaust presents us with the spectacle of an inhuman
drama: we sit in the audience and witness the unfolding of what we will never
"know," even though the tales are already history. The tradition of fate encourages identification: we may not achieve the stature of an Oedipus or a Phaedra,
but their problems of identity, of passion, of moral courage, or retribution, are
human—are ours. The tradition of doom—a fate, one might say, imposed on
man by other men against his will, without his agency—forbids identification:
for who can share the last gasp of the victim of annihilation, whose innocence so
totally dissevers him from his end? We lack the psychological, emotional, and
even intellectual powers to participate in a ritual that celebrates *such* a demise.
We feel alien, not akin. The drama of fate reminds us that Man, should he so
choose, can die for something; the drama of doom, the history of the Holocaust,
reveals that whether they chose or not, men died for nothing.

This is not a comfortable theme for the artist to develop, or for an audience to
absorb. Traditions of heroic enterprise, in literature or in life; conceptions of the
human spirit, secular or divine; patterns for imagining reality, whether written
or oral—all have prepared us to view individual men and women in a familiar
way. Hence it should not be surprising that some of the best known attempts to
bring the Holocaust theme to the American stage—Frances Goodrich and Albert Hackett's *The Diary of Anne Frank*, Millard Lampell's *The Wall*, and
Arthur Miller's *Incident at Vichy*—as well as films like *Judgment at Nuremberg*
and the TV "epic" *Holocaust*, should draw on old forms to reassert man's fate

213

instead of new ones to help us appreciate his doom. To be sure, visually we have progressed in thirty years from the moderate misery of a little room in Amsterdam to execution pits and peepholes into the gas chambers of Auschwitz in *Holocaust;* but imaginatively, most of these works still cling valiantly to the illusion that the Nazi genocide of nearly eleven million human beings has not substantially altered our vision of human dignity. When Conrad's Marlow in *Heart of Darkness* returns from the Congo to speak with Kurtz's Intended, he brings a message about Kurtz's inhuman doom to a woman who wishes only to hear about his human fate. And Marlow submits: the truth "would have been too dark—too dark altogether. . . ."

How much darkness must we acknowledge before we will be able to confess that the Holocaust story cannot be told in terms of heroic dignity, moral courage, and the triumph of the human spirit in adversity? Those words adhere like burrs to the back of a patient beast, who lacks the energy or desire to flick them away lest in doing so he disturb his tranquillity. Kurtz's Intended pleads with Marlow for "something—something—to—live with." The Holocaust—alas!—provides us only with something to die with, something from those who died with nothing left to give. There is no final solace, no redeeming truth, no hope that so many millions may not have died in vain. They have. But the American vision of the Holocaust, in the works under consideration here, continues to insist that they have not, trying to parlay hope, sacrifice, justice, and the future into a victory that will mitigate despair. Perhaps it is characteristically American, perhaps merely human, but these works share a deafness (in varying degrees) to those other words that Conrad's Marlow brings back only to find that he has no audience prepared to listen: "'Don't you hear them?' The dusk was repeating them in a persistent whisper all around us, in a whisper that seemed to swell menacingly like the first whisper of a rising wind. 'The horror! The horror!'"

There is little horror in the stage version of *The Diary of Anne Frank;* there is very little in the original *Diary* itself. Perhaps this is one source of their appeal: they permit the imagination to cope with the idea of the Holocaust without forcing a confrontation with its grim details. Like the *Diary*, the play (though even more so) gives us only the bearable part of the story of Anne and the other occupants of the secret annex; the unbearable part begins after the final curtain falls and ends in Auschwitz and Bergen-Belsen. An audience coming to this play in 1955, only a decade after the event, would find little to threaten their psychological or emotional security. No one dies, and the inhabitants of the annex endure minimal suffering. The play really celebrates the struggle for harmony in the midst of impending disruption, thus supporting those values which the viewer instinctively hopes to find affirmed on the stage. To be sure, in the *Diary*, Anne is not oblivious to the doom of the Jews, despite her limited access to information; but there is no hint in the play of this entry from October 1942: "If it is as bad as this in Holland whatever will it be like in the distant and barbarous regions [the Jews] are sent to? We assume that most of them are murdered. The English radio speaks of their being gassed."[1] In the *Diary*, however, Anne does not brood on the prospects of annihilation; she devotes most of her reflections to her aspirations as a writer and her passage through adolescence and puberty to young womanhood. Nevertheless, a certain amount of ambiguity lingers in her young mind (absent from her character in the play) that at least adds some complexity to her youthful vision. "I see the world being turned into a wilderness," she writes, "I hear the ever approaching thunder, which will destroy us too, I can feel the sufferings of millions and yet, if I look up into the heavens, I think that it will all come right, that this cruelty too will end, and that peace and tranquillity will return again."[2] But for all but one of the inhabitants of the annex, nothing came right, cruelty grew worse, and neither peace nor tranquillity ever returned.

Yet this is not the feeling we are left with in the play, that accents Anne's mercurial optimism at the expense of the encroaching doom, which finally engulfed them all. Upbeat endings seem to be *de rigueur* for the American imagination, which traditionally buries its tragedies and lets them fester in the shadow of forgetfulness. The drama begins with Mr. Frank, a "bitter old man," returning to the secret annex after the war and finding that Anne's diary has been preserved. His "reading" of excerpts becomes the substance of the play, which after the discovery and arrest fades back into the present, revealing a calm Mr. Frank, his bitterness gone. Considering the numerous "last glimpses" of Anne we might have received from this epilogue—one eyewitness in Bergen-Belsen, where she died, described her like this: "She was in rags. I saw her emaciated, sunken face in the darkness. Her eyes were very large"[3] —one wonders at the stubborn, almost perverse insistence in the play on an affirmative epigraph, almost a denial of Anne's doom. Why should the authors think it important that we hear from Mr. Frank, in almost the last words of the play, the following tribute, *even if those words were quoted verbatim from Anne's real father:* "It seems strange to say this," muses Mr. Frank, "that anyone could be happy in a concentration camp. But Anne was happy in Holland where they first took us [i.e., Westerbork detention camp]."[4]

The authors of the dramatic version of Anne Frank's *Diary* lacked the artistic will—or courage—to leave their audiences overwhelmed by the feeling that Anne's bright spirit was extinguished, that Anne, together with millions of others, was killed simply because she was Jewish, and for no other reason. This theme lurks on the play's periphery, but never emerges into the foreground, though one gets a vague hint during the *Hanukkah* celebration that ends Act One. That Anne herself, had she survived, would have been equal to this challenge is suggested by her brief description of a roundup of Amsterdam Jews witnessed from her attic window: "In the evenings when it's dark, I often see rows of good, innocent people accompanied by crying children, walking on and on, in charge of a couple of Germans, bullied and knocked about until they almost drop. No one is spared—old people, babies, expectant mothers, the sick—each and all join in the march of death."[5] But the audience in the theater is sheltered from this somber vision, lest it disrupt the mood of carefully orchestrated faith in human nature that swells into a crescendo just before the play's climax, when the Gestapo and Green Police arrive to arrest the inhabitants of the annex. One is forced to contemplate Anne's restive intelligence at its most simple-minded, as Goodrich and Hackett have her reply to Peter Van Daan's irritable impatience at their dilemma with the pitiful cliché: "We're not the only people that've had to suffer. There've always been people that've had to. . . ."[6] Anne's mind was more capacious, if still undeveloped, but a probe into the darker realms that Conrad and Marlow knew of, an entry like the following from Anne's *Diary*, would have introduced a discordant note into the crescendo I have mentioned: "There's in people simply an urge to destroy, an urge to kill, to murder and rage, and until all mankind, without exception, undergoes a great change, wars will be waged, everything that has been built up, cultivated, and grown will be destroyed and disfigured, after which mankind will have to begin all over again."[7]

This view of the apocalypse before any fresh resurrection appears nowhere in the stage version of Anne's *Diary*. Indeed, its presence in the other works I will examine will be one test of their authenticity as Holocaust literature. If in the end even Anne Frank retreated to a safer cheerfulness, we need to remember that she was not yet fifteen when she wrote that passage. The line that concludes her play, floating over the audience like a benediction assuring grace after momentary gloom, is the least appropriate epitaph conceivable for the millions of victims and thousands of survivors of Nazi genocide: "in spite of everything, I still believe that people are really good at heart." Those who permit such heartwarming terms to insulate them against the blood-chilling events they belie need to recall that they were written by a teenager who could also say of her situation: "I have often been downcast, but never in despair; I regard our hiding as a dangerous adventure, romantic and interesting at the same time."[8] Her strong sentimental strain, which was only part of her nature, dominates the drama, and ultimately diverts the audience's attention from the sanguinary to the sanguine, causing them to forget that the roots are identical, and that during the Holocaust man's hope was stained by a blood more indelible than the imaginary spot so distressing to Lady Macbeth. By sparing us the imaginative ordeal of such consanguinity, the drama of *The Diary of Anne Frank* cannot begin to evoke the doom that eventually denied the annex's victims the dignity of human choice.

The play presents instead a drama of domestic pathos; it begins and ends with the figure of Mr. Frank, a *paterfamilias* without a family who nevertheless is inspired, like the rest of us, by his dead daughter's steadfast devotion to hope. Bruno Bettelheim's needlessly harsh criticism of the Frank family for failing to recognize the crisis for Jews in Europe and to increase the prospect of survival by seeking separate hiding places, nevertheless implies an important truth for anyone seeking to portray the Holocaust experience with insight. The family unit, that traditional bulwark in moments of familiar stress, was worthless and occasionally injurious to individual survival in the unpredictable atmosphere of the deathcamp. The tensions that sundered such ancient loyalties are absent from *Anne Frank*; they begin to appear in Millard Lampell's play *The Wall* (1960), based on John Hersey's novel, but even here, under the pressures of life in the Warsaw Ghetto, family unity finally asserts itself and triumphs over the strains that threaten to crack it.

The American imagination seems reluctant to take the non-Kierkegaardian leap into unfaith that might reveal a vision like the following, from the Auschwitz stories, *This Way for the Gas, Ladies and Gentlemen*, of the Polish survivor Tadeusz Borowski:

> Here is a woman—she walks quickly, but tries to appear calm. A small child with a pink cherub's face runs after her and, unable to keep up, stretches out his little arms and cries: "Mama! Mama!"
>
> "Pick up your child, woman!"
>
> "It's not mine, sir, not mine!" she shouts hysterically and runs on, covering her face with her hands. She wants to hide, she wants to reach those who will not ride the trucks, those who will go on foot, those who will stay alive. She is young, healthy, good-looking, she wants to live.
>
> But the child runs after her, wailing loudly: "Mama, mama, don't leave me!"
>
> "It's not mine, not mine, no!"[9]

One has only to immerse oneself in this situation to understand how thoroughly the Nazi system of terror and genocide poisoned that vital source of human dignity, that made man an instrument in his fate: the phenomenon of choice. Mother and child is a comforting image when the mother can do something to comfort her child; but how does one comfort her child when both are on their way to the gas chamber? Futility drives the mother in this fictional passage— though we have eyewitness testimony to prove the historical bases of moments like these—to a repudiation unthinkable for the civilized mind. But Auschwitz introduced the realm of the unthinkable into the human drama, and no representation of the Holocaust that ignores this realm can be considered complete.

Lampell's *The Wall* peers into its dark recesses, but finally withdraws to reassert a familiar moral view. It is too dark—too dark altogether. "Man as a helpless victim," writes Lampell in his introduction to the play. "I do not deny that this is a truth of our time. But it is only one truth. There are others. There is understanding, and indomitable faith, and the rare, exultant moments when one human finally reaches out to accept another." But can one truth be severed from the other? And how do those rare exultant moments affect the doom of the eleven million helpless victims who did not survive to appreciate them? Lampell chose to avoid this question by searching for flickering rays amid the brooding gloom. His initial response to the plan to dramatize the Hersey novel was to immerse himself in documents and writings about the Warsaw Ghetto. When he discovered—to his dismay—that "what was unique in Warsaw was the scope of man's inhumanity to man," he was reduced to "an overwhelming sense of ashes and agony" and almost abandoned the project. His reason would be ludicrous, were the subject not so grave: "I am a writer chiefly concerned with life, not death." By temporarily retreating in despair from the ruins of the Ghetto because "I simply could not recognize human life as I knew it," Lampell unwittingly refused the higher challenge of the Holocaust experience—its utter transformation of human life as we know it. By finally accepting the "lower challenge" and building his play about the safer theme of men "in spite of it all, stumbling toward a possible dignity," he still writes an honest play, better theater than *The Diary of Anne Frank*, but one not governed by the inner momentum of the Holocaust toward extermination. Instead, Lampell restores to men an instrumentality in their fate; a handful of Jews, he insists, "exposed the fullest potential of the human race."[10] Whether this is solace for the 300,000 other Jews of the Ghetto who were deported to Treblinka (not Auschwitz, as the play suggests) and murdered, Lampell does not consider; but the impact of the dramatic spectacle is to affirm the heroic fate of the few, and to mute the unmanageable doom of the wretched rest.

The consolation of the *Hanukkah* celebration at the midpoint of *The Diary of Anne Frank* has its analogue at the exact midpoint of *The Wall:* the wedding of Mordecai and Rutka. But Lampell has established an effective tension between joy and terror, for while the wedding ceremony proceeds indoors, the first roundups of Jews for deportation to "labor camps" occur in the streets outside. The counterpoint between the grave Chassidic dance of Reb Mazur and the confused screams of terrified Jews fleeing for their lives in disorder, between the lively *hora* of the celebrants and the thudding boots of the Nazis, defines two alienated realms—and suggests the futility of the Jews' trying to inhabit both. Bruno Bettelheim had charged that the Franks' refusal to abandon family ritual and tradition had cost them their lives, though he seemed unable to admit that after twenty-five months of security in their haven, with the Allies moving on Paris and soon to be in Belgium, the Franks had sufficient reason to believe that their strategy for survival would work. Lampell assumes a more complex view, acknowledging how insidiously the Nazi threat of extermination could infiltrate the family unit itself. The desperate dependence on stability represents almost willful blindness on the part of the Ghetto inhabitants, and to his credit, Lampell makes this "refusal to see" the dramatic focus of the second half of the play.

What it amounts to, for the historic individual as well as the dramatic character, for the artist, the reader, and the audience, is accepting the credibility of doom (extermination in the gas chamber for being a Jew) when all our lives we have struggled to absorb the painful truth of our mortality, "merely" the necessity for our death—man's fate. Against that fate we can mount consolations, and even some forms of transcendence—faith, love, children, creative endeavor, some communion with the future that liberates us from the prison of our mortality. But what promised to free the human spirit from the deathcamp, the gas chamber, and the crematorium? This is the question to which Lampell is committed—*before* the act of creation—to finding an affirmative answer. Such commitment requires him to manipulate probability and distort the balance between heroism and despair, as if a prior espousal of human community, even amidst the rubble of the destroyed Ghetto, were the only way to make the Holocaust acceptable on the stage. To be sure, violations of that sense of community appear in the play. The *paterfamilias* here, Pan Apt, the father of Rachel,

Halinka, David, and Mordecai, repudiates his Jewish heritage and with forged papers flees to the Polish side of the Wall, deserting his family. Stefan, Reb Mazur's son, joins the Jewish Ghetto police because of the Nazi promise that he and his family will be safe from deportations. But in order to save himself, he is reduced to pleading with his own father to consent to "resettlement." Nazi doom left the individual no simple way of surviving with dignity: one had to pay a human price for his life, and in *The Wall*, that price is usually a disruption of family integrity. The one place where such integrity *is* preserved is one of the least probable (though most reassuring) moments of the play, infringing on the authenticity of history and of human doom in the Holocaust. Huddled in their bunker as Nazi troops are rooting out the scattered remnants of resistance, Mordecai, Rutka, their baby (born in the Ghetto) and a few other underground fighters are about to make their way through the sewers to safety outside the Wall, when a detachment of German soldiers spots them. Withdrawing into the bunker again, they wait in silence, when suddenly the baby begins to cry. We have ample evidence of parents smothering their infants to protect themselves and often larger groups from detection, but Lampell flinches before this ultimate rejection of the family bond: it, too, would have been too dark—too dark altogether. His scene direction reads: "Mordecai puts his hand over the baby's mouth. Rutka stands it as long as she can, then shoves his hand away."[11] The baby cries again, and of course the Germans hear him. Verisimilitude, human as well as aesthetic truth, would require the capture of the Jews at this point; instead, in an utterly unconvincing denouement, Berson leaves the bunker undetected and draws the soldiers away with the sound of his concertina. The heroic impulse triumphs over truth, Berson sacrifices himself that others may live (assuming they do: otherwise his gesture would be doubly futile), and man proves himself still in control of his fate, willing to surrender the life of a man in order to assure the continuity of the Life of Men.

One of the paradoxes of this play, and of much Holocaust literature, is that it tries to serve two masters. When Rachel reports to her horrified fellow Jews about evidence that the deported victims—men, women, and children—are not being resettled, but murdered, they are unable to believe her. "It doesn't make sense," cries Reb Mazur. "All right, they're not civilized," objects Mordecai, her brother. "But they're still human." And the rabbi later affirms: "Yes, I am calm—because I know that any faith based on love and respect will outlive any faith based on murder." One "master" which this play serves is a familiar but weary vocabulary, words like "sense," "civilized," "human," "faith," "love," and "respect," which desperate men and women cling to, to shore up the ruins of their crumbling world. They lead finally to the heroic if ultimately futile resistance that concludes the play—futile because the Jews possess neither numbers nor weapons sufficient to defeat the Germans. The other "master," mouthed but not acted upon by the briefly cynical Berson, represents a subterranean truth of the Holocaust that art has not yet found an adequate vocabulary to explore: "Love. What does it mean? When they come with the guns, I have seen a son beat his own mother. A mother throw her child out of the window, her own child that she bore inside her." We get a glimpse later on of the motive that leads Berson to a moral reversal, bringing him back into the Ghetto after he has left it: "I always thought that just to live was enough. To live *how*? To live *with whom*?"[12] But fine sentiments cannot replace the searching psychological analyses art must provide us with if we are to understand how the human creature reacts when he realizes that his enemy is neither "civilized" nor "human," and when the reality threatening to consume him resembles nothing his mind or soul has ever faced before.

The handful of survivors of the Warsaw Ghetto left behind them a world destroyed, one that their lives could not redeem, their memories not revive. The Nazis did their work thoroughly. Nevertheless, like *The Diary of Anne Frank*, *The Wall* reverberates with its memorable line, its token of hope, its verbal gesture of affirmation: "the only way to answer death is with more life."[13] And abstractly, conceptually, philosophically, it is a noble refrain; but whether Rachel will indeed survive to bear a child in defiance of all these atrocities, we will never know. An even more significant hiatus is the absence of some notion of how such new life "responds" to the multitudinous-deaths of the Holocaust. The teasing hint that somehow the future will bring palliatives for such anguish deflects our attention from a harsher truth of the Holocaust, which the play flirts with only to retreat from: that sometimes, many times, the only way to answer your own possible death was with someone else's life. John Hersey, in one crucial episode in the novel at least, does not flinch from this harsher truth: when the baby begins to cry, an underground leader takes it from its mother's arms and smothers it. Doomed people do not behave like men and women in charge of their fate. Lampell was probably correct in assuming that his audience would not tolerate such agony: but *The Wall*, like all art, pays a price for such compromise.

Moral oversimplification is one of the many sins afflicting writing about the Holocaust. We find comfort in schemes of cause and effect: villains destroy, victims submit or resist. We will never understand the behavior of the victims until we gain greater insight into the motives of their murderers. The courageous fighters of the Warsaw Ghetto, too few and too late, with scant help from the Polish underground and virtually none from the world outside, knew in advance that they were not choosing life but exerting minimum control over the manner of their death, rescuing a fragment of fate from a seemingly unassailable doom. That doom is personified by their enemies, but in *The Wall* they are mechanized, dehumanized, transformed into robots called merely German Private, German Sergeant, and O. S. Fuehrer. They differ little from the loudspeaker attached to a linden tree, barking orders for assembly and "resettlement." But the Jews were killed by men and women like themselves, not by automatons; one of the play's major faults is its failure to confront the challenge of characterizing those instruments of doom who, through a combination of ruthlessness and manipulation, deprived their victims of moral space to maneuver with dignity.

Regardless of their artistic merit, the plays and films we are examining share one common purpose: they bring us into the presence of human beings searching for a discourse commensurate with their dilemma. In order to recognize that dilemma (the threat of extermination), they must find a language adequate to express it; but in order to find that language, they must first be able to imagine the dilemma. Without such perception, without the words to articulate it to others and make it credible, the individual remains totally vulnerable. Even *with* such "ammunition," after a certain point in time, the Jew had few meaningful alternatives (though many hopeless ones); those left with moral space to maneuver with dignity were the non-Jews, and to his credit Arthur Miller in *Incident at Vichy* (1964) shifts the center of moral responsibility for the situation of the Jews from the victims to the well-intentioned spectator, who begins by dismissing Nazism as "an outburst of vulgarity" but ends by realizing that a more precise definition must move him from language and perception to deeds—a process similar to the one followed by the Warsaw Ghetto fighters, though their decision to act could not support anyone's survival.

Except for a gypsy, all the characters in *Incident at Vichy* have been rounded up because they are suspected of being Jews. How is the Jew to protect himself against such danger, psychologically, without supporting his enemy's view of him as a menace to society? He was vulnerable precisely because he was *not* able to see himself in this way: "You begin wishing you'd committed a crime, you know? Something definite," says Lebeau, the painter. "I was walking down the street before, a car pulls up beside me, a man gets out and measures my nose, my ears, my mouth, the next thing I'm sitting in a police station—or whatever the hell this is here—and in the middle of Europe, the highest peak of civilization!" Kafka could impose on life the discontinuities of art and the courageous reader might follow his vision with impunity; but when life imposed on the Jews Kafkan discontinuities like the one Lebeau describes, the confused and terrorized victim could not retreat for insight or relief to the sanctuary of art. Indeed, *Incident at Vichy* may be seen as concisely dramatized dialogues between points of view which question the power of art—on the Holocaust theme—to achieve these ends. Insight and relief are allied to meaning, but when one of the prisoners mouths the cliché that one "should try to think of why things happen. It helps to know the meaning of one's suffering," the painter—recalling that he has been arrested and possibly doomed because of the size of his nose—acidly replies: "After the Romans and the Greeks and the Renaissance, and you know what this means?"[14]

When humanistic precedents collapse, the individual loses the security of collective identity; neither family nor group nor profession protects: the prisoners in this play are isolated, alone, searching for private strategies to insure their release—unaware that the Nazi determination to destroy all Jews has deprived them of choice. The contest is unequal before it begins. If art is an illusion we submit to for greater insight, life—the life depicted in *Incident at Vichy*—is an illusion we submit to from greater ignorance. Habitual ways of thinking become parodies of insight; to rumors about Auschwitz the actor Monceau replies: "Is that really conceivable to you? War is War, but you still have to keep a certain sense of proportion. I mean Germans are still *people*." His naiveté about the equivalence of words to facts breeds futile hopes. Incapable of suspecting that the Germans will identify Jews by ordering them to drop their trousers, he urges his fellow prisoners not to look like victims: "One must create one's own reality in this world. . . . One must show them the face of a man who is right." Unlike the authors of *Anne Frank* and *The Wall*, Miller has the artistic integrity to expose the impotence of such facile rhetoric. Even more irrelevant is the electrician Bayard's conviction that one must not respond personally to the Nazi threat: they may torture the individual, but "they can't torture the future." Only Von Berg, the non-Jew "spectator" who knows that he can secure release by identifying himself, moves toward a clear perception of the future: "What if nothing comes of the facts but endless, endless disaster?"[15]

Miller has a lucid sense of the impotence of the Jewish victims, once they have lost the flexibility of their freedom. They talk of overpowering the solitary guard and fleeing, but a combination of fear, uncertainty, and lack of weapons frustrates this plan, especially after a sympathetic major warns them that armed guards stand outside. They berate themselves for not having been more wary *before* their arrest. But as Von Berg implies, decent men do not possess an imagination for disaster, especially one ending in gas chamber and oven. This is the source of Nazi strength, he argues: they do the inconceivable, and "it paralyzes the rest of us." The consequences for values, for human behavior, are alarming, if not revolutionary: "You must not calculate these people with some nineteenth-century arithmetic of loss and gain. . . . in my opinion, win or lose this war, they have pointed the way to the future. What one used to conceive a human being to be will have no room on this earth." One would like to believe that this is merely the language of fashionable despair, coming from an Austrian aristocrat who can still describe the Nazi menace as "the nobility of the totally vulgar." The doctor Leduc, Prince Von Berg's chief disputant and interlocutor as the others "disappear" into the inner office, refines the Austrian's observation by describing how the Nazis capitalize on their victims' habit of projecting their own reasonable ideas—like the impossibility of extermination—into their enemy's head. "Do you understand?" he pleads. "You cannot wager your life on a purely rational analysis of this situation."[16]

As they wait in this anteroom to deportation and death wears on, façades begin to fall away, and certain truths emerge which, if organized into a system of belief, would indeed transform our vision of what it was like to have been alive in that time—to say nothing of our own. Miller provides insight into the psychology—not necessarily of the Jew—but of the *hunted*, the humiliated, the disenfranchised, the abandoned, the scorned. Lebeau the painter admits to believing in the disaster that threatens, and to exposing himself to danger nonetheless: "you get tired of believing in the truth. You get tired of seeing things clearly." To perceive with the illogic of the Nazis, to endorse, for example, the impossibility of being a Jew in Hitler's Europe, was to accept the erosion of one's own humanity. Unwilling to embrace this course, *unable* to do so in the absence of model precedents, the victim was driven through sheer moral weariness to accept his own mortality, his vulnerability: "one way or the other," says the doctor, "with illusions or without them, exhausted or fresh—we have been trained to die. The Jew and the Gentile both."[17]

But even this seemingly final view is only one in a series of carefully orchestrated positions in *Incident at Vichy:* until the play's last moment, Miller withholds the heroic gesture that we have encountered in *Anne Frank* and *The Wall,* and which even he cannot ultimately resist, though he shrouds it with some ambiguity. Holocaust writing itself serves two masters: a clear intellectual perception of how Nazism shrank the area of dignified choice and reduced the options for human gestures; and the instinct to have victims survive heroically even within these less-than-human alternatives. When the German Major (who has been struggling, as a military man, against his own association with the S.S. inquisitor) asks Leduc whether he would refuse, if he were released and the others kept, the doctor murmurs No; and to the more complex (and deliberately nastier) question of whether he would walk out of the door with a light heart, he can only reply: "I don't know." The confrontation is a *locus classicus* for understanding how the Holocaust undermined what Von Berg would have called the "nineteenth-century arithmetic of loss and gain"—or right and wrong. "One man's death is another man's bread" ran a bitter slogan in the deathcamps, and it represents a far deeper and more painful truth than the principle that in spite of everything, men are really good at heart, or that the only way to answer death is with more life.

In the end, Miller concedes, perception changes little: the non-Jew will live not because he is a better man, but because he is not Jewish; the Jew will die, simply because he is Jewish. Such "logic" fits no moral scheme, generates no satisfactory mode of behavior. Viable attitudes may strengthen the moral will, but only viable acts save the physical self. Miller discovers such an act to end his play—Von Berg gives his pass to Leduc, allowing the Jewish doctor to walk safely past the guard while he himself remains behind to face the wrath of the Nazis—but the gesture simply imposes on a hopeless situation the temporary idealism of self-sacrifice. Von Berg has learned how to share the anguish of the Jew, to cross the terrain separating the complicity of silence from the helplessness of the victim. But as the curtain descends, more men rounded up as suspected Jews appear. One can hardly believe that Leduc will get far with the police in close pursuit, and the routine of identification and deportation is about to begin again.

The motive for Von Berg's gesture is left in doubt: has he tried to save another man, or his own soul? At least he has acknowledged a vital truth of the Holocaust: to be alive while others perish innocently in the gas chambers is itself a form of complicity. The Jew, as Leduc insists, has learned a grim lesson about the nature of man: "that he is *not* reasonable, that he is full of murder, that his ideals are only the little tax he pays for the right to hate and kill with a clear conscience." *He* has seen into the heart of darkness. Despite his lucidity about the "vulgar" Nazis, Von Berg clings to his ancient idealism, as the only prop that still supports his flagging life: "There are people who would find it easier to die than stain one finger with this murder." One might interpret this dialogue as a confrontation between the voice of a doomed man and one who still believes that he can master his own fate. But the irony of the moment is Von Berg's slow realization that he can restore the challenge of fate to Leduc only by surrendering his own, and submitting to the doom that the Jew now hopes to escape. One would feel more elated about this tribute to the human spirit were it not surrounded by the disappearance of the other Jews and the arrival of new victims who will have no one to "save" them. Von Berg has repudiated the idea of man's right to hate and kill with a clear conscience. A world without ideals, as he said earlier, would be intolerable. But how does one measure his private deed of generosity against the slaughter of millions? Does it invalidate Leduc's melancholy charge, only too familiar to survivors of the deathcamps, that "Each man has his Jew . . . the man whose death leaves you relieved that you are not him, despite your decency"?[18] Miller at least pays homage to the ambiguity of efforts to redress the imbalance between justice and suffering imposed by the Nazi atrocities. But the magnitude of the sorrow and loss dwarfs the deed, however noble, of one man for one man; *Incident at Vichy* illuminates the difficulty, perhaps the impossibility, of affirming the tragic dignity of the individual man, when it has been soiled by the ashes of anonymous millions.

If *Incident at Vichy* exposes the dilemma of measuring the private deed of generosity against the slaughter of millions, Abby Mann's script for the Stanley Kramer production of *Judgment at Nuremberg* (1961) raises the issue of measuring the public act of justice against that same slaughter. If Miller's play complicates the problem of redressing the imbalance between justice and such suffering, Kramer's film simplifies the question of establishing a connection between mass atrocity and individual responsibility. The force of idealism in *Judgment at Nuremberg* resides not in the faith of a young girl, or a beleaguered Ghetto fighter, or an Austrian aristocrat, but in a principle: that in a court of law, with only relevant testimony allowed, where defendants have counsel who may cross-examine witnesses, a just verdict against an unjust act somehow satisfies the conscience even though political expediency—in this instance, the Berlin Airlift and its consequences for German-American relations—may afterwards undermine its durability. Just before the final fadeout, the audience is treated to the unsavory irony that by July 14, 1949, after the last of the so-called second Nuremberg trials, of "ninety-nine sentenced to prison terms, not one is still serving his sentence."

I suppose that for those who still see the Holocaust as a situation of violated justice, this announcement is as exasperating and offensive as the news in 1980 that 200 alleged Nazi war criminals are still living safely in the United States. But both truths are accompanied by an overwhelming sense of futility, especially to those who have already understood that the logic of law can never make sense of the illogic of extermination. The film tries to do exactly the reverse; how else are we to interpret its final episode, with its unqualified assumption that the perversion of justice necessarily leads to genocide? The trial over, the guilty verdicts in, the life sentences proclaimed, the Chief Judge Dan Haywood

(Spencer Tracy) confronts the chief defendant, former Nazi Minister of Justice Ernst Janning (Burt Lancaster), who "doomed" himself in court by honorably announcing that "if there is to be any salvation for Germany those of us who know our guilt must admit it no matter what the cost in pain and humiliation." The two representatives of justice, now and then, face each other, and Janning says to Haywood: "I want to hear from a man like you. A man who has heard what happened. I want to hear—not that he forgives—but that he understands." The kind of insight (if not charity) demanded by this question, the film does not know how to dramatize. Whether because of a failure of nerve, of dramatic sense, or of artistic imagination, the author and director have not solved the problem of exploring this difficult psychological issue in their courtroom drama. Judge Haywood gropes for a response in a scene direction in the script, but this is conveyed to the audience only through the inarticulate furrows of Spencer Tracy's brow: "understand, Haywood says to himself. I understand the pressures you were under. . . . But how can I understand the deaths of millions of men, women, and children in gas ovens [a common technical blunder fusing and confusing gas chambers with crematorium ovens], Herr Janning?" A shrewd interpreter of furrowed brows, Janning replies in stereotypical and (as we shall see) self-contradictory justification: "I did not know it would come to that. You must believe it. You must believe it." The judge's rejoinder is the closing line of the film: "Herr Janning. It came to that the first time you sentenced a man to death you knew to be innocent."[19] A melodramatic riposte, precise and compact: but are we expected to be content with this explanation of the murder of six million Jews and five million other innocent human beings? When decent men, through tacit or active consent, from personal gain, weak will, or false patriotism, authorize (as in this film) the sterilization of a Communist's son or the execution of an elderly Jew on the trumped-up charge of cohabiting with an Aryan, they participate in a totalitarian manipulation of the law against certain individuals—but do they lay the groundwork for the annihilation of a people?

That annihilation is central to the historical truth behind the film, if not to its artistic logic: no serious treatment of the Holocaust can avoid it. But *Judgment at Nuremberg* introduces evidence about Buchenwald and Belsen in an almost gratuitous fashion, though the impact of these actual Army films on cast and audience is unquestionable; indeed, instead of establishing continuity between the horrifying events and the deeds of the defendants, the images of atrocity on a screen within a screen create a psychological distance: what system of justice can render homage to the mounds of corpses being shoved into a mass grave by a giant British bulldozer? The real event of atrocity and the subsequent film using it as a background do not cohere in a satisfying image of deed and consequence, uniting the twisted bodies of the victims with the acts of the four men on trial. At the end, Janning protests "I did not know it would come to that." But earlier, during his moment of "confession," he is more precise: "Maybe we didn't know the details. But if we didn't know, it was because we didn't want to know." The space between these two statements, between denial and equivocation, forms a psychological desert that the film doesn't begin to explore. Yet that wasteland is exactly the area whose detailed examination would make a film like *Judgment at Nuremberg* worthy of our attention. Three of the four German judges on trial are puppets in the dock, masks of contempt, indifference, or apprehension, but never human beings. The unrepentant Nazi, the timid collaborator, and the perennial self-justifier are familiar stereotypical figures whose presence in the film offer no insight whatsoever into the nature of the genocidal impulse. And Ernst Janning doesn't help us by denouncing himself as worse than any of them "because he knew what they were and went along with them." Nor does his self-portrait, shaded with aristocratic disdain—he "made his life . . . excrement because he walked with them"[20]—suggest any of the moral chiaroscuro that might fall from the master hand of a Rembrandt. Janning's declaration of guilt is not enough, psychologically or aristically: not enough for himself, because he still has not penetrated his motives, and not enough for us, because we still do not know how such a decent man came to lend his judicial prestige to the Nazi cause.

Admission of guilt neither restores decency—the lingering horrors of Belsen insure this in the film—nor explains its perversion, any more than Albert Speer's acknowledgment (at the primary Nuremberg trial and in his memoirs) of responsibility for Nazi crimes he claims to have known nothing about restores our faith in him or explains the tangled motives that led him to embrace the aspirations of the Third Reich. Nor does the eloquent speech of Rolfe the defense attorney, ably portrayed by Maximilian Schell, take us any deeper into the heart of Holocaust darkness. By expanding the perimeters of guilt—"The whole world is as responsible for Hitler as is Germany"[21]—Rolfe seeks to mitigate blame for his client; but under the burden of eleven million innocent victims, the structure of this argument collapses too. Although the immediate thrust of the film is to leave the audience feeling the irony of the conflict between political expediency and absolute justice, the perhaps unintended momentum of its subterranean current—reinforced by the impact of the documentary views of the camps—is to oppress the audience with the irrelevance of absolute justice to the collective crime of mass murder. In the aftermath of such "indecent" dying, the courtroom as *mise en scène* for a comprehension of its enormity seems pitifully inadequate. Like most Hollywood efforts, this admittedly serious film scants the more complex interior landscape of the mind, where Judge, Victim, and Accused surrender the clear outlines of their identity and wrestle with a reality that subverts the very meaning of decency. *Judgment at Nuremberg*, with its concluding irony that by July 1949 none of the 99 sentenced to prison at the last of the second series of trials was still behind bars, renders a judgment *of* Nuremberg, of Nazism, and of the contemporary world that it probably never wished to impose: that uncorrupted justice, the highest expression of law, order, morality and civilization, is only a charade in the presence of atrocities literally embodied by the mounds of twisted corpses in mass graves at Belsen. The film uses the Holocaust theme only to misuse it; it focuses momentarily on the original horror, then shifts our awareness (thereby once more warming our hearts) to the admirable probity of an amiable American judge. If the irony of history, allying Germany with one former enemy against another former one, has the last word, what happens to the responsibility of art, which must avoid the trivialization of that horror despite history's insensitivity? This is the real weakness of *Judgment at Nuremberg*, which mirrors that insensitivity while pretending that the temporary triumph of justice over expediency—German or American—can make a difference.

"To produce a mighty book," Melville says in *Moby Dick*, "you must choose a mighty theme." Perhaps modesty kept him from adding that a mighty talent was also necessary. Few contemporary themes present "mightier" challenges to the imagination than the Holocaust, the implacable, mesmerizing White Whale of our time; but when American television committed millions to produce Gerald Green's documentary drama, *Holocaust*, those who provided the money did not suspect that they had invested in a dolphin, though having been promised a whale. Had the makers of this mammoth enterprise been more attuned to sacred scripture, they might have been forewarned of the danger of trying to draw out leviathan with a hook.

When a famous survivor of Auschwitz, Elie Wiesel, protested in print that, whatever its intentions, *Holocaust* "transforms an ontological event into soap-opera,"[22] Green defended himself by citing the contrary views of distinguished critics like John Rich, Tom Shales, and Harriet Van Horne. To justify himself against the charge of large-scale mingling of fiction with historical fact, he cited the earlier example of *War and Peace*, compounding his sponsor's mistake of confusing dolphins with whales. The real issue was lucidly raised by *Time* writer Lance Morrow: "one senses something wrong with the television effort when one realizes that two or three black-and-white concentration-camp still photographs displayed by Dorf [fictional SS officer]—the stacked, starved bodies—are more powerful and heartbreaking than two or three hours of dramatization." Morrow goes on to complain that the "last 15 minutes of Vittorio De Sica's *The Garden of the Finzi-Continis*, in which Italian Jews are rounded up to be taken to the camps, is more wrenching than all the hours of *Holocaust*"[23]—a judgment with which I happen to agree. At least two crucial issues are raised here, both of which need to be addressed before anyone can respond intelligently to the television drama *Holocaust*.

The first is the question of whether that "ontological event" *can* be transformed into a form of artistic experience carrying it beyond its historical moment and making it accessible in all its complexity to those who have not directly experienced it. Can representation rival the immediacy of contemporaneous photographs, diaries dug up after the war in the ashes surrounding Auschwitz, or even survivor accounts—unromantic emotions recollected in disquietude? Nothing can rival the chaotic masses of undifferentiated corpses, the token of men's doom in the Holocaust; but I would suggest that only art can lead the uninitiated imagination from the familiar realm of man's fate to the icy atmosphere of the deathcamps, where collective doom replaced the private will. Holocaust art is transitional art, a balloon, as it were, straining to break free from its inspiring reality but always moored by a single stubborn strand to the ontological event that gave it birth—the extermination of millions of innocent human beings. It is a necessary art, ever more necessary as that event recedes in time and new generations struggle to comprehend why a civilized country in the midst of the twentieth century coolly decided to murder all of Europe's Jews. The documents themselves do not answer this vital question for us.

Does television's *Holocaust?* Many who celebrate the film argue that for the first time, at least in America, viewers will get a sense of what it was like to suffer being Jewish during the Nazi period. Nothing before on American stage or screen had faced so "fearlessly" the fact of genocide, and the process which led up to it. The uninitiated imagination is offered Kristallnacht, the euthanasia program, the Warsaw Ghetto, Buchenwald, Theresienstadt, Auschwitz, Sobibor, and Babi Yar—to say nothing of Eichmann, Heydrich, Ohlendorf, Biberstein, Blobel and several others in the hierarchy of Nazi executioners. One sees Jews being beaten, starved, tortured, marching primly into the gas chambers of Auschwitz, tumbling docilely into the murder pits at Babi Yar. One hears Erik Dorf and his historical counterparts speaking of Jews as if they were vermin, superfluous equipment, detritus on the shores of Europe. Why is it then that even Kurtz's Intended might have watched this spectacle without feeling that it was too dark—too dark altogether? Why is it that nothing in the drama equals or even approaches the unmitigated horror of the actual films of Nazi executions which Dorf shows his superiors? One might argue that art never matches history; but in the case of *Holocaust*, it is more valid to conclude that talent has not matched intention. The failure of *Holocaust* is a failure of imagination. The vision which plunges us into the lower abysses of atrocity is not there. We do not know what is was like, in the Warsaw Ghetto and elsewhere, to have been reduced to eating dogs, cats, horses, insects, and even, in rare unpublicized instances, human flesh. We do not know what the human being suffered during days and nights in sealed boxcars, starving, confused, desperate, sharing one's crowded space with frozen corpses. We do not know of the endless rollcalls in Auschwitz, often in sub-freezing temperature, when men and women simply collapsed and died from exhaustion. We have abundant examples of husbands and wives clinging together in adverse conditions, but we never glimpse—as I mentioned earlier—mothers abandoning children or fathers and sons throttling each other for a piece of bread. We see well-groomed and sanitized men and women filing into the gas chamber, but what does this convey of the terror and despair that overwhelmed millions of victims as they recognized the final moment of their degradation and their powerlessness to respond? Perhaps art will never be able to duplicate the absolute horror of such atrocities: but if it cannot recreate at least a limited authentic image of that horror—and *Holocaust* does not—then audiences will remain as deceived about the *worst* as young Anne Frank's lingering words on the essential goodness of human nature deceive us about the *best*.

A second crucial test of all Holocaust art is the question of insight. Having viewed *Holocaust*, do we have any *fresh* insights into the Nazi mind, the victim, the spectator? The drama chooses the least arduous creative path, tamely following chronological sequence, though the disruption of time-sense (and place-sense) was one of the chief features of the deathcamp experience: tomorrow vanished, and the past became a dim, nostalgic echo. It adopts the safe strategy of externalizing the event. A doctor sends Anna Weiss to Hadamar, notorious euthanasia center in prewar Germany, but neither he, nor her sister-in-law (who consents to let her go), nor the nurses who receive her, nor the group of puppet-like figures who join her in the walk to their death, reveal any vivid anguish, any searing conflict, any terror, pain or even dislocation of the moral center of their being. If extermination *is* such a simple matter of banality (and I do not believe it), it is hardly worth writing about. Even more impoverished (in terms of fresh insight) is the spectacle of Dr. Weiss and his friend Lowy lamely walking to their doom in the gas chambers of Auschwitz. What do men think or feel at that moment? In this critical instant of an "ontological event" that remains an abiding trauma to the modern imagination, the Doctor mutters something about his never having time now to remove his friend's diseased gall bladder. Do we have a right to expect more, before we bestow the laurel of insight upon *Holocaust?*

Could Gerald Green and his producers have done better? Consider this brief portrait of two human beings, about to die in the gas chambers of Auschwitz, recorded by Salmen Lewental in a diary exhumed from the ashes after the war:

> A mother was sitting with her daughter, they both spoke in Polish. She sat helplessly, spoke so softly that she could hardly be heard. She was clasping the head of her daughter with her hands and hugging her tightly. [She spoke]: "In an hour we shall die. What a tragedy. My dearest, my last hope will die with you." She sat . . . immersed in thought, with wide-open, dimmed eyes . . . After some minutes she came to and continued to speak. "On account of you my pain is so great that I am dying when I think of it." She let down her stiff arms and her daughter's head sank down upon her mother's knees. A shiver passed through the body of the young girl, she called desperately "Mama!" And she spoke no more, those were her last words.[24]

Perhaps "last words" like these are not dramatic; certainly they are not commercial; undoubtedly, they are not American. But they are authentic, and they are what the Holocaust was all about. The upbeat ending of *Holocaust*, minimizing the negative impact of all that has gone before, typifies the absence of insight and the externalization of horror that makes the entire production meretricious in its confrontation with disaster: wormwood and gall are mollified by aromatic spices from the orient. To leave an audience of millions with an image like the one of mother and daughter bereft of hope, of life, of speech would have been too dark—too dark altogether. The American theater and screen, the American mind itself, is not yet ready to end in such silence. The heroic gesture still seizes us with its glamor, tempering the doom of men and women who have lost control of their fate. Salmen Lewental has recorded an epigraph for all writing about victims of the Holocaust, whether as art or history—and it may serve as epitaph too: "On account of you my pain is so great that I am dying when I think of it." The memory of eleven million dead echoes as a symphony of pain: in that denial of final triumph lies our acceptance and understanding of the Holocaust experience.

NOTES

1. *Anne Frank: The Diary of a Young Girl*, trans. B. M. Mooyart-Doubleday (New York: Doubleday, 1967), p. 51.

2. Ibid., p. 287.

3. Ernst Schnabel, *Anne Frank: A Portrait in Courage*, trans. Richard and Clara Winston (New York: Harcourt, Brace & World, 1958), p. 177.

4. Frances Goodrich and Albert Hackett, *The Diary of Anne Frank* (New York: Random House, 1956), p. 172.

5. Anne Frank, *Diary*, p. 66.

6. Goodrich and Hackett, p. 168.

7. Anne Frank, *Diary*, p. 245.

8. Ibid., p. 245.

9. Tadeusz Borowski, *This Way for the Gas, Ladies and Gentlemen*, trans. Barbara Vedder (New York: Penguin Books, 1976), p. 45.

10. Millard Lampell, *The Wall* (New York: Alfred A. Knopf, 1961), pp. xiii, xiv, ix, xxiii.

11. Ibid., p. 158.

12. Ibid., pp. 99, 108, 124, 153.

13. Ibid., p. 156.

14. Arthur Miller, *Incident at Vichy* (New York: Viking Press, 1965), pp. 3, 6.

15. Ibid., pp. 19, 29, 30, 31, 33.

16. Ibid., pp. 38, 39, 46.

17. Ibid., pp. 50, 51.

18. Ibid., pp. 65, 66.

19. Abby Mann, *Judgment at Nuremberg: A Script of the Film* (London: Cassell, 1961), pp. 148, 180–81.

20. Ibid., pp. 149, 151.

21. Ibid., p. 153.

22. Elie Wiesel, "Trivializing the Holocaust: Semi-Fact and Semi-Fiction," *New York Times*, Sunday, 16 April 1978, Sect. 2, p. 29.

23. *Time*, 1 May 1978, p. 53.

24. Jadwiga Bezwińska, ed., *Amidst a Nightmare of Crime: Manuscripts of Members of Sonderkommando*, trans. Krystyna Michalik (State Museum of Oswiecim, 1973), p. 145.

Woody Allen: The Failure of
the Therapeutic

Mark Shechner

IT APPEARS TO BE THE FATE OF COMEDIANS IN AMERICA TO EITHER GROW ashamed of their humor or sputter out in a barrage of stale routines and stock responses. How many of our comedians have gone around the bend as prophets or reformers—like Mark Twain, Mort Sahl, Dick Gregory, and Lenny Bruce— or, after the fashion of Don Rickles, Jerry Lewis, Joey Bishop, and Redd Foxx, retired to Caesar's Palace or the Dean Martin Celebrity Roast as show biz personalities, wearily impersonating each other and, in the end, themselves. The burnout rate for comics approaches that for poets, rock stars, and relief pitchers, vocations for which the mealtickets are heat and velocity. Unlike the actor or the novelist, the comedian is not normally geared to go the distance.

The familiar figure of the *tummler maudit* has nothing to do with the re- nowned American contempt for genius that "crushes the artist," though Lenny Bruce may give us cause to think otherwise. But Bruce, it is clear, stood at the edge of the cliff and dared the authorities to push him off: the melancholy that suffuses Albert Goldman's book about him is the melancholy of a man who is determined to be beaten. The truth is that comedy is a form of insurgency that thrives on opposition and the comedian who has powerful enemies should consider himself blessed. Indeed, the more immediate problem for the come- dian in America is to find something substantial enough to push against. Maybe that is why our political cartoonists—Mauldin, Herblock, Conrad, and, now, Gary Trudeau—have fared best over the long haul, since the world of power and policy is so unredeemed in its folly that the cartoonist can never run short of examples. But for the specialist in social manners, the satirist of social preten- sion, the moment of truth commonly arrives when the *beau monde* opens its arms to him. When the bouquets start landing at his feet faster than he can clasp them to his warm breast, his irony is most in danger of collapsing into *gemut- lichkeit* and his sneers into tears of appreciation. It was not mere snottiness that kept Woody Allen away from the Academy Awards in 1978 when *Annie Hall* was the toast of the Academy. He was being understandably wary of the afflictions of the rebel-turned-celebrity, who looks so terrific in his ruffled shirt and blow- dried hair that he's liable to forget to bite the hand that feeds him and content himself with licking it a little. For the moment—in the wake of *Stardust Memories* in which his admirers are uniformly depicted as fools and gro- tesques—there seems to be little danger of Allen's doing that.

Yet Allen shares with his contemporaries the universal affliction of the come- dian, a weakness for upward mobility. Sooner or later the comedian wants to move up, to become a satirist of modern life, a director, a social critic, a novelist, an "auteur," even, Heaven help us, a crooner, like Jerry Lewis. The exceptions are few and celebrated. Groucho Marx and W. C. Fields stayed gratefully sour in the face of stardom, and one suspects in both cases reserved supplies of tension and spite to keep the comedy flowing and make the world's blandishments feel like assaults. One thinks also of more modest but no less durable talents like Jack Benny, S. J. Perelman, Mae West, and Mel Brooks, who have known how to pace themselves and how to reject all temptations to overreach the known ranges of their abilities. (Brooks's version of upward mobility is to make the same *knaydelach* out of bigger matzos; Bob Hope's is to justify the ways of gas and oil cartels to America.) In general, however, this year's sensation is next year's trivia question. What ever became of Tom Lehrer? Vaughn Meader? Allen Sherman? Red Buttons? Jackie Mason? Marshall Efron?

Woody Allen is not so perishable as these. All the same, his last four films, as of Fall, 1981—*Annie Hall, Interiors, Manhattan,* and *Stardust Memories*— give evidence that he is anything but immune to the universal crisis of the comedian. The side of Allen that wants to make a major statement has begun to edge forward, elbowing the comedy into the corners and even, in *Interiors,* smothering it altogether in wet blankets of *significance*. Having stepped up from laughs to values and having turned for dramatic concepts from Chaplin and the Marx Brothers to Bergman, Strindberg, and Fellini, Allen is now an "auteur," who shows a distinct weakness for a line of thought that has been flitting in and out of his comedy for years as an element of his standing routine: God is dead; life has no meaning: man is a lonely speck in a vast, impersonal void. In short, high-school existentialism. The apprehensions are familiar to anyone who knows Allen's earlier films or the books in which his *New Yorker* sketches and several of his one-act plays have been collected: *Getting Even, Without Feathers,* and *Side Effects*.[1] There they are usually employed as lead-ins to the basic Allen joke: the hifalutin' sentiment brought crashing to earth by the absurd juxtaposition. "My parents were very old world people. Their values were God and carpeting." "I have an intense desire to return to the womb. Anybody's." In *Play It Again, Sam,* Allen (as Allen Felix) attempts to pick up a young woman in the Museum of Modern Art, as both stand before a Jackson Pollock.

> Allen: What does it say to you?
> Woman: It restates the negativeness of the universe. The hideous lonely emptiness of existence. Nothingness. The predicament of Man forced to live in a barren, Godless, eternity like a tiny flame flickering in an immense void with nothing but waste, horror and degradation, forming a useless bleak straightjacket in a bleak absurd cosmos.
> Allen: What're you doing Saturday night?
> Woman: Committing suicide.
> Allen: What about Friday night?[2]

In one of the best routines in *Getting Even,* "Mr. Big," a clever parody of a Sam Spade detective story, Allen's private detective, Kaiser Lupowitz, is called in to investigate the death of God. Some of the interplay between coffee-house nihilism, home-cooked theology, and Hammett hardboiled-dom is brilliantly improvised, permitting Allen lines like "God is dead. The police were here. They're looking for you. They think an existentialist did it," and "Oh yes, baby. When the Supreme Being gets knocked off, somebody's got to take the rap." In "God" (in *Without Feathers*), a one-act play on the death of God, what was to be a modern rendition of a Greek tragedy goes haywire and gets away from both cast and playwright, until Zeus is lowered from on high to put things in order and is accidentally strangled by the machinery. "God is dead," announces an actor. "Is he covered by anything?" responds a physician who has rushed up from the audience.

These are classic American gags of a kind that Hope used to do in his sleep and Groucho and Perelman stored up in their cheek pouches like acorns. They are also soaked in borscht. The Yiddish theatre was afloat in that sort of humor, the Yiddish language being fine-tuned for ironic deflation and an ideal medium for the homely punch line, even when God himself was the butt of the joke. The little Yid who talks back to God and gets in the last word is a stock figure in Jewish humor, and Allen has a routine that is very much in this line: a brilliant sketch entitled "God Knocks" (in *Getting Even*) in which Nat Ackerman is visited by Angel of Death and challenges him to a game of gin rummy in the hope of gaining an extra day of life, *and wins*. Of course, this Angel of Death is no big shot; he is a klutz who trips headlong over the windowsill upon entering Ackerman's house and cries out, "Jesus Christ. I nearly broke my neck." And he is a terrible gin player; Ackerman not only beats him for a day, but takes him for twenty-eight dollars. Death has to leave empty-handed, but not before warning: "Look—I'll be back tomorrow, and you'll give me a chance to win the money back. Otherwise I'm in definite trouble." Nat answers him: "Anything you want. Double or nothing we'll play. I'm liable to win an extra week or a month. The way you play, maybe years." The *moloch ha movitz* [Angel of Death] takes a beating here along with Ingmar Bergman, whose *Seventh Seal* is being playfully parodied. Such comedy is built upon the particular genius of Yiddish comedy, and the Yiddish world view, to domesticate the exalted and cut the marvelous and the awesome down to human scale.

Elsewhere I've described a particular Jewish attribute of mind, which I think of as "ghetto cosmopolitanism,"[3] as an underlying motif in Jewish-American fiction, but it is something that can be found in comedy as well. Like the temper of mind it bespeaks, Jewish comedy specializes in inner juxtapositions and gets its effects through the collision of contradictions within the Jewish character and the conditions of Jewish life. The Yiddish world view was adapted to dissonance, and the literature of the Yiddish renaissance in the late nineteenth century and the early years of our own was founded upon a life brimming with vivid contrasts. Its typical figures were the *schlemiel* who was also a saint, the victim of misfortune who was also a hero of endurance, the impecunious scholar or rabbi who was the exalted moral arbiter of his community, the peddler, shopkeeper, or *luftmensch* down on his luck who was also a visionary. A story by Sholem Aleichem, "Dreyfus in Kasrilevke," for example, gains its particular pathos from the disparity between the isolation of the *shtetl* Jews from the greater world and their passionate involvement in that world.[1] As the Jews of Kasrilevke follow the Dreyfus case in the paper that Zaidle gets in the mail, they collectively pray, cheer, and lament as Dreyfus's fortunes change from day to day. They nominate Émile Zola the hero of Kasrilevka and declare that if he would only have come there "the whole town would have turned out with a wild welcome, they would have carried him on their backs through the dirty, muddy streets." When, at last, they learn from Zaidle that Dreyfus has been convicted, "There arose such a roar, such a protest, that the very heavens must have split," though, as Aleichem tells us, the protest was against Zaidle himself who *had* to be lying, since "truth must always come out on top."

This is not comedy as Woody Allen practices it, but it is humor as the Jews have long known it, an attitude that lies precariously close to desperation as laughter for them is always close to tears. Here the comedy is released by the superimposition of the tragic upon the trivial. These Jews, in one of earth's wretched backwaters (Kasrilevke may as well be Tierra del Fuego for all it matters to the world), behave as though they are at the heart of it, as if their own lives are being played out in the same major key as Dreyfus's. And, in some ways, they are right, since the religious and racial heritage of these provincial Jews is the taint that dooms Dreyfus, and his fate (though neither they nor Sholem Aleichem can know this in the same way we do) is a prefiguration of their own.

The effect of such a story is ambiguous, but its mechanism is plain; the Jews of Kasrilevke are marvelous hybrids, provincial but worldly, up to their necks in circumstances as thick and dark as the mud of Kasrilevke, yet, by sheer effort of mind and will, transcendent, as closely in touch with the great world as with the small, and really as much a part of the larger currents of history as they imagine. In disbelief they cry out to Zaidle, "If you stood here with one foot in heaven and one foot on earth we still wouldn't believe you," and that is exactly where Zaidle stands, straddled between heaven and earth, just like the rest of them.

This special consciousness is formed out of what the Yiddish scholar, Max Weinreich, spoke of in a famous formulation as the "internal bilingualism" of the Ashkenazi Jews,[5] their simultaneous existence in sharply contrasting worlds, each embodied in its own language, Yiddish or Hebrew. To quote Maurice Samuel, this bilingualism made available to Yiddish writing "a charming transition from the jocular to the solemn and back again. Well-worn quotations from sacred texts mingle easily with colloquialisms, and dignified passages jostle popular interjections without taking or giving offense."[6] Such linguistic effects represented a fundamental fact of Jewish life—that it was lived simultaneously in two worlds: *galut*, or exile, *and* Jerusalem.

Although American Jews are no longer bilingual and the striking antinomies of ghetto life are nowhere to be found in the smooth-as-velour continuities of the American middle-class, habits of mind that were fostered in the Old Country stubbornly persist as deep structures of consciousness. The habit of self-irony remains long after certain ironies native to the ghetto have been eradicated, gaining reinforcement from new discrepancies that are uniquely American, discrepancies that attend upward mobility and cultural assimilation. The contradictions of the ancient Semite, who, in the words of the British Arabist C. M. Doughty, "sits in a cloaca up to his neck, but his brow touches the heavens," has been replaced in some measure by the ironies of cultural change and generational succession. The modern Jew sits in Brooklyn up to his neck, but he works in Manhattan. (Invent these as you go. The Jew is up to his neck in Scarsdale but his brow touches the East Village.) The scale of irony is infinitely reduced and the distance is now spanned by the IRT instead of prayer and ceremony, but the form is familiar. As Woody Allen has advanced its techniques, such irony produces the comedy of the modern Jew versus his ancestors, or Beverly Hills in light of Warsaw, or, so foreshortened is the scope of our history, Beverly Hills in light of New York. In purely diagrammatic form it is the comedy of Allen's "Hasidic Tales" (in *Getting Even*), in which Rabbi Baumel of Vitebsk embarks on a fast "to protest the unfair law prohibiting Russian Jews from wearing loafers outside the ghetto" or Rabbi Yitzchok Ben Levi, the great Jewish mystic, applies cabalistic numerology to horse racing and hits the daily double at Aqueduct fifty-two days running. Now, such inventions are sheer formula: place the ancient and the modern side by side and you've got a joke. And it is precisely in such cases where the humor is nothing more than the routine application of technique, and not very funny, that its machinery is most clearly visible.

Yet when Allen lets the habits of self-irony and cultural aggression float free and create their own fiendish combinations, fantastic scenarios begin to emerge, such as Fielding Mellish's dream, in *Bananas*, in which two monks bearing enormous crosses come to blows over a parking place on Wall Street, or the routine in *Everything You Wanted to Know About Sex But Were Afraid to Ask* in which Gene Wilder takes an Armenian sheep to a hotel for a night of lovemaking, or the wonderful lobster-chasing scene in *Annie Hall*, where the gourmet in Alvy Singer suddenly yields to the nervous boy from Brooklyn who isn't quite ready to handle the aggressive, snapping *traif* [unkosher food] that his dreams of *savoir faire* have conjured up.

That the Yiddish element in Allen's comedy merges so easily with the American tells us something about the current state of American comedy and culture. Allen's humor almost never puts the Jewish side of him against the American; it customarily levels both barrels side by side against Europe and *Kultur*: Ibsen and Strindberg, Tolstoy and Dostoevsky, Ingmar Bergman, Kierkegaard and Freud. Bogart and baseball, gin rummy and the protracted sexual adolescence stand for much the same thing, Brooklyn, which is as distant from Manhattan as it is from Europe culturally, making it a convenient base of operations for strikes on both. What Americanness and *Yiddishkeit* have in common is a sense of cultural inferiority before the high culture of *Mitteleuropa*, making their assaults upon that culture exercises in *ressentiment*.

The dialectic at the heart of Allen's comedy recalls in rough outline Van

Wyck Brooks's conception of American culture as a realm divided between the spiritual and the practical, the incorporeal and the commercial, the highbrow and the lowbrow. But where Brooks, in "America's Coming of Age," was describing the broader antinomies at work in American life, the Jewish version of the dialectic appears to be at work within the individual Jew, who is highbrow and lowbrow unto himself. A substantial line of humor that runs through comedians as different as Jack Benny, Henny Youngman, Morey Amsterdam, Harpo Marx, and Allen himself is built upon the standoff between *Kunst* and candy store. Each of them carries or carried a musical instrument as a prop, though Allen's clarinet is a hidden prop that has never been introduced into his comedy, and Harpo didn't always drag out the harp. But we know about them in any case; the instruments are their credentials as artists, the signs of their sensitivity. In all cases the musical props indicate a prior, and abandoned, vocation that has specific cultural weight. These violins, cellos, and clarinets are the remnants of that particular version of European high culture that Jews sought to adopt, starting in the nineteenth century, as an avenue of escape from the confines of their narrow community. Such aspiration produced in our own day the great Jewish performers of German and Russian music—David Oistrakh, Jascha Heifetz, Yehudi Menuhin, Isaac Stern, Itzhak Perlman. Vladimir Horowitz, Artur Rubenstein, Vladimir Ashkenazi, et al.—and the comedy that alludes to them is the token of how successfully, and with how much guilt, their example has been evaded. In carrying his instrument on stage with him, the comedian carries his past as a sight-gag, a mechanical straight man that testifies to the stringencies of the ghetto and the dreams of Jewish parents. The Jewish comedian and his violin are not unlike the ventriloquist and his dummy, though the roles are reversed. Whereas the ventriloquist plays straight man to his dummy, it is the comic who plays dummy to his violin, which is also his muse, his superego, his better half. He brings it on stage in order to defy its sole command: play me.

As we now know from watching Woody Allen's career, the logic of cultural subversion is reversible, and comedy can be unmasked to reveal *its* latent content, which may be depression or despair or terror. It is abundantly clear by now that Allen, in bringing his comedy to bear on the great masters of gloom like Kafka, Kierkegaard, and Bergman was not just dropping banana peels in the path of Western thought but mulling over concerns that had been dredged up by his own distraught imagination; setting up troublesome preoccupations of his own and then pulling out the rug.

Allen has been something of a closet tragedian all along, and the air of cosmic befuddlement that now colors his thought was there from the start. He has taken to telling interviewers, "My real obsessions are religious," and, "Death is the big obsession behind all I've done," and "The metaphor for life is a concentration camp. I do believe that."[7] This last, he told *Time* magazine after *Manhattan* was released, was a line he had cut from that film but intended to use in his next. And despite efforts on Allen's part to keep *Manhattan* from drowning, as *Interiors* did, in too metaphysical a view of the modern condition, the void sneaks inexorably in. So, when Isaac Davis (Allen) and Mary (Diane Keaton) take refuge from a storm in Hayden Planetarium and conduct a flirtatious tête-à-tête amid lunar and nebular skyscapes, Allen, as director, is not just having fun with his sets; he's also reminding us that "we're lost out here in the stars."

Since depression, as everyone knows, is the special malaise of intellectuals, the comedian who admits to being even mildly depressed is bound to be taken for an intellectual comedian, as Allen often is, despite his frequent pleas that he is nothing more than a funnyman out in pursuit of the next laugh. It is true that his exploitation of ideas can scarcely conceal his ambivalence toward them, even now that he has taken to brooding in public over God, death, and *l'univers concentrationnaire*. He has the autodidact's contempt for formal schooling, and his comedy employs general ideas in much the same way that a hamburger employs meat.

That too marks Allen as a typical practitioner of the line of comedy that runs from Henny Youngman to Don Rickles by way of Grossinger's, The Copa, and Caesar's Palace. Jewish and from Brooklyn, he is urban though scarcely urbane, shy but aggressive, brainy but rebellious, neurotic and sensitive. And he works under a stage name, fearing that a name like Allen Stewart Konigsberg would not get him very far in show business. A profile like that comes right out of the do-it-yourself manual for comedians. Allen started out with a routine apprenticeship, ghostwriting one-liners for Earl Wilson and Walter Winchell, doing gags and *shticks* for Garry Moore, Herb Shriner, and *Your Show of Shows*, where he worked with Mel Brooks, Neil Simon, Sid Caesar, and Carl Reiner. He has worked nightclubs, gone on the road, played Las Vegas, and turned out reams of humor on contract under Hollywood conditions—tight schedules, confusion, humiliation—while writing *What's New, Pussycat?* for Charles Feldman. Little in that outline suggests anything special in Allen's initial orientation as a comedian. First and foremost he has been an entertainer who has learned the classic tools of his trade—the pratfall, the throwaway, the sight gag, and the strategic pause—from the masters: the Catskill comics like Youngman and Berle and the Hollywood funnymen like Groucho and Hope. He has even invented a comic persona for himself, the sexual loser (lately turned sexual narcissist), which, like Benny's cheapskate and Chaplin's little tramp, has done much of his thinking for him. About all in the standard repertoire of gimmicks he has shied away from are insults, impressions, and giving regards to Broadway; in most other respects he is the child of his profession.

But for all that, Allen has clearly taken leave of the mainstream of nightclub humor and its special redolence of alcohol, sweat and Arpége. He doesn't score points on Gentiles or mothers-in-law or chorus girls, and when he gets around to sex, the joke is on him. This choice of the comic high road owes something to Mort Sahl, whose brand of political satire Allen discovered in San Francisco in the 1950s. Sahl's example, reinforced by Lenny Bruce and the Second City comics, especially Mike Nichols and Elaine May, demonstrated that a come-

dian could deal in social values instead of social stereotypes and bring tren-
chant satire into popular comedy without bludgeoning his audiences over the
head, though Bruce himself wound up doing just that toward the end. But, while
some comedians, Sahl and Dick Gregory in particular, lent their voices to
political causes, and Bruce's martyrdom became totemic to a movement, what
impressed Allen was not their social attitudes. Neither Sahl's anger nor Bruce's
cynicism had an effect on him. Allen was fairly immune to the events of the
sixties; his concerns were, as they remain, too self-contained to be penetrated
by issues. Rather, what he learned from the coffeehouse comics were professional tricks of the trade, such as how to pitch material toward educated audiences without getting too dangerously involved with ideas.

He also learned from them how to bridge the gap between life and material by
becoming one's own material, looking at one's own life through the prism of
irony (and how Jewish a practice that is!). That, too, is a kind of faking, since it
involves free improvisation around an invention, a self that is not strictly one's
self but a concept of one's self. Allen's *schlemiel*, like Fields's hustler, West's
vamp, and Groucho's madcap, has origins in his own personality but is first and
foremost a *shtick*, a theatrical relationship to life. You needn't *be* a *schlemiel* to
calculate the advantages of *behaving* like one.

Every comic needs some such theatrical self to be not only his trademark but
his muse, the inventor of the jokes he tells. The comedian plays host to his other
self which lives off him as much as he lives off it, and, unless he collapses into
his persona entirely, he is by profession a case of split personality. Allen the
comic, we are led to understand, is by no means the same man as Allen the
clarinetist; and such a self-division, it appears, is something of a professional
standard. It is not only for purposes of ethnic whitewashing that nearly all
Jewish comedians perform under stage names. So dependent is the comic on his
other self that he comes to seek shelter in it, and asking any comedian to step
out from behind the mask is a little like asking Harpo Marx to speak. Woody
Allen's efforts to adopt a new identity starting with *Annie Hall*, then, is a rare
event in show business, all the more so for reflecting an effort on his part to grow
up, since the *schlemiel*, as he has played the type, had the character of a child
in a world of adults. But now the sexual incompetent of the early films has given
way to the sexual narcissist, and the bewildered, precocious kid has grown up to
be the urban neurotic.

Allen's world of late has been of singles in distress, who are predominantly
urban, affluent (or, at any rate, not pressed for money), educated, divorced,
schooled in breakup and breakdown, for whom the analysis is a substitute for
the marriage and the analyst a surrogate for the family. It is, then, a social
enclave that best exemplifies what Christopher Lasch calls "the culture of
narcissism." As such, it is not a place at all (New York) but a way of life that has
taken hold wherever the middle class has graduated from sufficiency to surplus
and found the end of the rainbow to be also the end of the rope. It is here that
success breeds despair, leisure yields to boredom, and the cost of modern life is
more visible for being so much higher than that of the goods that are conspicu-

ously consumed. ("I ran into my ex-wife the other day, and I hardly recognized her with her wrists closed.") In a faltering monologue at the beginning of *Manhattan,* Allen's Isaac Davis speaks portentously of Manhattan as "a metaphor for the decay of contemporary culture," as though to prepare us for a tour through the city of dreadful night. Scarcely. There isn't an act of terror in the film and not even a subway joke, let alone a subway mugging. Culture decomposes at the highest tax brackets, among tea rooms and sculpture galleries, to the strains of Gershwin. And Central Park is still for lovers. What distresses Allen is not what is happening to society but what is happening to that social class whose dreams were once scored by Gershwin, and which, having ascended to the skyline, has nothing left to look forward to save sexual adventurism. What do you give the man who has everything? A divorce.

We might well ask what is so Jewish about any of this, since Allen plays this as a Jewish drama. At first glance, little is. Jews have no patent on success and despair, and a footloose Jewish bachelor like Allen's Isaac Davis is scarcely going to reflect on the Torah or the tragic history of his people while cruising the Dalton School for a pickup. In fact, what is most Jewish about *Annie Hall,* *Manhattan,* and *Stardust Memories* is what is most American about them. The Jews, having found a home in the heart of the American middle-class, have inherited its conflicts: ambition vs. ethical probity, commerce vs. spirit, family vs. career, and it makes some sense to see Allen's recent films as footnotes to the history of immigrant success and therefore as reflections of the life that began on the Lower East Side and eventually arrived uptown by way of Brooklyn. It might well be said that Allen's ambiguous celebrations of uptown Manhattan are predicated upon a boyhood spent in Brooklyn, from which the Brooklyn Bridge must have seemed like a stairway to paradise. In a sense, Allen is following the lead of Abraham Cahan's *The Rise of David Levinsky* and, more recently, Saul Bellow's *Humboldt's Gift,* both examinations of the ironies of Jewish success. If his talents permitted, Allen might become the tragic historian of Jewish achievement.

I scarcely think, however, that Allen is conscious of so bold an intention, unless he is more socially conscious than he lets on. In *Manhattan,* a film basically about class and taste, he appears to take up social themes whose full ironies elude his grasp. But social history isn't always recorded best by those who have reflected on it most. The migration from Brooklyn to Manhattan may put a man in touch with the social drama of a culture without granting him any conceptual understanding of it. Allen plays catch-as-catch-can with his social themes, attacking them with whatever weapons come to hand: the one-liner, the cameo, the throwaway, the fragments of overheard conversation. But largely he approaches society through the bedroom door, as though the sexual habits of a culture could stand for its entire life, which, in some measure, they can. After all, the history of psychoanalysis is also the history of a particular phase of Western civilization, and psychoanalysis itself has been instrumental in forming the values of the modern world. Whether it is true or not that, as John Murray Cuddihy argues in his book, *The Ordeal of Civility,* Freud's sexual interpretation of culture is a special manifestation of Jewish alienation and rage, it does seem the case that both psychoanalysis and Jewish comedy share in common a genius for debunking social pieties by calling attention to their hidden motives. But whether Allen's brand of bedroom analysis is equal to the job of social analysis is another question. Consider *Manhattan*. It opens to find Isaac Davis twice-divorced, unemployed, about to have his private habits exposed in print by his second wife (now a lesbian who left him for another woman), and taking refuge in the arms of a seventeen-year-old senior at the Dalton School named Tracy, whom he is, in embarrassment, trying to dump. Enter Mary, a dippy, neurotic critic (of everything, it would seem) who is involved with Isaac's married friend, Yale, and romance slowly kindles between them, presided over by the lush strains of Gershwin's "Embraceable You," "Lady Be Good," and "Someone to Watch over Me." It culminates in a brief affair that lasts only until Yale can summon up the courage to leave his wife, claim Mary, and leave a heartbroken Isaac alone, full of regrets, and feeling very much the fool. The conclusion finds him at Tracy's door, begging for a reconciliation as she is preparing to depart for London and drama school. This sort of bed-swapping, home-breaking, breakup, makeup, 'cause I love you brand of living is Allen's version of the "decay of contemporary culture," and it does seem fairly bleak. Allen tries to play it as a romance, but there aren't enough moonbeams to go around. Post-Freudian culture, we're meant to understand, frees us for pleasure at the cost of loneliness and guilt; and modern guilt, unlike its Victorian antecedent, is not over the impulses we've repressed but over those we've acted out. This is a film about freedom and its discontents, and Allen never once has to invoke the death of God in explanation. Sex and boredom explain everything.

There is material here for a substantial criticism of the culture of narcissism, but Allen turns out to be doing something different, writing a romance (albeit a depressive one) and a comedy of manners in which the narcissism of taste that is under attack finally wins out because, it seems, Allen wants it to. Allen appears to be uncertain whether he wants to denounce middle-class ennui or exalt it, and so he does both, as though George Gershwin could be assimilated to, say, Herbert Marcuse without anyone's noticing the difference. Let us accept for the moment the film's romantic premise—that Isaac, at forty-two, has been foolish to give up his seventeen-year-old Tracy for the neurotic Mary, who was bound to drop him just as soon as Yale could get up the gumption to leave his wife. What are the appeals of Tracy that prompt Isaac to tell her at one point that she is "God's answer to Job?" Of course there is her low threshold of arousal, which makes her want to do most of her homework in Isaac's bed. She does respond passionately, much to the relief of Isaac, whose last wife has charged him with having changed her from a bisexual into a lesbian. But you needn't be seventeen to be embraceable. It is not for nothing that Allen's sex goddess is a kid, because the film's deepest idea, which is quite apart from any of that stuff about the decline of values, demands it. The underlying myth of *Manhattan* is that in a world of corrupt adults, redemption may come through the love of a child, or, since the redemption is sexual, the love of a teenager. *Manhattan* is a fairy tale for an age of sexual freedom, in which the hero is released into innocence *and* orgasm, providing a new twist to an old moral: *And they came together happily ever after*. Only thinking stands in the way of this; it is known as "intellectualizing," and it blocks the avenues to self-realization and erotic fulfillment. We recall that during their flirtation at the Hayden Planetarium Isaac chides Mary for relying too much on her brain to the detriment of her feelings. As a would-be intellectual (and all of Allen's intellectuals are would-be) she has thought her way into her neurosis and can't feel her way out of it. Tracy, on the other hand, being unencumbered by ideas, is uninhibited in her feelings. She has no opinions, no tastes in art, that region of corruption, and nothing to say except "I love you," which usually comes out sounding like, "Gee whiz, why can't I stay over tonight?" You have to wonder what they teach at the Dalton School. What Allen seems to fear is that the bedroom may be confused with the classroom, no minor fear given the way doctrines proliferate in the most private recesses of modern life. Learning, he believes, interrupts pleasure, and all the while he is giving us this Marin County credo straight from the hot tub, he pretends to have nothing but disdain for California.

Allen has often been compared to Philip Roth, though it might be more pertinent just now to compare him to J. D. Salinger, a *New Yorker* writer of another generation in whose books a similar irony lends cover to an overwhelming sentimentality. For Salinger, too, sex is a threat, intelligence invariably a pretentious show of bogus erudition, and innocence a cherished and elusive virtue. Of course, Allen can admit sex while Salinger can only deny it frantically. But when Allen celebrates the adolescent love goddess in *Manhattan* he gives us an unwitting parody of *The Catcher in the Rye*, in which Phoebe Caulfield, by her innocence, proves to be her brother's only refuge. The fact that Allen's heroes, unlike Salinger's Seymour Glass in the story "A Perfect Day for Bananafish," use the bedroom for love and not death, doesn't mitigate their fear of women; it only promotes their terror a few grades, from junior high to high school level. The innocence Allen yearns for is that of the eternal sexual high school, while Salinger's is that of the threshold years, where all is yet a vast and terrifying portent. The latter trades on the kind of sexual mystification that points the way to the monastery or the ashram, while Allen's sexual mythos takes him to the playground. In *Manhattan*, Tracy is seventeen because Isaac Davis is scarcely older than that himself. Perpetual adolescence is Allen's great secret and his weapon. His film persona is nothing without it. He is the eternal kid.

Great comedy can be launched from that position, because the kid is granted special insights into the follies of the adult world, and because he has a dispensation from that world to be as sentimental or as belligerent as he pleases. Boys will be boys. Thus armed and vulnerable, he gives free rein to his imagination. Now, the kid's-eye view of the adult world won't always give you a persuasive criticism of society, since its powers of analysis are likely to be primitive, but it does permit explosive combinations of outrage and wit. Yet Allen has chosen to repudiate the imaginative advantages of playing the kid overtly, as he did in his earlier comedies, for more sober points of view. The kid is still very much there steaming with envy and resentment, but he is now cunningly disguised as a social critic. The resultant inflation of perspective and deepening of voice have not pleased everybody. Vernon Young, in reviewing Allen's *Interiors* for *Commentary* early in 1979, took note of Allen's "Puritan hunger for High Seriousness, the discontent with authentic veins of American subject matter," and complained of the snobbishness inherent in the belief that comedy is an inferior art.[8] "What on earth compelled him to settle for less by aping a mode of cinema in which he has to inhibit himself instead of releasing his better inspirations is a problem for him to resolve; the movies may be the last place in which he can resolve it." The tepid compromises of *Manhattan*, in which random one-liners ("my mother, the castrating Zionist") struggle in vain to bring light to a gloomy situation, hardly disprove Young's strictures. In an effort to lend his work more contemporary significance, Allen has managed, in *Interiors* and *Manhattan*, to go off the shallow end. Taking leave of comedy, he has taken leave of his imagination as well.

This leap from the plane of Yiddish to that of Hebrew, to return to our old metaphor, is not a sudden development in Allen's work. As early as *Sleeper* in 1973, Pauline Kael remarked that his abandonment of the loose, manic highs of *Bananas* and *Everything You Always Wanted to Know About Sex* for a controlled and paced humor signalled an "overvalued normality."[9] Allen, she complained, "still thinks that that's the secret of happiness. He hasn't come to terms with what his wit is telling him."

We can't measure the gains to Allen personally of this new frame of mind that places personal development in charge of artistic growth. But for myself, Allen's films grow less entertaining and less significant as they strain to become more mature and "responsible." Allen has misjudged how rich a statement he was already making back when his humor seemed more desperate and his extraordinary imagination was broadcasting its own nervous messages. "Surreal comedy is chaos," Kael reminds us. "To be really funny, you have to be willing to let your unconscious take over." It is the sign of Allen's midlife maturation that where id once was now only ego is visible, and we can only lament the passing of a rare and gifted childhood.

POSTSCRIPT

This essay was initially drafted in 1979, just after *Manhattan* had its run and a year before the release of *Stardust Memories*, but there is nothing in that film to persuade me that Allen's work will soon take a turn for the better. *Stardust Memories* is a cloyingly narcissistic film that concedes nothing to life or vitality or humor. Not even the liberal allusions to Fellini's *8½* relieve the monotony of Allen's self-recital. Allen has only two themes now: his own beleaguered self (or perhaps it is self-beleaguerment) and the history of film, and he carries on with both as though even he found them exhausting.

BIBLIOGRAPHIC NOTE

Because Allen's career has so many dimensions as both literature and popular entertainment, his humor has become more available and less perishable than that of most of his contemporaries. Many of his best jokes and routines can be found on record and in the three books I've noted: *Getting Even* (New York: Warner Books, 1972), *Without Feathers* (New York: Warner Books, 1976), and *Side Effects* (New York: Random House, 1981). A fourth book, *Non-Being and Somethingness*, has been announced but as of October, 1981, had not been released. Souvenir books have also been made of some of his films. See, for example, *Woody Allen's 'Play It Again Sam'*, edited by Richard J. Anobile (New York: Grosset and Dunlap, 1977).

Much has been written about Allen, possibly too much when one reflects on the poor quality of the great bulk of it. There are two biographies and one book of criticism, all three of which are long on anecdote and short on reflection. The biographies are Eric Lax, *On Being Funny: Woody Allen and Comedy* (New York: Charterhouse, 1976) and Lee Guthrie, *Woody Allen, A Biography* (New York: Drake Publishers, 1978), and the critical book is Maurice Yacower, *Loser Take All: The Comic Art of Woody Allen* (New York: Ungar, 1979). None of these books probes very deeply into the sources and meanings of Allen's humor, but all are useful in recalling highlights from his films and in filling in the backgrounds of his career. Chatty books of this sort are amply supplemented by chatty articles; film reportage is dominated by efforts to "get to know" the celebrity. The best of these are Richard Schickel, "The Basic Woody Allen Joke," *New York Times Magazine*, 7 January 1973, p. 10; Penelope Gilliatt, "Guilty, With An Explanation," *New Yorker*, 4 February 1974, p. 39; Michael Dempsey, "The Autobiography of Woody Allen," *Film Comment* (May–June 1979): 9–17; Jack Kroll, "Funny, But He's Serious," *Newsweek*, 24 April 1978, p. 62; and Richard Schickel, "Woody Allen Comes of Age," *Time*, 30 April 1979, p. 62.

By contrast, incisive criticism of Allen's films is fairly hard to find. The best pieces I have come across are Pauline Kael's review of *Sleeper* in her *Reeling* (New York: Warner Books, 1976), pp. 240–244; Vernon Young's strictures on *Interiors* in *Commentary* (January 1979): 60–64; Alan Spiegel's essay on "American Film-Flam" in *Salmagundi* (Spring 1978): 153–169; Joan Didion's review of *Annie Hall, Interiors*, and *Manhattan* in the *New York Review of Books*, 16 August 1979, p. 18; and Pauline Kael's bitter and unsparing remarks on *Stardust Memories* in the *New Yorker*, 27 October 1980, p. 183.

NOTES

1. Woody Allen, *Getting Even* (New York: Warner Books, 1972), *Without Feathers* (New York: Warner Books, 1976), and *Side Effects* (New York: Random House, 1981).
2. For this and other splendid comic bits see Richard J. Anobile, *Woody Allen's 'Play It Again Sam'* (New York: Grosset & Dunlap, 1977).

3. Mark Shechner, "Saul Bellow and Ghetto Cosmopolitan," *Modern Jewish Studies Annual* 2 (1978): 33–44.

4. "Dreyfus in Kasrilevke" appears in *A Treasury of Yiddish Stories*, ed. Irving Howe and Eliezer Greenberg (New York: Schocken, 1973), pp. 187–91.

5. Max Weinreich, "Internal Bilingualism in Ashkenaz," in *Voices From the Yiddish: Essays, Memoirs, Diaries*, ed. Irving Howe and Eliezer Greenberg (Ann Arbor: University of Michigan Press, 1972), pp. 279–88.

6. Quoted in *A Treasury of Yiddish Stories*, p. 47.

7. Such pronouncements can be found almost anywhere, but see especially the cover stories in *Newsweek*, 24 April 1978, p. 62, *Time*, 30 April 1979, p. 62, and *Film Comment* (May–June 1979): 9–17.

8. Vernon Young, "Autumn Interiors," *Commentary* (January 1979): 60–64.

9. Pauline Kael, *Reeling* (New York: Warner Books, 1976), pp. 243–44.

Mel Brooks and the Cinema
of Exhaustion

Sanford Pinsker

"TRANSPOSE THE SOLEMN INTO THE FAMILIAR AND THE RESULT IS PARODY."[1]
Transpose the familiar into the solemn and the result is academic criticism. The
first position is Henri Bergson's; the second is mine. I begin by turning Bergso-
nian parody inside-out, partly because my subject will, indeed, be versions of
the parodic imagination and partly to hedge some objections in advance. With
regard to the latter: The general proposition that nothing is duller than a joke
explained seems doubly true if one imagines a discussion of Mel Brooks's humor
conducted in scholarly tranquility. At the same time, however, nothing would
please him more, especially if the article put him in good, literary company,
appeared between hard covers and was destined for the library stacks.

During the same year that Mel Brooks was editing *The Producers*, an intriguing literary essay—at once literary criticism and aesthetic manifesto—appeared
in *The Atlantic Monthly*. The piece was entitled "The Literature of Exhaustion"
and its author was a tall, bookishly funny man named John Barth.[2] The year was
1967. It was an age that had a keen ear for the death rattle and one that took a
particular glee in announcing the End of Nearly Everything: the Establishment
and business-as-usual, the Old Guard, the Old Politics, the Old Left, one's Old
Man. And, of course, linear print and the Novel. Small wonder, then, that Barth
felt his ox being gored. As he saw it, the heart of the matter was that "the very
idea of the controlling artist has been condemned as politically reactionary,
even fascist."

Needless to say, SUNY-Buffalo (where Mr. Barth taught courses in fiction-
writing) was no place to be an elitist. It was probably not even a good place to
insist that people keep on *writing*, albeit in their own way. Given the widespread appeal of junk art and the shrill rhetoric of its defenders, one was hardly
surprised when Barth reaffirmed the old Aristotelian verities. His own inclination, he chided gently, was to "prefer the kind of art that not many people can
do, the kind that requires expertise and artistry as well as bright esthetic ideas
and/or inspiration." Given a choice between, say, the pop art of Buffalo's
Albright-Knox collection and the jugglers at the old Hippodrome theatre, Barth
would opt for his memories of the Baltimore vaudevillians every time. They
were, as he put it, "genuine virtuosi" because they did things anyone can dream
up and discuss but almost no one can do.

For Barth, the issue was less the current state of aesthetic chit-chat than the
kinds of actual work still possible. The used-upness of certain forms, the
exhaustion of certain possibilities, struck him as the central fact of life that
contemporary writers had to face. To be sure, there were authors who simply
chugged ahead, spinning out turn-of-the-century novels with something like

mid-century language and situations. But that clearly would not do. A more ingenious way of handling the dilemma of the novel's exhaustion might be to write a novel about it—which, of course, is exactly what our most ingenious artists have done:

> If you happened to be Vladimir Nabokov, you might address that felt ultimacy by writing *Pale Fire:* a fine novel by a learned pedant, in the form of a pedantic commentary on a poem invented for the purpose. If you were Borges, you might write *Labyrinths:* fictions by a learned librarian in the form of footnotes, as he describes them, to imaginary or hypothetical books. And I'll add, since I believe Borges's idea is rather more interesting, that if you were the author of this paper, you'd have written something like *The Sot-Weed Factor* or *Giles Goat-Boy:* novels which imitate the form of the Novel, by an author who imitates the role of Author. [p. 275]

As Barth would have it, our most contemporary "contemporary writers" turn form into subject and self-consciousness into a narrative posture. They are, in a word, reflexive. They also have a way of being in the forefront of consciousness, of knowing things before they happen in the culture at large.

This much said, let us return to the Mel Brooks we left on the cutting room floor of *The Producers*. It, too, was an extended exercise in parody, albeit one that was American-Jewish to its very bones. Brooks's film not only saw the Broadway musical through Hollywood eyes, but, more important, it saw the creators of that culture through eyes at least one generation removed. Henry Bech, the composite (psychologically projected?) Jew of John Updike's *Bech: A Book*, puts it this way:

> . . . the artistic triumph of American Jewry lay, he thought, not in the novels of the fifties but in the movies of the thirties, those gargantuan, crass contraptions whereby Jewish brains projected Gentile stars upon a Gentile nation and out of their immigrant joy gave a formless land dreams and even a kind of conscience.[3]

What Barth and Brooks shared was a felt sense that traditional forms had worn thin. For John Barth, this meant the world of Richardson and Fielding, Austen and Eliot; for Brooks, it was more likely to mean the cowboy movie and the gangster film, Fred Astaire and Ginger Rogers. The difference between them had to do with the relative independence of the novelist as opposed to the large capital investment that movie-making requires.

The days of the old scenario in which Mickey Rooney gazes into Judy Garland's eyes and says: "Let's put on a show!" are over. To make a production happen, you need money. And to make it happen on Broadway, you need a producer like Max Bialystock. At least that is the premise of the film Brooks tried to sell Joseph E. Levine. But entitled *Springtime for Hitler?* With Nazi chorus girls, to boot? Ironically enough, Levine settled for *The Producers*. Perhaps he thought that the sleazy world of Max Bialystocks was not at all like the dealings of Hollywood. No matter. What Brooks had in mind was a portrait of the artist as part con-man, part artistic genius. Stephen Dedalus proudly boasts that he will *"forge* the uncreated conscience of his race on the smithy of his soul" while James Joyce relishes the pun. I belabor these Joycean connections because Brooks chose Leopold Bloom (the protagonist of Joyce's *Ulysses*) as the name for his nervous accountant-hero. In Brooks's words:

> I don't know what it meant to James Joyce, but to me Leo Bloom always meant a vulnerable Jew with curly hair.[4]

Enter Gene Wilder.

But given the "Springtime for Hitler" motif, Brooks's notion of Bloom as "vulnerable Jew" takes on special meanings. If a black comedian like Dick Gregory tries to deflate the sting in the word "nigger" by making it serve as the title of his book, Brooks does much the same thing by reducing the grotesquerie of the Holocaust world to screamingly bad theater. His humor is at once a defense mechanism, one that holds the heinous event at arm's length, and a weapon designed to beat Nazism senseless. To be sure, providing a rationale for what some will *always* consider tasteless is tough, thankless work.

Fortunately, when Zero Mostel plays Max Bialystock, the notion of a *lovable* con-man becomes easier to explain. Unlike Bloom, the nebbish, Max Bialystock is the Id: "Bite, kiss, take, grab, lavish, urinate—whatever you can do that's physical, he will do." Enter Zero Mostel. He is, in short, libidinal energy with a Jewish heart. By that I mean, he waves his arms and shrieks, but he is, at best, a parodic version of the hedonist. On the other hand, what's so wrong, he might ask, with a laugh or a little pinch before his elderly female backers tumble into their graves? Like Buddy Hackett, the roly-poly Zero Mostel "gets away" with questionable material by hiding it under layers of baby fat and behind a boyish grin.

The partnership of Leo Bloom and Max Bialystock was arranged in that peculiarly Jewish heaven where there is a lid for every pot. Their secret-sharing not only accounts for the plural in the compromised studio title, but it puts the emphasis on the *making* of *Springtime for Hitler*. Without Leo Bloom's creative accounting, Max Bialystock is simply one more down-at-heel producer with a long string of flops. With it, he is back in business beyond even *his* wildest dreams. The premise of overselling shares and then consciously setting out to produce the worst play in history makes for some biting, very funny satire. Kenneth Tynan likens the effect to that of Ben Jonson's *Volpone:*

> In the early scenes, Mostel and Wilder play together like figures out of a Jonsonian comedy of humors. Cupidity (Mostel) seduces Conformity (Wilder): in each, a single trait is exaggerated to the point of plethoric obsession, and beyond. [*NYP*, p. 114]

The result is a chorus line of Stormtrooper maidens (garbed in leather) who sing *Springtime for Hitler* as they parody Busby Berkeley routines, this time in the shape of swastikas. It is Bad Taste in bold relief, Vulgarity so shrill that audiences, real and imagined, were overwhelmed. It is also very funny stuff.

Sophoclean ironies account for part of the reason that the wacky premise of *The Producers* works. Try *too* hard to engineer a failure and the world will insist your play is a smash—which, of course, means that your multiple backers will insist on their cuts of the profit. The world will also insist that future dance routines be choreographed behind prison walls.

Mel Brooks is, in the vernacular, a yeller. In Brooks's own words: "My comedy is big-city, Jewish, whatever I am. Energetic, nervous, crazy."[5] He shrieks, *shpritzes*, goes crazy, flails his arms, dissolves in a heap. He also has a fine ear for the rhythms of immigrant speech and an even sharper feel for the no-nonsense wisdom lying just behind their broken English. His Uncle Joe, for example, was

> . . . a philosopher, very deep, very serious. "Never eat chocolate after chick'n," he'd tell us, wagging his finger. "Don't buy a cardboard belt," he'd say. Or he'd warn us—we're five years old—"Don't invest. Put da money inna bank. Even the land could sink!" [*PI*, p. 49]

Being an American-Jewish comic is often a delicate balancing act between keeping in touch with these voices and incorporating them into one's act. In his comic short, *The Critic* (1963), Brooks juxtaposes the intonations of a pickle-barrel philosopher like his Uncle Joe against a background of abstract cartooning by Norman MacLaren. The incongruities that result are, of course, very funny, but they also tell us a good deal about the American-Jewish comic behind the camera. Not surprisingly, Brooks felt equally at home—or uncomfortable—in both camps. He was at once a parody of the Wise Old Jew and an interloper at the watering holes of High Culture.

Such people learn early that Language is Power. As Brooks remembers it:

> I was scrawny. I was the last one they picked to be on the team. . . . But I was brighter than most kids my age, so I hung around with guys two years older. Why should they let this puny kid hang out with them? I gave them a reason. I became their jester. Also, they were afraid of my tongue. I had it sharpened and I'd stick it in their eye. I read a little more than they did, so I could say, "Touch me not, leper!" "Hey! Mel called me a leopard!" "Schmuck! Leper!" Words were my equalizer. [*PI*, p. 53]

No doubt, other fast-talking, wisecrackers would agree: the Word was, indeed, the great equalizer against the angry fist and well-aimed rock. To survive the best and the worst the streets had to offer, one became a verbal jouster, if not "jester," and fended off the bigger boys with one's mouth.

Becoming a pool *tummler* roughed up whatever polished surfaces remained. To break into the Borsht Belt circuit, one was expected to do everything: wash dishes, wait tables, clean up the tennis courts, rent out the rowboats and, if one were lucky, make the guests at the poolside laugh. A *tummler* was, in Brooks's phrase, a "busboy with tinsel in his blood." Mel Brooks had a keen instinct for what the trade calls Catskill *shtick*. As a fourteen-year-old, one of his favorite bits involved dressing up in an overcoat and derby, *shlepping* two large suitcases—filled with rocks—and edging his way toward the end of the diving board. There he would scream at the top of his lungs: "Business is terrible!"— and jump off. Hardly sophisticated stuff, but, then again, the Borsht Belt was not a sophisticated place in 1940. Perhaps this nervous, driving energy accounts, in part, for Brooks's brief career as a drummer. It, too, meant hitting, meant noise.

In any event, Brooks brought his American-Jewish legacy to Hollywood. He had assimilated the best (some would be quick to add: also the worst) that had been thought up and *shpritzed* out on the vaudeville stage. Words continued to be his special equalizer long after the old gang had left the corner candy store and Brooklyn for parts unknown. At times—as in *The Producers*—energy alone carried the day. Playwriting took a second place to the outrageous parody of that art. The victory was sealed the following year when Brooks won an Academy Award for the screenplay of *The Producers*. The rest, with the exception of *The Twelve Chairs*, becomes parodic history. Or to apply the Barthian formula, *Blazing Saddles, High Anxiety* and *Silent Movie* are: films which imitate the form of Film, by a filmmaker who imitates the role of Filmmaker.

Evidently, cinema exhausts itself more quickly than linear print. The Western, for example, had already etched its clichés into the American psyche. As a mode it reeked with used-upness; as a "possibility," it was exhausted. *Blazing Saddles*—a film Brooks once described as "a Jewish Western with a black hero"—is about the making of itself. Put another way: It is Jewish Camp, that special brand of spoofing which wrenches the expected out of context and makes it fend for itself somewhere else. The zigzagging alternations are symptomatic of deeply divided impulses in American-Jewish life—to swallow the popular culture which surrounded it, to, in a word, assimilate *everything;* at the same time, to remain separate, slightly superior, culturally intact. The result is pastiche, a phenomenon Ronald Sanders describes as a "Jewish specialty," the gift of a people forced to live in culturally ambivalent situations.[6] So, too, is parody. Both are built from nearly equal shares of imitative reverence and ironic distancing. The voice that shouts its allegiance to things American—to stickball and movies, to wisecracks and the candy store where Heshie dwells—never quite drowns out that other voice whispering *goyishe nachas* [Gentile happiness].

Blazing Saddles constantly shifts between expectation and surprise, between the Americanness of its original form and the American-Jewish nature of its parody. It is *the* Western, as seen through urban eyes. When a bigoted straw-boss demands that a black railroad gang serenade his cronies ("Sing one of them songs you people just loves to sing. . . ."), the discontented darkies burst into Cole Porter. When the camera zooms in on a group of cowboys with tin plates and beans, an anvil chorus of farts is sure to follow. In this film, Gucci provides designer saddlebags, the local Howard Johnson's is a one-horse/three-flavor operation and nice old grannies throw wicked punches and know all the four-letter words.

In short, *Blazing Saddles* had a "just-*once*-we'd like to-see" flavor; it was an amateur's romp on a seven-figure budget. Nothing of the Old West—or more correctly, the traditional Western—escaped unscathed. The exorcism was as complete as it was unrelenting. Predictably enough, the critics panned it as sophomoric and "tsk-tsked" about the money it was raking in at the box offices. Gary Arnold's review was typical: "When people claim that a comedy like *Blazing Saddles* broke them up, I like to believe they've gone a long time between movies. Brooks imagines he's being killingly funny when he's just painfully facetious."[7]

One scene has been singled out for special attention. As a wagonload of Blacks move across the prairie, a group of Indians (headed by Mel Brooks, in redface) investigate the intruders. When Brooks realizes who they are, he looks befuddled, then aghast . . . and then shouts his way into celluloid immortality: "*Schvartzers?*" It is a page out of Leslie Fiedler's *Love and Death in the American Novel:* black and white interchange; and, at bottom, all men—even Indians—are secretly Jews.

The early moguls knew what they wanted and, more often than not, it was pious, conventional, if you will, "orthodox." The Age of Hollywood demanded that established forms be followed, that every *t* be crossed, that every *i* be dotted and that every performer be "American." The *shtick* done on Brooklyn corners was one thing; an industry that peddled its films throughout the Midwest was another. Things changed when economic realities whistled a different tune. By the time Melvin Kaminsky (born 1926) transmogrified himself into Mel Brooks, a parodic career was not only possible, but probably necessary. So was *Blazing Saddles*. After more than three decades of horse operas and shoot-'em-ups, after straight horror films and comic chasers, it was high time Hollywood learned to laugh at itself. Besides, the blandness of the fifties threatened to drown America in white bread and gray flannel suiting. If Mel Brooks did not already exist, a freer-swinging, hipper America would have had to invent him.

Young Frankenstein (1974) continued Brooks's love affair with cinematic parody, but this time he narrowed the object of his affection to a single film: James Whale's 1931 classic—*Frankenstein*. Scope became less important than the homage paid in that flattery called comic imitation. From *Young Frankenstein* onward, reverence about movies had a strong Mel Brooks thumbprint. Other filmmakers—one thinks especially of Woody Allen—reserved their awe for serious giants like Ingmar Bergman or François Truffaut. Brooks, on the other hand, is more plebeian. His parody requires neither footnotes nor scholarly introduction. *Frankenstein*, after all, is part of our collective unconscious: *The Sorrow and the Pity* is not. Mel Brooks's loving attention to the details of James Whale's film (including his resurrection of the original laboratory equipment) triggers small bombs in our nostalgic imaginations. That the Woody Allen persona in *Annie Hall* has an obsession with *The Sorrow and the Pity*—a hard-hitting documentary about occupied France during World War II—makes for decidedly smaller orbits of resonance.

But that much said, let me hasten to add that Brooks's parody has its share of "personal" touches, albeit not of the autobiographically confessional sort we associate with Woody Allen. To make the point both dramatic and clear, I cite the following anecdote from Kenneth Tynan's *New Yorker* profile:

> Brooks quickly established himself as the clown of the classroom. One of his favorite movies was *Frankenstein* (the 1931, James Whale version), and he discovered at the age of eight that he could reduce his closest chum, a boy named Gene Cogen, to uncontrollable hysterics by singing "Puttin' On the Ritz" in the manner of Boris Karloff. [*NYP*, p. 68]

Forty years later, Peter Boyle—as the Monster—cracked up America with the same gag.

Indeed, *all* the minor roles in *Young Frankenstein* are brilliant: Madeline Kahn as the Doctor's fiancée (shrieking into orgasm, at last, in the Monster's arms), Marty Feldman as the hunchbacked, popeyed Igor (here pronounced *Eye-gore*), Kenneth Mars (the Nazi playwright in *The Producers*) as the thick-headed Inspector Kemp and Gene Hackman, in cameo, as the blind man. But Gene Wilder as Young Dr. Frankenstein (or, as he insists, *Fron-ken-shteen*) provides the greatest share of on-screen hysterics. Writing the screenplay (along with Wilder), directing the film, and, presumably, running the omnipresent fog machine was involvement enough for Mel Brooks. In Hollywood, there is no greater love than he who effaces himself out of awe for the original version. The result is a film widely praised as cohesive, artistically unified, consistently whole—all proffered with the left hand. Which is to say, *Young Frankenstein* was a Mel Brooks film without Mel Brooks.

The mayhem of *Blazing Saddles* ended at the studio backlots, as the shootout with the bad guys spilled over into other movies-in-progress. Punching holes in the conventions of the Western—where, for example, cardboard fronts make a "fake" town indistinguishable from the *real* one and a hastily erected turnstile can stop pursuing villains dead in their tracks—ended with *Blazing Saddles* stepping completely out of its artifice. It was a moment not unlike the magician revealing the trap door or Hamlet stepping out of character to tell us he is really an acting student from Bayonne, New Jersey. For Brooks, a phrase like "self-conscious parody" became increasingly redundant.

Silent Movie (1976) is, in this sense, as much a parody of itself as it is of those Great Salad Days before sound. Like Marcel Proust's *Remembrance of Things Past*, it is the story of its own composition. Everything moves toward that climactic moment when we join Mel Funn (played by Mel Brooks) as he rushes, breathless, into the theater and down the aisles to watch the movie we have just seen made. The effect is akin to Chinese boxes, where opening one leads to the discovery that yet another lurks inside. And opening *that* one reveals yet another, etc. etc. Such solipsistic mirroring can—and in modernist literature, often does—go on to dizzying lengths. Outdoing the modernists at their own game is not easy, but in books like *Lost in the Funhouse* and *Chimera*, John Barth raises frame-tales to the fourth power. In an age of exhausted narrative forms, *more* is More and authors must dazzle if they are to be seen at all.

Unfortunately, in *Silent Movie* the *idea* outstrips the execution. By taking a vow of silence—broken only by Marcel Marceau's "No!" in thunder—Brooks restricts himself to sight gags and subtitles. Ironically enough, Barth had more freedom, more *possibilities*, in old-fashioned, linear print. Even so, Brooks did well enough with the subtitles (*shpritz* though he might, the man is a "writer"). Sight gags are not Brooks's strong suit. All too often the visual mugging in *Silent Movie* was a pale copy of the Real Goods. After all, silent films were *already* exaggerated; indeed, that was part of their appeal. Fiction might be able to parody a Parody—especially if its author is John Barth—but *Silent Movie* by Mel Brooks could not.

Nor did the ironies stop there. It is bad enough when the grayer heads in the audience start comparing, unfavorably, the straining gags on the screen with funnier ones they remember from Chaplin and Keaton, but it is even worse when Sid Caesar continues to play Master to Mel Brooks's continuing apprenticeship. Brooks, after all, worked as a writer for "Your Show of Shows" (in a stable that included the likes of Neil Simon, Woody Allen, Mel Tolkin, *et al.*) and watched as Sid Caesar performed the best sketches ever seen on television. In *Silent Movie* Caesar plays a patient whose cardiac monitor is turned, by degrees, into an electronic ping-pong game. His eye-rolling and overly dramatized gasps are what *Silent Movie* needed throughout.

Silent Movie is loaded, perhaps *over*loaded, with cameo performances to insure a box-office draw. Once again, reflexivity is the premise: Mel Funn desperately tries to lure Big Names into his film, which, of course, is what we are watching. Moreover, rather than, say, the disguised role Gene Hackman played in *Young Frankenstein*, each of the "stars" in *Silent Movie* plays a comic version, a *parody* if you will, of himself: Burt Reynolds as a preening narcissist, James Caan as a vain, chauvinistic jock, Paul Newman as a race car driver with twinkling, baby-blue eyes.

Silent Movie tried hard to rekindle some of the naive magic which would have the audience cheering as Mel Funn (presently a washed-up alcoholic, but once a brilliant director) tries to save his studio from the clutches of a conglomerate called Engulf and Devour. A couple of years later, *Rocky* would do a better job by playing it old-fashioned, corny and very, very straight. Nonetheless, the figures on *Silent Movie* were well in the black. The old saw about one's second million being easier to make than the first is doubly true for comedies. After *Blazing Saddles* and *Young Frankenstein*, Mel Brooks was, in the lingo, bankable.

Establishing yourself is the hard part. For stand-up comics, recognition has become synonymous with an identifying tag-line. Rodney Dangerfield "gets no respect" and Henny Youngman asks us, for the hundredth time, to "take my wife . . . *please!*" It is the all-too-familiar, rather than the unexpected, the incongruous, which is demanded. Steve Martin need only proclaim himself a "wild and crazzzzy guy" and his audiences "crack up." A "Mel Brooks film" does much the same thing. It has come to mean parodic fun at Hollywood's expense, yet another romp through old flicks.

All of which put *High Anxiety* (1977) under considerable pressure. Rather than being seen as one who equated parody with love, Brooks had to face continuing charges of piracy and cannibalism. Evidently movie audiences had a bigger stomach for zany parody than film reviewers. The former bought tickets and laughed; the latter kept urging Brooks to move on, do something else, make different films. And too, his race with Woody Allen was heating up. Each had achieved a share of independence in the film industry (no small trick), each had developed something akin to a repertory company (Brooks's included Gene Wilder, Dom DeLuise, Madeline Kahn) and, most important of all, each was beginning to hit full, confident stride. In short, there was a lot riding on *High Anxiety*.

The results were mixed: As a parody of Hitchcock films, *High Anxiety* did not have quite the "lunatic class" (Brooks' term) he had hoped for, nor did the title find its way into our psychoanalytic vocabulary, but in it Brooks gave perhaps his best performance as a comic actor. Rather than the quick cabaret-paced blackouts and/or sight gags of *Silent Movie*, *High Anxiety* had longer stretches for Brooks to be funny in. For example, with enlarged photographs of the discipline's giants—Sigmund Freud, Carl Jung, Dr. Joyce Brothers—hanging behind him, Dr. Robert H. Thorndyke (Mel Brooks) addresses a meeting of fellow psychiatrists. It promises to be a thoroughly conventional affair, one filled with the sort of glib jargon that comes with the territory. That is, until a member arrives late, with his young children in tow. Thorndyke becomes unglued and a shower of euphemisms follow, as one sort of double-talk is replaced by another. Or that wonderful moment in the piano bar when Thorndyke fairly takes off on a devastating parody of Frank Sinatra. The song (words and music by Mel Brooks) is first-rate, but the phrasing ("High an-*xie*-etee") is the stuff of which classic parody is made. Every gesture, every nuance of the saloon singer's art is so lovingly evoked that the scene could almost double as a Las Vegas training film.

High Anxiety allowed Brooks the luxury of ranging through the Hitchcock canon (see especially *Vertigo, North by Northwest, Rebecca, The Man Who Knew Too Much*) and, at the same time, not feel constrained as he was in *Young Frankenstein*. There was enough raw "plot" for those who might miss the allusions, but this was a film of Hitchcock by Brooks and for buffs of both. Flashes of recognition—as the audience matched the parodic Brooks against the Master—were important. Moreover, Hitchcock is a filmmaker who fairly aches to be parodied. His psychological thrillers generate less from overt violence than by allowing the imagination full rein. Give this sort of "terror" a quarter-turn and the result crosses that thin, mental line into comedy.

There was, of course, still plenty of "sophomoric" Brooks in the Establishment upperclassman. The same mind that insisted on demonstrating the cause and effect relationship between bean-consumption and breaking wind also knew the *real* truth about birds. In the Hitchcock original, *The Birds* attack without apparent reason, their beaks pecking through human flesh. At the end, they are perched, ominously, on the overhanging branches, a powerful symbol of the apocalypse to come. It is a chilling vision of a benign Nature gone haywire. By contrast, Mel Brooks's parody is earthier, even somehow reassuring: Dr. Thorndyke is pelted by bird-droppings. The world—or at least the *birds* of the world—have a habit of doing exactly that. And if you are Mel Brooks, they will do it on your head. But the world is not an inherently evil place, nor should one reject it out of hand in favor of more spiritual, presumably less scatological realms. The vision that can see both the bird-dropping and the world's beauty strikes me as very Jewish indeed. After all, birds have tormented Jewish heads since the days of Tobit. Mel Brooks has simply found a new wrinkle for a very old, very Jewish story from the *Apocrypha*. In both cases the human condition is not an Either/Or proposition; rather, it is likely to be both/and. Somehow, Jews learn to make an uneasy accommodation to that reality.

At the same time, however, Brooks is not restricted to scatological humor for his laughs. The shower scene from *Psycho* generates parody of a very different stripe. Like the laboratory equipment in *Young Frankenstein*, Brooks has an uncanny knack for reduplicating the look, the *feel*, of the original. Even Dr. Thorndyke's movements remind us of Janet Leigh. The effect is carbon copy, with a difference. And as the shadow (holding a knife?) once again falls across the plastic curtain, its chilling ambience is recreated. At that point, Brooks pulls out the rug and our expectations/memories are replaced with comic surprises: The "murderer" is, in fact, merely an irate bellhop; his "knife" is, in truth, a rolled-up newspaper and however often he might plunge it into an increasingly nervous Dr. Thorndyke, the result will be anxiety, not death. Meanwhile, we watch the scene transfixed, caught between our lingering sense of the Hitchcock original and the parodic versions being played out before our eyes. The tableau ends, as it must, with ink from the soggy newsprint swirling, blood-like, down the drain.

Another element is worth mention: Unlike Woody Allen, Mel Brooks makes a distinction between film and autobiography. He recognizes an obligation to be funny (as a publicity release put it: ". . . I don't want to sacrifice a single laugh"), but not to turn each successive movie into an installment of his personal history. Nonetheless, *High Anxiety* is closer to felt concerns than the relatively "academic" exercise called *Silent Movie*. At the back of Mel Brooks's best humor one hears the modern counterparts of Marvell's "winged chariot" hurrying near: pain, guilt, floating anxiety, the Whole Works. Brooklyn was a hard, demanding place to learn how comedy *really* works:

> The corner was tough [Brooks remembers]. You had to score on the corner—no bullshit routines, no slick laminated crap. It had to be, "Lemme tell ya what happened today . . ." And you really had to be good on your feet. "Fat Hymie was hanging from the fire escape. His mother came by. 'Hymie!' she screamed. He fell two stories and broke his head." Real stories of tragedy we scream at.

The story had to be real and it had to be funny. Somebody getting hurt was wonderful. [*PI*, p. 53]

The difference between comedy and tragedy is a subtle line, rather than a wide gulf. It depends upon emphasis, perspective, the teller as opposed to the tale. Or as Kenneth Tynan reports:

> . . . when Reiner challenges him [Brooks] to define this difference . . . his reply is as memorable as any I have ever heard on this ancient subject: "Tragedy is if I cut my finger. Comedy is if you walk into an open sewer and die." [*NYP*, p. 94]

Parody, I might add, is a way of holding an obsession with death at arm's length. By propping the death threat on some*one* or some*thing* else, tragedy is deflected. And who knows, if you kid Death long enough and hard enough, maybe he'll forget to collect on your I.O.U.

All of which is to suggest that Mel Brooks's career has not been the lucky accident, the *fluke*, it appears to be at first glance. Nor is he the "brilliant amateur," the man chock full of nervous, improvisational energy. Mark Twain once insisted that humorists of the "mere" sort do not survive; the same thing holds true for comics of the "simple" variety. Granted, *some* things about Mel Brooks have not changed: He is still short and that, presumably, still matters. He is still the professional "Jew-boy" and that posture still serves as both his shield and his weapon. But for all the patois of immigrant speech, for all the urban-Jewish-manic craziness, Brooks now faces the very real danger of parodying himself. His latest film, *History of the World: Part I* (1981) brings a career that began with the staccato quips of the 2000 Year Old Man full-circle. Put baldly: *History of the World: Part I* cannibalizes the Brooks canon—the farting scene from *Blazing Saddles*, the "walk this way" joke from *Young Frankenstein*, the effeminate Hitler from *The Producers*. To be sure, films like *Star Wars*, *2001*, and *The Ten Commandments* make cameo appearances by way of parody, but there is no dazzling premise, no unifying vision, to link one blackout to another. Instead, the gags remind the world of vaudeville transmogrified onto celluloid. Brooks has assembled old cronies from triumphs past (Dom DeLuise, Madeline Kahn, Harvey Korman, Cloris Leachman, Sid Caesar) and added a generous assortment of veteran (read "aging") Jewish comics (Jack Carter, Shecky Greene, Jackie Mason, Jan Murray, Henny Youngman *et al.*), but the result is sophomoric wit, bush-league comedy.

Not surprisingly, the R-rating (the direct result of Brooks's heavy dose of doodie/caca jokes) kept Brooks's credentials as a Bad, Tasteless Boy in good order. There are, after all, some fans who like their humor broad and prefer their brows low: for them, Cheech and Chong's *Up in Smoke*, Bill Murray's *Caddyshack* and Mel Brooks's *History of the World: Part I* are interchangeable comic parts. There is, however, a more disturbing, genuinely subversive film hiding just beneath the façade of adolescent rebellion. As Brooks would have it,

History is the record of religious oppression—namely, what They (i.e., the Christians) did to Us (i.e., the Jews). Nowhere has this whispered truth been more blatantly shouted than in the part (about a third of the whole movie) of *History of the World: Part I* that deals with the Spanish Inquisition. Mel Brooks as Torquemada sings his way through a lavish production number called "The Inquisition" (lyrics and music by Mel Brooks and Ronny Graham). It is humor with a cutting edge of sarcasm and paranoia, reminiscent of the "Springtime for Hitler" number from *The Producers*, but, this time, aimed at the mass audience Brooks both fears and hates. In short, Brooks can feel that he is a victim and a superior person simultaneously. *History of the World: Part I* is, in effect, a record of how that condition is generated.

History of the World: Part II will, presumably, continue the saga—in the best Hollywood tradition of exploitive sequels and Brooks's brand of parody. In fact, three tongue-in-cheek "previews of coming attractions"—"Hitler on Ice," "Viking Funeral" and "Jews in Space"—are included in Part I, to seed clouds, whet appetites and bankroll the next Brooks film, whatever it might be. Meanwhile, the possibilities of parody grow increasingly exhausted. *History of the World: Part I* ends as Brooks punctures whatever willing suspension of disbelief has been created and he reminds us, via the large, conventionally block-cut letters spelling out THE END that this has been, after all, only a movie. It is also to remind us of how fragile, and how exhausted, this mode of comedy can become.

NOTES

1. Henri Bergson, "Laughter" in *Comedy*, ed. Wylie Sypher (New York: Doubleday Anchor Edition, 1956), p. 140.

2. John Barth, "The Literature of Exhaustion," in *The American Novel Since World War II*, ed. Marcus Klein (New York: Fawcett Premier Edition, 1969), pp. 267–80. Subsequent references to Barth are to this essay.

3. John Updike, *Bech: A Book* (New York: Alfred Knopf, 1970), pp. 17–18.

4. Kenneth Tynan, "Mel Brooks: Frolics and Detours of a Short Hebrew Man," *New Yorker* (October 30, 1978), 108. I am indebted to Mr. Tynan's "profile" for many of the biographical facts in this article. Hereafter it is abbreviated as *NYP*.

5. "*Playboy* Interview: Mel Brooks" (February 1975), 49. Hereafter abbreviated as *PI*.

6. Ronald Sanders, as cited in Irving Howe, *World of Our Fathers* (New York: Harcourt Brace Jovanovich, 1976), p. 563.

7. Gary Arnold, in *Movie Comedy*, ed. Stuart Byron and Elizabeth Weiss (New York: Viking, 1977), p. 119.

The Vanishing Act:
A Typology of the Jew in the
Contemporary American Film

Alan Spiegel

IN OLD HOLLYWOOD, WHEN GOD SPOKE TO HIS PUBLIC, HIS MESSAGE WOULD usually be mediated through a special-effects team in any one of six or seven different ways: burning bush, roiling cloud, disembodied voice, colored nimbus, clap of thunder, shaft of light, speckled spiral of fanned sand—in most cases the inspirational fires stoked by whatever clue from Old Testament imagery could be finagled into New World technology. Nowadays Hollywood—"New Hollywood"—usually gives us the Word with much less audio-visual mystification: lately God seems to do his talking in the form of George Burns. In the immensely popular *Oh, God!* (1977) the Almighty shuffles about in sneakers, fishing cap, golfiing sweater, and thick, black-rimmed glasses—just "like an ordinary man," he says—and compacts his wisdom as a series of gelded bromides that could not stir a poster of protest from the most rabid of sectarians (e.g., "You may find it hard to believe in me, but I believe in you," etc.) But what is most interesting about this divine old codger, who cares not a smidgen for racial or religious affiliation, who stands opposed to Priest and Rabbi alike, is that he unburdens himself in the gravel-voiced, shoulder-shrugging, ironically inflected, sweet curt manner of a tired Borscht circuit comedian, unflappable, streetwise, and unmistakably Jewish. Not *very* Jewish, mind you, not the way George Jessel or Myron Cohen might have played it, but Jewish enough so that more than a tincture of chicken broth adheres to the gesture, and more than enough to insure the necessary recognition and good will from a contemporary audience.

Now the unstated and only semi-conscious point of this charade is that the Jewish mannerisms of the Deity are to be understood as the essential index neither of his holiness nor least of all his Jewishness, but rather of his ordinariness, the visible and audible tokens of his transfiguration into a common man. Rather than specializing the character, Burns's Judaism provides a nondenominational Almighty with a conduit to a shared communal property, a patch of ethnic coloring that paradoxically enhances the ecumenical point. Nowadays producers know something that would have astounded their predecessors: the more Jewish, the more universal.

It's no secret that in the last two decades the Jew has wandered all over the topography of the American film, not merely in the countless movies depicting Jews or recounting Jewish experience but even in those works where the material does not warrant his presence, where Jews and Jewish interests would seem to have no necessary relation to the subject at hand. The Jew appears as Jew and also as a specific type of nonspecific quotidian humanity, the most unillusioned, least pretentious, common-clay side of any member, Jew or Gentile, of the current moviegoing public. The ubiquity of this figure and his world has made him virtually indistinguishable from the larger non-Jewish community that once served to differentiate but now increasingly serves to define him. Back in 1959, Leslie Fiedler, one of the leading mythographers of American Jewish culture, could state with justifiable confidence, "The notion of the Jewish cowboy is utterly ridiculous, of a Jewish detective . . . nearly as anomalous."[1] Twenty years later, however, we have seen not only many "anomalous" Jewish detectives (*The Exorcist*, 1973, *The Boys from Brazil*, 1978, etc.), but the "utterly ridiculous" Jewish cowboy (*The Frisco Kid*, 1980), as well as the equally "ridiculous" Jewish Indian (*Blazing Saddles*, 1974). Lately we learn that Charley Chan's grandson, the number one son of the number one son, has a Jewish mother (one Brenda in *Charley Chan and the Curse of the Dragon Queen*, 1981) which, in the current shorthand of movie conventions, conjugates this fabulous child from oriental intrigue through domestic comedy to an up-to-date American mean.

Moreover, films like *Funny Girl* (1968), *Fiddler on the Roof* (1971), *The Way We Were* (1973), and some of the Mel Brooks comedies, are not merely popular entertainment, but according to *Variety* tabulations, high among the "all-time" top-grossing American films, and their success, as well as that of *Goodbye, Columbus* (1969), *Lenny* (1974), and *Funny Lady* (1975), cannot be entirely explained in terms of the ethnic loyalty of what amounts to little more than 2% of the population. In a similar manner, Woody Allen, Barbra Streisand, and Bette Midler are something more than celebrities; they are demi-mythic figures, heroes and heroines of mass culture; Midler is "divine"; Streisand is "bankable"; "Woody Allen" is, the ultimate pop accolade, a comic strip. Equally remarkable, they have acquired these stations not by underplaying Jewish looks, manners, and backgrounds, and not in spite of them, but precisely by exaggerating these characteristics almost to the point of iconic abstraction. They have become majority heroes by italicizing minority profiles and now reside on the "inside" without seeming to have ever left the "outside."

Obviously to broach the character and situation of the Jew in American film is one useful way of broaching the character and situation of the Jew in America and the whole matter of American Jewish identity (that obsessive and fateful problem that the Jew has solved and unsolved so often that merely to pose it once again already determines the asking itself as one not-so-small part of the answer). At the present moment, the Jew seems so thoroughly swallowed by the demotic American dream of Jewish men and women that one may legitimately ask how much of his person and manner still belong to himself? I want to offer a few remarks on the origins, development, and ramifications of this curious situation, this terribly mixed blessing; to sort out the different roles that Jews have been asked to play in American films, particularly those of the last thirty years; and to examine what these roles tell us about America's notion of the Jew and the Jew's notion of himself.

The first and most extraordinary fact about Jews in the movies is not their recent emergence, but rather their longstanding dominance; how so few have managed to acquire so much authority and influence in a medium deeply touching so many is one of the great socioeconomic phenomena of big business in our century. The next most important fact, however, is that until recently this extraordinary influence—creative, fiscal, and social—was largely exerted behind the cameras by Jewish directors, writers, and producers rather than in front of it. This situation has resulted in many films by Jews and even almost as many with Jews (i.e., Jewish actors), but until the last fifteen years, it has not resulted in a comparable number of films about Jews. Nor has it resulted, even in the last fifteen years, in (what might be called) Jewish-American films of particularly high artistic quality and certainly none that bears evidence of a distinctly Jewish style or sensibility. By the standards of Griffith, Keaton, Chaplin, Ford and Welles—that is, by measure of the best work done in America—films about Jews while frequently vivid as entertainment, have been generally dim as art. The major Jewish directors, Lubitsch, Wyler, Wilder, and Kubrick, did not make or have not yet made, major films about Jews; and some directors like Wilder and Kubrick have to date not made any films about them. The richest area of Jewish achievement on camera (as opposed to behind it) has been in performance (acting, singing, joking), some of the most affecting work often appearing in the most indifferent contexts. At best, and most of it recently, the interest in Jewish life has translated to the screen in a number of busy, likable, skillful, various, observant, and on occasion, robust and powerful productions. All things considered, not an undistinguished record: in a mass art like American movies, rigged to cast nets of the widest possible appeal, it isn't surprising, though hardly commendable, that almost none of its many moments of formal and dramatic radiance centrally embody the experience of any racial or religious minority.[2]

Still, from Edison's fragment *Cohen's Advertising Scheme* (1904) and Griffith's two-reeler *Old Isaacs, the Pawnbroker* (1907) to Neil Diamond's dry tea recycling of *The Jazz Singer* in 1980, it's safe to say that no period in American film has been without some depiction, however meager, of Jewish life. But perhaps only in the early and middle twenties, before the consolidation of the big studios at the end of the period and the beginning of a protracted ethnic slump, do we find a proliferation of films comparable to the Jewish flowering in the late sixties and seventies. Ethnic tearjerkers (*Humoresque*, 1920), transmogrified vaudeville burlesques (*Potash and Perlmutter*, 1923), and domestic sitcoms advocating both assimilation and intermarriage (*The Cohens and the Kellys*, 1926) were popular and plentiful.[3] One may speculate, however, that while the appeal of these films went beyond that of a minority public, it could not have gone far beyond it. In spite of the assimilationist zeal expressed in many of these stories, the range of character types was still too heavily marked by an odd mingling of prayer shawls and pushcarts, of Eastern European *shtetl* life and Hester Street family clannishness; landlords, merchants, and rabbis; skinflints, kindhearts, and greybeards; weeping mothers and gossipy aunts; wayward sons and blooming daughters: figures at once too exotic and too unglamorously gritty to enter the deepest imagination of the large American audience. The fantasies of the majority public veered away from immigrant swarm life and toward extremities of soulful optimism, heavy-lidded glamor, and far-flung romance—cowboys and swashbucklers, Ruritanian counts and Latin lovers, go-getters and flappers, tramps, hoydens, and sweethearts. The Jewish comics, the most popular of the early ethnic types, were also the least threatening and the ones most shorn of Old World and ghetto associations; but even the much admired George Sydney, Alexander Carr, and George Jessel could not hope to rival the popularity of the reigning WASP clowns, Chaplin and Lloyd, or approach the oneiric force of the period's leading romantic stars, Fairbanks, Pickford, Valentino, and Barrymore. Moreover, of the many "Jewish" films that were produced, only one has become part of our permanent legacy from this period (though I don't mean to reject the possibility that others will, or even should, emerge): *The Jazz Singer* (1927) with its reputation based almost entirely on an innovative sound technology and all but ignored as the story of a cantor's son (Al Jolson) who leaves his father's Orchard Street synagogue in order to sing in blackface at the Wintergarden. Cited everywhere as the film that marked the end of the silent period, it is rarely remembered as the film that also marked the close of the wide-ranging Hollywood gallery of major Jewish portraiture and genre study for the next twenty years.

This new de-Semitized situation was created by a somewhat promiscuous mixture of fresh marketing values, political idealism, and personal anxiety on the part of the men who ran the studios that made the movies. Starting in the late twenties and early thirties, six or seven giant factories (e.g., Metro, Warners, Columbia, Universal, etc.), controlled, streamlined, and homogenized each phase of the entire filmmaking process from conception to distribution in conformity with the stipulations of new economic guidelines: one movie for everyone, and the subordination of specific interests of special groups to the common interests of a mass audience; thus, put baldly, a film designed to reach the largest number would not be fashioned of ingredients pertaining only to the smallest. In this manner, the hero of such a film would often be a vague, idealized American who, as played by, say, Gary Cooper or James Stewart or Henry Fonda, was often assumed to be a WASP largely because he did not seem to *look* like a member of any specific minority. But actually his church often went unmentioned, for the goal was primarily neither to conceal minorities or glorify majorities but ideally to dissolve both in an official studio ideology of democratic idealism, of the ultimate homogeneity of all human beings. So industry economics (one movie for everyone) and industry politics (the essential sameness of everyone) went hand in glove; and the producers themselves—in the main, either Jewish immigrants or the sons of Jewish immigrants (Mayer, Goldwyn, Thalberg, Cohn, Selznick, the Warner Brothers, etc.)—while never ignoring their Judaism, hastened to underscore their allegiance to national ideals in preference to immigrant roots. They did this both as a gesture of gratitude, for command of an industry whose affluence for a time was competitive with that of U. S. Steel, G. M. and Standard Oil, and as a strategy for outflanking their numerous anti-Semitic critics. "I'm an American," said David Selznick in one extreme instance, "not a Jew."[4] On other occasions he was pleased to be both; but he, like other successful Jewish producers, knew how to smother Jew-baiters in a conciliatory bearhug of appreciation, loyalty, and frantic flag waving.

Under these circumstances, the studio produced one of its more evasive creations in the figure of the Nominal Jew, a minor character even more abstract and anonymous than the idealized hero, who bore a Jewish name, and sometimes even looked Jewish, but was rarely referred to as a Jew either by others or himself and evinced little or no ethnic habits; his race and religion were not seen or even inferred as part of his intrinsic condition, but along with most other ethnic traits, as something entirely separate and detachable from his quintessential and non-denominational personhood. If he appeared in a war film, he would be a member of a bomber crew (as in *Air Force*, 1943) or an infantry platoon (as in *A Walk in the Sun*, 1945) and you would know he was probably Jewish because he would be named Corporal Weinberg or Pvt. Friedman; but his values, needs, and aspirations would be exactly those of the Italian rifleman Tranella or the Polish bombardier Wynocki or the tall WASP flight commander Quincannon. He would see himself exactly as the others saw themselves, a member of a team whose special and private interests were entirely subsumed by national democratic interests, and he fought to destroy an enemy who stood in opposition to those interests. The plight of European Jewry, for example, would make no particular appeal to his general concerns (for his only concerns were general ones); Hitler was the enemy not because he was anti-Semitic, but because he was anti-egalitarian.

Within this ethnic vacuum, there were a few rule-proving exceptions: George Arliss's Anglo-Jewish embalmings in *Disraeli* (1929) and *The House of Rothschild* (1934); David Selznick's little known soaper about a Jewish surgeon, *The Symphony of Six Million* (1932); a pair of Elmer Rice theatricals that glance lightly at American anti-Semitism, *Street Scene* (1931) and *Counsellor-at-Law* (1933); and Chaplin's direct confrontation of Jewish persecution in Europe— perhaps the only one of its time—*The Great Dictator* (1940).[5] As a whole, however, the presentation of the Jew in the period from roughly 1927 to 1947 was both peripheral and so ethnically blurry that James Agee, the leading film critic of his decade, could observe in 1947 at the opening of *Crossfire*—a study of American anti-Semitism in the form of a manhunt thriller—that "millions of people will look forward [to films about anti-Semitism] if only for the questionable excitement of hearing actors throw the word 'Jew' around."[6]

The aftermath of World War II, however, produced two international events, a death and a rebirth, the effects of which inevitably changed the depiction of Jews in film as they inevitably changed the consciousness of Jews everywhere: these were the dissolution of the European Jewish community and the creation of the state of Israel. Naturally the long-range repercussions of these events on every phase of American Jewry can hardly be overestimated, but in Hollywood in the late forties and fifties, the immediate repercussions, while very discernible, were relatively modest: an end to the moratorium on Jewish characters in major roles, and two important modulations, though no radical transformations, of existing stereotypes. In a post-Holocaust atmosphere, the Nominal Jew gave way to the Jew as Innocent Victim, and in the wake of Israel's independence, there appeared the Jew as Biblical Exotic.

The Jew as Innocent Victim appears most notably in the *Cav* and *Pag* of anti-anti-Semitic social drama of the late forties, *Crossfire* and *Gentleman's Agreement* (1948), both of which added essentially one palpable touch to the old portrait of the Nominal Jew: in place of the figure who was a Jew because he had a Jewish name stood a figure who was a Jew because an anti-Semite defined him as such; the Jew was now forced to declare his Jewishness but only by means of prejudicial insistence, the presumption being that without bigotry the issue as well as the fact of one's Judaism need never arise. The corollary presumption of a film like *Gentleman's Agreement*, in which a Gentile (Gregory Peck) exposes pockets of anti-Semitism in middle-class suburbia by masquerading as a Jew, was that without bigotry, the American Jew left to his own devices would want nothing more, better, or different than to live exactly as the WASP did, to stay at the same hotel, play on the same golf course, and buy a house in the same neighborhood.

The Victimized Jew was not only as ethnically ill-defined as the Nominal Jew, but in both *Crossfire* and *Gentleman's Agreement* he was still essentially a supporting player (Sam Levene in the former, and John Garfield and Sam Jaffe in the latter), fading off behind either the character of the bigot (Robert Ryan in *Crossfire*) who would proceed to nail him to his ethnic cross, or his Gentile benefactor (Peck in *Gentleman's Agreement*, Robert Young in *Crossfire*) who, like Ivanhoe for Rebecca, would frequently make speeches on his behalf. The character of the Victim had to remain vague and recessive dramatically, for he had to remain blameless morally, not only of what he was accused, but of anything that might make him appear either complicated or difficult or ornery or abrasive or even slighty unsavory (i.e., *fully* human)—indeed, as if the presence of any of these qualities might actually constitute an argument *for* anti-Semitism.

To be fully innocent he also had to be rendered fully harmless, and so his sexuality was thoroughly muted as he stepped aside to let the Gentile protagonists (Peck and Dorothy McGuire) occupy the central love interest. When a Jewish Victim did fall in love as Montgomery Clift's Noah Ackerman did, later in the period, with Hope Lange's *shiksa* in *The Young Lions* (1958), his lovemaking was glazed over with such childlike awkwardness, so much stammering gratitude and teary apologetics that his Gentile lover's passion instantly converted itself into a form of maternal commiseration; and when Clift entered army boot camp, he could only gain the respect of bigots like Lee Van Cleef by allowing them to beat him up repeatedly and consummately until the outlines of his saintly archetype, the Christlike Suffering Servant, rose up from its ancient depths below the agonized visual surface. The Man of Constant Sorrows (Isaiah

53: "He was oppressed and he was afflicted, yet he opened not his mouth") merges with the mythic aspect of the Victimized Jew, a tolerant stranger lost amid his intolerant neighbors, who in his neutered sexuality, indefatigable passivity, and almost bottomless gluttony for punishment, never seems to have lost favor with the public or producers (e.g., *Ship of Fools*, 1965; *Cabaret*, 1972).

Far more flashy and virile, though no more ethnically lucid, was the Jew as Biblical Exotic. This figure was less a fixed character type than a daub of Levantine color in an epical canvas derived from Hollywood raids on the Old Testament in search of visual spectacle, lavish garments, and photogenic miracles. Beneath these immensely lucrative gobbets of exotic splashiness—zebra-striped caftans, shepherd's crooks, stubby broadswords, clangorous desert battles, sprayed beards like silver bibs, etc.—like *David and Bathsheba* (1951), *The Ten Commandments* (1956) and *Solomon and Sheba* (1962), there resided a spiritual and cultural void, the entire social, moral, and religious complex of ancient Judaism reduced to a simple principle: the Jews believed in one, invisible Supreme Being while their polytheistic enemies worshiped idols. The films did not say that this God also believed in the Jews, that they were his "chosen" by covenant, but rather implied that this God was available to anyone who could acknowledge his omnipotence; in other words, all one could learn about the whole spiritual structure of Jewish life was that one part of it was continuous with, and easily converted to, Christianity. But when the Biblical Jew was not busy adumbrating another dispensation, he was usually depicted as emerging victorious from his many trials (lapses of faith, Egyptian Pharaohs) and dissolving into the tribe of his people, a nation united and invigorated by its unswerving belief in its own ultimate survival. No matter how extraneous or shallow the Biblical Exotic seemed in relation to any contemporary reality, he embodied one topical overtone that could not be mistaken: the Jew in the audience knew that the Jew on the screen represented the Hollywood establishment's mandate to the State of Israel.

With Jewish characters now appearing in the movies once again, it was only a matter of time before the quality of portraiture would deepen and intensify. Two films probably did more to transform or at least considerably aggravate existing formulas than any others—*Exodus* (1961), a contemporary transformation of the biblical spectacle, and *The Pawnbroker* (1965), a spawn of the social-problem dramas of the late forties. Neither the Jew as Innocent Victim or Biblical Exotic could do much to challenge the security or enlarge the range of expectations of the majority public; the former figure was simply too passive, indeed virtually castrated, the latter too remote in both time and custom. But with *Exodus*, the first major Hollywood production devoted to the Jewish struggle against British colonialism and the winning of Israeli independence, there were Jewish freedom fighters and terrorists in modern dress, festooned with ammo belts, shouldering Tommy guns, storming Arab fortresses, and planting bombs in the King David Hotel. And above all, there was the young Paul Newman, athletic and bellicose, rising out of the surf like a sea demon in his frogman's black rubber body suit, and later making love to a Gentile nurse, the ermine-haired Eva Marie Saint, in a manner that was anything but childlike and apologetic. Diffuse, longwinded (well over three hours), populated by characters of a single dimension, *Exodus* was nevertheless with its big stars and big budget equally big at the box office; *The Pawnbroker*, unglamorous, low-budget, downbeat in every way, was generally admired only by critics, but in the utter seriousness of its conception (if not its realization) and in the toughminded treatment of its central character, became even more dramatically than *Exodus*, the immediate and emphatic precursor of a new era in Jewish portraiture. Often pretentious and hamhanded in the dramatization of its themes, and glitzy and derivative in its fractured narration—flashframes, flashforwards, jump cuts; the difficult and elliptical methodologies of Godard and Resnais simplified and traduced for native consumption—this film still had at its center one memorably disturbing reason for being: an unloving and unlovable Jew (in a stong performance by Rod Steiger). Along with its ponderousness the movie had at least the modest gumption to present a protagonist whose major function was not dedicated to wooing the audience, who even risked connection with a prejudicial stereotype, Shylock the usurer; it also had the good sense to account for this nightmarish association by the more authentic nightmare of historical and political circumstance that transforms a European Professor into a Harlem pawnbroker; Sol Nazerman loses his wife and child in a Nazi death camp and protects himself from this unbearable memory by freezing his feelings. The viewer keeps waiting for the obligatory sweetness to flow, for the rush of charity or magnanimous heroism one assumes to be on tap just beneath the icy exterior—but this doesn't happen. Surviving into the present, Nazerman denies love, friendship, and commiseration from relatives, mistress, social worker, and employee. When feeling finally does come—after the sacrificial death of his young assistant who during a robbery attempt stops a bullet meant for him—it is a silent howl of pain. In his thaw, Nazerman finds neither serenity nor reconciliation, but an awakening to an old agony in a new context. Whether in Dachau or in Harlem, there is no remission from either history or suffering, and Nazerman comes back to life only to clutch at those very (necessary) conditions that drove him from it in the first place.

As a marker in the history of the Jew in film, *The Pawnbroker* was probably only the most notable and virulent wave of what toward the end of the sixties proved to be a floodtide of Jewish characters, issues, and performers. The end of the decade saw two of its biggest hits, *Funny Girl* and *Goodbye, Columbus*, as well as Woody Allen's *Take the Money and Run* (1968) and Mel Brooks's *The Producers* (1968), initiating fresh trends in American Jewish comedy. From this point to the present moment major and minor Jewish characters appear with such regularity that one is tempted to recall their previous absence as one of the curiosities of ancient film history. What had been happening throughout the late forties and fifties was that the hegemony of the big studio had begun to fall apart and a new marketing concept began to find its place alongside the old one: Hollywood still tried (as it continues to try) to make one movie for everyone, but since everyone was watching television, it became increasingly more practical to try to make a movie for someone; to try, that is, not just to think in terms of a single, homogeneous audience, but from time to time, to also think in terms of many different audiences; and to acknowledge that in a fragmented and anomalous market, a "special-interest" film might have a somewhat better chance than a "general-interest" film. But while the hunt for new audiences might account for the presence and even the sheer quantity of films about Jews, it could not account for their popularity, which often went beyond the patronage of special interest groups. In this matter, social history played its part.

Throughout the sixties and, to some extent, into the seventies, in both the palaces of culture and the flea markets of the economy, there emerged an unprecedented fascination with the personality, manners, anxieties, hungers, ecstasies, and follies of the contemporary American Jew (with more than a nod to his European origins). Responding in 1961 to the first and unexpected gust of adulation, Philip Roth wrote, "I find that I am suddenly living in a country in which the Jew has come to be—or is allowed for now to think he is—a culture hero."[7] It wasn't simply that half the idols of the marketplace seemed to be Jewish (Norman Mailer, Lenny Bruce, Harry Golden) or that the other half seemed ripe for conversion (Marilyn, Elizabeth, Sammy): but that in the sixties, Jewishness itself became a mass culture concept, a hot ticket, an eminently transportable commodity, a way of thinking and living thoroughly accessible, if not entirely applicable, to practically anyone. "Negroes are all Jews," said Lenny Bruce in his autobiography, *How to Talk Dirty and Influence People*, "Italians are all Jews, Irishmen who have rejected their religion are Jews. Mouths are Jewish. And bosoms . . ."[8] In the context of the times and at the level of cultural iconography, the Jew appeared most immediately as a paradoxical and bifurcated figure, at once a figure of critical agitation and orderly repose, both a problem and solution. On the one hand, in a period of race riots, student demonstrations, political assassinations, and a disastrous and escalating foreign war, he could be viewed as a young radical, a dissident gesture against the Establishment, one of the disaffiliated and the disaffected, a political satirist (Bruce, Mort Sahl), a black humorist (Heller, Friedman), a hippie poet (Ginsburg) and a white Negro (Mailer). On the other hand, in the same context, he could also be perceived as an older traditionalist, a stabilizing force, a paragon of moral obligation (Bellow's Mr. Sammler), of family piety (Harry Golden), of Old World loyalty (Chaim Potok), of middle-class security (Paddy Chayefsky, Herman Wouk)—in short, the very mirror of those social postures one saw challenged, and eroding from the textures of America's private and public affairs. But whether one perceived him as outsider or insider, radical or conservative, Lenny Bruce or Harry Golden, he was among the first contemporary American heroes of the sixties never to be perceived as a social or moral novice; whatever he was, he had tasted of the tree of knowledge. Americans in the first shock of disillusionment with a country that had been wrong about race, sex, property and foreign policy, turned to the Jew as both exile and survivor, as someone who seemed to live with fewer illusions about himself and his circumstances than they did; "as if," as Robert Warshow put it, "[he was] a day older in history than everybody else."⁹ In the crisis context of the moment, the Jew provided the model of a survival kit for the future of Americans who wanted to learn how to live beyond their own historical innocence; he was Europe's Job to America's Adam.

Accordingly, Hollywood, too, during this period begins to modulate beyond its own historical innocence in a hunt for tougher, less sentimental images of experience. As against the older heroes and heroines, the new protagonists become odder, earthier, funkier, slightly uglier and less fabulous, if no less charismatic. If one turns from a typical sampling of the top box-office stars of the studio era—say, Rooney, Temple, Astaire, Rogers, Cooper, Tracy, Hepburn—to a similar scattering from the seventies—say, Nicolson, Pacino, Streisand, Hoffman, Allen, Travolta, Bronson—one immediately perceives a general loss in toniness, symmetrical beauty, prairie elegance and picket-fence wholesomeness as well as a gain in streetwise and roadwise professionalism, caustic humor, bumpy ethnicity, and aggressive sexuality. And along with these new performers, there has evolved a new social geography to contain them: after the Western and Midwestern idealizations of the thirties and forties, movies of the sixties and seventies begin to discover harsher and grittier regional fantasies in the highways and backroads of the South and Southwest (good ole boys, truckers, moonshiners, warbling Nashvilleans, etc.) as well as in the manners of the Urban East—city *tummlers*, Broadway careerists, white-collar drones, Manhattan neurotics, and American Jewish families. Urban Jewry in particular quickly becomes a territory staked out by a cadre of creative specialists (who of course work in other areas as well): directors like Sidney Lumet, Herbert Ross, Paul Mazursky, Woody Allen, Mel Brooks, and James Toback; writers—who in a genre notable for its loquacity become even more important than directors— Paddy Chayefsky, Neil Simon, Carl Reiner, Jules Feiffer, Marshall Brickman, Arnold Shulman, Elaine May, and (again) Brooks and Allen; and many stars, Barbra Streisand, Dustin Hoffman, Richard Dreyfus, Walter Matthau, Elliot Gould, George Segal, Richard Benjamin, Alan Arkin, George Burns, and (once again) Woody Allen.

Now in terms of Jewish character, the major contribution of these artists has thus far consisted largely in the replacement of two or three stock figures by a plurality of types and situations. These new types are often more elaborate and varied and ethnically precise than the old ones; they are also more likely to be presented in terms of social personalities—with manners, speech, and social backgrounds scrupulously observed—rather than melodramatic abstractions bearing ten-ton messages. These new characters are still fashioned for as general a general audience as can be imagined nowadays, but an audience no longer thought to be so certain or so vain of its national pedigree, or so guarded or sectarian in its ethnic preferences. The Jewish types of the studio era were essentially fantasies for Gentile consumption—the form a Jew might take to allay the anger, suspicion and querulousness of an outsider both feared and adored—and in this sense, were partly Gentile creations. The new types are fantasies, too, but ones more freely and indigenously dreamt, less defensive and less overdetermined, more directly concerned with what contemporary Jews imagine themselves to be apart from alien surveillance. Jewish directors and writers are now obviously comfortable enough in their identity as Americans to feel openly curious about their identity as Jews.

But the confidence of these creators and the surface veracity of their creations should not deceive anyone (and especially Jews) as to the "reality" of these new characters and situations: the new types may be more sensuously and topically detailed than the old ones, but beneath the quasi-factualist veneer, they are no less typological in their general profiles, no less formulaic in the pattern of their actions. In the past fifteen years, the Jew in film appears most often as a middle-class city dweller (often a New Yorker, sometimes an Angeleno) who is characteristically defined within or in opposition to a family situation. A Jew is a Jew because he or she is the son or daughter of a Jew, always the last member in a family declension traveling backwards through a litany of begats to the time of the Patriarchs, a divine contract, and two figures in a garden. Because of its obvious family "coding"—and to facilitate discussion—the range of the prototypical Jewish characters can conveniently be divided into fathers, mothers, sons and daughters (with the latter two often being equivalent versions of the same type). What follows makes no attempt to be exhaustive but simply representative of what I take to be the most notable figures within each grouping.

Since the movies of the last fifteen years are frequently fashioned for the young, and frequently by the young, it isn't surprising that most recent movies about Jews are also usually about the young, that sons and daughters appear more often than their mothers and fathers. Mothers in particular appear even less often than fathers, and almost always in advanced years, and almost never at screen center. Since the "Jewish Mama" has made extravagant appearances just about everywhere else (in fiction, theater, etc.), it is no wonder that in all but perhaps the most shameless of movies—like *Enter Laughing* (1967) or *Where's Poppa?* (1970)—she isn't allowed to venture much beyond her tiny treadmill of space that usually extends from the stove to the kitchen table. When occupying a somewhat larger turf and often in the person of Shelley Winters or Ruth Gordon or Maureen Stapleton, she is a powerhouse of love and concern, and overconcern, Hagar-like in her protectiveness, forever meddling and fussing with spouse or child over minutiae of health, clothing and food— serious concerns in Old World contexts (and thus betraying her roots in European literary soil) but only forms of comic relief in affluent America. In a Jewish setting, her engulfing warmth can often be perceived as a threat to the survival of her children (as in *Where's Poppa?* or *Next Stop, Greenwich Village*, 1976); but in a Gentile setting, the same quality can be perceived as redemptive, a hot compress to a chilly Goyish brow (e.g., Maureen Stapleton, in *Interiors*, 1979, mouth-to-mouth resuscitation of her Gentile stepdaughter after a failed suicide attempt). Because, however, she is the most notorious of stereotypes, the mother's greatest threat is actually to the credibility of any movie in which she appears.

As the mother opens up and flows, the father bottles up and freezes; as the passion of the mother urges her toward centrifugal envelopment, the obligations of the father bid him stand pat and toe the mark. The father may anchor himself in steadfast obedience before an altar of law and tradition, as Tevye does in *Fiddler on the Roof;* or he may honor a grey round of middle-class responsibilities, like those aging, Paddy Chayefsky heroes in *The Hospital* (1971) or *Network* (1976)—respectively George C. Scott and William Holden—who seek out young *shiksa* lovers only to drop them in the end and return to the same bludgeoning job *(The Hospital)* or arid family life *(Network)* that originally sent them looking; or he may enter into a bearded ritual of fussy and contested orderings, like Walter Matthau and George Burns in *The Sunshine Boys* (1975), two ancient vaudevilleans trying to rehearse a forty-year-old act and fighting like Talmudic pedants over every cue, prop, and chalk mark.

When childless, the father often links up with a young male accomplice to whom he dispenses advice as if to a son—as George Burns does to John Denver in *Oh, God!,* as Zero Mostel does to Gene Wilder in *The Producers,* and as Lee Strasberg does to Al Pacino in *The Godfather, Part II*. The accomplice may take or leave this advice without irreparably damaging the father's vanity, for the father is less committed to the accomplice than to the advice which he fully believes will outlive both of them. This commitment often makes him a static figure in relation to the youngsters who often bustle about him and have ideas of their own, but ones less precise and firmly fixed than his; still, this intellectual dewiness usually makes them less resistant to change than he is (as in *The Chosen,* 1982). But sometimes even the father must change. And this is the lesson of *Fiddler on the Roof* in which the figure of the father reaches something very like a mass-culture apotheosis. A gold mine of public relations as well as theater rentals, this one film has probably evoked more mass-audience goodwill for the European sources of American Jewry than any other ever made; and thus constitutes at the least a social phenomenon that could not have taken place at any previous period in American film history. I doubt if anyone would want to call the *Fiddler* art (often what moves crowds most—deepest and longest—has little to do with art); it's too blatant and corny, the language pagebound, much of the acting Broadway stagebound. Yet the subject has tragic grandeur—the dissolution of *Shtetl* folkways and the consequent immigration to America—and the film itself has great gusto. The dancing is vigorous and picturesque (with one superb image of rows of bearded men in ankle-length black coats balancing tall wine bottles on their heads and whirling like dreidels.) And there is Tevye, the linchpin of the show and its main attraction. Even if Topol's performance were less solid than it actually is, much of Tevye's strength, which is the strength of the original Sholem Aleichem concept, would still come through: the secret of this impoverished milkman's appeal resides in his composite nature, a mingling of the spiritual and the practical, the strict and the yielding, the ancient and the modern. Tevye's prototype is the austere Father Abraham—whose shadow follows most of the figures in this category—the first of the Patriarchs and the most obedient, the one most conversant and convivial with the Lord. Tevye, too, continually chats with God (his remarks addressed to the camera) and while God never chats back, this fact never deters the milkman from worrying out loud about the horse that is lame, the daughters who disobey, the wife who nags, the Czar who wants to—and eventually does—remove him from his beloved village of Anatekva. In the Abramic manner, "tradition" is his mainstay, and his deepest aspiration, beyond wealth, is to luxuriate in prayer, scripture, and Talmudic dispute. In 1971, audiences were ready to be interested in such a figure, but were only ready to love him if they could be sure that his severe shell protected a kernel of liberal permissiveness. As it did. Not everyone remembers Tevye's one-sided conversations with the Lord or the fringe of prayer shawl that peeps out beneath his black vest, but no one forgets the uncorseted and very un-Abramic joy he takes in dancing and crooning, fingers snapping, breasts shaking, great black boots stomping in the barnyard dust. Abraham sees only one side, God's side; Tevye sees at least two, God's and man's. He wants what God wants, but his strength is in accepting whatever he gets from life—or doesn't get, for in the end he loses just about everything, and his blessings, however begrudgingly given, are upon his losses—his three daughters who marry against his initial wishes (the second to a radical, the third a Gentile) and his village home that he must leave behind. His genius isn't for theology, but for survival, and his truest intimate isn't God, but "the fiddler," his daimon, his life force, a symbolic double whose ecstatic music accompanies him through every adversity, including the silence of the heavens.

A substantial smattering of Abramic rectitude, however, did nothing to undermine Tevye's immense popularity. During the seventies, the Jewish shelf in the house of American culture becomes so securely fastened that any forbidding or even outright sinister portrayal of its holdings could only seem but another index of its snug vantage. This situation pertains even to the darker side of Abraham, the father who at God's bidding held a knife to his son's throat, the figure who became the wicked slayer archetype of European anti-Semitic folk legend and literature (cf. Chaucer's "The Prioress' Tale"). The Abramic knife resurfaces in the coke bottle that the Jewish gangster Marty Augustine (Mark Rydell in *The Long Goodbye*, 1973) smashes across the face of his blond mistress; and Abramic Oedipal jealousy surges again in the Jewish Mafia lord, Hyman Roth (Lee Strasberg in *The Godfather, Part II*) who betrays his young business associate Michael Corleone and becomes his deadly rival. But neither of these portraits was construed as prejudicial: both "villains," after all, were spellbinders with the seductive menace of the stylish exploiter (as opposed to the impotent pathos of the drab exploited); Augustine was a funny man with the non-stop spritz of a Vegas lounge act, and Hyman Roth was a kindly white-haired daddy with kingly influence. Most members of the Jewish community weren't any more offended by them than wealthy citizens of Dallas would take umbrage at J. R. Ewing. Apparently the Jew had acquired enough comfort and authority in American culture to become worthy of its ultimate homage— lampoon and vilification (though he might very well sigh, and with more rue than Harry Golden, "only in America").

But Marty Augustine is a young man while the Abramic figure is traditionally old, and his high energy hustle brings him closer not to Abraham, but to Abraham's grandson, Jacob. This figure is easily the most driven of the Patriarchs who, before he settles down to a responsible fatherhood, at which point he turns static and contemplative, is perceived as the son who has to struggle, connive, and even cheat, for every scrap that comes his way. A trickster and a battler, with strong links to Joshua the warrior and Samson the muscleman, Jacob is the one who cons his dull-witted older brother out of their father's blessing, who works seven years to get a wife he doesn't want and then another seven to get the right one; he wrestles all night with the Lord's angel, suffers a sprained thigh, but still won't let him go until he gets a new name, one that defines his whole life: "Israel," striver with God. Unlike the steadfast Abraham, Jacob is a man in motion, as active as Abraham is contemplative, as hungry as Abraham is patient. While the Abramic figure is characteristically involved in a drama of social change where old ways must either give way or hold the line before new ones, the Jacobean figure usually appears in a drama of achievement, a struggle to the top (not always successful) against many obstacles: who else but Jacob would dream of angels ascending and descending a ladder that climbed to the stars?

A great hero in the Bible and one of the abiding projections of the Jewish imagination, Jacob surfaces first in American fiction and theater, decades before he enters film, in the novels of Budd Shulberg, Jerome Weidman, and Ernest Lehman, and the plays of Arthur Miller and Clifford Odets—but often in terms of disapprobation. The pre-war and early postwar version of the Jacobean striver is often selfish, greedy, materialistic, the anti-hero of a cautionary parable about the perils of sucess (sensual, material) and failure (ethical, emotional) in America, the dark Semitic side of Horatio Alger who rushes from rags to riches to grief, loneliness, and the corruptions of the spirit. This theme is spelled out in the titles of the two best film versions of the classic American pusher, *Body and Soul* (1948) with John Garfield as the Jewish boxer who finally sees the light, and *The Sweet Smell of Success* (1957) with Tony Curtis as the scheming press agent who remains in darkness. Even as late as 1975, the type reappears in *Hester Street* (1975). Here the aptly named Jake, a greenhorn garment worker in New York's lower East Side at the turn of the century, wants to trade his skull cap for an American derby, and divorce his wife Gitel, who won't abandon either her Yiddish or her orthodox wig, for a brassy dancehall instructress. "I don't care for nobody," he cries, "I'm an American fella." And Gitel bitterly agrees and after a divorce immediately pairs off with Jake's anti-type, Bernstein, an orthodox Abramic scholar, as fastidious as Jake is bumptious, as much a European traditionalist as Jake is an American assimilationist.

On the whole, however, most films of the last fifteen years have managed to treat the Jacobean striver more favorably than does *Hester Street*. In a contemporary situation where virtually all Jewish types are indulged, the passionate needs of the hustler are admired even while his acts are deplored. If he's a "bad boy," the world in which he operates, one *he* never made, is far worse; his sass, his heat, his high velocity, the self-seeking of his independence stand in opposition to the sterility, conformism, numbness, abstraction, and technocratic deep freeze of the contemporary social structures. Down a cold, mean street where "nobody cares," where "we have forgotten how to feel," who would disvalue this hungry, running man who still knows how to sweat for what he wants? At worst he is treated with wobbly ambivalence and equivocation so that the judgment of his character becomes nearly impossible; as it does, for instance, in the fuzzily motivated *The Heartbreak Kid* (1973) in which the manic but honestly dazed Lenny (Charles Grodin) callously but understandably ditches his helplessly gauche but truly innocent Jewish bride on their honeymoon to race off with a cool but really nice *shiksa* goddess. On the other hand, the fraudulently argued *Save the Tiger* (1973) recycles the problems of Arthur Miller's *All My Sons* but reverses its morality by absolving the hero of responsibility for his crime, and cops a special plea for Harry (Jack Lemon) the humane, decent, hard-driving Los Angeles garment manufacturer, who is driven to commit arson to save his business by "bad times" and a "corrupt system." "They're making jock straps out of the flag," weeps Harry, "There are no more rules." In *The Apprenticeship of Duddy Kravitz* (1974), the most rambunctious and authentic of these "revisionist" works, the ambiguities emerge from a rich, headlong immersion in a complex central figure and not from any confusion on the part of the filmmakers. Giggling, scratching, sweating, eating, running, eating *and* running, rumpled shirt tail eluding his belt, Richard Dreyfus' Duddy is an impulsive, likeable, Montreal chiseler (circa 1940) who steps on every toe, makes a bundle, but loses his girl, his best friend, and the respect of his Abramic grandfather who dearly loves him. We watch Duddy choose against his own natural impulse towards generosity and for this, the film never lets him off the hook. We, however, do. The movie doesn't fudge its final condemnation of Duddy, but its judgment is without force. Not only does Dreyfus' bustling performance draw us up into the sheer giddy joy that Duddy takes in his own outrageousness, but the Mordecai Richler script cannot create a satisfactory moral alternative to rival Duddy's chubby hilarity and wayward high spirits. The "virtuous" characters are either trite (his grandfather), wan (his girl), sickly sentimental (his friend) or strangely sabotaged by the author (e.g., the cultured Uncle Benjy, a Cold-Blooded Intellectual and sexually impotent to boot). In such company, Duddy becomes a man wrong in his acts, but right in himself.

There is nothing morally evasive, however, about the heroine of the Barbra Streisand cycle: she is the "greatest" and everyone knows this; the other characters know it and there always seem to be obligatory scenes in her films where one or more of them will tell her just that; her fans know it and that is why they turn out in droves for her films (which in themselves are often of no very special consequence); and Barbra, of course, has always known it and this is the not-so-secret knowledge that the Streisand heroines have in common, what makes them not really characters at all, but vehicles for the demonstration of their author's self-rapture. Streisand is probably the most admired of all the incarnations of the Jacobean striver and represents the ultimate contemporary ratification of the type. Her ambition is more imperious and soaring than that of any other go-getter, and far more strenuous than the ostensible struggle indicated by the plots of her most popular films. Certainly this ambition exceeds Fanny Brice's no-sweat drive to fame and fortune *(Funny Girl)*, or her triumph over two bad-luck marriages *(Funny Lady)*, or a rock singer's speedy ascension to the top of the record charts while her husband goes to pieces *(A Star is Born,* 1976), or a Jewish socialist's attempt to keep a shaky union with an apolitical WASP *(The Way We Were)*. Streisand's real goal is always to drive past these plots, to purify herself of the fiction in which she toils, and deliver herself to the audience, the one object she has never stopped wooing just beyond the arms of the pallid, or feckless, or self-destructive, or in any event, fully unworthy movie lover of her immediate attentions (e.g., Omar Sharif, Robert Redford, Kris Kristofferson). And each of her four most famous films allows her to lose this lover and gain herself and the one liaison fully commensurate with the force of her talents and her own vast sense of everything she has and is. One awaits the almost ritualistic climax of each film (sometimes at a performance where she sings, or in *The Way We Were* distributing "ban the bomb" pamphlets to passersby) the moment after the marriage has failed, after she realizes she can go on by herself, triumphant in her grief, the moment when she stands alone before the crowd whose rapport she is so confident of that it becomes her exalted mirror: Streisand asserting her tragic self to her heroic self. Within this perspective, her real obstacles aren't the "humble beginnings" of the traditional Jacobean figure, but ones far more intimate: that is, her cosmetic imperfections (the big red mouth, the Borzoi profile), her raffish inflections (the George Jessel and Jackie Leonard intonations, the red hot mama parodies), the idiosyncratic singing mannerisms. Her struggle becomes to make audiences see that what at first might appear too irregular, or too coarse, or yes, too precociously Jewish is actually just right, radiantly necessary. In her final tragic-heroic moments, or in those arias of self-intoxication like "Let's Hear it For Me" *(Funny Lady)* or "Don't Rain on My Parade" *(Funny Girl)*, we see Jacobean self-interest pushed to a pitch of delirium where author cuts loose from character, swan from duckling, and the striver discovers in herself the most direct and unencumbered way to hustle for idolatry.

"You push too hard," Robert Redford says to her in *The Way We Were*. But Streisand doesn't always play a pusher: As the neglected New York housewife in *Up the Sandbox* (1972), she spends so much time daydreaming it's hard to determine whether anything concrete could actually satisfy the amorphousness of her needs. When Jacob stops running, cools off, gets meditative, and takes stock, he begins to merge into *his* biblical son, Joseph, a dreamer and a reader of dreams, and a young man who never really has to run after anything. Joseph is the brightest, the worldliest, the most naturally gifted and self-assured of the early Patriarchs, the prototype of the artist, the intellectual, the scientist, the statesman, the Jewish "Prince" who rises to high power in foreign courts (with historical avatars in the lives of Disraeli, Rothschild, Thalberg, Oppenheimer, and Kissinger). Joseph, too, like Jacob, is the hero of a success story, one of the greatest in the Bible—from slavery to Prime Minister in one swift, inexorable ascent. Perhaps it is *too* inexorable and thus just a trifle bland; Joseph seems to expend so little to get so much. Unlike Jacob who must create his own fate and sweat for his victories, Joseph seems to let things happen to him, good things as well as bad (sold into slavery by his brothers, accused by Potiphar's wife). He is always less agonized in his own behalf than Jacob is in his; and final good fortune seems to follow him like a birthright. In the mythology of Jewish culture Joseph plays "nice boy" to Jacob's "wayward son," a Tom Sawyer to his father's Huck Finn. And just as Jacob's tale flows like the dream of an "unloved child" (i.e., his father's blessing belongs to his brother) in which special favor is never easily attained or willingly given but must always be acquired by transgression, so Joseph's becomes a fantasy of the caressed and the pampered, a father's best-loved son, in which triumph is inevitble and conscious transgression impossible; rather the child himself is surrounded by transgressors, enemies who envy his gifts, his favored condition, and despise his assumption of these as his natural rights. (In their neurotic manifestation Jacob becomes manic, Joseph paranoid.)

Because of his many facets, Joseph is perhaps the most porous and elusive of the traditional prototypes and in his contemporary translation, takes on many different roles. One of these is that of the artist figure or the Jewish intellectual encircled by hostile opponents, like Dustin Hoffman's Lenny Bruce *(Lenny)*, a gifted social satirist destroyed by moral censors, or Hoffman's Babe Levy *(The Marathon Man,* 1976), a doctoral candidate tortured by Nazi agents, or James Caan's Axel Freed *(The Gambler,* 1974), a City University Professor hounded by loan sharks and underworld debt collectors. Perhaps Joseph's most tragic incarnation to date has been Monroe Stahr *(The Last Tycoon,* 1976)—in Robert DeNiro's immaculate and elegant portrayal—a brilliant movie czar, a maker as well as an interpreter of celluloid dreams, "a Vine Street Rabbi" (as one enemy calls him), cut down by avaricious producers and a Tennessee Baptist union organizer. But then this version of the artist can easily turn lighter and somewhat soured in those self-pitying heroes of the recent Woody Allen films, the successful comedian *(Annie Hall,* 1977), the television writer *(Manhattan,* 1979), the filmmaker *(Stardust Memories,* 1980), none of whom can seem to turn a corner without crashing into an assortment of importuning boors and noisome grotesques.

In this somewhat negative vein, it isn't hard to see how Joseph in his dreaminess and intense self-absorption can easily fall prey to narcissistic navel-gazing or self-indulgent rumination (i.e., prophecy as chatter). We watch him, for example, make comic alliances with his spoiled but basically innocuous sub-type, the less gifted but no less self-centered Jewish Bubbie and his "J.A.P." sister (the Jewish American Princess): as in the addled Brenda Patamkin (Ali McGraw in *Goodbye, Columbus*) who prefers material security to her boyfriend's affections; the caviling Alex Portnoy (Richard Benjamin in *Portnoy's Complaint,* 1973) who makes love to his fist, the hysterical Jeffrey Rosenbloom (again Benjamin in *Love at First Bite,* 1979) who cries after his departing fiancée: "I almost love you!"; and the helpless Judy Benjamin (Goldie Hawn in *Pvt. Benjamin,* 1980) who only begins to think for and beyond herself when she joins the army. A spoiled Joseph's mantic qualities, however, can also move him in the direction of social commentary on which occasion he can become as didactic as his great grandfather Abraham, though in every way less disciplined and principled; his lectures tend to be woolly and diffuse, and by Abramic standards, generally trivial, as in the monologues of Woody Allen's recent alter-egos, or more egregiously in the tirades of Alan Arkin's Simon Mendelsson (*Simon*, 1980) who, for some mysterious reason, threatens the entire military and technological establishment just by raging for ninety minutes against Muzak, billboards, velvet paintings and the like: for this chopped teakettle, however, he triumphs over his enemies, and for more mysterious reasons, is awarded a Nobel Prize. Perhaps only in the genial and ramshackle *Bye Bye Braverman* (1968)—thus far Sidney Lumet's most ingratiating treatment of urban Jewish material—are Joseph's metaphysical pretentions treated with the proper blend of light affection and gentle kidding: here four New York Jewish intellec-tuals of the "distinctly second rank" philosophize all over the city while search-ing for the funeral parlor that houses the recently deceased body of their pal, the critic Leslie Braverman, but wind up benightedly attending services for a total stranger.

Actually most versions of the Joseph figure, serious and comic, don't make a point of attending Jewish rites. In fact, the most significant and curious aspect of the whole Joseph tale is this hero's lack of communication with Jehovah and the meager amount of time he actually spends with the Jewish people (indeed, Joseph is partly instrumental in bringing the Israelites *out* of the Promised Land and into four centuries of bondage in Egypt). A recurring motif in some films is to link a meditative, uptight, or searching Joseph figure with a black man or an Italian who often accompanies, or leads him towards, a more sensual, liberated, and frequently inchoate form of existence where one's Judaism matters only in the degree to which it is cast aside (e.g., Harvey Keitel and James Brown in *Fingers*, 1978, or Alan Arkin and Peter Falk in *The In-Laws*, 1979). In Paul Mazursky's *Willie and Phil* (1980), Willie (Michael Ontkean), a high school English teacher with longings for a career as a concert pianist, hangs out with Phil (Ray Sharkey), an Italian Catholic who in turn has always wanted to hang out with "a Jewish intellectual" like Willie. But later when Willie is asked, "Are you Jewish?", he replies, "Well, sort of . . ." He was *bar-mitzvahed*, once a year he attends a Passover dinner with his parents—and with this Willie exhausts his stock of ethnic affiliation. Like many Mazursky heroes, Willie is "searching"; he wants "answers"—but his Judaism won't provide them. Nothing else does either. Willie wanders to California, to India, back to California, tries yoga, joins religious cults, and settles down in the end, a narrator informs us, to lead "an ordinary life". In Mazursky's fuzzy concept and in Michael Ontkean's laid-back performance, Willie becomes a parody of the Wandering Jew, a wandering Non-Jewish Jew, a character in search of qualities, or that is, no character at all—a man who's been rubbed out.

Nowadays it's a common experience to go to the movies and find many "sort of" Jews, characters with not much more ethnic specificity than the old Nominal Jew of the studio era (e.g., Mazursky in particular—*Alex in Wonderland*, 1970, *Blume in Love*, 1973—seems to have become a specialist in this area). It is also just as common to attend other movies and find the equally ubiquitous comple-ment of this figure, a character who looks, acts, and talks like a Jew, but isn't—

in other words, a Jewish Non-Jew (which brings us back to *Oh, God!* or those Neil Simon films like *The Prisoner of Second Avenue*, 1975, or *Chapter Two*, 1980). In both kinds of movie, one sees how, say, the Joseph figure, or for that matter any traditional prototype, might die into a new figure that is neither really type nor coherent character, but rather a speaking, ambulating smear too porous and anomalous to have any specific identity at all.

Odd: Jewish non-Jews and non-Jewish Jews. In view of this, is it indiscreet to wonder to what degree the recent Jewish emergence in film has "failed" by virtue of its success? If "Jewishness" seems to be everywhere in general, where—or better, what—is it in particular? Aren't we witnessing to some extent the process whereby a Jewish style unmoors itself from a Jewish content, and both vanish into the social sea? And how legitimate is it when Jewish identity becomes just another all-purpose insignia of urban contemporaneity? We have seen how marketable a commodity Judaism can be, but does marketable also mean exportable? Surely in many respects this new situation is better than the old one of either general neglect or wholesale charade. And as we have also seen, there are plenty of vivid and legitimate types around, and ethnic exactitude may not be perfectly necessary in every instance (though from an artistic perspective, *any* kind of exactitude is never beside the point). Still one may wonder why, on current evidence, some Jews seem so eager to trade their ancestral and familial uniqueness for cultural anonymity?

NOTES

1. Leslie Fiedler, "The Jew in the American Novel," in *To the Gentiles* (New York: Stein and Day, 1972), p. 102.

2. I would remind the reader of some very few exceptions to this beefy generalization: Ford's Irish (*The Informer*, 1935; *The Quiet Man*, 1952), Howard Hawks's treatments of Italo-Americans (*Scarface*, 1932), Martin Scorsese's best work (to date) (*Mean Streets*, 1973), and the best work of Francis Ford Coppola (*The Godfather*, 1972; *The Godfather, Part II*, 1974).

3. According to Patricia Erens, "Within the decade Jews appeared in over ninety-five films, mostly in major roles." *The Jewish Image in American Movies*, p. 19 of the unpublished manuscript.

4. Selznick preserved a *Time* magazine article which referred to "the crafty and extraordinary methods of one time fur-peddlers, garment dealers and second hand jewelers . . . Jews . . . who padded their payroll with relatives, settled their biggest deals over all-night poker games and . . . discussed the motion picture business in comic strip dialects." Quoted by Ronald Haver in *David Selznick's Hollywood* (New York: Knopf, 1980), p. 73.

5. Here I omit the largely New York-based Yiddish Cinema (1924–61), some fifty films the majority of which appeared during the thirties—a rich subject, to be sure, but one beyond the frame of my Hollywood focus.

6. James Agee, *Agee on Film* (Boston: Beacon Press, 1964), p. 270.

7. Philip Roth, "Some New Jewish Stereotypes" in *Reading Myself and Others* (New York: Farrar, Straus and Giroux, 1977), p. 125.

8. Quoted by Fiedler, "Some Jewish Pop Art Heroes" in *To the Gentiles*, p. 138.

9. Robert Warshaw, "Clifford Odets: Poet of the Jewish Middle Class" in *The Immediate Experience* (New York: Atheneum, 1970), p. 63.

The Contributors

Enoch Brater, Associate Professor of English at the University of Michigan, Ann Arbor, has published widely in the fields of modern and contemporary dramatic literature. He is a specialist in the works of Samuel Beckett.

Jules Chametzky, Professor of English at the University of Massachusetts, Amherst, and former editor of the *Massachusetts Review,* is now Director of the Institute for Advanced Study in the Humanities at that University. Publishing widely in the field of modern American literature, he is the author of *From the Ghetto: The Fiction of Abraham Cahan.*

Sarah Blacher Cohen, Associate Professor of English at The State University of New York at Albany, is the author of *Saul Bellow's Enigmatic Laughter* and the editor of *Comic Relief: Humor in Contemporary American Literature.* She is the general editor of the SUNY Press series *Modern Jewish Literature and Culture* and one of the editors of the journal *Studies in American Jewish Literature.* Currently, she is writing a book on Cynthia Ozick.

Leslie Field, advisory editor of *Modern Fiction Studies* and *Studies in American Jewish Literature,* is Associate Professor of English at Purdue University. His publications include edited books on Thomas Wolfe, Robert Penn Warren and Bernard Malamud. His current projects are book-length studies of Jewish-American writers and a critical evaluation of Thomas Wolfe's fiction.

Lawrence L. Langer is Alumnae Professor of English at Simmons College in Boston. He is the author of *The Holocaust and the Literary Imagination, The Age of Atrocity: Death in Modern Literature* and *Versions of Survival: The Holocaust and the Human Spirit.* He is presently writing a book titled *Heroic Discontent: From Manfred to Moses Herzog.*

Anthony Lewis, Professor of English at the State University of New York College at Buffalo, teaches courses in Shakespeare and comedy writing. He regularly appears as a stand-up comedian on stage, television and radio. In addition to publishing many articles on Shakespearean comedy and comedy in general, he is presently writing a book on the humor of Lenny Bruce.

Bonnie Lyons is Associate Professor of English at The University of Texas at San Antonio and a recent Fulbright lecturer to Greece. She has written articles on Margaret Atwood, Saul Bellow, Abraham Cahan, Delmore Schwartz, Isaac Rosenfeld and Isaac Bashevis Singer, and she is the author of *Henry Roth: The Man and His Work.*

Keith Opdahl, Professor of English at DePauw University, is the author of *The Novels of Saul Bellow,* and has published in such periodicals as *Nation, Commonweal, Modern Fiction Studies,* and *The Iowa Review.* Currently he is completing a book on the realistic style.

Sanford Pinsker chairs the English Department at Franklin & Marshall College. His books include *The Schlemiel as Metaphor; The Comedy That "Hoits": An Essay on Philip Roth; The Languages of Joseph Conrad; Between Two Worlds: The American Novel in the 1960's;* and *Critical Essays on Philip Roth.* He is currently at work on a study of three Northwest poets.

Nahma Sandrow, Professor of English at the City University of New York, has written the highly acclaimed *Vagabond Stars: A World History of Yiddish Theater* and the book for the off-Broadway musical dramatization of it. Her prior scholarly book is *Surrealism, Theater, Arts, Ideas.* Her book in progress will deal with a variety of ethnic theaters.

Mark Shechner, Professor of English at the State University of New York at Buffalo, is the author of *Joyce in Nighttown: A Psychoanalytic Inquiry into Ulysses.* His essays and reviews appear regularly in *Partisan Review, Salmagundi* and *The Nation.* He is currently at work on a book about Jewish-American writing since the war.

R. Baird Shuman is Professor of English, Director of the Rhetoric Program, and Director of English Education at the University of Illinois at Urbana/Champaign. In addition to his books on English education and approximately three hundred articles ranging from Old English to current American literature, he has written book-length studies of dramatists Clifford Odets, Robert E. Sherwood, and William Inge.

Mark Slobin, Associate Professor of Music at Wesleyan University, has shifted from writing books on the music of Afghanistan and Central Asia to working on aspects of Eastern European Jewish music in Europe and America. He is the author of *Tenement Songs: The Popular Music of the Jewish Immigrants* and *Old Jewish Folk Music: Collections and Writings of Moshe Beregovski.*

June Sochen, Professor of History at Northeastern Illinois University, Chicago, has written extensively on women's social and cultural history. Her books include: *Consecrate Every Day: The Public Lives of Jewish American Women, 1880–1980; Herstory: A Record of the American Woman's Past; Movers and Shakers: American Women Thinkers and Activists, 1900–1970;* and *The New Woman: Feminism in Greenwich Village, 1910–1920.*

Alan Spiegel, Associate Professor of English at the State University of New York at Buffalo, teaches courses in literature and film. He is the author of *Fiction and the Camera Eye: A Study of Visual Consciousness in the Modern Novel* and is the regular film critic for *Salmagundi.* His essays on books and films have appeared in a variety of journals and anthologies including *Novel, Georgia Review, Virginia Quarterly Review,* and *Modern European Filmmakers and the Art of Adaptation.* At present he is finishing a book on James Agee.

Daniel Walden, Professor of American Studies at Pennsylvania State University, is the author of *On Being Jewish: American Jewish Writers from Cahan to Bellow*, five other books and more than forty articles. The founder and general editor of *Studies in American Jewish Literature*, he is currently writing a book on the influence of technology on ethnic literature.

Stephen J. Whitfield, Associate Professor of American Studies, is the author of *Scott Nearing: Apostle of American Radicalism* and *Into the Dark: Hannah Arendt and Totalitarianism*. Book review editor of *American Jewish History*, he has published articles in *South Atlantic Quarterly*, *Journal of Popular Culture*, *Moment*, *Jewish Social Studies* and *Midstream*.